FRANKIE McINTOSH
and the Art of the Soca Arranger

FRANKIE McINTOSH
and the Art of the Soca Arranger

Frankie McIntosh and Ray Allen

University Press of Mississippi / Jackson

The University Press of Mississippi is the scholarly publishing agency of
the Mississippi Institutions of Higher Learning: Alcorn State University,
Delta State University, Jackson State University, Mississippi State University,
Mississippi University for Women, Mississippi Valley State University,
University of Mississippi, and University of Southern Mississippi.

www.upress.state.ms.us

The University Press of Mississippi is a member
of the Association of University Presses.

Copyright © 2024 by University Press of Mississippi
All rights reserved
Manufactured in the United States of America

∞

Library of Congress Cataloging-in-Publication Data

Names: McIntosh, Frankie, author. | Allen, Ray (Professor of music and
American studies), author.
Title: Frankie McIntosh and the art of the soca arranger / Frankie
McIntosh, Ray Allen.
Description: Jackson : University Press of Mississippi, 2024. | Includes
bibliographical references and index.
Identifiers: LCCN 2024030249 (print) | LCCN 2024030250 (ebook) | ISBN
9781496854001 (hardback) | ISBN 9781496854018 (trade paperback) | ISBN
9781496854025 (epub) | ISBN 9781496854032 (epub) | ISBN 9781496854049
(pdf) | ISBN 9781496854056 (pdf)
Subjects: LCSH: McIntosh, Frankie. | McIntosh, Frankie—Interviews. |
Arrangers (Musicians)—Biography. | Jazz musicians—Biography. |
Arrangers (Musicians)—Interviews. | Jazz musicians—Interviews. |
Soca—Trinidad and Tobago—History and criticism. | Calypso
(Music)—Trinidad and Tobago—History and criticism. | Popular
music—Trinidad and Tobago—History and criticism.
Classification: LCC ML410.M4528 A5 2024 (print) | LCC ML410.M4528 (ebook)
| DDC 782.421640972983 [B]—dc23/eng/20240703
LC record available at https://lccn.loc.gov/2024030249
LC ebook record available at https://lccn.loc.gov/2024030250

British Library Cataloging-in-Publication Data available

CONTENTS

vii   Acknowledgments

3   Introduction: Finding the Arrangement in the Song

13   Chapter 1: Making Music in Saint Vincent and Antigua

43   Chapter 2: Brooklyn Is Meh Home

73   Chapter 3: The Saint Vincent Connection—Alston "Becket" Cyrus and Granville Straker

90   Chapter 4: The Art of the Soca Arranger

114   Chapter 5: Arranging with the Small Island Calypsonians

155   Chapter 6: Arranging with the Trinidad Stars

207   Chapter 7: Jazzing Up Calypso in the New Millennium

237   Epilogue: Our Calypso Tags

253   Appendix 1: Small Island Calypsos and Soca Songs

275   Appendix 2: The Trinidad Calypsos and Soca Songs

299   Appendix 3: Jazzing Up Calypso

315	Notes
325	Interviews
327	References
333	Index

ACKNOWLEDGMENTS

The past four years have flown by as this book project moved from a nascent idea to a final published work. Thankfully, after several hundred hours of conversation and tedious coediting, we are still standing and talking to each other. Working together over such an extended period has posed challenges, but the collaboration has proved tremendously satisfying for both of us. For Ray, it has been a privilege to have helped tell the story of one of the Caribbean's most esteemed and beloved musicians. For Frankie, it has been an honor to have had a music professor from his old alma mater, Brooklyn College, deem his life and music deserving of such thorough documentation.

Many colleagues and friends have contributed along the way. Frankie's circle of musicians and associates who offered up their insights include Garvin Blake, Charles Dougherty, David "Happy" Williams, Alston "Becket" Cyrus, Dr. Hollis "Chalkdust" Liverpool, Leston Paul, Pelham Goddard, Linda "Calypso Rose" McCarthy Sandy Lewis, Maclean "Short Shirt" Emanuel, Paul "King Obstinate" Richards, Caldric Forbes, Errol Ince, and Rawlston Charles. We are indebted to calypso historian Ray Funk, *Everybody's* magazine editor and long-time Carnival observer Herman Hall, and poet/historian Dawad Philip for their thoughts and advice along the way, and to Caribbean music scholar Jocelyne Guilbault who originally suggested the idea of this book to Ray. Our gratitude to those who read and critiqued various portions of our manuscript: Phil Rupprecht, Jeff Taylor, Denise Stephens, Fred Wasser, Nancy Berke, Laurie Russell, and the readers at the University Press of Mississippi. Our appreciation to editors Lisa McMurtray and Laura Strong, and to designer Jennifer Mixon, for advising and shepherding our manuscript across the finish line.

Frankie's special thanks go out to all the musicians who played his music, whether in the studio or on live shows, and to the music lovers who supported it in various ways. Without them there would be no book. The work stands as a tribute to the extended McIntosh clan: his father Clarence Arthur

"Tom" McIntosh; his mother Belle Cordice McIntosh; his siblings Cheryl, Arlene, Anthony, and Sonja; his first son Ahmad and his children Kaylah, Nasir and Nina (twins), and Ethan; his second son Omar and his children Rashid, Aiden, and Jasim; his daughter Jamilah and her son Jaiden; and his youngest son Hakim and his recently arrived son Kymani. Frankie hopes his nine grandchildren, and perhaps their children, will read this book someday and be reminded of where they came from.

And finally, from Frankie and Ray to their spouses, Patsy and Laurie: your love and support have kept us going through it all!

—Frankie and Ray
Brooklyn, November 2023

FRANKIE McINTOSH
and the Art of the Soca Arranger

INTRODUCTION
FINDING THE ARRANGEMENT IN THE SONG

Frankie and Ray originally crossed paths some twenty years ago. "I first heard Frankie McIntosh play at Restoration Plaza" recalls Ray. "It was a steamy August evening back in the early 2000s, just prior to the recent wave of gentrification, back when central Brooklyn was predominantly Black and West Indian. The occasion was a lively calypso tent run by Trinidadian producer and poet Dawad Philip. It turned out to be a memorable night."

Philip had chosen the locale wisely, showcasing his artists in a neighborhood that was heating up for Brooklyn's annual Labor Day Caribbean Carnival celebration. The Restoration Plaza complex, located on Fulton Street near Nostrand Avenue, included a studio where many hit soca (soul/calypso) records were recorded, as well as the Billie Holiday Theater, a popular venue for West Indian music and dance productions. Just down the street from Restoration was Charlie's Calypso City, a record shop and recording studio that produced many of Brooklyn's greatest soca recordings during the 1980s and 1990s. The store's owner, Trinidad expatriate Rawlston "Charlie" Charles, was permitted to shut down a section of Fulton Street on the Saturday of Labor Day weekend to run a Carnival block party featuring performances by visiting calypso dignitaries. Less than a mile to the south lay Eastern Parkway, the main route for the annual Carnival parade that drew millions of spectators on Labor Day afternoon. The Parkway parade culminated in front of the venerable Brooklyn Museum, whose outdoor grounds hosted the annual Dimanche Gras concert and Panorama competition held over Labor Day weekend.

Ray continues: "I had been attending Brooklyn Carnival events since the mid-1980s, and eventually began researching and writing about Brooklyn's steelband scene in collaboration with Trinidadian journalist Leslie Slater.[1] As my interests shifted toward the calypso and soca side of Carnival music, I began frequenting calypso tents that popped up in Brooklyn around Labor Day." Dawad Philip's tent that season featured a number of big-time calypsonians, among them Gypsy, Sugar Aloes, Short Shirt, and Swallow. In addition, his house band included a lineup of crack instrumentalists—Frankie on keyboards, Dane Gulston on steel pan, Errol Ince on trumpet, Jeff Granum on saxophone, Wayne Walcott on trombone, and Terrance Shaw on guitar. At the opening of each set, the band jammed around on a jazz or R&B standard, affording Frankie and the others the opportunity to showcase their improvisatory chops. "I was impressed with Frankie's keyboard skills, both his rich harmonic accompaniments and his cool, lyrical soloing," recalls Ray. "I had heard of Frankie McIntosh, the arranger responsible for the music behind the soca hits 'Don't Back Back' by Sparrow, 'Lorraine' by Explainer, 'Is Thunder' by Duke, and 'Coming High' by Becket, to name just a few. But I had no idea that he was so well-versed in jazz and R&B as well as soca and calypso. I approached him at the end of the show to say hello. As I recall our conversation that night was brief, but right then and there I knew this was a musician I needed to get to know if I wanted to understand more about Brooklyn soca music."

Frankie remembers it this way: "If memory serves, I first ran into Ray at a calypso event, a tent at Restoration Plaza. The last act had just finished and the audience was heading toward the exit, except for this gentleman walking in the opposite direction. Now, as with most musicians at the end of a long gig, I was tired and not eager to engage in lengthy conversation. But before I could get away, he introduced himself as Professor of Music from my old alma mater, Brooklyn College. That got my attention! He went on to compliment my playing and asked a question about one of the songs we had performed. As we briefly chatted, I realized this fellow was quite knowledgeable about calypso, not just someone with a passing interest in the music who somehow ended up at the show looking for exotic Carnival music. I told him I hoped to see him again sometime, but didn't think much about the encounter until a few days later when I was browsing through some books in my home library. When I came across the volume *Island Sounds in the Global City*, edited by Ray and Lois Wilcken, I realized that this was the Ray Allen I had met at the concert. The article on Brooklyn steelbands in Brooklyn that he had cowritten with Les Slater confirmed my earlier appraisal that here was someone who knew quite a bit about the music through his academic research and who was out there attending events in the community. I later asked Les about Ray, about what it was like working with him. He described the experience as 'gratifying,' characterizing Ray as 'honest and diligent,' someone who was open to others' ideas and someone you could trust. Les's comments would have been a sufficient recommendation, but when my daughter Jamilah returned home from a music lesson at Brooklyn College and announced: 'My professor saw my name and asked if I was related to you; his name is Ray Allen,' I became further convinced that Ray was no dilettante, but someone with experience and a genuine interest in the musical culture to which I belonged. So, sometime later when Ray finally arrived at my home for a series of interviews in connection with his Carnival book project, I was ready and willing."

Following that chance meeting at the Restoration calypso tent, Frankie and Ray ran into each other on occasion, but it was not until the summer of 2013 that they finally sat down to have a serious chat about Frankie's life and career as a soca arranger. Ray recalls: "I had just begun work on my next book project, a history of Caribbean Carnival music in Harlem and Brooklyn. Soca would be front and center, and Frankie's work with Brooklyn record producers Granville Straker and Rawlston Charles were critical to the story. I was totally taken by Frankie, whose exuberant love and knowledge of all things musical lay quietly below his outwardly modest demeanor. His friends and bandmates often described him as a humble musical genius, and I quickly understood why. We hit it off right away, perhaps because he was eager to talk with someone who really wanted to dig deep into his music. And we bonded over our serendipitous connection to the Brooklyn College Conservatory of Music, where I had been teaching for the past twenty years and he had received his bachelor's degree back in the 1970s. It quickly became apparent that we shared a great admiration for the Conservatory that had provided him with first- class musical training, but also a lingering frustration with the program's Eurocentric vision of music that too often treated jazz and world music as second-class citizens. More on that later.

Frankie picks up the story: "I was happy to speak with Ray. In previous interviews, most journalists tended to dwell on a narrow range of interests: 'What was it like playing with my father's band as a twelve-year old?' 'Which calypsonian did I enjoy arranging for the most?' But Ray asked more challenging questions, focusing on my arranging process and how I put things together, probing for my aesthetic philosophy. Right away he wanted to discuss specific examples from my previous recordings, so I couldn't wander off into vague generalities. Above all it was quite clear that he respected my music and my artistry as an arranger. Those initial interviews were gratifying for me, and later I was pleased with the chapter he wrote about Brooklyn soca music in his *Jump Up!* book. The acknowledgments he gave me and record producer

Granville Straker were greatly appreciated. But at that point, ten years ago, I was not thinking about a biography or memoir."

The seed for that idea, as it turns out, was planted a year after their initial interview sessions. Ray remembers: "In 2014 I presented a paper at the Society for Ethnomusicology on my preliminary research on Brooklyn soca. Afterwards I was fortunate enough to have a cup of coffee with Jocelyne Guilbault, the widely admired Caribbean music scholar who had just finished a terrific cowritten biography with Trinidadian soca bandleader Roy Cape. Upon hearing more about my work in Brooklyn, she looked me in the eye and said quite emphatically: 'Ray, you should really write a book about Frankie McIntosh, or better yet, a book with Frankie McIntosh.' That was great advice, and Frankie and I thank her for it, emphatically!"

The Art of the Soca Arranger tells a story of Caribbean music in the diaspora through the eyes and ears of pioneering soca arranger Frankie McIntosh. Soca music, an offspring of older Trinidadian calypso, emerged in the late 1970s and early 1980s, and today is recognized worldwide as one of the English-speaking Caribbean's most distinctive styles of popular vocal music. Fans are no doubt familiar with famed singers Lord Kitchener, the Mighty Sparrow, Calypso Rose, David Rudder, and a host of other bards whose poetic wit and wisdom became the defining hallmarks of the music. But much less is known about the arrangers and instrumentalists who created the musical setting in which those vocalists plied their craft. This work will fill that void by focusing on the life and music of one of the most celebrated soca arrangers and keyboardists of all time.

Franklyn "Frankie" McIntosh was born on the Caribbean Island of Saint Vincent in 1946. Like many Caribbean people, he was of mixed descent, tracing his ancestry to West Africa, India, Scotland, and possibly Germany. He cut his musical teeth as pianist and arranger for his father's calypso dance orchestra in Kingstown before establishing his own band at the age of fourteen. In 1968 he joined the wave of Caribbean immigrants who landed in Brooklyn, where he studied and earned a BA degree in classical piano from Brooklyn College and an MA in jazz studies from New York University. For nearly a decade he made a living playing with Brooklyn calypso dance orchestras and small jazz ensembles, before joining forces with fellow Saint Vincent expatriate and record producer Granville Straker. Serving as the company's musical director and leader of the studio band the Equitables, Frankie composed musical arrangements and oversaw the recordings of hundreds of calypso/soca albums for Straker's Records as well as Brooklyn's two other calypso companies, Charlie's Records, and B's Records. His list of musical collaborators reads like a who's who of calypso and soca in the 1980s and 1990s: Chalkdust, Calypso Rose, the Mighty Sparrow, Lord Kitchener, Duke, Shadow, Machel Montano, Becket, and Swallow to name but a few. Today Frankie is recognized as a member of the esteemed pantheon of arrangers whose musical visions were indispensable in crafting the modern soca sound.

Most of the biographical writings on the music of the English-speaking Caribbean have focused on star vocalists, with little attention to the musicians and arrangers who played essential roles in shaping popular styles. Scholarly works on calypso and soca have emphasized social history and song lyrics while paying little attention to the music.[2] With the exception of Jocelyne Guilbault's 2014 co-biography, written with and recounting the life of Trinidadian bandleader Roy Cape, little has been said about calypso orchestras, soca bands, and their musicians.[3] Likewise, the individuals who created the musical accompaniments have been ignored, save for Guilbault's chapter on early calypso arrangers Frankie Francis and Art de Coteau, and in Ray's own work on more recent Brooklyn soca arrangers.[4] To date, no in-depth study of an influential calypso or soca arranger and his/her music exists.

The *Art of the Soca Arranger* places Frankie McIntosh at the center of several overlapping narratives of immigration and musical diaspora. There is Frankie's personal voyage from the Caribbean to Brooklyn and his efforts to hammer out a career in music while raising a family in his newly adopted home. His immigrant tale is intertwined with his musical journey, from popular Caribbean dance bands through formal studies in Western classical music and jazz to his work as a gigging jazz pianist and calypso/soca arranger. Along the way he embraced the varied musics of Brooklyn's African American and West Indian communities. His story provides a unique lens for viewing Brooklyn Carnival music, and brings into sharp focus the borough's rise to prominence as the transnational hub of the soca music industry in the 1980s.

The initial chapters of *The Art of the Soca Arranger* are arranged chronologically to coincide with Frankie's life and musical experiences. The first chapter focuses on his childhood and young adulthood growing up in Kingstown, Saint Vincent. The story begins with his years of classical piano studies, follows his apprenticeship as pianist for his father's calypso dance orchestra, the Melotones, and moves forward to his founding of the Frankie McIntosh Orchestra at the age of fourteen. In this rich musical environment, he became familiar with an array of Caribbean dance genres, from calypsos to tangos and boleros, as well as American jazz standards imported by records and written scores from the United States. After graduating from high school and a year's teaching English literature in a local intermediate secondary school, Frankie relocated to Antigua in 1967, where he played piano for the popular Laviscount Combo that specialized in calypso as well as American R&B, funk, and pop tunes.

The second chapter turns to Frankie's immigration to the United States in 1968 and his experiences upon arrival in central Brooklyn's burgeoning West Indian community. He recounts his formal studies of classical piano and jazz performance at Brooklyn College and New York University, his introduction to the 1970s New York City jazz scene, and his memories of Brooklyn's early Carnival celebrations. He was, by then, equally at home with the music of Claude Debussy, McCoy Tyner, James Brown, and the Mighty Sparrow. His challenge was to combine his skills as a performer and arranger in order to support his family upon the arrival of the first of four children in 1974. The second section of the chapter covers Frankie's work as a keyboardist for a variety of local calypso orchestras, jazz ensembles, and R&B bands during the 1970s. Brooklyn's calypso dance orchestras led by Sid Joe, Lio Smith, and Ron Berridge, provide an introduction to the borough's vibrant Caribbean dance scene. In addition, he recalls his experiences playing in small clubs in Brooklyn and Queens that were frequented by Black American audiences in search of jazz and R&B.

The third chapter turns to Brooklyn's emerging calypso/soca recording industry with the introduction of producers Granville Straker (Straker's Records), Rawlston Charles (Charlie's Records), and Michael Gould (B's Records). Frankie's initial foray into the soca world came in 1976 through his work with Vincentian calypsonian Alston "Becket" Cyrus. In the late 1970s, Frankie became the musical director for Straker's Records and the leader of the Equitables, Straker's studio band with an international cast of players from Trinidad, Saint Vincent, Barbados, Puerto Rico, Panama, and the United States. In New York's advanced recording studios, he encountered the new multi-track recording systems and the latest synthesizer and drum machine technology that would become hallmarks of the emerging soca sound.

The first section of chapter 4 explores Frankie's early training and the musical influences that shaped his development as a calypso/soca arranger. The story pivots to his arranging process and philosophy, focusing on the specific methods he used to move from the skeletal melody he received from a calypsonian to a full-blown arrangement ready for recording sessions. Questions of overall form, harmonic language, and melodic improvisation that characterized his most popular arrangements are explored, as are his approaches to composing introductions, instrumental band choruses, and codas. Frankie ruminates on the process of "finding the arrangement" inherent in a song through contemplation of the lyrical message and overall mood of the material presented to him.

The next two chapters focus on Frankie's work with a number of the most influential calypso/soca singers of the 1980s. He describes in detail the collaborative creative process—how singers would visit his house in Crown Heights to drop off a cassette or to sing their latest offering while he began to work out chord progressions and horn lines on his old acoustic piano. Once the written instrumental parts were complete, he would contact musicians and set up separate rhythm, horn, and vocal sessions and oversee the studio recording. Chapter 5 centers on his early work with "small island" singers Alston "Becket" Cyrus (Saint Vincent), Winston Soso (Saint Vincent), Scorcher (Saint Vincent), Swallow (Antigua), Short Shirt (Antigua), and Obstinate (Antigua). Chapter 6 doubles back to Trinidad stars Chalkdust, Calypso Rose, Duke, Explainer, Shadow, Lord Kitchener, and Sparrow. Frankie recounts his experiences working with these artists, and discusses several favorite songs that he arranged for each. Ray's brief biographical introductions to the singers provide context for Frankie's commentary, and illuminates the roles these artists played in Brooklyn Carnival culture.

Chapter 7 jumps to Frankie's activities in the new millennium. With soca production shifting back to the Caribbean, his work as an arranger began to dwindle, which in turn prompted him to take a job as a music educator in a Brooklyn neighborhood school. But he also returned to his earlier interests in jazz, and began playing and recording with steel panist Garvin Blake, bassist and singer David "Happy" Williams, bassist Max Gouveia, and saxophonist Charles Dougherty. The music they made is discussed in the context of Brooklyn's Caribbean jazz scene, addressing the question of what constitutes the slippery categories of "calypso jazz" or "pan jazz." Frankie and his bandmates offer their observations on the current state of Caribbean-influenced jazz and new directions for popular calypso and soca music.

An epilogue and three appendices complete our story. The latter contain listening guides timed to YouTube recordings of all the music we discuss in the book, along with basic chord charts and musical highlights for each piece. Listening, or more specifically our colistening experiences with these recordings, lies at the heart of the second half of this book. For Ray, it was a matter of returning to a number of old favorite soca songs from the 1980s and 1990s while hearing others for the first time, as well as discovering Frankie's more recent jazzy calypso arrangements. For him, the sounds were fresh and exciting, music bursting with aesthetic pleasure and cultural agency waiting to be explored. That perspective clearly guided his questioning. For Frankie the experience was different—he was returning to songs he had helped create three to four decades earlier (and in many cases had not listened to in the interim), along with more recent jazz-oriented compositions. Revisiting one's own art, years later, can be simultaneously reaffirming and disappointing—a combination of satisfaction, regret, nostalgia, and even sorrow when listening to singers and musicians who have passed on. These colistening sessions were sometimes challenging for Frankie, especially when pushed to comment on his original motivations, compositional strategies, personal aesthetic preferences, and finally for self-evaluation from his current perch, some forty years later. We hope the results are revealing, at times even illuminating, but they must be understood as our take on how the songs resonated with us at the moment, in the early 2020s, not necessarily back in the day when they were written and arranged. The passing of time may add perspective, but historians take heed.

The Art of the Soca Arranger is a coauthored project. We take inspiration from scholar/musician collaborations such as those by Jocelyne Guilbault and Trinidad bandleader Roy Cape, Kyle DeCoste and the Stooges Brass Band of New Orleans, and Stan BH Tan-Tangbau and Vietnamese jazz saxophonist Quyen Van Minh.[5] We are both longtime residents of Brooklyn, and bring our individual backgrounds and particular skills to the task: Ray, a white, New York–born researcher, writer, and academic trained in ethnomusicology and folklore; Frankie, an Afro-Caribbean professional pianist and arranger with formal background in Western classical and jazz music and a lifetime of experience with Caribbean Carnival music. Voicing our parts to tell the story emerged organically through an ongoing process of dialogue and negotiation during over a hundred hours of recorded conversations and colistening. The first three chapters are primarily Frankie's first-person accounts of his childhood and early musical career, with brief contextual interludes by Ray. The remainder of the work presents our in-depth discussions of musical practice and commentary on specific recordings. Because the conversations in these later chapters came about during our colistening sessions, we determined it best to present them as a running dialogue between us, broken up by snippets of history from Ray.

Together we approach this project as partners and aim to obviate the asymmetrical power relations that characterize more conventional biography and scholarship based on the traditional scholar/subject relationship. This is certainly a worthy and long overdue goal for music scholars who aim to decolonize knowledge. That said, we recognize the difficulties in totally transcending the traditional scholar/subject relationship with its innate power inequities when writing a book like this for an academic press. Consider our respective positions in this project: Ray, a full professor and published author; Frankie, an independent musician operating in the world of Caribbean popular music

Frankie and Ray, Brooklyn, 2022. Photo by Laurie Russell.

and jazz. That configuration creates certain expectations regarding authoritative voice and the division of labor. After all, Frankie is first and foremost a musician—his fingers at the piano keyboard yield beautiful music for us to relish and ruminate about. Ray is a teacher, writer, and amateur pianist, not a practicing musician—his digits click away at a keyboard attached to a computer in order to produce the final written product before you. But these scholar/subject, writer/musician binaries are by no means cut and dried in our particular situation. Keep in mind that we both hold advanced degrees—Frankie in jazz studies and Ray in folklore/ethnomusicology. Moreover, Frankie's formal training in piano technique and music theory exceeds Ray's (as does his knowledge of Latin and classical European history, among other things, due in part to the exacting nature of the British-style colonial education he received in Saint Vincent). Ray is more conversant with the scholarly literature on Caribbean music, but Frankie is well read, and he brings a lifetime of musical and cultural knowledge to the table. So, who is it that really speaks with the authoritative voice? Perhaps both in different ways? Frankie's memories and musical oeuvre are at the core of the work, while Ray's primary responsibility has been to organize those memories into a cohesive narrative. That recognized, the process has been dialogic throughout, from the early planning stages and choice of musical examples through the joint editing and reediting of Ray's initial drafts and Frankie's revisions. The final narrative is Frankie's story, shaped by Ray's queries and interludes.[6]

Although our work appears on an academic press, we write for a broad audience, particularly those in the Caribbean community for whom Frankie is a cultural icon. In this spirit we couch our discussions of the music in language that we hope will be accessible to nonmusicians and those with broader interests in Caribbean studies and cultural diaspora. All the music examples we cover are readily available on the YouTube channel "Art of the Soca Arranger,"[7] and we have included timed listening guides in three appendices for those interested in the more formal aspects of the music. We hope that you, dear readers, will become listeners, regardless of your musical backgrounds. Our words can only go so far in describing the ineffable magic of music—only by engaging with the recordings can you gain a deeper appreciation of the art of the soca arranger.

CHAPTER 1

MAKING MUSIC IN SAINT VINCENT AND ANTIGUA

When Franklyn "Frankie" McIntosh came into the world on August 19, 1946, Saint Vincent was still a Crown Colony under the rule of Great Britain. Outside the capital of Kingstown, most of the undereducated, agrarian population labored as subsistence farmers and workers on plantation-style estates producing arrowroot starch, sea cotton, and bananas. The majority of the island's approximately 65,000 inhabitants were the descendants of African slaves who had been stolen away to the Caribbean in the eighteenth and nineteenth centuries to work the early sugar and coffee plantations. Their ranks were bolstered by a smattering of East Indian and Portuguese indentured workers whose ancestors were recruited in the decades following the abolishment of slavery in 1834. A small upper class of planters and government administrators of British and mixed-race lineage controlled the agricultural estates and government.[1]

But the spirit of democratic reform and the desire for self-government had been percolating for some time throughout the English-speaking Caribbean. In 1935 Frankie's paternal grandfather, George McIntosh, led a group of working-class Kingstown Vincentians in protest against excessive colonial tax legislation. The gathering turned riotous and the elder McIntosh, after being charged and acquitted for treason, went on to lead the Saint Vincent Workingmen's Cooperative Association. That organization would push for land reform and the universal suffrage that was finally granted in 1951.[2] During Frankie's school years the struggle for independence continued, with Saint Vincent and other Caribbean British colonies attempting and failing to unite under the West Indies Federation (1958–1962). It was not until 1969, two years after he had left home to work in Antigua, that Saint Vincent attained Associated Statehood with the United Kingdom, and another decade before achieving full independence as Saint Vincent and the Grenadines in 1979.

Despite the colony's autocratic rule and widespread poverty, the post–World War II Kingstown that Frankie grew up in was a bustling port with an active cultural life and a small but aspiring class of businesspeople, artisans, and educators. A handful of secondary schools provided an elite British-style education for the most talented students, including Frankie, who won a merit scholarship to the Saint Vincent Boys Grammar School at the age of nine. The school featured a curriculum of math, science, literature, and compulsory French and Latin, but little in the way of music save a singing class.[3]

Fortunately for Frankie, Kingstown and the surrounding villages were rich in musical offerings. An ensemble of Black and mixed-race string, brass, and reed players known as the Kingstown Orchestral Society was established as early as the 1890s. Frankie's father, Clarence Arthur "Tom" McIntosh, his uncle Harold McIntosh, and trumpeter Shake Keane occasionally played with another group called the Saint Vincent Philharmonic Orchestra, which performed at outdoor concerts and colonial events.[4] The island boasted a number of talented classical piano teachers and performers, including pianist Pat Prescod who formed the Kingstown Chorale in 1956 and went on to teach at the Boys Grammar School and serve as the music officer in the Ministry of Education.[5] Prescod's instructor, pianist Miss Eunice Horne, was employed to teach Frankie and his brother Tony.

In the more vernacular realm, military-style and police marching bands were common, as were dance orchestras. The marching bands played standard European and American brass and wind compositions, while the dance ensembles' repertories included foxtrots, waltzes, boleros, merengues, calypsos, and American standard pop and jazz tunes. The Melotones orchestra, led by Frankie's father Tom McIntosh; the Blue Rhythm Orchestra, led by his cousin Syl McIntosh; and the Latinaires Orchestra, led by Kerwyn Morris, were three of the leading groups that entertained regularly at town and village dances and annual holiday celebrations. The brass and wind players, along with most of the other musicians, read music from charts imported from Great Britain and the United States. Nearly all, including the percussionists, were able to play by ear and to improvise "head arrangements" of local calypso and Latin pieces.[6]

Saint Vincent's rural and village areas were rich in folk music, ranging from African-derived big drum song/dance practices to hybridized "bum drum" ensembles of flutes and drums to more European-style string bands with flutes, guitars, cuatros, and scrapers. Various configurations of these groups would play for dances, weddings, and annual festivals, particularly around Christmas, Easter, and for Carnival celebrations.[7] Carnival linked earlier slave emancipation celebrations and French-Catholic pre-Lenten festivities and featured boisterous dancing, masquerading, and the singing of satire songs. As in Trinidad and throughout the Caribbean, Africans took over Carnival and placed their own distinctive stamp on the celebration, which became known for its transgressive masquerading themes, percussive music, and call-and-response kaiso songs.[8] Masking traditions and satire songs often lampooned the colonial elites who saw Carnival as a threat to social order—as early as 1879 the British authorities tried unsuccessfully to shut it down.[9]

Saint Vincent's small towns and villages held their own informal Carnival celebrations dating back to the decades following the 1834 emancipation. But as the twentieth century unfolded, Kingstown increasingly became the center of more organized festivities. As early as the 1930s, groups of masqueraders and singers paraded through the city to the Botanical Gardens to perform for the colonial administrator. The best singer received a wooden scepter called the "Pole," and was crowned the King of the Revelers.[10] The *Vincentian* newspaper reported that a Trinidad-style steelband led by Raphael Davison played in a Kingstown Carnival jump up in the mid-1940s, and informal steelband competitions were reported as part of the Monday morning J'Ouvert celebrations as early as 1949.[11] In 1948 a more organized calypso monarch contest was established in the city's downtown Victoria Park, followed by a steelband competition in 1962. These musical competitions, along with a Queen of the Bands costume contest, were usually held on the weekend prior to the Monday J'Ouvert celebration and the Shrove Tuesday parade of costumed bands, dancers, steelbands, and calypso singers.[12] A Carnival Development Committee (CDC) of local businesspeople and administrators was formed to coordinate activities.

A thorough history of Saint Vincent calypso has yet to be written, but the memories of calypsonian Peter "Caribbean Pete" Olson and Cauldric Forbes suggest a lively scene around Carnival time. During the 1950s and 1960s, singers with sobriquets Young Sparrow, Young Wrangler, Mighty Sheller, Lord Teach, Lord Hawke, Toiler, and Caribbean Pete dominated the calypso competition. Trinidad-style calypso tents were established where calypsonians would try out their latest songs for local audiences prior to the calypso monarch competition. The Melotones and similar calypso dance orchestras were often employed to provide instrumental accompaniments for the singers, and Frankie recalls that the island's top calypsonians would often visit his father's home to rehearse their latest songs. In addition to the monarch competition, calypso shows featuring local talent and visiting luminaries from Trinidad were held in downtown venues like the Russell Cinema and the Lyric Cinema during Carnival season.[13] Because Saint Vincent lacked professional recording studios and production facilities, few of its singers were known outside the island until the 1970s, when several went to Trinidad (Sheller and Hawke) and later New York (Alston "Becket" Cyrus, Winston Soso, and Cyril "Scorcher" Thomas) to record. For many years Trinidad calypsonians maintained a cultural dominance throughout the Caribbean, and it was not until 1971 that the Carnival Development Committee declared that the island's annual Road March should come from a Vincentian calypsonian. In hopes of attracting more tourists, in 1977 the CDC moved Saint Vincent's Carnival from its traditional pre-Lent date to early July to avoid conflict with Trinidad Carnival.

In addition to the island's abundance of live music offerings, the local music scene was heavily influenced by foreign radio and imported recordings. The Windward Islands Broadcasting Station (WIBS) offered limited hours, so most Vincentians depended on Radio Trinidad and Radio Guardian to keep up with the latest popular calypsos.[14] Likewise, music fans had to turn to calypso recordings produced in Trinidad as well as the latest popular tunes and jazz standards arriving on vinyl from the United States.

Despite Saint Vincent's robust local music cultures, many of the island's best players sought greater artistic and financial opportunities abroad. Some migrated to Trinidad's cosmopolitan Port of Spain with dreams of recording and expanding their performance possibilities. Still others, including famed trumpeter Shake Keane and other members of the Melotones ensemble, took advantage of the island's Commonwealth status and headed to Great Britain in the 1950s.[15] Following United States immigration reforms of the 1960s, many, including Saint Vincent's most heralded calypsonians of the next decade, "Becket," Winston Soso, and "Scorcher," headed north to New York.[16] Frankie would join that wave of out-migration in fall 1968, after a brief stint in Antigua.

• • •

Frankie: My Early Years in Kingstown and Pauls Lot

Mommy was fond of reminding me that I was born on a sunny Monday morning at the Kingstown General Hospital located in the British colony of Saint Vincent. I arrived, so I am told, around 9:00 a.m. on August 19, 1946.

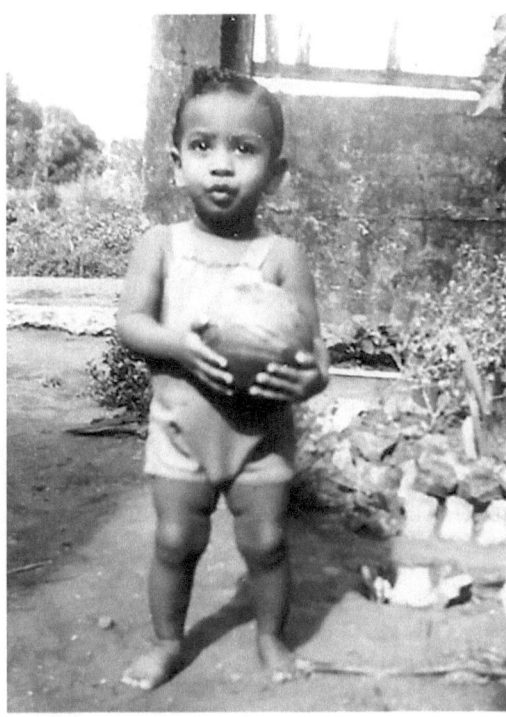

Frankie age 2, Pauls Lot, Kingstown, Saint Vincent and the Grenadines

As the anesthesia wore off, the first sound my mother became aware of was a hospital radio blasting the strains of Lord Kitchener's Trinidad Road march for that year: "Jump in the Line." She wished she could join her fellow nurses in song, but was still too weak.

Coincidentally, this was also the birthday of William Jefferson Clinton, the 42nd president of the United States. Although I was not destined to become a politician in the United States (or Saint Vincent for that matter), our powerful neighbor to the north would play an enormous role in my future.

Meanwhile, preparations for my grand homecoming were underway at my paternal grandfather's house in Pauls Lot, a working-class neighborhood adjacent to Kingstown's bustling business district. I would later learn that my grandfather, the Honorable George Augustus McIntosh (known to the family as "Papa"), was a famous labor leader who was almost executed for treason a decade prior to my birth, but that's getting ahead of the story. At his house my mother would have another opportunity to sing, but this time to the accompaniment of live music. My dad, Clarence Arthur "Tom" McIntosh, along with his siblings and musician friends, gathered for the celebratory jam.

The legendary jazz trumpeter Ellsworth Shake Keane, along with other members of my father's dance band, the Melotones Orchestra, were included in the assemblage of guests at Papa's home that afternoon. Daddy recalled they played Roaring Lion's "All Day, All Night, Mary-Ann" (the big song in Trinidad for the previous year, 1945), King Radio's 1944 hit "Brown Skin Gal," and Lord Invader's legendary 1943 "Rum and Coca Cola." As the level of the rum bottle declined, the faster-paced songs gave way to gentler ballads. (I should add that George McIntosh neither approved of drinking alcohol nor imbibed it himself—he acquiesced only owing to the reason for the celebration.) Mommy remembered my grandfather requesting "Cruising Down the River," his favorite waltz.

Shortly after my birth, the Trinidadian calypso icon Mighty Spoiler arrived in Saint Vincent to fulfill an engagement. Since the Melotones had been hired as the backing band, Spoiler visited my dad to discuss the repertoire. As related by my father, Spoiler picked me up from the crib, and improvised an a cappella calypso to the effect that "This baby shall grow to be a musician, following in his father's footsteps."

Family and Early Music Making

I was blessed to be born into a musical family. Indeed, my earliest musical memories come from my paternal grandfather's house in Pauls Lot. "Papa" McIntosh (1886–1963), the son of a Scottish planter and a Black Vincentian cook, worked as a chemist, mechanic, and most famously as political activist. My grandfather was well known in Kingstown as a leader who actually stood up to the planting class in support of the common folk, the poor, and the disenfranchised. He held meetings in the back of his pharmacy where he would encourage the local people to organize and demand their rights, especially the right to vote—back then only people who owned land could vote. A protest in downtown Kingstown over new taxes in 1935 turned violent and several people were killed. The British authorities blamed the whole thing on my grandfather and had him arrested. He was charged with treason, an offense that could have ended with him before a firing squad. His family and associates hired a famous lawyer from Trinidad, a fellow named L. C. Hannays, to represent him. He went to trial and was exonerated. Papa went on to form a political party, the Saint Vincent's Working Men's Association, and became a leader in the fight for adult suffrage, which finally came about in 1951, when I was around five years old.

I have fond memories of Papa and my paternal grandmother, Ethel Warren (known to us as "Granny"). She was also of mixed parentage—we believe she

Frankie age 7–8, Kingstown, Saint Vincent and the Grenadines.

George Augustus McIntosh circa 1940.

was African German. According to Joan McIntosh, my first cousin and family historian, the name Warren is a corruption of Worn. Granny's father was apparently a German resident in Saint Vincent, surname Wörn, her mother was a local Afro-Vincentian with the surname Bonadie. Granny was born in Pauls Lot, and as was true of many residents in that area, she survived by dint of entrepreneurial skills and tenacity. She became a trader of goods from Guyana—a country she visited frequently—to Trinidad and Saint Vincent. Granny was also the was proprietor of a small shop in Kingstown where she made and sold cocoa for tea, sugar cakes, marmalade jam, and other sweets. It was a popular hangout for us kids—there and Papa's drug store where a candy machine was located. Granny was stunning, comparable to photos of those Nigerian beauties found in travel guides. And she was musical, always singing. Of my four grandparents she was the one who most ardently embraced calypso, so I suspect that a good deal of my African heritage and musical tastes may have come through her.

Now back to my grandfather, Papa. In addition to being a druggist and a political leader, he was an accomplished musician. He played the piano and clarinet, and had a strong appetite for classical music, as evidenced by his private collection of gramophone records and his repertoire on piano and clarinet. I'm not sure how he learned to play, but he saw to it that my father and uncles had instruction from Eunice Horne, a classically trained pianist and family friend. She would later become my teacher, but it was Daddy who gave me my first music lessons.

My father, Clarence Arthur "Tom" McIntosh (1920–2011), was an accountant by profession who worked for the government's treasury department. He was also a talented athlete who represented Saint Vincent in track and football (soccer). But his first love, besides Mommy of course, was music. The saxophone was his instrument of choice. He told me that his first teacher was a musician named Griffith who was the captain of the local police band. Daddy was a good reader and could play everything from the classics to calypso. While most of his playing was with the McIntosh family dance band, he occasionally performed with the Saint Vincent Philharmonic Orchestra, whose repertoire included Sousa marches, Viennese waltzes, Bach chorales, hymns, and patriotic tunes. He also loved American jazz and idolized saxophonists Charlie Parker, Lester Young, Coleman Hawkins, and Illinois Jacquet. On Sunday afternoons he hosted jazz and calypso jam sessions at our McKies Hill home in Kingstown to which we moved when I was around six or seven years old.

But I'm getting ahead of myself. When I was around four years old his job required him to move the family from Kingstown to Barrouaille, a small town on the leeward side of Saint Vincent. In my first year of school there I met three boys who would become friends for life: Adrian Fraser, who became an esteemed professor of history and the author of a book about the 1935 Saint Vincent labour riots that my grandfather George was accused of fomenting; and Anselm Scrubb and Bing Oliver, who became distinguished musicians (on trumpet and bass respectively) and with whom I would later play in New York. Now it was in Barrouallie that Daddy taught me the rudiments of musical notation on a homemade piano fashioned from a toy xylophone. I also picked up the basics of the solfeggio method for sight reading by sitting in on the lessons he gave to local musicians. I did not realize it then, but the solfeggio techniques I absorbed as a youngster would prove vital to my future success as a musician. Later Daddy introduced me to the saxophone. I never mastered the instrument, but understanding its possibilities would be an immense help in my latter career as an arranger.

My father was loving, nurturing, and a great provider. We were fortunate; we were never wanting for food, clothing, and shelter, the three economic necessities. He was proud of my musical accomplishments and abilities. In fact, he would sometimes make me a show pony in the presence of musicians

Clarence Arthur "Tom" McIntosh circa 1950.

visiting from Trinidad and elsewhere. I remember I was in awe of the Trinidadian pianist Kelvin Finch, and I would hide under the bed when he came over on Sundays because I knew what would happen, my father would say, 'Oh, have you heard my son Franklin play? Franklin, come and play the piano for Finch.' And I would crawl out from under the bed and play with trembling fingers. But there was never any competition between my father and me. As they say, the son is supposed to sit on the parent's shoulders, and that was what happened! My father put me on his shoulders, he never had me below his knees.

My Mother, Belle Cordice McIntosh (1918–1990), came from an East Indian family. Her grandparents arrived in Saint Vincent sometime in the late nineteenth century as indentured workers. Her father's original name was Balusingh, but it was changed to Cordice, the name of the estate owner, when the family settled in Saint Vincent—that was standard practice back then. They had a rough life, and several of her aunts and uncles were among the nearly 1,600 people who perished when the Soufrière volcano erupted in 1902. Her family was not very musical, but they were successful professionally, rising up as doctors, lawyers, and teachers. Mommy did love to dance and sing, and was always a big fan of calypso and my father's dance band. She was

Belle Cordice McIntosh circa 1950.

apparently thrilled when Daddy's friend Eddie Payne from Trinidad brought his dance band, the Merry Makers, to play for their wedding.

Mommy was devoted to all her children, but to this day my siblings say I was her favorite—I suppose because I was the first. She was very protective of all of us, always concerned about the way we looked and dressed when we went to school. She made sure the part in my hair was straight, presuming there was some connection between a straight part in your hair and walking a straight path in life. My mother was a strict disciplinarian; if she got angry, we might get a whipping with the belt. Nothing too bad, nothing approaching child abuse. But you know, a lot of us from the Caribbean thank our parents today for spanking our butts when we were little, because it made us what we are today. Of course, in the States you can't spank your kids today but the cops can shoot them! She was very loving to me and my brother Anthony (whom we called Tony) who came next, and then my two sisters, Cheryl and Arlene. There was also my half-sister Sonja—Daddy's daughter with Amy Providence—who came along before he met my mom. Sonja visited often and my mother always made her welcome. In addition to raising the four of us, she was employed as a nurse, and was very particular about who she would allow to look after us when she was at work.

When Mommy and Daddy married in 1946, intermarriages between East Indians and Africans were not that common. Saint Vincent's East Indian population was small compared to that of, say, Trinidad or Guyana, where such unions between Africans and East Indians were more widespread. Now my brothers, sisters, and I were obviously of mixed West African, East Indian, and Northern European heritage. But going by the definition of the "one drop of Black blood rule," I figured I had a couple of gallons, so I always identified as Black both in Saint Vincent and later in Brooklyn. In any case, it was not much of an issue at school, as there were plenty of other mixed kids of various ethnic persuasions.

My parents were married at the Anglican church in Calliaqua a few months before I was born. But growing up, I do not recall them being "Sunday morning churchgoers." Attendance was pretty much limited to funerals and occasional christenings. Nonetheless, when I was about nine, my mother decided that if I went to church on Sundays, that would make me a better person. Her decision was shocking, since to my mind, I was already a model kid. So off to the Kingstown Anglican church I journeyed. For the first few weeks, a couple of like-minded friends and I gathered berries from a tree in the churchyard, climbed the stairs to the upper level of the church, and threw those berries onto the heads of unsuspecting worshippers below. Then we scurried down the stairs and out of the church's back door. Somehow word of this got back to my mother, who insisted that from then on, I must sit in the lower level, in sight of my old piano teacher, Eunice Horne. The next Sunday I entered the church from the main entrance. Spotting a pew with only one occupant, an elderly gentleman, I took a seat there. Within seconds the cranky curmudgeon bellowed: "This is my pew, I paid for it, get out!" You see back then the churches gained revenue from renting pews—the fee was sixpence a year, and the renter was granted the authority to decide who could occupy it. Quickly bewilderment gave way to elation as I merrily jogged out the church and back home. I related the experience to my parents. Mommy was skeptical that I had gone to church at all. Daddy's take was "You do not have to pay for seats in heaven. Do not go back to that church!" My dad's reasoning seemed sound, so I followed it.

Education in later years did little to endear me to church, especially when I learned that the Anglican Church had been founded by King Henry VIII of England, infamous for his beheading of two wives. I also found out that within the nave of the Kingstown Anglican church lay the remains of Alexander Leith, an English officer who, in the late 1700s, murdered Saint Vincent's national hero, Carib Chief Joseph Chatoyer (whose body was never recovered). The thought of worshipping in such a precinct rubbed against the grain. To whom was I really praying?

My two sisters were musical, they sang, but they never showed much interest in playing instruments. But it was my brother Tony who joined me in taking up the family musical mantle. He had piano lessons, and would grow up to be a proficient keyboardist, saxophonist, and bass player—a real multi-instrumentalist. He played a little percussion with my ensemble in Saint Vincent when he was young, and later he followed me to Antigua to play for a band that the famous calypsonian Short Shirt put together. When I left in 1968 to come to Brooklyn, Tony replaced me as keyboardist for the Laviscount combo, the group I had played with in Antigua for more than a year. They just swapped McIntosh brothers! Eventually Tony moved to Brooklyn and lived with me for a while; he and I were always very close, being just three years apart.

Now back to my early musical training. When Miss Horne first encountered me as a five-year-old in Barrouallie, she had a look at my hands and told my father, "he has the hands of a pianist—you must promise me that I will be his teacher when you move back to Kingstown." So I started my piano lessons with her after we moved—I was around nine or so. Miss Horne was fair complexioned, very British in manner and speech, and a strict disciplinarian. You had to do exactly what she said, use the correct fingering and so forth. She would sit on the right side of the piano and observe what you were doing, and the penalty for consistent wrong notes was a crack on the knuckles with this heavy pencil. I always kept one eye on her hand and one on the keyboard.

Now Miss Horne taught only the classical repertoire, and was never a lover of local calypso music. In fact, she sorely reprimanded my father when she discovered that he had inducted me into the Melotones dance band. "How dare you, Arthur! This will impair Franklyn's immaculate touch!!" she intoned while standing quite erect. Fortunately, Daddy did not take that advice seriously.

I loved to play the piano, but as a young boy I was not always wild about going to my twice-a-week lessons. And at one point I guess I could be accused of truancy. My mother would send my brother and me off to Miss Horne's house for lessons, but we would end up at the Anglican school where we would play ping pong, or down at my grandfather's pharmacy where he had a candy machine. And sometimes I'd sneak into the big Anglican church with my friends who would pump the organ while I'd play calypsos on the keyboard. When the deacon finally appeared from his back office we had to scoot. This went on for a few months until my mother got wind of what was going on and enlisted a neighbor to drag me to Miss Horne's house. But looking back, I'm grateful for Miss Horne's efforts—she gave me the basic foundation in piano technique and theory that I would need to advance, and a real appreciation of the classics. I was honored to join the Philharmonic Orchestra, playing my saxophone alongside my father and uncle, at her brother's funeral in the early 1960s.

All in the Family: The Melotones

Sometime back in the late 1930s my father Tom and my uncles started a dance band called the McIntosh Brothers—later they changed the name to the Melotones Orchestra. Daddy and my uncles Donald and Harold were the saxophone players; Ben Prescod (brother to the celebrated classical pianist Patrick Prescod) and later my Uncle Jim were the pianists. Shake Keane, the renowned jazz musician and poet, defected from his family band to play trumpet for my father. Shake had left the Melotones for England by the time I joined, but I recall as a young child his broad arms carrying me up the stairs to rehearsals at the Working Men's Association Hall. That was the building that my grandfather had constructed for meetings with his political party. I did not have any idea back then of the fame Shake was destined for in Europe, or that decades later we would reconnect in Brooklyn and play together on recording sessions and jazz jams.

Besides the Keane Brothers, there were other dance bands on the island and we were all in competition with one another. There was a country band called the Jack Brothers, and several Kingstown-based groups—the Blue Rhythm Orchestra led by my cousin Syl McIntosh and Olson "Caribbean Pete" Peters; the Latinaires led by Kerwyn Morris and Raul Soso; and the Lime Light Orchestra, led by my Uncle Harold after he left my father's group. When I was growing up the Melotones were the best known through their association with my grandfather and playing for his political rallies.

All of the bands played for village dances. Now, none of the musicians did it professionally, no one depended on music for a living. They all had daytime jobs, a carpenter or plumber or a teacher or whatever. But most bands played on Saturday night dances, sometimes sponsored by schools and church groups. There also were New Year's Eve balls and occasional dances at the Association Hall in central Kingstown.

The dance orchestras played a wide repertoire of music, and I really benefited from being exposed to all that different music as a youngster. They played Latin boleros, merengues, waltzes, fox trots, American popular jazz arrangements, and of course calypsos—even a polka or two. Interestingly, nearly all the music back then was instrumental; you hardly ever heard singers. Cauldric

Forbes did sing in front of the Latinaires on occasion, but that was a newer group, formed after the Melotones. So as time progressed, I suppose you could say that more groups did start using singers. It was the same as in Trinidad. I don't recall a single record by any of the older, well-known dance orchestras like the Dutchy Brothers and the Clarence Curvan Orchestra, on which a vocalist was featured. We were all basically instrumental bands for people to dance to, and that is what the audience expected, they didn't ask for singers. Thinking back, I would divide the dancing into two main categories. Sometimes couples would dance close, holding each other, say on slower boleros and fox trots. During the breakaways on the faster calypsos and merengues couples would separate and dance facing each other but not touching. That is when things would get hot and individual dancers would strut their stuff.

The Melotones Orchestra was set up in similar fashion to American swing bands of the era—you had trumpets and saxophones, and a rhythm section of acoustic piano, string bass, and drum kit. Occasionally they would add a conga drum for the calypsos and boleros. Everybody in the band, except for the percussionists and a few of the bass players, knew how to read music. Same for the other dance orchestras, except for the Jack Brothers who played exclusively by ear. They had a looser sound and did lots of calypsos and waltzes for dancing, melodies that were easy to memorize. But they did not play jazz or popular song arrangements from scores. You see, most of the written arrangements were ordered from the United States—swing pieces by Count Basie, Duke Ellington, and the like.

Another thing—instrumental solos were really important back then! After the scored-out themes were played by the whole band, the saxophone, trumpet, or piano might take a solo. That is, they would improvise something new that was not written down. The more experienced musicians would improvise over the harmonic form of the song—maybe the verse/chorus chord changes or a simple blues form. Those who were less skilled would only solo during what we called the montuno, or tag sections—when you just repeated two chords over and over near the end of the song. They would go to town on that. But those who understood the harmonies, like my father and Uncle Harold, would play mostly on the chord changes. In the American jazz tradition, they would embellish and come up with new lines that were not directly connected to the original melody. This was similar to what Lester Young and Charlie Parker were doing at that time, playing on the changes and coming up with new melodic material. I remember that Daddy loved to play "Body and Soul," a tune on which Coleman Hawkins took a classic solo. Of course, he did not try to imitate Hawkins, he just played what he felt.

Melotones Orchestra circa 1946. Arthur McIntosh, fifth from left with saxophone; Shake Keane second from left with trumpet.

That's how music was in those days, when I was coming up in the 1950s and early 1960s. There was lots of emphasis on instrumental work, and not only in Saint Vincent but in Trinidad and all around the Caribbean. I have to say I was fortunate to grow up in those times—there was such variety, and it was a challenge to play the theme and then play a solo, you really had to think about the melody and the chords and how to put them together. You just do not get that in what's going on today in soca and a lot of pop music. It seems that instrumental soloing eventually fell out of favor in much calypso and Caribbean music. With the rise of the singer as the front man a lot was lost, both in terms of repertoire and instrumental practice, most notably the decline in any sort of virtuosic improvising. There was more emphasis on the theatrical presentation by the calypsonian, who in order to entertain and win competitions was expected not only to sing but also to dance and clown around. So, in those sorts of performance settings, especially the competitions, the music became subservient, which was a shame from the instrumentalist's perspective.

Back to the Melotones. I joined the group after I had entered the Boys Grammar School. I must have been around ten years old—that would have been sometime in 1956. My Uncle Jim was the pianist at that time. He was one of the best pianists on the island, but because of that he developed something of an attitude. When we had a gig he might say, "Well, y'all might need to send a special taxi to pick me up." Now by that time we were rehearsing in our house in McKies Hill back in Kingstown. Things would get going when my father got off from work, but some of the members would arrive early and run through the material before he got there. That is when I would sit at the piano and rehearse with them, until Uncle Jim came, if he came, and then I'd get up and go inside. Eventually Uncle Jim stopped coming to rehearsals regularly, and he was always demanding a cab for jobs. So finally, a few of the other band members said to Daddy, "Look Tom, Frankie knows the repertoire, why are you going through all this with Jim when we can use Frankie?" He said "no he doesn't," and they said "yeah he does." My father asked me to play at one of the rehearsals and I knew the music. So finally, there was this important gig coming up on New Year's Eve, and Uncle Jim was waiting for the taxi but they never sent one. I played the gig myself, and I got ten dollars—can you imagine? So that was it; from then on, I was the designated pianist for the Melotones.

Now, not all the Melotones' music was written down, some was played by ear. The calypsos, for example, were mainly head arrangements. After we ran through the verse and chorus several times the song would end with the montuno section. One player, often one of the saxophonists, would start a riff and everyone else would join in, and then someone else might start to solo and on and on. The more challenging melodic pieces like the boleros and the fox trots, or some of the waltzes, those we would need music for. But the calypsos were done by ear, and maybe some of the familiar waltzes, like the "Blue Danube." So, the players needed to be able to do both, read scores and play be ear.

When it came to soloing on the piano, it was easier for me to be more adventurous with the band because there was no one looking over my shoulder to crack my knuckles if I played the wrong note. And I am sure I played a few wrong notes! But it was a matter of refinement, you learned and you kept trying and developing things. It was easier to solo with the band, because you had the bass and drums for accompaniment. I did fiddle around with the chord progressions when I was by myself, but most of the solos were worked out with the band in rehearsal, or even at a gig.

A few folks have asked me about recordings of the Melotones, but I don't know that any exist today. They never made a commercial recording as far as I know. In fact, the groups that did record in the 1960s—the Latinaires and the Blue Rhythm Orchestra—had to travel to Trinidad to find adequate studio facilities. Daddy told me that sometime in the 1940s an American outfit stopped in Saint Vincent and recorded the band for the Voice of America radio program. A few people evidently heard the broadcast, but no one ever received a copy of the recording. This is a shame, and if anyone out there runs across some old tape with the music by the Melotones please let us know!

Stepping Out: The Frankie McIntosh Orchestra

A few years after I joined, the Melotones began to go into decline—I think my father just did not want to be bothered with all the rehearsals and arranging for gigs anymore. This would have been around 1960. Meanwhile I had won a scholarship and was attending the Saint Vincent Boy's Grammar School. I received a first-class education there, with a curriculum that included Latin, French, English literature, chemistry, geography, and so forth. But there was not much in the way of formal musical training other than a singing class on Friday afternoons. So, by the time I was a teenager, say thirteen or fourteen years old, a few of my schoolmates who played instruments and I began meeting around the main hall after school to play. Fortunately, they had an old piano in the building. At the end of the term, there was a function that they called a social, for the sixth form boys from my school and the girls from the high school next door. When someone suggested that we should play for the dance, well, we jumped at the opportunity. We were so happy to play! Even though we did not get paid, we didn't fuss. I played the piano, my friend Darnley Dublin guitar, cousin Ardon McIntosh trumpet, cousin Joseph McIntosh drums, and another friend, Clem Ballah, played conga drum and later graduated to string bass. We called ourselves the Frankie McIntosh Orchestra, although we were hardly that big a group at first. But eventually we acquired more instruments, adding two saxophones, an electric bass, and timbales. So, we ended up with a whole little dance orchestra, similar to what I was used to with the Melotones.

After that first dance at the school, we played for teen talent shows at the Lyric and Russell Cinemas and in Kingstown. By the time the second school social came around we were getting well known. We were a young group, and the teenagers were always on our side, especially the crew from the Devil Street neighborhood that was home to our timbales player, Dennis Davidson. The more mature audiences tended to gravitate toward my cousin Syl's Blue Rhythm Orchestra. Some of those talent shows were recorded by the local radio station "705," but unfortunately, they were recorded over and erased because the station was low on tape at the time. As far as I know, no recordings of the Frankie McIntosh Orchestra exist.

Besides the regular school socials, we played for debutant dances, what we call proms here in the United States. For private parties we would cut the band down to a small combo—the piano and rhythm section but no horns. The full orchestras would play at the bigger dance venues in Kingstown including the Peace Memorial and Association Halls, the Conway House, and the Sea View

Frankie McIntosh Orchestra circa 1965. Frankie on far right in front of piano.

Hotel. We also traveled to community centers in the smaller villages such as Layou, Barrouallie, and Chateaubelair on the leeward side, and at the dance halls in Georgetown, Calliaqua, and Mesopotamia on the windward side of the island. Besides these socials and dances, we were hired to accompany local calypsonians in the annual competition in Victoria Park, and for shows at the Lyric and Russell Cinemas when Trinidad calypsonians like Blakey, Lord Melody, and Bitterbush came to town. We kept busy, playing on weekends, and several times we even traveled to St. Lucia where we played at the Palm Beach Club and the Gaiety Club.

Some of the places we played had old pianos, but they were not in very good shape, especially in the schools. So sometimes we would rent an upright acoustic piano, which was quite laborious to move around. We would have to load it in the back of a pickup truck, sometimes drive for as much as twenty miles, then unload, and finally carry it up stairs. It was not until the mid-1960s, a year or two before I left, that I finally got an electric organ, which was much easier to carry around.

Hard as this was, I gained a lot of valuable experience playing with my band, and sometimes in unexpected ways. I remember one time our bass player disappeared after a mid-show break, so I had to take over. I sat the bass on my lap and played it by depressing the strings with my left hand while playing the piano parts with my right hand. I never advanced on the bass

Frankie in Saint Lucia with members of his orchestra and the Tru Tones, 1965.

guitar, but as with my early saxophone lessons, that experience helped me understand the instrument's potential when later I had to write out bass lines for my soca arrangements.

During the 1960s our repertoire would have been a little different from what we played in my father's band, because we were more geared toward the younger generation. Now we did maintain some of the standard jazz and pop arrangements like "Misty," "One O'Clock Jump," "The Stars Fell on Alabama," stuff like that. But we expanded things by taking on more contemporary pop songs from the UK and the United States, and putting them to a calypso beat. For example, we would take a song by the Beatles, like "Yesterday," and retain the original melody and chords, but put a calypso beat to it. That is where the subtle use of the Caribbean three-beat *tresillo* and four-beat *habanera* rhythms would come in. As far as the standard calypsos went, with my father's band we would play instrumental versions of songs by the older calypsonians like Spoiler, Kitchener, and Lion, while my band did songs by Sparrow, Rose, and the other younger singers of the 1960s.

I had a little experience writing out charts for the Melotones. Daddy had taught me the fundamentals of harmony, and when the orchestra charts arrived from the United States, I would examine them closely. There was always one chart, the conductors score, with all the parts, everything was laid out for you. So, I could see how the parts interrelated with one another, say how far the first saxophone would be from the second saxophone and so forth. If the parts were close, you got a tighter sound than if they were more spread out. So, I got a lot of ideas about how music could be orchestrated and arranged from studying those scores, and if I had a question Daddy would help.

Right from the beginning I was doing all the arranging for my band. Here is how it would work. When I was getting ready to leave for school in the morning, I might hear a new Sparrow song on Radio Guardian or Radio Trinidad. I would listen to it, press whatever record button was in my head, and attempt to memorize it. When I got home, I would start sketching a chart based on what I remembered. Then hopefully I would hear it again on the radio that night or the next morning, allowing me to check if what I had written corresponded to what I was hearing. If all went well, I would have a basic chord chart for the different sections of the song, along with initial melodic material for the introduction and instrumental sections that would be played by the horns and keyboard. Occasionally I would write instrumental melodies based on motives from the vocal verse or vocal chorus that Sparrow sang—but more often they were material of my own invention. I also wrote outlines for the ending montuno, or jam section as we called it. Those were usually my own creations that had nothing to do with Sparrow's original melody. I will go into this process in considerably more depth in chapter 4, but this should give you a taste of my youthful ventures into writing arrangements.

Once I'd handwritten all the parts, I would call a rehearsal and try out the arrangement. The other band members pretty much relied on me because they knew I understood what was going on, musically speaking. If there were difficult lines I would often sing or play them because their levels of reading really varied. Sometimes I would have to clap the rhythm to demonstrate how it should be played or phrased. So, that is how we would put it all together at a rehearsal, and then we would be good to go.

Carnival in Saint Vincent

Carnival was a busy time for us. Back then Saint Vincent's Carnival coincided with Trinidad's, on the days leading up to Ash Wednesday. It was not until 1977, years after I had left for Antigua and Brooklyn, that our Carnival was changed to early July to avoid the scheduling conflict. Now I recall Mommy dressing me up for Kiddie Carnival, and Daddy played in one of the adult masquerade bands. The whole family would go to downtown Victoria Park in the afternoon and evening to watch the Mas and Queen competitions. And of course, we ate well that day—everyone brought food and shared with everyone else. During the competition a small band with horns and rhythm section would play and the audience would sing along when they struck up a familiar calypso. I remember them singing "We Want Ramadhin on the Ball"—a reference to Sonny Ramadin, one of Trinidad's most legendary cricket players who happened to be of Indo-Caribbean heritage. Most of the calypsos we heard on the radio at that time were from Trinidad—our own singers had not made records and were seldom heard outside of the local calypso tents or the competition.

Now, after the big parades and daytime festivities, the Melotones always played for evening Carnival dances and balls that were held in places like Association Hall or Peace Memorial Hall. But bear in mind we had to be done by midnight on Tuesday, because the next day was Ash Wednesday, and you would be punished by God if you played on that day! We were warned by the serious church folks that the whole place might blow up and be consumed by fire.

Saint Vincent Carnival had our own local calypso competitions, where singers like Mighty Hawk, Sheller, Young Sparrow, Sun Blaze, and Toiler presented their original songs. I don't recall my father's band ever being part of that, but cousin Syl's Blue Rhythm Orchestra, and eventually my own band, would accompany the calypsonians during the competition. Typically, the Calypso Monarch contest would take place on the Saturday evening before Carnival Monday, usually on a stage in Victoria Park. There was seldom much rehearsing. The way it would work, the band would be on stage, and the calypsonian would come over to me by the piano and sing the first line so I could get the key. Once I had the key and the chord sequence established, he would start singing and the bass player would follow me, and then the horns would come in. Everyone played by ear, it was just a head arrangement, no charts. We really did not have time to rehearse everyone, and the Carnival Development Committee could not pay for a venue to rehearse. They might have up to ten finalists on Saturday evening, and each one would sing two songs, so the final competition might last three or more hours. We were paid to perform, but not rehearse.

We also had steelbands in Saint Vincent, but in my day, they were limited in size and scope. Their musical arrangements tended to be simpler than they are today—no extended introductions, multiple sections, and so on. And the availability of pans was limited—we did not have a lot of builders and tuners, so we had to depend on Trinidad for pans. Not surprisingly, the pans were not well tuned back in those days; the sound of the pan is much more refined today thanks to the advanced techniques of the tuners. I don't remember any big pan yards, but I do recall bands would gather outside on a street corner to rehearse. And we did have a steelband competition that took place in Victoria Park on Carnival weekend. There were small bands, what we called pan sides, set up in different corners of the park, and they would play in their designated order.

Now, I will tell you my experience with the competition and one steelband, led by this gentleman with the last name Woodley. I was in grammar school at the time, maybe sixteen years old. And Woodley asked me if I would arrange a piece for his Tuborg Band—I think they were sponsored by a beer company. He had six, maybe eight guys, and he was the single tenor pan player. I went to the Bay Street neighborhood to rehearse the band, in which I also played double tenor. So, I arranged two songs, I think one was a Beatles song. Everything was done by ear because they did not read music, but we finally got the arrangement down. I was playing the harmony. But Woodley was a fierce drinker, and I remember going down to Bay Street Friday night for the last rehearsal and telling him, "Now Woodley, remember the competition is tomorrow night, so no drinking!" And he said "Man I know how important this competition is, I ain't gonna drink!" There were three bands that competed the following night, and let's just say we came in third. When we all got up on stage, everyone was there except Woodley, who was responsible for the main lead part on tenor pan. Then we looked out and saw him stumbling across the park, with a rum bottle sticking out of his pocket. He mounted the stage and started to play. I do not know what he played, but it certainly did not have any relevance to the arrangement! So, all that time was wasted, and we came in last. That was pretty much the beginning and the end of my involvement as a pan arranger and player.

Later on, I had requests from band leaders to arrange for pan, there in Saint Vincent and up here in Brooklyn. But few of the players read music and I did not like having to teach them by rote. It just took too long. I was used to working with reading musicians in the Melotones and my band, and I just did not want to go through the task of having to drill people over and over on their parts. I had heard that arrangers were not always paid what they were promised, especially if the band did not win the competition. Raf Robertson, the great Trinidad pianist, told me a story of how he once arranged for a steelband up here in Brooklyn. After the competition, when he asked for his money, the band captain said: "Which money you asking for? We ain't win!" So, I just did not want to deal with that sort of thing. Now don't get me wrong—I love pan, and I hold pan arrangers like Clive Bradley, Ray Holman, and Boogsie Sharpe in highest regard. Sometimes I have even tried to write soca bass lines that I thought would sound good on bass pan, and of course, playing with pan soloist Garvin Blake up here in Brooklyn has always been a joy.

The Frankie McIntosh Orchestra stayed together until I left for Antigua in 1967, after which their name was changed to the Symphonettes. Now here is how my departure came about. After finishing at the Boys Grammar School, I took a position at the Intermediate School in Kingstown, teaching English literature. My Uncle-in-law, Bertram "Timmy" Richards, was the headmaster there, so I had a connection. I think I was making around $165 a month, and still playing weekends with my band. But I really wanted to go to college, and there was no university in Saint Vincent—the nearest was the University of the West Indies, which had branches in Trinidad, Jamaica, and Barbados. Unfortunately, none of these schools had full music degree programs at that time. Meanwhile, a friend of mine, Cooper Prescod, who played trumpet for my cousin's Blue Rhythm Band, had moved to Antigua and joined a popular group called the Laviscount Brass combo. Cooper wrote me and said the band was in dire need because their regular pianist, Carver James (who happened to be my brother-in-law), was travelling to Canada over Carnival season. This was 1967. So I told Uncle Timmy that I wanted to go to Antigua for a week or so, and he agreed to give me a leave of absence. I remember the members of my band were all sullen and sad faced because they didn't believe I was coming back. They had a little get-together and send-off for me at the Haddon Hotel, a popular dance spot. The trumpeter, Vernon Coombs, played this piece called, "For All We Know, We May Never Meet Again." And the kids at school said, "Mr. McIntosh, don't go for long, we'll miss you."

Antigua

When an ambitious twenty-one-year-old Frankie McIntosh arrived in Antigua in 1967, he found a society that was both familiar and dissimilar from what he had experienced growing up in Saint Vincent. Like its neighbor to the south, Antigua is a small Caribbean island with a population of just over 60,000 individuals who are mostly of African descent. Antigua shares Saint Vincent's history of slavery, sugar production, and British colonial rule. The island was also a member of the failed West Indies Federation, eventually becoming an Associate State of the United Kingdom in 1967 before gaining full independence in 1981. But unlike Saint Vincent, Antigua chose to move from an agricultural to a tourist-based economy in the 1950s. By the time Frankie landed in the late 1960s, the island's beautiful beaches and St. John's luxury hotels were attracting tourists from North America and Europe. The benefits and dangers of tourist-based economies were then, and remain today, complex, but in the 1960s the result in Antigua was a bourgeoning entertainment business ripe with opportunities for musicians.[17]

As part of the tourism effort Antigua established an official Carnival in 1957. Based on the Trinidad model but held in early August, the celebration included steelband and calypso contests that attracted both locals and tourists. Antigua had developed its own steelband tradition early on, with the popular Hell's Gate band winning the first official competition that took place at the St. John's Girls School in 1949. In 1955 the Hell's Gate, along with Brute Force and the Big Shell Steelband, were the first Caribbean steelbands to be recorded and featured on commercial records thanks to the efforts of the American record producer Emory Cook.[18]

By the 1950s Antigua boasted a strong indigenous calypso scene. The first official Calypso King contest, staged as part of the 1957 Carnival, was won by Samuel "Styler" Richards, who was accompanied on the stage of St. John's De Luxe Cinema by the Hell's Gate Steelband. The competition was later moved to the outdoor Carnival City venue, where brass bands, often the Mason Brothers Orchestra led by saxophonist Oscar Mason, provided instrumental accompaniments for the calypso contests. Following Trinidad's precedent, during the months prior to Carnival, tents were organized where local calypsonians would try out their latest songs for fans and tourists.[19] In 1970, the first road march title for the most popular calypso heard during the street parades was awarded to Calypso Joe's "Bum Bum."[20] During the 1970s and 1980s several noteworthy Antiguan calypsonians traveled to Trinidad and Brooklyn to record. McClean "Short Shirt" Emmanuel, Rupert "Swallow" Philo, Paul "Obstinate" Richards, and Rupert Blaize were among the most influential singers for whom Frankie would later arrange in Brooklyn.

While demand for calypso was high during Carnival season, Antigua's hotels and restaurants provided work for singers and musicians year-round, opportunities that were simply not available in Saint Vincent or the other small islands. For Frankie, Antigua offered the chance to finally work as a full-time musician.

Onward to Antigua

As soon as I landed in the port of St. John's, Antigua, I was scooped up by Cooper Prescod and the other members of Laviscount. I hardly had time to catch my breath because the band was scheduled to play for Saturday, Sunday, and Monday fetes as well as a big evening Carnival dance. The following day we gathered at Cooper's house to be paid, and he hands me $600 Eastern Caribbean Currency. I could not believe it—I had never held $600 in my hand before! I ran into my room and spread it out on the bed to count it again. And later Cooper tells me, "Look Frankie, Carver is not coming back from Canada, so there is an open job here in the band for a pianist full-time. We have so much work here we could be playing seven nights a week!" You see, they liked me because like Carver, I played calypso and was also conversant with the jazz standards that the American audiences often demanded at the hotels. So, I told Cooper of course I would stay after he showed me how much money I could make.

You could do much better in Antigua as a musician than you could back home, or even in Trinidad for that matter. In fact, I met several musicians who had come there from Trinidad for the work. At the time, Antigua boasted a thriving economy based on tourism, with four- and five-star hotels such as the Anchorage and the Jolly Beach that catered to American and European customers. Back in Saint Vincent, musicians played mainly at dances that were sponsored by sports clubs and other civic organizations. They tended to coincide with holidays such as Easter, Christmas, and of course Carnival. But in Antigua there was work all the time if you knew the standard jazz repertoire, some American R&B and rock tunes, and the popular calypsos. For a gigging Caribbean musician, Antigua was the place! So, I asked my mother to tell Uncle Timmy back in Saint Vincent that I would not be coming back. I regretted it, but I knew that for my career and future as a musician it would be more beneficial for me to stay in Antigua than to go back home. I remained there for a little over a year, before setting my sights on the United States.

I believe that Laviscount was, back then, the most popular band in Antigua, because the players were so versatile and we could play various genres of music. We did American R&B songs by James Brown, Wilson Pickett, and Otis Redding; recent calypsos by Sparrow and Rose; and American standards like "Satin Doll" and "Body and Soul." There was plenty of work, not just at Carnival season. We ended up playing six nights a week (Cooper gave us one night off to rest)—maybe three at hotels like the Anchorage, two at local nightclubs like the Strip, and often a weekend dance at the Country Club or Michael's Mount. At the big hotels we played mostly for American and European tourists who would be sitting and drinking, or maybe eating dinner. Once in a while a couple would be moved to get up and dance, but mostly it was music for listening. So, we played jazz standards and contemporary pop/R&B stuff that they would be familiar with. Occasionally we would throw in a calypso. But at the smaller clubs and dance halls the audiences were mostly local Antiguans who came to dance. So that's where we'd roll out the calypsos, sometimes with the long jams when the music got hot and the dancing intense.

Laviscount had a somewhat unique setup, sort of a hybrid. It was smaller than the dance orchestras like the Melotones, but bigger than the combos that were becoming popular at the time around the Caribbean. Those smaller combos used electric guitars and organs, and focused mainly on their interpretations of American-style rock songs. Our front line was only two trumpets, no saxophones or other reed instruments. Now, neither Cooper, the first trumpeter, nor Lucian (that is what we called him, he was from St. Lucia), the second trumpeter, read music fluently. They played by ear, so I could not write out parts for them the way I did back in Saint Vincent. But those two fellas just really seemed to click together. Cooper would play a melody and Lucian would naturally harmonize it, usually in thirds or sixths. The sound of those two trumpets locked in together was very satisfying, and both Cooper and Lucian memorized their parts and could play in any key. We had several Antiguan drummers who came in and out of the band. Cooksy was more of a rock and roll drummer. He was replaced by Chubby, who could play and sing. Finally this fellow Dodsey came along who was versatile and had a nice feel for calypso. So, the rhythm section was drum kit, a conga drum, electric guitar, electric bass, and me playing the Farfisa electric organ. Although I did not write out formal arrangements, I would coordinate things at rehearsals, like establishing the proper key and the chord progressions. We used an American Fake Book for the jazz standards, so everyone could follow the chords and the vocalist the lyrics. Which reminds me, the other big difference from my older bands was that we always had a singer in Laviscount.

The jazz standards we played came from the Fake Book, but the American R&B and pop stuff were mostly covers we had learned from records or heard on the radio. Songs like "I Feel Good," "Mustang Sally," "Soul Finger," "I'm Your Puppet," and "Whiter Shade of Pale" always went over well. We played them pretty much like the original, employing a straight 4/4, R&B/rock beat rather than a calypso bounce. Our singer would try to imitate the same soul inflections of the original Black American vocalists, with no Caribbean accent. The calypsos we played were the most recent ones from Trinidad that we heard on the radio or perhaps from a record that someone had bought. Interestingly, many of the singers were well versed in both R&B and calypso—I suppose they had to be in order to please the different audiences at the hotels and dance halls. Occasionally a guest singer would sit in for our last set. Rupert Blaize, a fantastic pop and soul singer, would sometimes join us. I really loved his voice, and years later would arrange for his R&B and calypso recordings in Brooklyn.

When Trinidadian calypsonians like Rose would visit Antigua, they would always have Laviscount accompany them, because we were the local band most conversant with calypso style. Maybe it was because Cooper, Lucian, and I were from the southern islands that we shared a feel for calypso's distinctive rhythm and linear phrasing. The other Antigua bands were heavier on American R&B, soul, and funk, perhaps due to their closer proximity to the United States and the preferences of all the American tourists they played for.

Of course, Carnival was a big deal in Antigua, but we were so busy playing for dances and at clubs that first week that I did not have time to attend many of the major events like the calypso and steelband competitions. I did hear Oscar Mason's band that first year. They had a full brass and reed horn line like the Melotones did, so they were the band of choice to accompany the calypsonians on stage at Dimanche Gras. When I first met Oscar, he tried to impress me by playing the trumpet, saxophone, and flute on the same song. Cooper whispered to me to be respectful because Oscar was a feared boxer. I was, and we became good friends—I visited his house often that year.

I also recall hearing two of the Antigua's top steelbands, Brute Force (when Bum Jardine was the leader) and Hell's Gate. Antigua had a much bigger

Frankie and Laviscount guitarist Paps, Antigua, 1968.

steelband scene than we had back home in Saint Vincent—they had an oil refinery and access to the necessary drums to make the steel pans. Hell's Gate and Brute Force played during the day at this St. John's open-air venue called the Town House, usually with a good-sized group of twenty-five or so players. Laviscount would usually play there in the evenings for dancing. That was one place where there was lots of mixing between the tourist and the local audiences.

I met a few of Antigua's foremost calypsonians during my stay. Short Shirt (McClean Emmanuel), who dominated the Antiguan Calypso Monarch competition during that period, was a friend of Cooper, and he had a little club, more of an outdoor bamboo tent setup called the Calabash. He had food, drink, and a makeshift bar. It was one of the small local clubs where Laviscount played, and occasionally Short Shirt would join us. The arrangements were always impromptu—he would come over and sing a bit of the song to me, and I would set the key and then the rest of the band would join in. Most of the clientele were local Antiguans because the club was located along Briggins Road, in a neighborhood of St. John's that was outside the normal tourist zone.

I had a number of other new experiences in Antigua, including my first recording session. A record company came to Antigua and talked to Cooper about recording Laviscount. I am not sure, but I think they were from the US. Now, back then there were no recording facilities in Antigua, so they took us into an empty club. They didn't have any elaborate equipment, just a reel-to-reel tape recorder with one or two microphones—just enough to pick up the band acoustically. There was no individual miking of instruments through a fancy mixing board or anything like that. It was a two-track recorder, so whatever we played was going onto the record. We rehearsed three pieces—the popular Sparrow calypso, "Crazy John You Can't Dance," and the pop tunes "Love Is Blue" and "Whiter Shade of Pale." There were no written arrangements, I just ran through the chords with the band and they rolled the tape. I did not think much about it until a while later, when Cooper called the band together and presented each member with a 45rpm record. I do not recall the record getting any real distribution or radio airplay—it might have been a vanity recording that was never released on a real label. In any case, hearing ourselves on Cooper's record player was amazing, and I knew that making records was something I wanted to do!

Antigua put me in touch with musicians that I never would have met if I had stayed in Saint Vincent. It was during an engagement at the Anchorage Hotel that I was introduced to the legendary American jazz pianist Teddy Wilson. His trio was booked for a few weeks and Laviscount was fortunate enough to play alternate sets with him on Wednesday nights. During the breaks I pestered Teddy with questions about technique, solo work, and chord voicings. He loved to expatiate, and I imbibed all! His bass player, Alex Layne, was American born with a Vincentian father, so we immediately hit it off. He was really into modern jazz and had played with Ahmad Jamal, Horace Silver, and Nina Simone among others. He would laugh that Teddy was too "old school" for him. So, Alex would hang out with us sometimes, and one day I remember him sitting at the piano and showing me how Silver had voiced the piano chords with his left hand to the piece "Nica's Dream." This was a true epiphany for me! I finally had a sense of the modern jazz sound I had heard on record but could never capture. I was exhilarated—I felt like a different pianist. Those informal lessons with Teddy and Alex reminded me just how much more I wanted to learn about modern jazz, music theory, and piano technique.

Then one day I met "Montego Joe" Sanders, the famous percussionist who had played with Art Blakey, Max Roach, Dizzy Gillespie, Monty Alexander, and a bunch of other well-known jazz artists. He lived in New York and was in St. John's for a gig. I started talking to him about my aspirations to continue my music studies, and he recommended Brooklyn College. I asked him what about Juilliard or Manhattan School of Music, and Joe said that those institutions specialized exclusively in music. But at Brooklyn College I would get music and a whole lot more in terms of literature, history, philosophy, science, math, and so on. Given my background, I guess what you would call a "liberal arts" education in Saint Vincent, he thought maybe Brooklyn College might be a good fit for me. That turned out to be great advice.

The money I earned gigging with Laviscount was terrific, but I knew that if I was going to progress as a performer and teacher I needed to expand my experiences and musical knowledge beyond the Caribbean. Looking back, I realize Antigua was a stepping stone to come to America. I think I knew, even before leaving Saint Vincent, that I was not going to make Antigua my long-term domicile. But meeting those musicians and getting a sense of the broader world out there really brought it home for me. I turned my attention toward New York and wrote to Brooklyn College.

CHAPTER 2
BROOKLYN IS MEH HOME

When Frankie McIntosh landed at JFK airport in October 1968, New York was a city in transition and fraught with social unrest. Amidst accusations of racism and anti-Semitism, city teachers were on strike over demands for community-based control of schools in Brooklyn's Ocean Hill–Brownsville neighborhood. That spring, anti–Vietnam War student activists had shut down Columbia University, and tensions flared in Harlem and Brooklyn following the April assassination of Martin Luther King Jr. In the wake of King's civil rights legislative successes, Black power advocates were clamoring for self-determination and the overhaul of public and private institutions where the vestiges of racism persisted. In more mainstream politics, Shirley Chisholm, a second-generation Afro-Caribbean of Barbadian parentage from Brooklyn's Crown Heights neighborhood, was elected in November 1968 as the first Black (and West Indian) woman to serve in the US Congress. Meanwhile, significant numbers of white New Yorkers were abandoning their old city neighborhoods for the greener pastures of the suburbs, eventually leading to a loss in tax revenues and the deterioration of public services including schools, police, subways, and sanitation.

Brooklyn College, a part of the City University of New York (CUNY), had become a center of controversy when Frankie arrived there in the fall of 1969. In response to CUNY admissions policies that resulted in its senior colleges remaining overwhelmingly white despite the city's growing racial diversity, Black and Puerto Rican student activists had organized a strike in the spring of that year that paralyzed the Brooklyn College campus. One of their demands, reform of a perceived Eurocentric curriculum, resulted in the establishment of Departments of African Studies and Puerto Rican Studies. Similar protests across CUNY campuses led to the implementation of the controversial open-admissions, tuition-free policies in 1970. The number of nonwhite students more than doubled in the early 1970s, resulting in a far more diverse student body. But increased enrollment exerted tremendous pressure on an already financially strapped system and in response to the city's 1976 financial crisis, tuition was reinstated (the first year that the number of nonwhite students exceeded that of whites).[1]

While concerns about the Vietnam conflict and racial inequity were mounting, the city's demographics, and Brooklyn's in particular, were rapidly changing. The 1965 Hart-Celler Immigration Reform Act made significant modifications in the old quota system and opened the door for immigration from the Caribbean, Latin America, and Asia. Small West Indian countries, including Saint Vincent and Antigua, benefited from these reforms. In the early decades of the twentieth century, New York's original West Indian immigrants had settled in Harlem, with smaller enclaves in the Bronx and in Brooklyn's Bedford-Stuyvesant neighborhoods. Looking for better and more affordable housing, the post-1965 surge of West Indian migrants headed for central Brooklyn's neighborhoods of Crown Heights, East Flatbush, and Flatbush, as well as areas of southeastern Queens. According to the 1980 census, some 300,000 West Indians lived in New York City, a five-fold increase from 1965.[2] By the turn of the millennium, West Indian immigrants constituted 8 percent of New York's population, making them the largest immigrant group at that time.[3] The central Brooklyn that greeted Frankie in 1968 was rapidly transforming into New York's own "Little Caribbean" as the older Italian and Jewish occupants headed for the suburbs. Immigrants from Saint Vincent formed a relatively small percentage of the new arrivals, with Jamaica and Trinidad leading the way. However, a shared British colonial heritage, language, food, and music allowed Vincentians to comfortably intermingle with other English-speaking islanders.[4]

The relationship between the newly arrived West Indians like Frankie and their native-born African American neighbors was complicated and not always copacetic. On one hand, there were times when some Caribbean immigrants sought to maintain a social distance between themselves and their African American neighbors, due in part to their perception of native-born Blacks' low-class standing in the United States. Not surprisingly, some African Americans resented what they took to be the newcomers' "uppity" attitudes and saw them as competitors for jobs and real estate.[5] On the other hand, America's one-drop racial caste system failed to differentiate between native and foreign-born Blacks. As a result, most whites simply lumped the two groups together as "Black," and naively assumed they should live side-by-side in segregated, nonwhite neighborhoods. Caribbean immigrants and African Americans thus found it advantageous to form alliances to fight against racial discrimination and the high crime and drugs that too often plagued their communities. A shared African heritage gave them a degree of familiarity when it came to each other's music, dance, folklore, and worship practices. This social reality further underscored the complexity of identity politics for Caribbean immigrants. Could they assimilate into mainstream America, or at least into Black America? Should they maintain a pan-Caribbean identity, or should they cling to their island-specific cultures?[6] Would Frankie and his extended family become Americans, Black Americans, Caribbean Americans, or Vincentian Americans, or all the above? And where did his East Indian background fit into the puzzle? Music would play a key role in the process, as a cultural expression that could both differentiate and unify Black Americans and Caribbean people.

Despite its economic woes and social tensions, New York City at the time of Frankie's arrival remained a vibrant center for diverse musics. The opening of the Lincoln Center for the Performing Arts (1962–66) cemented the city's position as the citadel for classical symphonic and choral music, opera, and ballet, and the downtown scene was bursting with experimental new music. Midtown and downtown Manhattan clubs and lofts supported the world's most renowned and innovative jazz musicians. Harlem's legendary Apollo Theater remained a leading venue for Black music of all stripes, and the 1969 Summer of Soul Festival series attracted more than 300,000 fans to Harlem's Morris Park to hear the leading stars of soul, funk, jazz, and salsa. Broadway rolled on, breaking new ground with the 1968 premiere of the rock musical *Hair*. In the churches, clubs, and dance halls of the outer boroughs one could hear jazz, Black gospel and R&B, Latin jazz and Nuyorican salsa, Dominican merengue, Jewish Klezmer, Irish ceili, and Greek rebetika music. Caribbean Carnival music, reggae, and hip hop would be added to the list in the 1970s and early 1980s.

With the migration of Harlem's Labor Day West Indian Carnival to Brooklyn in the late 1960s came calypso and steelband music. Sparrow, Trinidad's most popular calypsonian of the era, prophesized the rise the borough's celebration with his 1969 classic "Mas in Brooklyn." The chorus's bold pronouncement, "Brooklyn is meh home," surely resonated with the many newly arrived islanders and sounded out the formation of a Caribbean-Brooklyn identity. On Labor Day of 1971, the West Indian American Day Carnival Association (WIADCA) staged its first big Carnival parade down Eastern Parkway, Fredrick Olmsted's grand boulevard that ran from Grand

Army Plaza east into the Caribbean neighborhood of Crown Heights. Steelbands and calypso singers mounted on trucks provided the soundtrack for colorfully costumed Mas (masquerade) bands who danced up the Parkway for what would soon become the city's largest outdoor ethnic celebration.[7] WIADCA quickly established steelband, calypso, and reggae concerts, and local dance halls featured calypso orchestras led by islanders Lio Smith, Syd Joe, Ron Berridge, and Daphne Weeks. Calypso tents and outdoor concerts attracted star singers from Trinidad who visited to perform and record during Labor Day Carnival season. Several, including Sparrow, Calypso Rose, Lord Melody, Becket, and the Mighty Duke would relocate in Brooklyn and Queens and record for recently established Caribbean-owned record companies. By the early 1980s Brooklyn would emerge as the leading production center of Caribbean calypso/soca music, a development that would indelibly mark Frankie's musical career.[8]

In addition to Brooklyn's blossoming Carnival music scene, Frankie found himself in a borough overflowing with African American jazz and R&B. The scores of small clubs and bars that dotted Black neighborhoods in Brooklyn and Queens offered local instrumental and vocal music. The Blue Coronet (Fulton Street), Putman Central (Putnam Avenue), Club La Machel (Nostrand Avenue), and Tony's (Grand Avenue) presented jazz luminaries Miles Davis, John Coltrane, Dizzy Gillespie, and Thelonious Monk. La Machel was the site of the now-legendary 1965 live recording, *The Night of the Cookers*, featuring iconic trumpeters Freddie Hubbard and Lee Morgan. Brooklyn native Randy Weston and his neighbor Max Roach organized musician collectives, and in 1969 a Black cultural center and jazz venue known as The East (Claver Place) opened in Bedford Stuyvesant. But this was only the tip of the iceberg; as one musician told historian Robin Kelley regarding Brooklyn's neighborhoods, "The music was everywhere. Every little corner bar had jazz."[9]

When Frankie began his musical studies in 1969 the formal study of jazz in the United States was on the cusp of unprecedented growth, with programs in American colleges and universities beginning to expand their offerings in jazz history, criticism, theory, and ensemble playing. In 1972 only fifteen institutions offered degrees in jazz studies, but by 1982 the number had swelled to seventy-two.[10] Drawing on New York's aging population of major jazz figures who were ready to turn their attention to teaching, City College and New York University were able to establish graduate degree programs in the 1970s, while the New School and the Manhattan School of Music followed suit in the 1980s. Despite these advances there remained resistance to jazz in many quarters of higher education because elite, Eurocentric notions of culture that downplayed the seriousness of all musics outside the Western classical canon.[11] The Brooklyn College Department of Music that Frankie joined as a student in 1969 was typical of this conservative approach, cementing its Western-classical focus by adopting the title of Conservatory of Music in 1972. The following year, as Frankie was completing his classes for a bachelor's degree, the Conservatory organized its first jazz ensemble, although it would not establish an official master's program in jazz until 2016.[12] Fortunately for Frankie, City College and New York University were more forward thinking, providing him the opportunity to study jazz at the graduate level.

When President Gerald Ford refused to provide federal government funds to bail out New York City from its financial crisis, the now infamous headline "Ford to City: Drop Dead" appeared in the October 30, 1975, edition of the *Daily News*. The phrase resonated with many Americans, who at the time had come to see the nation's largest city as a rapidly deteriorating cesspool of crime, drugs, and corruption. But many new immigrants, especially those from the West Indies, viewed New York through different eyes. Yes, the city was big, dirty, and dangerous, but in the 1970s it offered enormous opportunities for work and study that simply were not available to them back home in the islands. And for artists like Frankie, who straddled the worlds of classical, Caribbean, and Black American music, honing his craft through advanced instruction and using his skills to earn a viable living were no longer just dreams.

Frankie: Touching Down in Brooklyn

I remember hearing stories about famous calypsonians and musicians traveling from the Caribbean to New York by steamer, back in the 1930s and 1940s. But these were modern times, so in October 1968 I found myself on a BWIA flight from Antigua bound for Kennedy Airport. As the plane took off, I experienced conflicting emotions: leaving the known for the unknown; abandoning a vibrant, existential reality to pursue an uncertain dream. I tried to turn my attention toward the cockpit, the direction of my future. And with an occasional glance out of the plane's window I could see the past vanishing in the distance. But the past never disappears from consciousness; it forever serves to guide the future.

As my flight approached our destination, my apprehensions gave way to anticipation. I knew New York was where I needed to be. At that time, it had the reputation of being the jazz center of the world, and I was fascinated by all the stories of musicians like Dizzy Gillespie and Charlie Parker, playing at these renowned jazz clubs. I wanted to see all these places. And of course, New York was a melting pot with lots of people from the Caribbean and from all over the world. I suspected there would be opportunities to play Caribbean music and maybe jazz while I was studying classical music. As far as music, the arts, and education went, I was sure I could benefit from being in New York more than anyplace else.

And I had a plan. Getting a tourist visa to the States had been no problem. I'd received an acceptance letter from Brooklyn College, and I understood that once I arrived and registered for classes I could apply for a student visa that would be good for several years. Meanwhile I had exchanged letters with my Uncle Harold, the saxophone player with my father's band who had moved to Brooklyn. He assured me I had a place to stay with him and his family when I arrived.

Just before we landed, the stewardess came along and offered everyone tea or coffee. I do not usually drink coffee because it tends to make me sick. However, most of the passengers were American, and they were all having coffee, so not wanting to be the odd one out as I approached my new home, I accepted. And wouldn't you know it, after the first few sips I was retching in the plastic-lined bag—welcome to New York! Things did not improve once I got off the plane. I called my Uncle Harold, and whoever answered put his wife on. I said "Hello, this is Frankie," and she replied, "Oh, Harold isn't here right now. I know he was talking to you about staying with us, but would you believe six of your cousins just arrived from Canada so that room is no longer available." So, there I was, right off the plane with my suitcase, all alone at Kennedy, and nowhere to stay!

Fortunately, my friend Lee Olivacce and his brother Ken had planned to come to the airport to greet me and carry me to Uncle Harold's place. I knew Lee from Saint Vincent—he was originally from Curaçao and Grenada, but was working at Radio 705 in Kingstown, where I met him in the mid-1960s. When they arrived, I explained what had happened with my uncle and said, "Look Lee, I have a return ticket and I think I'm just going to jump on the plane and go back to Antigua tomorrow. You know, I have a job there and social connections. And I don't even have a place to stay here!" Lee and Ken responded in unison, "What, are you mad, man? You're going back to Antigua when you're in New York already? That does not make any sense, you come and stay by us!" So, we got in the car and drove to his parents' place in the Cypress Hills neighborhood in Brooklyn, right on the Queens border. They owned a frame house on Glenmore Avenue near Euclid. When we arrived, I saw their mother, Mrs. Olivacce, standing on the steps to the doorway of the house. I greeted her as I went in but and she did not say a word to me, and I remember thinking, "Ought-oh, she probably doesn't like them bringing this strange guy in here." I got inside and put down my suitcase and she came in and said, "Oh wait, that was you who just passed? I'm sorry, I thought you were one of my sons." And that was prophetic, because I would become one of her sons soon enough—she was my future mother-in-law.

Lee took me around the house and to this room where he said I would be staying. There were three beds in there, and they just brought in a fourth. Lee said, "This will be your bed." So I slept in the room with Lee and his brothers, and later moved to the basement where I was a little more comfortable. Meanwhile here comes this pretty little girl with two ponytails, and I looked at her and she smiled back at me. And Lee says "Oh, that's my sister Patsy." So that is how I met my future wife, but more on that later.

Uncle Harold appeared the following day with an apology and an enjoinder to move to his residence. But I had already seen Patsy, so I politely declined his invitation with no further explanation. You might say I had an ulterior motive at the time. Now, the Olivacces were a typical, hard-working Caribbean family. The mom, Clarion Olivacce, was East Indian and originally from Anguilla. The dad, Connell Olivacce, was from Dominica—he could speak French creole. Lee and Patsy and their siblings were born in Curaçao but later moved to Grenada, before coming to the States sometime in the early 1960s. At the time that I arrived, Mr. Olivacce was working as a medic at Fort Hamilton, Lee had landed a job at NBC as a tape editor, and Patsy was just finishing up high school. I recall that Mr. Olivacce was impressed when he learned that I had been accepted to Brooklyn College. He was especially elated when I read his medic reports and could identify $CuSO_4$ as copper sulphate, and $NaNO_3$ as sodium nitrite. I was immediately dubbed a budding Einstein and Toscanini rolled into one. Mrs. Olivacce became even more maternal when she discovered that her closest friend in Curaçao was my Great Aunt Isa, who too had moved there from Saint Vincent for work. I felt right at home in this big Caribbean family, even though they were not from Saint Vincent, and I lived with them for my first two years in Brooklyn.

One thing that really impressed me was that they owned their own house! The goal of most Caribbean people has always been to buy or build a home for the family; this aspiration was the norm, not a dream that began in the United States among immigrants. Back home in Saint Vincent most of my family owned their own homes. You see, folks travel with their culture. Now, the Olivacces did not have a fancy Brownstone like you might find on some blocks in Crown Heights—it was just a modest frame house. But it was theirs to do with as they pleased. They could bring in family (or future family like me), rent out rooms, whatever they wanted. I thought to myself that someday I would buy a house in Brooklyn.

Getting Settled in Brooklyn

Honestly, I was a little disappointed in Brooklyn when I arrived in the fall of 1968. I recall that initially the air smelled musty, and the sky was not so clear and clean as it was back home. In fact, on the first night I was alarmed that I could not see the stars due to pollution. And fast-food establishments like White Castle and Benson Burgers produced an unpleasant chemical odor. There were no curry, onion, garlic, or chive aromas except in the house when Mrs. Olivacce was cooking delicious Caribbean food.

Out on the streets I immediately experienced clear cultural differences. I was appalled that instead of returning a "good day" greeting, passersby would look at me askew, with a puzzled expression. And children seemed to show little respect for elders, using profanity in their presence without concern. Surprisingly, that did not seem to bother the elders either. That sort of language from children would never have been tolerated back home.

I noticed that the houses in the immediate neighborhood looked a little raggedy. Back in Saint Vincent, or at least in most of Kingstown, the houses were well kept, both wood and stone. We had some great architects and builders in Saint Vincent. The colors of the Brooklyn buildings were not as vivid—overall they struck me as grey and drab. There was a sameness from block to block, every house in its own space, separated from the neighbor by a wall or fence. In the Caribbean, open yards were common. The school playgrounds of concrete called "parks" amazed me. Where was the green grass for kids to roll in?

After a few tours around Brooklyn with Lee and his brothers, it became apparent that this was not the great melting pot I had read about. There were distinct ethnic neighborhoods: Jewish, Italian, Hispanic, Black, and so on. But in this diversity lay a certain richness and character peculiar to New York. A resident of this city could experience the world without leaving: a Jewish falafel in Flatbush, a Greek gyro in Astoria, Italian pizza and chicken cacciatore in Bensonhurst, Caribbean curry chicken and roti on Nostrand Avenue, and so on. Although my nostalgia for the Caribbean lifestyle never waned, I found myself being slowly assimilated to New York culture and consequently appreciating such conveniences as supermarkets and bodegas within a block or two of my residence, easy access to medical practitioners, and efficient taxi and phone service. Never having ridden a train in my life I found the subway fascinating, although the gun-toting transit police were a bit intimidating at first. Back home the only weapon the police ever carried was a club.

And of course, there was the music, so much music! A few days after I arrived Lee took me to hear the famous jazz pianist Ahmad Jamal at the Village Gate in Manhattan. He really impressed me, and I realized there were some real benefits to being in New York—I never would have heard Jamal in Saint Vincent. Shortly after that I went to a show in Madison Square Garden that I will never forget—it was the Count Basie Band, the James Brown Band, the Ramsey Lewis Trio. Each band did a set, and then they all came back on the stage and played together. It was so awesome, the quality of the sound! Meanwhile I discovered that on nearly every corner of my neighborhood around Glenmore there was a little bar or club, and many of them had a jazz trio or an R&B band on the weekends. You could hear some outstanding musicians there, people who were not necessarily going to become famous recording artists, but talented singers and players in their own right. So, at that point I knew that I did not want to go back to the Caribbean, at least not right away.

The neighborhoods out in Cypress Hill and Brownsville were not all Caribbean at the time of my arrival in 1968. In fact, I think the Olivacces were one of only two Caribbean families on the block at that time. It was mostly Black and Latino, with a few Italians, and I remember one German family. Halsey Street in Bedford Stuyvesant, where I moved in 1971 to rent a room from my Aunt Hilda, was mostly African American. There I lived with my cousins and two Trinidadian renters. It was an extremely comfortable Caribbean kind of setup; we all spoke with the same accent and we shared food. On occasion one of the Trinidadians would cook a big pot of stew and we would all eat together. Unfortunately, I came home one day from Brooklyn College and found an eviction note on the door—apparently Aunt Hilda had not been paying the landlord the rent we were giving her, so I was out on the street and had no choice but to go back to the Olivacces' house on Glenmore.

Shortly after this happened, Aunt Hilda somehow managed to buy a house at 1297 St. Marks Avenue in Crown Heights. Then I got together with my mother, who had arrived in Brooklyn shortly after me, and together we rented small apartments next door at 1299 St. Marks in a building owned by a Trinidadian lady named Idlett who also lived in the neighborhood. Mom, who was a registered nurse, had been working at St. Mary's Hospital, across the street where Aunt Hilda also worked. Soon after that my father, my brother Tony, and my

Frankie, Patsy, Ahmad, and Omar, St. Marks Place, Brooklyn, 1975.

younger sister Arlene came up. Tony had experience as a lab technician and got a job at St. Mary's. It seemed like the whole family was working there; it was so convenient, right across the street. Later my older sister Cheryl joined us. So, we all ended up living in 1299, with Hilda and my cousins right next door. I married Patsy in 1974, right in my apartment with a Baptist minister named Reverend Hallet. When my son Ahmad came along later that year and Omar arrived in 1975, I realized that we could use more room.

One morning in 1981 I was sleeping in after a gig. Patsy came in and said, "Frankie the people down the block told me they want to sell their house at 1287 St. Marks, right down the street. Now I know we do not have any money to buy a house, but they gave a price of something like $20,000." And I woke up, jumped out of bed, and told her, "Go find that person right now, whoever it was!" The owners were Leo and Mafalda Squeri, a very nice Italian couple who had lived on the block before I moved into 1299. They just could not maintain a second house at 1287, so they decided to sell it and I was quite happy to relieve them of that burden. I took out what in those days they called a passbook loan. I had money in the bank, and the passbook loan was only around 4 percent at that time. A conventional mortgage would have been more expensive, maybe at the time something like 10 percent. They froze my account at the Flatbush

Federal Savings Bank, and I could keep the loan as long as I wanted as long as I paid the interest. I was able to pay the whole thing off in good time, because I was doing pretty well financially, playing several nights a week with an R&B group called The Wonderful World of Charlie Brown and Yvonne, freelancing on my nights off with jazz ensembles, and building up my arranging career with Granville Straker and Rawlston Charles.

Patsy (who was pregnant at the time with our daughter Jamilah) and I, my young sons Ahmad and Omar, my Mom and Dad, my two sisters, and my brother Tony, all moved into the new house at 1287 St. Marks. And with Hilda and my cousins a few houses down in 1297 it started to feel like living in the Caribbean again. We would go to each other's houses to eat and for celebrations. The neighborhood was really starting to change around then. When we first moved in 1981, we were the only two Caribbean families on the block. Most of our neighbors back then were Black Americans. But then more people from the islands started moving in, and today, forty years later, I would say the block is probably 80 percent West Indian. Now some young white people are starting to move in; things keep changing.

You know, the dominant opinion of white people who do not live in the community is that this is a "Black neighborhood," that we are just one homogenous group of dark-skinned people and that and everyone gets together and there is all this love. Well, that was not always the case, because sometimes things could get tense between the Black American and the West Indians in our neighborhood. I remember one time that a few of my cousins, they were just youngsters then, got in some sort of argument with some Black kids around the block, and a fight broke out. And there was this gang of Black people, folks who we thought were our friends, coming up the street with pitchforks and shovels and God knows what else shouting: "Get them damn West Indians off the Block. Them damn West Indians want to take over!" And this fight broke out and the cops had to come to break it up. It was really troubling, because these were people who always smiled at us and we smiled at them. But after that I was on my guard.

I think there was a degree of jealousy based on the perception that we Caribbean people placed such a premium on education and hard work. The public schools were not so great back then and a lot of the Black kids ended up dropping out. Then here come these West Indian kids staying in school, studying to be nurses and doctors. Given those realities, I really pushed to get my kids into private schools. We were fortunate to enroll them into St. Ann's and Brooklyn Friends, they were both terrific educational institutions. Thankfully, all four of my children were good students and ended up with scholarships, which was the only way we could afford it. Brooklyn was a bit rough back then, and a number of Vincentians and other Caribbean folks who had the financial means were moving out to Queens and Long Island where the schools were better and they thought it might be safer. But with our kids' education taken care of, I wanted to stay in Brooklyn because this was where all the music was happening for me.

I do not want to paint too bleak a picture here, because despite these conflicts Black Americans and Caribbean folks often did get along. If there was a common cause, like fighting for higher wages or something to do with the schools, things that would apply to all of us, people would come together and unite on that front. And the younger people did socialize and some intermarried. Our landlords at 1299 were a Black American man and a Trinidadian woman, and I ended up playing with many Black American and mixed Black/Caribbean musicians. It depends on whether you look at the situation with a telescope or a microscope—with the more microscopic view you can see some of the divisions.

On a positive note, establishing residency in the United States and eventually becoming a full citizen proved to be relatively simple. You see I had maintained my student visa for a number of years until Patsy and I got married in 1974. Her family had come to Brooklyn in the early 1960s and she had acquired citizenship through naturalization. So, about a year after we married, she filed for me to get a green card, because if you were married to a US citizen your application went right to the top. It did not take long after that. I remember I had to leave the country—I went to Canada for one day—and then came back and got the card. I decided to continue with the green card for work and travel so I could maintain my Vincentian citizenship, and it wasn't until 1996 that I officially became a dual US/Vincentian citizen.

You know, attitudes toward immigrants were different back in the late 1960s and 1970s, not like they are today. US policy recognized the need for immigrants and the contributions of immigrants to America, especially coming from the Caribbean. We worked in the hospitals and health care, in the construction trades, and of course a few of us in music and education! The average Caribbean person, male or female, came to the US with skills; we did not come to live off the government. Take my mother, for example. She was a registered nurse in Saint Vincent, and when she came to Brooklyn, she took a test and then went to work as a nurse for the rest of her career. You see, back then there was not this fear that the Black population would outstrip the white population and that we had to limit the number of visas the government would issue to Black immigrants. That is what some politicians are

Frankie with Ahmad, Omar, Jamilah, and Hakim, Brooklyn, 1982.

trying to do today, and I think that sort of fear is at the root of our current immigration debate. Thankfully it was easy for me back then.

Classical Music and Jazz Studies— Brooklyn College and New York University

By the time I touched down in New York I had already been accepted at Brooklyn College, but I was not to start until the fall semester of 1969. So, my first trip to the campus was for registration that August. I took the train to Flatbush Avenue and found my way into Boylan Hall to the registrar. And I ran into this guy from Trinidad—he picked me out because I was one of the few Black students. So he walks up and engages me in conversation, and from my accent he must have figured I was from the Caribbean. He enquired: "So you're coming to Brooklyn College, so what are you going to study here, steelpan?" I laughed and answered, "I doubt it." But that made me feel a little more at home because nearly all the students around me were white Americans.

This was certainly a different experience from my schooling back in Saint Vincent, where everyone was Black, East Indian, or mixed. I remember that in my initial music classes I was the only Black student, although that would change later. I can't say I was treated any differently—I think my professors quickly figured out that I was eager to learn about music and that was all that mattered. That first introductory class was a listening course in which we had to identify the forms and themes of the great works of the classic repertoire. And the music we listened to was strictly from the Western classical canon—Bach to Beethoven to Brahms to Wagner to Debussy and everything in between. Back in 1969 no one was taking about jazz or world music—all other music was considered second-rate compared to the classics. Jazz was not respected back then. I remember one professor told the class that anyone playing jazz was probably a C student at best, because they were not up to our classical standards and values (I was careful not to let him know about my jazz interests). And of course, I did not go to Brooklyn College to study jazz or calypso; who would teach it? I came expecting to study primarily European music, I wanted to gain knowledge in the areas in which I was lacking, especially in Western music history and classical piano repertoire.

My second or third year I did take one class in African music from a white professor named Kennedy. It was basically a history and culture course and I really enjoyed it. But I remember the first day when he entered the classroom several of the Black students complained that Professor Kennedy should not be teaching the class because he was white. They ended up walking out and dropping the class. I was surprised, but things were tense back then, with a lot of complaints from the Black American students about the way the college was being run. With the new open admissions policy there were a lot of first generation Black and Puerto Rican students trying to figure out how things worked. But as I said, this was not a big issue in the music department. Nearly all the students were white, but more Black and Caribbean students like me were starting to show up. There was a real sense of comradery among the music students, supporting one another, and many of my friends were white.

Looking back, it seems strange to me that people would rank different musics, or say that only someone from a particular culture could teach that music. Maybe it was because of the American cultural and racial divide, that people presumed this was supposed to be jazz and this was supposed to be classical and ne'er the twain shall meet. But I did not think of it that way. Coming from the Caribbean I had a more holistic view of music and culture. We were exposed to a wide variety of music, and for me, everything was all connected. I had grown up playing classical piano pieces, calypso dance music, R&B pop songs, and big band and modern jazz, and loved them all. And there were groups like the Dutchy Brothers, from Trinidad, who were playing Tchaikovsky's *Waltz of the Flowers* and Chopin's *Piano Bolero (Fantasie-Impromptu)*. They used the original melody and harmonies but interpreted them through the eyes and ears of Caribbean musicians, using calypso rhythms and occasionally improvising. In any case, I had to learn a lot more about European music, especially about its origins and history, because it drew from musics from other parts of the world—from Asia and Africa, and of course there was the influence of American jazz in the early twentieth century. So I felt I had the same right to learn about European music as Europeans had to learn about other cultures. It was a global, open way of looking at it.

I did not get involved in any protests or political organizations, but I wholeheartedly supported the new open admissions policy, and thought it was a great opportunity for students who did not have the right academic diplomas from high school. As far as free tuition went, I was all for it, and eventually would myself benefit, at least indirectly. I always believed that money should not be a factor when it came to imparting knowledge! But I was bothered by some students who abused the privilege by not going to classes, who just hung around socializing and looking for financial aid. I had to pay $18 per credit for my first year at Brooklyn College, which I could afford, and foreign students were not supposed to be eligible for the new tuition waivers. But then at the end of the year the dean called me into his office and told me that because of my excellent grades I had been put on a special list of foreign students of color and would no longer have to pay tuition. Of course, I greeted this news with great delight! But those "excellent grades" would slip slightly over the next few years when playing music and touring caused me to occasionally be late with papers and to miss important exams. You could say that work sort of took over. In any case, I was fortunate not to have to ever pay tuition at Brooklyn again!

I came in as a piano performance major. But during my first year at the college I realized that although my technique was up to college level and my knowledge of harmony above average, my classical repertoire on piano needed to be extended. Some students had begun studying classical piano as early as age three, and there was one girl whose parents were concert pianists. Her playing was more mature than some of the instructors! Fortunately, I was assigned to Zenon Fishbein as my primary piano instructor. He was a distinguished concert pianist originally from Argentina and who was on the faculty of the Manhattan School of Music. In fact, several of my professors also taught at Manhattan and Juilliard Schools of Music, so we had access to them without the hefty tuition charged at those places. Fishbein gave me a number of challenging new pieces to work with. There was no piano at Glenmore Avenue, so I'd have to go to the practice rooms on campus after class and just stay until it got dark. I was hungry to learn. That was my routine. I'd be in the practice rooms between and after my classes.

I also took private lessons from two other excellent pianists, Anne Dodge and Robert Harris (who also taught at Juilliard). Dodge was an accomplished classical performer, but she also loved jazz. So, we worked on Joplin and other ragtime pieces as well as the standards by Beethoven, Chopin, and Debussy. She really helped me with repertoire.

As far as technique and interpretation went, I learned a lot from Fishbein. His approach was not to worry so much about specific technical factors. He would ask me to imagine how different sections of my piano piece would sound if they were orchestrated. Would this line be more adaptable to a flute, a bassoon, a violin, or whatever? Then he might urge me to try to get a flute sound, a flowing legato sound from the piano. Do this and the technique would take care of itself. At some point he would guide me. If you want to get a more legato sound you hold your fingers closer to the keys. Or you pull against the keys rather than striking them straight down. Things like that. He was very helpful.

I really got a lot from my theory and composition classes, analyzing on the one hand, and synthesizing or constructing on the other. When you listen to a musical work, what are you really hearing? For the trained musician, it is not enough to say "the trumpet is really playing sweetly." I began to think about how the composer approached form and structure. Everything, I began to realize, came from a conceptual plan—like an architect would have before he erects the Empire State Building. So those classes really helped me to listen analytically, to identify the various sections within pieces, and how they functioned. I also developed a deeper understanding of the intricacies of melody, things like which notes were primary, passing, upper or lower neighbors, which were ornamental and which structural, how motifs combined to form phrases, and so forth. Now, we never actually talked about the music of Charlie Parker, or John Coltrane, or McCoy Tyner in my classes—the examples were drawn strictly from the classical Western repertoire. But I could use those analytical techniques to better understand what modern jazz players were thinking and doing. Once I determined those principles, I could apply them analytically in a broad sense rather than trying to copy note-for-note, say a Coltrane or Tyner solo. This knowledge had a positive impact on my own improvisation and composition.

Down the road I was able to use these methods to analyze and arrange calypso music. Of course I recognize the African contributions, particularly when it comes to melodic and percussive rhythm, preference for certain instrumental timbres, vocal delivery, syncopation, melodic contour, phrasing, and the like. But calypso, as it emanates from the calypsonian as composer, is essentially tonal, in a rudimentary sense. Use of western harmony among Blacks in North America and the Caribbean is one example of the syncretism that tends to occur when cultures clash. Enslaved Africans did not sing 'do re mi," "Yellowbird," or "Go Down Moses" on the slave ships. Western harmony was learned, in churches and schools. But whereas Black American jazz musicians have expanded the European tonal vocabulary while applying aspects of their African musical heritage, calypso tends to affirm tonality's basic I, IV, V harmonies.

That said, in terms of form, many calypso melodies develop in ways which the European masters would never have imagined. There is a sense of balance and proportion, often not as easily recognized in calypso as one would in a Beethoven sonata. The point is that the methods of "seeing and hearing things" that I learned at Brooklyn College were applicable to the calypso and jazz music I was and would be arranging, and I was able to employ those ideas. Maybe that's why people think my music sounds a bit different from that of other soca arrangers.

While I found the tools of Western music theory helpful in understanding some aspects of Caribbean music, I was disturbed to find that within so-called "higher academic circles," expressions like calypso simply were not recognized as music. I remember once in the college library trying to find "calypso" in a reference book and coming up empty under the music section. I had to go to anthropology to locate calypso, as if it were only a form of culture and not real music! I was alarmed that you could have students from places like Brooklyn College with music degrees who had never heard of Charlie Parker, or Art Tatum, or the Mighty Sparrow, or Lord Kitchener—how could that be possible? You call yourself a musician and you do not know what calypso, or jazz, or gospel is? I felt privileged to be exposed to all these different facets of American and European musical cultures, and still maintaining my own. Recognizing the contributions our local music made to the musics of the world was essential.

As I mentioned earlier, jazz was not part of the official Brooklyn College music curriculum when I arrived in 1969. However, I managed to find a few kindred spirits and we set up our own little informal jam sessions. One fellow student was Larry Feldman, a flute and saxophone player. He knew Chick Corea personally and had access to these handwritten piano voicings that Corea had made for him. So, he would bring Corea's music to me; this was back in the early 1970s. And I would play the Corea chord charts and Larry would improvise. There were often a couple of other students. One was Leslie Edwards, a terrific trumpet player. He was Black American, and more inclined toward jazz than classical music. Leslie never really embraced the Brooklyn College Conservatory program and what it was about as eagerly as I did. Miles Davis and Freddie Hubbard were more his focus. And there was another Black piano student named Harold Beasley who would come to the sessions. He had gone to Music and Art High School and was really a phenomenal classical player. He really wanted to learn how to play jazz, so he would come to the sessions and mostly watch what I was doing and at one point we discussed exchanging lessons, but as I recall we never got around to it.

Our little jazz sessions were strictly off the books, not for any kind of formal class or recital or anything. Larry, I, and the others would just find an empty practice room in the basement of Gershwin Hall. Of course, everyone could read, so we would play from charts, and Larry had a couple of fake books with transcriptions of the top jazz standards. Those basement sessions really paid off for me and Larry. He later carved out a successful career in jazz. It was a real learning experience, playing with musicians like Larry and Leslie, who like me, were studying classical repertoire and technique but also loved jazz. It was a welcome break from our other classes, so sometimes we would meet several times a week, whenever the occasion arose.

For my final jury piano recital at Brooklyn College, I remember playing Chopin's *Revolutionary Etude*, Beethoven's Sonata *Pathétique* in C Minor, several Bach fugues, and Debussy's *Reflets dans L'eau*. I passed the recital, but I was three credits short of graduation because I had handed in a final Music History paper late and the professor had left for Germany. I did not want to take the course over again at Brooklyn, and I was busy playing and traveling with these different jazz and R&B band by then, so I let it slide for two years. I finally made up those three credits at City College and officially graduated from Brooklyn in 1976. While I was at City College one of the professors heard me playing around at the piano and suggested I consider their Jazz Masters program where I could study with John Lewis of the Modern Jazz Quartet. At that point I wanted to do more formal jazz study, not only to learn but because a graduate degree would probably be necessary if I eventually want to teach. So I auditioned for Professor Lewis and was accepted in the program. But City College's schedule was not good for me, and I found out I could finish a master's degree much quicker at New York University.

Sometime in the late 1970s I auditioned at NYU. I remember they were impressed with my rendition of Art Tatum's *Tiger Rag*—something I am sure I can no longer play. Then they offered me a partial scholarship and I accepted.

Arranger and saxophonist Tom Boras was the head of the jazz program at that time. He taught the arranging and composition classes and I performed with several of the school's ensembles, including the one that Tom led. I also had the opportunity to take a wonderful series of aesthetics courses with Lawrence Ferrara in which we dealt with music from a philosophical perspective. Those discussions and research papers opened up a whole new vista for me, about the issue of referential meaning in music, and how cultural factors affect what we hear.

My main piano teacher at NYU was Jim McNeely. He was the arranger for Thad Jones and Mel Lewis, and often played with their big bands at the Village Vanguard. During lessons we would sit at the piano and he would play the bass line while I would improvise on pieces that I had prepared the week before. And then we would switch—I would play the bass line and he would take the solo. He might suggest certain things that I might incorporate into my solo, like modal ideas or other alternative ways of approaching the chord changes. Sometimes he would show me how he would do things, and other times the way pianists McCoy Tyner and Hank Jones might vary the harmonic voicings during their solos. This was quite helpful to me. I could see McNeely's way of looking at it, but he would never negate mine. When things went right, I could incorporate, or conjoin his ideas with my own, thereby expanding my improvisational skills.

I really valued the holistic approach to music and jazz that I experienced at the NYU program in those years. The faculty saw jazz as America's classical music, and while acknowledging its African American origins, they did not hesitate to use European techniques and methods as a lens through which you could understand and perform jazz. This was very much in keeping with my own convictions. As I mentioned earlier, all the music theory I was learning did not apply only to classical music, but could also illuminate the work of Charlie Parker, McCoy Tyner, and all the other jazz greats of that time. And now at NYU this was openly acknowledged and discussed in our classes on jazz arranging, composition, and history. Tom Boras was quick to point out that for an artist like Billy Taylor, this distinction between jazz and European music was minimal. And of course, Taylor, along with jazz players John Lewis, Miles Davis, and others, had studied Western classical music. On the other side, European composers including Stravinsky, Bartók, and Debussy incorporated elements of ragtime and jazz into their classical works, and American composers Gershwin and Copland later did the same. Curiously, early jazz was accorded an elevation in stature by music critics only when legitimate white composers like Debussy, Bartók, or Copland adopted it—a sudden transformation to "classical" art music. But when played in the ghettos by urban Black people it was still only "jazz," not serious, substantive music like the modern European composers were creating. The folks at NYU challenged that outmoded approach, taking as a given that jazz was serious art music. From a broader perspective, they saw the transmission, exchange, and influence of art among cultures as being universal and eternal. I agreed, and appreciated that stance!

Gigging to Make a Living— Caribbean Dance Bands & Brooklyn Carnival

All the time I was studying at Brooklyn College I was making a living playing in various groups around the city. By the time I arrived there was a vibrant Caribbean community here in Brooklyn, and not surprisingly there were several working dance orchestras similar to the ones I'd played with back in Saint Vincent. Within weeks after settling in at Glenmore Avenue I was rehearsing with the Tropicana Brass, the Olivacce family band. They were an amateur group that gigged occasionally on weekends, mostly for private parties for friends of the family. They did not stay together for long and I quickly moved on, but their guitar player, Mikey Lorrainey, became a close friend and musical partner with whom I would do a great deal of playing down the road.

In the local Caribbean music world, there were people who knew of me from my playing back home, including several who had played in my father's band. One was the saxophone player Lionel "Lio" Smith, who had immigrated to Brooklyn back in the 1950s and had organized his own orchestra. He and his brother Alan owned Alan's Bakery on Nostrand Avenue, a favorite shop for Caribbean people. So, when word got out that I was in Brooklyn, he invited me to come play with him. Now one day, this must have been sometime in early 1969, he stopped by my house on Glenmore and said "Frankie, my bass player cancelled, can you play tonight for a boat ride?" Calypso dance bands frequently played for evening cruises around Manhattan, mostly for Caribbean patrons. Now I didn't play much bass, but I was destitute and this would be my first chance to play with a professional ensemble in Brooklyn. So, of course I said yes! Now, I had played a little bass guitar by ear in Saint Vincent, and although reading bass clef on piano posed no problem, I had no clue where to find the notes on the fretboard of the instrument. But with grim persistence I took my place in the bassist's seat at the back of the band, next to the drummer. The frontline horns were all heavyweights including trumpeters Ray Copeland

Frankie and Olivacce Family Band with Mikey Lorrainey on guitar, Glenmore Avenue, Brooklyn, 1969.

and Pearson Tudor, and sax virtuosos Howard Kimbro and Charlie Brown. Lio distributed the charts about fifteen minutes before start time, and I was astonished to see that each bass part was at least six pages long. I was familiar with most of the basic melodies in the repertoire that included jazz standards like "Satin Doll" and "Shiny Stockings." However, Ray Copeland's arrangements, gems in their own right, were teeming with unexpected transitions, breaks, and unison passages that left me lost much of the time. The frontline players cast occasional disapproving glances in my direction as doggedly I plucked away. Somehow, I remained on board until the boat docked, and Lio even paid me! Fortunately, that was the last gig I ever did on bass for Lio. He had a Panamanian pianist at the time named Terry Pierce, but I guess he liked my Vincentian approach to things and he started to call me to play keyboards. I revisited those challenging bass parts with the same group on future gigs, but this time as organist, with left hand devoted to bass.

The Lio Smith orchestra was a big band, with four saxophonists, three trumpets, and two trombones. And he had some great jazz players, including

Copeland and the Panamanian saxophonist Carlos Garnett. You could say it was quite similar to the Melotones back home, so I just fit right in. We played for Caribbean audiences on weekends, especially Saint Vincent clubs and organizations that Lio had connections with. We performed at venues like Anton's Catering (Queens), Albermarle Towers (Flatbush), Wishco Manor (Eastern Parkway), Gayhart Ballroom (Nostrand Avenue), and a few Manhattan ballrooms including the Audubon. In those halls we played mostly calypso arrangements, and a little big band jazz. Occasionally we would play for white audiences in Long Island or Connecticut—they wanted to hear mostly big band jazz for dancing, so that's what we gave them.

Eventually I did some arranging for Lio, including Sparrow's "I'm a Robot" and Lord Melody's "Rasta Man," that his orchestra recorded in the late 1970s. We did that at Art Craft Studio in Brooklyn and Lio released it on his own label. "Robot" was a hit by Sparrow the previous year—it was one of Lio's favorite calypsos and he asked me to write the charts for it. I probably used the Sparrow recording from the radio as my source for ideas. The basic harmonic framework was a I-VI-II-V loop (C-Am-Dm-G7 in the key of C). Sparrow's melody was transcribed for the horns, with some embellishment. Near the end of the arrangement, I freed up a little (as we say in the Caribbean), improvising around on the monophonic synthesizer over the chords and a stop time figure. The flip side of the recording was Lord Melody's "Rasta Man," a calypso he had put out in 1978. As with Sparrow's song, Melody's tune was rendered on the horns, with call and response sections divided between high and low brass, or reeds and brass, all interspersed with the vocal line "Rasta man be careful," taken from the original song. Then toward the end, the tag opens things up with a trombone playing a jazzy solo against punctuated horn riffs (4:03). This was the sort of "montuno," or coda section, that that we would end a song on at a dance, but in that setting we would stretch it out longer, especially if the dancers were into it. On the recording the engineer just faded us out when he determined the song was long enough. Those two recordings give a good sense of how, early on, I would arrange a popular calypso tune for a dance band.

My name was beginning to get around and eventually another Caribbean dance band leader, Syd Joe, started calling me for gigs when his regular pianist was not available. I knew his Trinidadian guitar player, Leslie Sargent, who probably recommended me. Now, the Syd Joe Orchestra did not do any American jazz, the repertoire was nearly all Caribbean dance music. We would usually play a few calypsos, and then slow things down with a bolero or waltz. The boleros were slow, in 4/4, with the bass playing a characteristic one/rest/three/four, and people would dance close. Syd did most of the arranging

"Rasta Man," 45rpm record by the Lio Smith Orchestra, 1979.

himself, but sometimes used Frankie Francis. He would get the latest calypso records from local music stores like Straker's or Charlie's, and then he would write out the parts. For the piano it was mostly filling in with chords and a few unison lines. Once in a while the band would employ a singer, but it was mostly instrumental. The horns did take solos, although as I recall they were not as jazzy as they were in Lio's band. It was more of a simple triadic approach, staying close to the original melody and adding light embellishments. Honestly it was more playing from the heart, what you felt, not thinking about a solo in terms of harmonic extensions or modes, the way a modern jazz player might.

Syd Joe had a set band made up primarily of Caribbean musicians, not all of whom were conversant with American jazz. Lio's outfit, on the other hand, consisted of a looser personnel that often included Black American jazz players. The calypso dance gigs paid well, maybe two or three times more than you could make playing at a small club, so Lio was able to attract all these top-notch jazz players who wanted the higher-paying jobs.

Labor Day Carnival was a busy time for the orchestras led by Syd and Lio and others who played for dances, calypso tents, and other events around Brooklyn. Looking back, the funny thing is that the first few years after my arrival, I did not have anything to do with the Eastern Parkway Carnival parade—in fact, I did not realize it was happening. Then, sometime around 1974 I got the call to play with Syd Joe's band for the parade. So, of course I accepted, and we motored down the Parkway on a flatbed truck with speakers and guitar amps, all powered by a generator. At that time, the parade was not as big as it is now, but there was a modest crowd behind our truck, and there were other trucks and small steelbands. There were no DJs or big sound systems like you have today, it was all live music. I played with Syd's band on the Parkway a few times, but one year someone got shot in front of our truck and I decided not to do it anymore.

Then the next year I was resting in bed on Labor Day morning and my friend Anthony "Buggs" Niles calls me and begs me to come down to the Parkway because his group really needed a keyboard player. Begrudgingly I agreed, but when I got there, I found out it was only Buggs, who played drums, and a bass player—no horns, guitar, or singer. So, I had to carry all the melodies and strum the chords myself on this cheap keyboard they had for me. It was a tough gig, very hot out there on the Parkway for two or three hours. And at the end wouldn't you know it, the Trini bass player, who they called "Bass," went into a club to collect our pay and disappeared! We never got paid, and I decided that was the last time I was playing the Parkway.

It was good to see Caribbean people get together and to participate in a Caribbean festival, but you did not feel that sense of togetherness or community that I'd experienced in Saint Vincent or Antigua. Each island group had its own truck and flag. To me it was not really like a Carnival in the Caribbean, it was a New York Carnival—wider spaces, people not greeting one another. In Kingstown you would know pretty much everyone! Another thing I noticed about Eastern Parkway was that there was not much sense of musical unity. Each island played its own songs. Here you might have Syd Joe's band playing Sparrow, an Antiguan band playing Short Shirt, a Dominique or Haitian band with someone singing in French patois, and eventually a Jamaican band playing Bob Marley.

I did enjoy playing with bands at the Dimanche Gras show behind the Brooklyn Museum. Many of those gigs were with Sparrow—we would play somewhere on Sunday afternoon in a park in Queens or a school yard in the Bronx, and then go to the Museum for the evening show. The band was made up mostly of Sparrow's regular players: Sunshine Diaz on bass, Jimmy Brown on guitar, Buggs Niles drums, Erol Ince on trumpet, Denis Wilkinson on sax, Wayne Walker on trombone, and myself on keyboards. We would accompany whichever big-name calypsonians were there that year—Sparrow, Shadow, David Rudder, and Rose. We knew most of the songs, but they usually handed out charts, so there was never a problem and we did not have to rehearse. Even though we were outdoors it was a sit-down sort of situation, so the audience was by-and-large attentive, they would listen, and applaud. I had some memorable times at the Brooklyn Dimanche Gras concerts, but getting back to the issue of Caribbean unity, that whole scene was heavily Trinidadian. When singers would ask the audience to wave if you were from Saint Vincent, you would see a few hands, but when they asked the Trinidadians to wave, you would see maybe 80 percent of the people jumping up.

I did occasionally play at Brooklyn calypso tents during the Labor Day season. They were not generally that well supported, although attendance improved around Labor Day weekend. The tent we mentioned earlier run by Dawad Philips at Restoration Plaza usually did well, and he often alternated calypso and jazz shows. There was also the Vincentian-run Graduate Calypso tent, now organized by Carlos "Rejector" Providence, originally located on Nostrand Avenue. That endeavor was generally not that successful, in part because the top singers would not usually compete. The best show came on the final night, around Carnival weekend, when Becket, Soso, or Scorcher might make a special guest appearance, and the other, lesser-known singers would engage in a competition. Judges would be flown in from Saint Vincent to select the top three performers who would qualify to compete in Saint Vincent's national competition. Thing was that the local New York committee, and calypso contestants themselves, had to put the money up to bring these judges in. Not surprisingly, the singers who were not picked would always be grouchy. One year they wanted two rehearsals with the band I put together, but they could not afford it so we only had one. As you might imagine, the ones who did not get picked blamed the band (and me) for not having enough rehearsal time. The fact was that some songs were just better than others, but they did not see it that way. So eventually I decided to stay out of organizing bands for the tents.

Gigging to Make a Living—Jazz and R&B

My New York jazz playing started in the large band format, but as time passed and word got around, I started forming networks of friends with connections, and several Brooklyn jazz players started calling me for small-group gigs. Lio himself occasionally got requests for a quartet in a local bar or something and he would have me play with him. American saxophonists Jimmy Tyler, Howard Kimbro, Carlos Ward, Joe Walters, and Barry Calimese would call me when they needed a keyboard player. Most of these jobs were in small bars like the Blue Ice Lounge in Queens and several in Brooklyn—there was Tiffany's on Nostrand Avenue, the Playboy Lounge on Franklin Avenue, and several on Bedford Avenue. There was a club on Washington Avenue, whose name escapes me, but I remember we had to play downstairs where people would dance. Occasionally someone would yell "Stop, stop playing!" because of a police raid. I do not think the proprietor had the proper liquor license.

I especially liked playing with Howard Kimbro. He was an excellent saxophonist, well versed in the jazz repertories of Lester Young, Charlie Parker, and John Coltrane. He was a Black American, born here in New York, and his gigs were strictly jazz. In his trio I would play left hand bass, organ style, Howard played saxophone, and we had a drummer. Occasionally he would hire a bass and we would play as a quartet. The Blue Ice Lounge in Queens was one of our favorite haunts. There was also a club on Framers Boulevard near Jamaica Avenue, where Weldon Irvine (composer of the song "Young, Gifted, and Black") would sit in on keyboard and jam with us. Weldon was a good friend who occasionally referred me for gigs he could not make.

Most of the jazz gigs were in hole-in-the-wall establishments, often without liquor licenses, not big dance halls. Usually there was a bar, a small bandstand, a few tables, and maybe a little space for dancing. In some places folks could brown bag it and bring in their own liquor, but in other places they had to buy at the bar. Occasionally a lady might jump up and dance and entice some guy to join her, but mostly people sat, drank, and hopefully listened. The audiences at these local bars were predominantly African Americans, so we played mostly jazz and instrumental arrangements of R&B songs. Occasionally we would sneak in a calypso because the Black American crowd seemed to like them. We would do some Parker and Gillespie tunes; I remember "Ornithology" was a favorite. And of course, we did our share of jazz standards, things like "Autumn Leaves" and such. But the younger crowd would also want to hear R&B songs, things they would recognize by the Spinners,

Isaac Hayes, and James Brown. First, we would get their attention with the familiar verse and chorus melody and then improvise over the chords—it was all instrumental with those little jazz groups, seldom was there a singer. There were no formal arrangements, because the musicians on the set all knew the pieces. We generally adhered to a standard small jazz ensemble format, opening with an introductory head, followed by the horns, piano, and bass taking turns improvising solos over the chords, and closing by restating the original head. Of course, we would extend the improvisations if the crowd was into it or people were dancing. Remember, we would often have to play for three or four hours (with a few breaks). Stretching out the tunes allowed for more individual creativity, but here was also a practical function—that is, filling in the entire period for which we were being paid.

Sometime around 1970 I teamed up with the Grenadian guitarist Mikey Lorrainey, whom I had met through the Olivacce family band shortly after my arrival in New York. Mikey had been working with Tony Williams and the Platters back then, and he had contacts with New York booking agents Norby Walters and Marvin Herman. Marvin started booking us at Manhattan establishments like the Lorelei on 72nd Street. From there we moved to the Copacabana—we played in the small lounge that was upstairs from the big hall and stage where the stars would perform. It was just a trio with me playing bass with my left and the organ lead with my right, Mikey on guitar, and a drummer. Sometimes we would use an American singer. For that crowd we played mostly soft jazz stuff and popular R&B, and occasionally a calypso.

As our reputation grew, we could move from club to club, so I had work every weekend—Friday, Saturday, and often Sunday nights. With the small group I would make between $25 and $50/night, and with the big bands up to a $125. Later, when I started playing fulltime with the R&B group headed by Charlie and Yvonne Brown, I was making a steady $250/week. With a side gig or two on our off nights that number would get as high as $300/week. Now that was good money back then, especially because I did not have to pay tuition at Brooklyn College after my first year, and the Olivacces never pressured me for rent. They took me in and became sort of surrogate parents (even before I got serious with their daughter Patsy); I was treated as a member of the family. I never wanted to take them for granted, so I would give money to Lee regularly to help pay for food and shelter. But of course, you can never repay people for that worth of kindness. I was fortunate to be able to scrape by and make a living playing these gigs while I was single and a student. Unlike many musicians, I never had to have a day job working in a store or restaurant.

Things really started picking up for me around 1972 when I began playing with singers Charlie and Yvonne Brown, a husband-and-wife team from New Jersey who specialized in American R&B. They called themselves The Wonderful World of Charlie Brown and Yvonne. Pretty quickly I pulled Mikey Lorrainey into the group. He wanted me to join his band that was backing up the Platters, but there was a lot more work with Charlie, so we went with him. Norby Walters had us booked mostly at Italian restaurants and clubs in the Bronx, Queens, Staten Island, and once in a while in Brooklyn. We even did a little touring to Florida and Las Vegas. We kept very busy, usually playing five nights a week, and when they were off, I would often play a jazz gig. All this cut into my work at Brooklyn College. I remember studying for tests on the subway ride to and from gigs, and trying to read in between sets at clubs. It was a challenge to work and study at the same time, but one I liked—there was a certain self-propelling aspect to it all that was exciting. Most importantly, I was making good money and able to save enough to eventually buy the house in Brooklyn.

The band consisted of me on keyboards (playing the bass lines with my left hand), drummer Jerry Pierce who was from Panama, Mikey who was from Grenada, and African American singers Charlie and Yvonne. Charlie occasionally doubled on bass. We were basically a Black American R&B band with a little Caribbean flavor. We would often begin a set with some classic organ jazz by Jimmy Smith or Richard "Groove" Holmes, or a soul jazz guitar piece by George Benson. We might even venture into Emerson, Lake, and Palmer's multi-sectioned "Baba Yaga" or Focus's "Stones of Years." That would set up the appearance of Charlie and Yvonne, who would sing covers of popular R&B and funk hits of the day, stuff by Gladys Knight, the Spinners, Aretha Franklin, Kool and the Gang, and the lot. It was strictly American music, I played no calypso in that group. As a result, I developed a serious R&B repertoire from the early 1970s. In fact, I was better versed in the latest R&B hits of the day than I was with the most recent calypsos from the islands. Of course, that would change soon enough. In later years some of the younger players in the Caribbean bands were shocked when an R&B song was occasionally called and I knew it—they thought I was this old guy who only played calypso.

We made a recording of R&B songs with Charlie and Yvonne, but I don't think it was ever released. Things fizzled out after a few years with Charlie retiring and Yvonne continuing to do occasional solo jobs. When they moved to Atlanta that was it for local New York gigs and I lost touch with them. But the real tragedy was in 1973 when our guitarist and my close friend Mikey died during a Florida tour. We were staying at a motel in Miami called the

Charlie and Yvonne with Frankie on Farfisa organ and Mikey Lorrainey on guitar circa 1972.

Apache Motor Inn and playing downstairs in the Polo Lounge. Mikey was a very outgoing guy and sometimes consorted with the female guests, including this Italian girl he had met at the club. And one evening he went out on this supposed double date with her and this local guy and his girlfriend. The next morning, we got a call from Charlie Brown from the adjoining room, in tears, wailing "Mikey's dead." According to the police report, their car had run off the road into a canal and Mikey and the Italian girl were found dead in the water. We thought there might have been some foul play but it was never proven. You know, in Florida in 1973, no one was going to do an investigation of a Black man found floating face down in a canal. In any case that really soured me on touring, I preferred staying closer to home.

Thinking back, most of the musicians I played with in New York were quite versatile in terms of repertoire and playing styles. They were equally at home at a dance or seated club situation. On the other side of the bandstand, most local audiences were receptive to different genres of music, American and Caribbean. But sometimes there was a bump in the road. I remember one dance in a Community Hall in Queens, not far from Farmers Boulevard and the Conduit. Now the band that had been booked for the event was led by Jimmy Tyler, a fabulous jazz saxophonist who had played in a band with

Charlie Parker back in the late 1940s. Tommy Potter, the acoustic bass player, had also made numerous recordings with Parker. Drummer Marvin Muller hailed from the Virgin Islands, but jazz was his favored genre. With me on keyboards, this was strictly a jazz quartet, but somehow, we found ourselves playing for a younger R&B crowd who came expecting to dance. By the time the band struck up, about two thirds of the guests had already arrived. Jimmy played a blues and the crowd just stood and watched. Another blues, then "Confirmation" by Parker, followed by the slow ballad "Stardust." Still, they just stood there staring, and no one even attempted to dance. Finally, one of the promoters approached the band and asked in a concerned and caring voice whether we were hungry. After our next piece, Parker's "Scrapple from the Apple," the same promoter insisted that we take a break and eat something. Within minutes of our being backstage, someone hooked up a turntable and everyone was dancing to Sly and the Family Stone's big funk hit "Thank You (Falettinme Be Mice Elf Agin)." Fortunately, we still got paid, and Jimmy learned from that experience to be more accommodating on future gigs.

I liked working with Jimmy because it gave me the chance to play the piano and dive into the more challenging jazz repertoire. The R&B gigs paid more generously, and I was grateful for them because that is how I was able to actually save a little money. But I always felt a little bogged down playing the organ in that context, having to constantly support the singers while always carrying the bass line with my left hand. That really limited me as a soloist, and the pop material we played was not that conducive to much sophisticated improvisation in the first place. After I left Charlie and Yvonne, I pivoted toward jazz piano gigs with Jimmy Tyler, Jean Jefferson, Barry Calimese, and others. I often subbed for Bross Townsend, former pianist with Art Blakey. Playing piano in those small jazz groups gave me more freedom as a creative artist. Of course, the problem was how to make enough money to survive and to support my growing family. As much as I loved playing and loved the music, I had serious doubts that working exclusively as a jazz pianist sideman was going to pay the bills. I suppose I could have started my own jazz trio or even a Caribbean dance band, but had no appetite for the business responsibilities that such an undertaking would demand. What to do?

Then I met two other Saint Vincent expatriates, Alston "Becket" Cyrus and Granville Straker. That changed everything.

CHAPTER 3

THE SAINT VINCENT CONNECTION

Alston "Becket" Cyrus and Granville Straker

When Frankie met calypso singer Alston "Becket" Cyrus in Brooklyn during the summer of 1976, calypso music was on the cusp of a transformation to what would soon be dubbed *soca* (short for soul/calypso). Shadow's 1974 Road March–winning "Bassman" (arranged by Art De Coteau) foregrounded a melodic bass line in unprecedented fashion, signaling a shift in textural emphasis to the low register. In 1976, Lord Shorty, who is most often credited for coming up with the term soca, released "Sweet Music" (arranged by Ed Watson), introducing modal synthesizer lines and cool vocals associated with Black American soul balladeers. Calypso Rose's 1977 "Tempo" (arranged by Pelham Goddard) raced along at 130 BPM over slinky synthesizer lines while the singer called for more tempo and swore her allegiance to Carnival revelry. Lord Kitchener's 1978 hit "Sugar Bum Bum" (arranged by Ed Watson) was distinguished from his earlier material by its catchy melodic bass line, airy synthesizer theme, and compact lyrics. *Sparrow's 25th Anniversary* LP, released in 1979 (arranged by Art De Coteau), announced the master calypsonian's pivot to the new soca sound with the raucous song "Don't Drop the Tempo." Sandwiched between these iconic recordings came Alston Becket Cyrus and Frankie's 1977 release "Coming High," built around jazzy chord changes and complex synthesizer lines, and clocking in at a lengthy eight and a half minutes.

Taken together, these songs signaled a shift from the older calypso style to what was becoming known as soca by the late 1970s.[1] The new music was generally faster paced compared to the older calypso's lilting, moderate tempos.

Syncopated, melodic bass lines, influenced by funk and reggae, grounded the groove for dancers. In contrast to the calypso's text-dense lyrics and propensity for ribald humor and witty social commentary, soca lyrics were built around short phrases addressing simple themes of love, sensuality, and celebration. The overall sound was more contemporary, replete with synthesizers, electric guitars, mechanical drum beats, and electronic sounds for timbral effects. As the "soul" in "soul/calypso" suggested, the new music drew generously on Black American soul, funk, and disco styles of the times, in addition to rock and occasionally jazz.[2]

The rise of soca also heralded the coming of a new generation of Caribbean music arrangers who wrote the instrumental accompaniments for the songs. While older calypso arrangers like Art De Coteau and Ed Watson were certainly influential in shaping the early soca sound, it was younger musicians Pelham Goddard, Leston Paul, Clive Bradley, and of course Frankie McIntosh whose innovations came to define the soca of the 1980s and early 1990s.[3]

The early collaborations between Frankie and Becket would eventually be recognized as harbingers of the bourgeoning soca revolution of the late 1970s. And for Frankie, they would prove crucial in his emergence as a soca arranger.

Frankie: Coming High with Alston "Becket" Cyrus

In the mid-1970s I was working with small jazz and R&B groups, and occasionally with Lio Smith and the other Caribbean dance bands. The steady gig with Charlie and Yvonne was over, but I was still making a living, at least marginally. Then came the arrival of my son Ahmad in 1974, and right on his heels Omar! I became seriously worried about the future, about my growing financial responsibilities. I also needed to finish my credits at Brooklyn College and think about further study in order to earn the teaching credentials that would qualify me for work as an educator. Or perhaps there was some other way forward to earn a living through my music?

Those concerns were in the back of my mind when the Vincentian calypsonian Alston "Becket" Cyrus approached me with a batch of new songs. That was in 1976. I had first met Becket the previous summer when he needed someone to help transcribe his scores for a boat ride engagement booked through the record producer Granville Straker. Becket had released an album in 1975 called *Raw Calypso* with arranger Art De Coteau, and was starting to get some attention here in the Brooklyn Caribbean community. Straker had evidently booked him to perform on a boat ride along

Alston "Becket" Cyrus, 1976. Photo courtesy of Alston "Becket" Cyrus.

with Ron Berridge's band—evening boat excursions in the summer with live calypso music were very popular with Caribbean folks back then. But Becket ran into some problems at the rehearsal because the original scores had been rendered so sloppily in pencil that the musicians complained they could not read it. So, he came to my house at 1299 St. Marks, rang the bell, introduced himself, and asked for help with his scores. We sat down with a cassette of the songs and I carefully rewrote the parts, this time in neat penmanship and with a sharp pencil. And that's how Becket and I got started working together.

The boat ride apparently went well, and the following year Becket contacted me about working with him on some new songs. He returned to my house with his guitar and sang several pieces, including one he called "Coming High." It was just a skeletal melody and a few lyrics alluding to smoking grass, but I remember thinking it was catchy and might be something I could work with, and began pondering an introduction and full arrangement. Eventually we went into a studio to record the song—mind you, Becket at that point was paying for everything, he didn't have a record label behind him. He figured he'd shop this recording around in hopes of getting someone to pick it up and finance a whole album. A producer named Buddy Scott, a friend of the recording engineer at the Hit Factory studio, got excited when he heard what we were doing with "Coming High." Scott had connections in the recording industry at that time and brought the song to the attention of the folks at Casablanca Records. They were a US label based in California that featured some big acts like Dona Summer and Kiss. Apparently, the Casablanca people liked the demo and ended up giving Scott and Becket a budget to produce an entire LP with the idea that some of the material might go into a movie they were working on, *The Deep*. We went back in the studio and recorded all the songs for the album that came out on Casablanca under the title *Disco Calypso*. In fact, one of the songs, "Calypso Disco," did make it onto the soundtrack, along with "Down Deep Inside" by Donna Summer. John Barry, who did the score for the film, found "Coming High" too slow, but he liked the faster "Calypso Disco" and thought it would fit well into this certain scene. In any case this was a big deal for a calypso singer at that time, back in 1977, to have an album of your music on an American record label and one of your songs in a Hollywood movie!

Disco Calypso was my first serious arranging and recording project in New York, and it was significant because we had a budget for musicians and the creative freedom to do pretty much as we pleased. Looking back, it was somewhat ironic because, even though the recording was backed by an American label and Buddy Scott was our producer, I felt no pressure to worry about the market or to produce a product with commercial appeal. I was just writing what I felt, and at that time I was immersed in jazz. That would change down the road when I began working for Brooklyn producers like Granville Straker and Ralston Charles, but we'll get to that soon enough. With that budget and freedom, I was able to do some unusual things. On "Coming High" I composed a jazzy bridge, employed a key modulation, and added bluesy interludes on the synthesizer, which was a new instrument for calypso at that time. On the songs "Calypso Disco," "Legalize the Grass," and "St. Thomas Mas" I scored parts for a string quartet we hired through the musicians union. "St. Vincent, I Love You" had a laid-back, cool feel, and I was able to stretch out on an acoustic piano solo (2:20–3:15), something I rarely got to do on soca recordings.

Disco Calypso was well received by the public in the Caribbean and here in New York, and "Coming High" got international airplay in Europe and South America. But neither Becket nor I made much from it, and apparently neither did Casablanca Records, because they were not interested in backing a second recording. That left Becket on his own once more, but he remained determined to press on. Fortunately, he was pleased with the music I had

Frankie at Becket "Coming High" session, 1977.

come up with for *Disco Calypso*, so he came to me with another set of songs that would become the material for his next LP, *Coming Higher*. This one was self-produced and self-funded, probably using what little profits he had garnered from sales from the earlier Casablanca album. We recorded at Platinum Factory and Hit Factory in Manhattan, and Beckett released the album in 1978 on his own label, First River Records. Even though he was paying the bills himself, Becket let me hire a big band—we had four saxophones, a flute, two trumpets, and two trombones, in addition to the rhythm section and vocal chorus. With all those players, I was able to write more expansive harmonies for the horns. I also brought in several talented jazz players, including trumpeter Ray Maldonado and alto saxophonists Sam Furnace and Jimmy Cozier. My old friend Lio Smith played tenor saxophone, and my brother Tony was on bass. Two of my favorite songs from the *Coming Higher* LP were "Wine Down Kingstown" and "Tony." I'll talk about my musical approach to these two tunes, as well as "Coming High," in chapter 5, but suffice it to say my arrangements made use of colorful harmonies, instrumental solos, and synthesizer layering not common in calypso at that time.

I was credited as the arranger on those early Becket LPs, but I probably should have had coauthorship on some tunes, especially "Coming High" and

"Wine Down Kingstown," where I composed a good deal of the music. In hindsight, I realize I was also serving as technical producer on those projects. I not only wrote the arrangements, but I decided which musicians to call and was in charge of running all the studio sessions. I really cut my studio teeth recording those first two LP projects with Becket, leaning how to direct the musicians to get the sound I was looking for, how to alter or add parts on the spot when necessary, and when and where to overdub an additional synthesizer or percussion line. This was my first serious experience with the new multi-track recording process that would become the norm as I moved forward.

Listening to these Becket arrangements more than forty years later, I hear New York and sense its influences upon me back then: the jazz and R&B in the air and on radio stations like WRVR; the solos of saxophonists Jimmy Tyler, Howard Kimbro, and bassist Tommy Potter; performing in small Black-owned clubs in Brooklyn; playing with Charlie Brown and Yvonne, Lio Smith, Eddie Payne, Jene Jefferson, Don Maynard, Jeff Medina, Snub Mosely, and so many others; rushing to make a gig on a last-minute call and the hustle of being a freelance musician. Attempting to write about it objectively today is so different from simply living it back then, when I had no clue that my artistic self was developing. Creation certainly does not end at birth!

Prior to my work with Becket, I'd done a little gratis arranging for family friend Lio Smith, but not much for real pay. I believe it was the experience with Becket and Casablanca Records that prompted a change. Singers who had heard my work with Becket began approaching me to arrange their material, and I realized this was a possible career path, even if it meant cutting back or giving up working as a freelance pianist. Unfortunately, my second venture into arranging and recording did not have such a positive outcome, at least not in terms of the finances.

The success of *Disco Calypso* and *Coming Higher* did not go unnoticed in Trinidad, and in addition to Becket, my name started to get around. This producer, whose name I will not mention, had recently married one of my cousins in Trinidad. He called and introduced himself as a "family" member. Right then I should have been suspicious. He asked me if I would be interested in arranging an album for the up-and-coming calypsonian Edwin Ayoung, who went by the stage name Crazy. We agreed on a fee and a few weeks later Crazy and this producer appeared at my house on St. Marks with a pile of songs. We picked out six, I wrote the arrangements, and we recorded at Music Farm studio in lower Manhattan. I called a number of the musicians for the session that had appeared on the Becket albums, including myself on keyboards, my brother Tony on bass, Anthony "Bugs" Niles on drums, Victor Collins on guitar, Sam Furnace on alto saxophone and flute, Ron Taylor on trumpet, and Lio Smith on tenor saxophone. The album, *Crazy's Super Album* (1979), sold well in Trinidad, and several of the songs, including "Parang Soca" and "Cricket Commentary," were very popular. In addition to those two songs, we did a few other noteworthy things like using a live steel pan on "Back to Pan." The song "Bachelor's," which was the longest (7:40) on the album, evoked a cool, laid-back vibe with a gorgeous guitar solo by Victor Collins (4:42) and elegant flute interludes by Sam Furnace (4:04).

Crazy was easy to work with and the music was overall to my liking. But a problem arose when it came to getting paid. My new "cousin" gave me only a pittance to start the work, promising the balance before I was finished. All of the sudden he was off to Trinidad on some type of emergency. He left me a letter saying "don't dig nothing, you'll get the rest of our oranges"—West Indian slang that translates "don't worry, you'll get the rest of the money I owe you." Well, I guess those oranges went rotten, because I never got paid the rest of my fee, even though the album was a big seller in Trinidad. So, when Crazy approached me the next year about arranging another album, I refused on principle. Since I didn't get paid for the first album, I didn't really want to work on a second, especially since he had the same producer.

That experience might have soured me on arranging, but around that time my fortunes changed. My fledgling career as an arranger took a big turn in the right direction when I met my fellow Vincentian expatriate Granville Straker, the owner of Straker's Records in Brooklyn. In the late 1970s we began an enduring working relationship that would result in hundreds of calypso and soca records.

Brooklyn Soca: Straker's Records, Charlie's Records, and B's Records

Around the time Frankie began collaborating with Becket and Crazy in the late 1970s, Brooklyn was emerging as an international hub of calypso and soca music. Trinidad's recording studios had been on the wane for more than a decade, and many small islands lacked professional recording facilities. Meanwhile, growing Caribbean diasporic communities in the United States and Canada offered new and lucrative markets for the music. With this in mind, a number of calypsonians began to look abroad for better opportunities to record, produce, and distribute their music. In Brooklyn, a handful of entrepreneurial Caribbean expatriates were waiting to help them.

Granville Straker (b. 1939), a native of Saint Vincent, arrived in Brooklyn via Trinidad in 1959. After working as an auto mechanic and opening up a car service he turned his attention to music. As Brooklyn's Caribbean community grew, so did demand for calypso, and by the early 1970s Straker was running three record stores in central Brooklyn. In 1971 he began releasing 45s on his own Straker's Records label, and over the next two decades built an impressive catalogue that included such calypso/soca luminaries as Shadow, Chalkdust, Calypso Rose, Lord Melody, Black Stalin, Winston Soso, Singing Francine, Lord Nelson, and Machel Montano. Moving between Brooklyn and the Caribbean, where he maintained record shops in Trinidad and Saint Vincent, Straker became a veritable one-man operation—transnational talent scout, recording/mixing engineer, record distributor, and concert promoter. Exact numbers are difficult to come by, but estimates are that he released hundreds of LPs and several thousand singles on his Straker's Records label over the two-decade period spanning the early 1970s through the mid-1990s. For much of that time Frankie would serve as Straker's main arranger and leader of the Equitables, a studio band that Straker assembled in the 1970s and employed on hundreds of his recordings.

Straker's main competitor was Rawlston Charles (b. 1946), a native Tobagonian who landed in New York in 1967 with a suitcase under one arm and a Lord Kitchener album under the other. In 1972 he opened a record shop at 1265 Fulton Street in Brooklyn, and the following year began to issue records on his own Charlie's Records label. Over the next decade Charles helped produce and distribute some of the most important early soca recordings, including Calypso Rose's "Give me Tempo (1977), Lord Kitchener's landmark "Sugar Bum Bum" (1978), and Arrow's international super hit "Hot, Hot, Hot" (1983). His catalogue would grow to be a who's who of calypso and soca in the late 1970s and 1980s, including recordings by the aforementioned Rose, Kitchener, and Arrow, as well as those by Sparrow, Shadow, Melody, Swallow, Duke, David Rudder, and many others. In 1984 Charles built his own recording studio above his Fulton Street record shop, which became a hub of activity for Caribbean musicians visiting Brooklyn. Like Straker, Charles possessed an exceptional ear for talent and a willingness to embrace the emerging soca sound in hopes of appealing to a broader international audience without losing his core Caribbean followers. Charles also looked to younger Trinidadian arrangers Leston Paul and Pelham Goddard who, in addition to their background in calypso, were well versed in contemporary American soul, funk, and rock music. In the late 1970s, in return for Charles's purchase of new high-end equipment for his group, Goddard changed his outfit's name from Sensational Roots to Charlie's Roots and rose to prominence as Trinidad's leading soca band.

A third influential Brooklyn soca label was B's Records, founded by Trinidadian American entrepreneur Michael Gould. He poured considerable money into recording, mixing, and jacket design, and was known for the generous fees he paid to artists and arrangers. This enabled him to recruit top calypsonians, including Sparrow, Kitchener, Duke, Melody, Lord Nelson, and Black Stalin to his label. Though short-lived, B's Records produced over 120 LPs and twelve-inch extended play discs. Gould's favorite arrangers were Leston Paul and Clive Bradley, the latter another Trinidadian who embraced American soul and funk music. Frankie would find occasional work with B's and Charlie's Records, as well as other smaller labels that sprung up in Brooklyn during that period.

Brooklyn's heralded position as a center of soca production was on the wane by the mid-1990s. The small Brooklyn companies were not able to transition to CDs, and cheap digital burners led to widespread music pirating that crippled their sales. Meanwhile the rise of advanced recording and mixing technology in Trinidad and other islands, along with more recent home recording capabilities, greatly diminished the need for Caribbean musicians to go abroad to produce high quality recordings. In hindsight it is clear that Frankie was certainly in the right place at the right time when he landed in the Brooklyn scene in the 1970s. For two decades he was able to employ his musical talents and arranging skills to help shape the new soca sound.[4]

Frankie: Arranging for Granville Straker, Rawlston Charles, and B's Records

I had heard of Granville Straker back in Saint Vincent, but never made his acquaintance until I moved to Brooklyn. By then his record company was doing well, thanks to his successful recording of high-profile calypsonians like Shadow and Chalkdust. Straker had organized a studio recording group, the Equitables, that was led by my cousin Syl McIntosh, who played alto saxophone, with Toby Tobias on drums, Nasser on bass, and Lubert Martin on keyboards. Before going into the recording studio, the group rehearsed at Straker's record shop on Utica Avenue—that's where I first heard them, and I may have sat in on one number. By the way, the first and only Equitables recording with those personnel was titled *Sugar and Honey*, released by Straker in 1973. On that album they played strictly instrumental arrangements

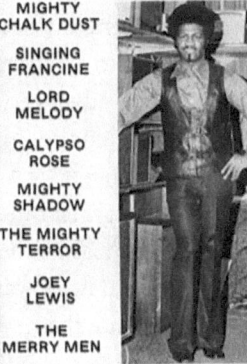

Straker's Records ad, 1975.

of popular calypsos and American pop songs. You see, back in the early 1970s many people still wanted instrumental music.

After Syl returned to Canada where he had been living, Straker kept the name Equitables and recruited me to lead the band and to arrange the music for recording sessions. We remained strictly a studio recording group with a rotating cast of players whom I could call on. Some of those recordings were instrumental, and others used singers like Winston Soso, Charmaine Yates, and Cauldric Forbes. Straker often decided to record covers of popular Trinidad calypsos, things like Blue Boy's "Soca Baptist," Sparrow's "Love African Style," and Scrunter's "Woman on the Bass." He even had the Equitables record a cover of Shadow's big hit "Bassman" several years after he released the original on his label! I was not happy doing cover arrangements because I didn't like the idea of cutting into an artist's sales. Imitating someone else just wasn't very creative from an arranging or performing perspective, and I was inclined to change the original arrangement. But Straker always wanted it to sound as close to the original as possible.

You see, Straker went by the numbers. By releasing dozens of records, and say making a little on each of them, then he could do OK financially. Now the downside to that approach was that the artists, who worked on a fixed percentage, only received a tiny proportion of the profits. Not surprisingly there was a lot of dissatisfaction, especially from the lesser-known calypsonians who didn't understand Straker's modus operandi. His decisions were more business than music oriented. He was interested in picking singers and songs that would sell, not in supporting musical innovation.

Fortunately, when Straker dubbed me leader of the Equitables in the late 1970s, he was producing popular calypsonians who brought in their original songs in need of original arrangements. Right off the bat I was able to work with Chalkdust, Winston Soso, and King Wellington, and a few years later Calypso Rose, Duke, Singing Francine, and many others who recorded for Straker. My first important recording project for him came in 1979 when we worked with Winston Soso, another fellow Vincentian. Here's what happened. Straker came to my place on St. Marks with two propositions. The first was to do a cover of Becket's "Coming High." I didn't think that was ethical, since I'd already done an arrangement of that song for Becket and Casablanca Records, so I said no. The irony was that before Becket hooked up with Casablanca, he had approached Straker with "Coming High," but Straker wasn't interested. Now Straker wanted to do a cover of a song he rejected in the first place! His second idea was to have me assist with the recording of Winston Soso's original song, "Soca Dianne." I admired Soso, a fellow Vincentian who was booked to perform at Labor Day Carnival that year, and was intrigued by the song when Straker played me a rough cassette recording. He had just heard Soso and his group Clymax at a Brooklyn dance and saw how people responded enthusiastically to the song. He thought there was potential here for a hit, and he was right. On my end, I figured this would give me a chance to work up some new material, not just do a cover of a popular calypso recording, so I encouraged Straker to go with "Dianne," and he did. I don't think I wrote out charts for that song, because Soso's group Clymax already had a head arrangement. We went into the Art Craft Studio, where I made a few suggestions to the horn players regarding phrasing and articulation and added several synthesizer lines. I recall we recorded the song in one session, with minimal overdubbing. "Soca Dianne" did very well and helped jump start Soso's career. Soso was definitely pleased, and a year later he asked me to arrange an entire album, *Too Much Corruption*, the first of about ten LPs I would do with him on Straker Records.

Around the same time as the Soso project, Straker invited me to arrange an album for Hollis Liverpool, aka Chalkdust, or simply "Chalky" as we called him. This was really big time, as Chalky was one of Trinidad's most popular singers, and the winner of the Trinidad Calypso Crown competitions in 1976 and 1977. This was the first time I had arranged and recorded an entire album of music for Straker, and we developed what would become our standard work routine for the next two decades. I'll get to Chalky's music and our first album together, *Origins*, in chapter 6, but right now let me focus on the production process we worked out.

Straker would send calypsonians (beginning with Chalkdust) to my house with their songs. We would sit in my basement and they would sing them to me, preferably accompanying themselves on acoustic guitar, with me at the piano. We would settle on a key, and I would sketch out some preliminary ideas on manuscript paper—the basic melodies, chords, and so forth. Sometimes singers would have a cassette recording of the song to leave with me. Then I'd go to work, sitting at the piano, composing an introduction, a band chorus, a bass line, and maybe an idea for a tag (coda). Occasionally the melodic horn lines and the bass parts would come from the initial melody of the verse and chorus, but usually I would compose original material that I thought was appropriate for the mood of the song. Next, I'd score out the different parts—the melody lines for each horn, the chords and melodic fills for the guitar and keyboard, and the bass line. With Straker I usually worked with two trumpets and a tenor saxophone. If the budget permitted, I'd add an alto saxophone and a trombone. I wrote out the master score and each individual part carefully by hand on music manuscript paper with pencil, then duplicates were made. I always did the transposing on the master score for the individual parts, and I usually employed a copyist to transcribe the scores for the individual instruments. Musicians like Shake Keane and Gene Jefferson were good at that. Remember this was before the days of computers, so everything was done by hand, which was very time consuming.

I called musicians and Starker booked the studio and paid them on the spot—that took the pressure off of me! Thankfully Straker rarely interfered with the process and left all the musical decisions to me, which resulted in a relaxed atmosphere and a quality musical product. The recording process required several studio sessions. First came the rhythm section that included the keyboards, guitar, bass, drums, and the calypsonian singing a "dummy" or "guide" vocal so that the musicians could get a sense of the whole song.

I'd hand out the parts for the bass and guitar and of course for my keyboard. The drummer played by ear, following my cues for tempo and accents. We would usually run through the piece once or twice and then roll the tape. By then most studios had twenty-four track capabilities, so every instrument was miked up separately. The second session was for the horns and keyboard overdubs. I would hand the horn players their parts (they were all excellent readers) and make any last-minute adjustments, which occasionally included a suggestion from one of the musicians. Next, we'd go do a brief run-though in the main studio area where they were set up. When we were ready to record, I would sit with the engineer while the musicians recorded over the rhythm track from the first session, which they listened to on headphones. We aimed for one good take per song, as Straker was always trying to keep studio time and costs at a minimum. A third and final session was booked for the calypsonian and backup vocalists, and a final mix session that included Straker and an engineer. In the early days I was often present for the vocal and mix sessions, but as I got busier and busier, I often skipped them because my work as an arranger was basically done at the point when all the instrumental tracks had been laid.

When I worked independently with an artist, or later for producers like Rawlston Charles, I would charge a flat fee depending on how many songs I would be arranging. Sometimes I was paid by the song, and other times for an entire album. But with Straker I worked out a different arrangement because I was often working on several recording projects for him at a time. Every two or three months he would call me down to his store on Utica Avenue, and tell me which of the records were doing well and which were not, and he would pay me a modest figure for the work. On the American R&B circuit, this would not have been considered adequate pay for the amount of work I was doing, but some of us put culture over dollars, and it was something steady to count on. Eventually I realized—unlike many calypsonians who had false expectations and constantly complained about being ripped off—that calypso records just weren't selling in the same numbers as were big American pop songs. From that perspective my financial arrangement with Straker was reasonable and, most importantly, dependable. The convenience of our both being in central Brooklyn helped. It was easy for calypsonians to visit my house on St. Marks Avenue, and it was a leisurely six block walk for me over to Straker's store on Utica Avenue.

One other thing that made me feel good about working with Straker was that he always supported small island singers, not just the big names from Trinidad. In fact, were it not for Straker, many Vincentian calypsonians—with the notable exception of Becket, who never worked with him—would probably not have been recognized. He had at least fifteen Vincentian calypsonians on his label, including Winston Soso, Scorcher, Tommy T, Walter Porter, and Darwin David. Many of them ended up living in New York, and on occasion Straker would take them back to Saint Vincent to put on a show. I traveled back with Straker for several of those programs and sat in with the local bands. I recall they were quite successful in the early years because the calypsonians he brought from New York represented the majority of Vincentian artists with recordings. But sometimes the local singers who hadn't left the island resented this, disparaging their returning expatriate brethren as "foreign based." Needless to say, Straker deserves a lot of credit for his efforts to promote Saint Vincent calypso back then.

I should add that Straker was not my only source of income. All along I continued to do limited freelance work as a jazz, R&B, gospel, and calypso keyboardist. As my reputation as an arranger grew, I landed work from a number of independent artists and producers, including singers from Saint Vincent, Grenada, and Antigua who regularly came to New York to record.

One of the most important Brooklyn producers I formed a relationship with was Rawlston Charles, the owner of Charlie's Records. His store and recording studio were not far from me on Fulton Street near Nostrand Avenue. I don't recall exactly how I first met him, but it might have been in 1981 when he recruited me to arrange *Man from the Ghetto*, an LP by the Trinidadian calypsonian Explainer (see chapter 6). I believe Explainer requested me, but Charlie was a little uneasy at first about hiring the same arranger that his competitor Straker was using. Eventually I gained his trust when he saw that I always put the music first no matter who I was working for. *Man from the Ghetto* did well, especially the song "Loraine," and I went on to do a few more LPs for Explainer, several for Swallow, and one for Kitchener, all on Charlie's label. The work expectation was similar to that for Straker—I met with the singer and scored out the arrangement, called the musicians, and oversaw the rhythm and horn recording sessions. I usually wasn't expected to be present for the final vocal or mix sessions, nor would I have been paid to do so. I do recall that during the few mix sessions I did attend Charlie always got dressed up in special attire for the occasion—he had a reputation for being a dapper dresser, and still does!

Straker and Charlie were quite different in the studio. Straker was pretty much hands-off, trusting me with all the music. His input would come in the final mix. But Charlie was more involved. We would usually have to run through the piece once for him before we pressed the record button. He would stand there, bob his head up and down a little, figuring out if this was something people could dance to. And occasionally he would make a small suggestion, maybe like "How about a more attacking bass line?" Or he might make some broader comments on the kind of "feel" he thought the song should have. He often wanted to hear more bass and drums, because he thought that was what sold records in the Brooklyn Caribbean community and back in Trinidad. I would usually make changes in correspondence with his suggestions, and I don't remember him ever not approving our final arrangement. I should mention that both he and Straker supervised the final mix—I was generally not there. Listening back, I think too often they overemphasized the bass, drums, and synthesizer at the expense of the horns, and their tendency to use the same approach year after year may have led to a certain homogenization of the calypso/soca sound. But they seemed to be aligned with what the public and the DJs wanted, and the records sold, so that was the bottom line. Be that as it may, it was a successful formula for delegating the work—I arranged the music and ran the rhythm and horn section recording sessions, and they took care of the final vocal session and the mix.

When it came to negotiating an arranging fee, Charlie was a hard bargainer, always reminding me how poorly calypso records sold. But once we reached an agreement, he was always good for the money, 100 percent. Overall, I had good business and personal relationships with Charlie and Straker. Both would drop off presents for my kids on Christmas morning. They were certainly in competition with one another and with the other small labels, but there was sense of a genuine shared culture among the members of Brooklyn's calypso community back then.

I also did some work for Michael Gould and Julian Williams who ran B's Records and J&W Records respectively, two other important but short-lived Brooklyn-based labels that specialized in calypso and soca. Through Gould I got the opportunity to arrange for Sparrow. His 1984 recording, "Don't Back Back," won the Trinidad Carnival Road March and was one of the best-selling arrangements I ever did. Of course, I would always freelance for calypsonians who were producing their own records, often for their own labels. In addition to Becket and Crazy I worked independently with Duke, Short Shirt, Gypsy, Obstinate, Rupert Blaze, to name just a few of the more prominent ones.

I continued to occasionally play with jazz musicians Jimmy Tyler, Don Maynard, and Snub Mosley, but as I got older my family obligations grew. By the time my son Hakim arrived in 1982 (our fourth and final), I had come to realize that arranging offered certain advantages over gigging five nights a week and touring. Playing a gig meant carting my electric keyboard and amplifier down the stairs, into the car, probably back upstairs in the club or dance hall, then actually playing (the fun part), and finally carrying all that stuff home late at night. I was getting older and starting to feel it—you get the picture. But arranging I could do sitting in my cellar or bedroom with pencil, paper, and piano—I didn't have to leave home! And when I did have to go to the studio, it didn't require hauling a lot of stuff, because the studio had all the equipment.

The most important advantages were financial. As a student and single, I didn't need much income to survive. It had been all about me, everything revolved around Frankie. But with four kids to take care of my priorities became family first. Now an average job with the big band paid around $100, or at most $150 a night; and as little as $50 at a small club. But you could do a calypso arrangement, right from your home, and get paid as much as $400 to $500 per song. Arranging was more lucrative, and I didn't have to be out half the night, or spend extended time touring away from the family. That suited me fine! It was more money for less work, which is something everyone aspires to, right? Hooking up with Straker helped boost my steady income.

The whole atmosphere in the recording studios was a more comfortable social situation for me than were clubs and dances. I could wear anything I wanted and could converse with the other West Indian musicians about what was going on in the Caribbean. We shared the same language, the same foods. It wasn't like a jazz gig—there you worked for someone like Jimmy Tyler and it was all business.

Artistic satisfaction was one more area of consideration, because when playing keyboards on most of my arrangements I continued to create and express myself musically. Composing and executing effective synthesizer lines was a challenge I relished, and I often left room in my arrangements for solos, although they did not demand the advanced technical and improvisatory skills of a jazz pianist. As discussed in the next chapter, the craft of arranging sometimes spills over into composition when creating original introductory passages, bass lines, horn phrases, and tags. I often looked at the process of arranging as a challenge to solve a problem—how to create a musical setting that would complement, indeed augment, the words and melodies that calypsonians brought to me. This would involve coming up with an overall framework for the piece, and then filling it in with the specific elements of instrumentation, melody, harmony, rhythm, texture, and so forth. The process of reifying the plan was always itself intriguing. When all the parts are in place and the musical result is desirable, the problem is solved, giving rise to a higher level of satisfaction for me as the arranger. Of course, that didn't always happen. There were times that Straker would only budget for a sax and a trumpet for a recording session—that would limit my harmonic possibilities for horns on the band choruses. Too often Straker left in the four-measure drum machine introductions that were supposed to set the tempo and were to be edited out in the final mix. He always wanted to extend the time of the tracks because he thought his customers wanted more for their money, that is, longer songs. And then there were mixing decisions I was not privy to and later regretted after hearing the results. But attending those sessions would have meant considerable additional unpaid time for me—every song required two or three hours of studio mixing. In that world I was the hired hand and this was work for pay. If the producer and calypsonian ended up doing well with the final product, they would likely come back to me next year with more work.

Arranging and recording would become my lifeblood for the next few decades, providing me with financial stability and a measure of artistic fulfillment. Now that readers have heard the story of how I got there, let's dig deeper into the more technical aspects of my musical arranging process and the singers I worked with.

CHAPTER 4
THE ART OF THE SOCA ARRANGER

American jazz and popular music arrangers have received relatively little attention from critics or scholars. Jazz and pop are predominantly performer-oriented traditions and, not surprisingly, star instrumentalists and vocal luminaries have been the primary focus. While a handful of jazz arrangers including Don Redman, Billy Strayhorn, Gil Evans, Nelson Riddle, and Quincy Jones have been critically acknowledged, they generally take a backseat to the players and singers.[1]

Jazz arrangers have historically been dismissed as mere practitioners of craft rather than acknowledged as creative artists. Musicologist John Wriggles notes that unlike composers, who are credited with creating original art, arrangers are generally thought to be about the business of "adapting a [pre-existing] composition to fit a specific performance format or ensemble," be it a vocal choir, symphonic orchestra, or jazz ensemble.[2] Jazz historians, he writes, have too often tied arrangers to the commercialization of the art form, claiming that they force the music into static, formulaic written scores that obviate the spontaneity and improvisatory practices central to "authentic" jazz. Wriggles pushes back against this stance, providing historical evidence that the skills of the arrangers often spill over into actual composition, suggesting the possibility that jazz arrangers can at times be creators. He quotes jazz legend Benny Goodman: "the art of making an arrangement that a band can play with swing—and I am convinced it is an art—that's something very few musicians can do."[3] At least one esteemed jazz historian, Gunther Schuller, agrees with Goodman. Schuller points out that while some jazz arrangements are simply standardized versions for commercial dissemination, in the hands of a skilled arranger the result may be "highly creative recompositions, which transform the basic material in a specific style or manner, in itself marked by a striking originality which may even surpass the quality of the original material."[4] One needs look no further than Edward Duke Ellington to realize that the roles of band leader, performer, arranger, and composer are often deeply intertwined.

Post–World War II arrangers of American popular music have also tended to remain in the shadows, leading music producer and historian Richard Niles to describe them as "invisible artists." Even though their contributions to popular recordings sometimes rose to the level of cocomposer, they generally received no credits on records or liner notes. He notes while songwriters, composers, and producers often received royalties, arrangers were usually paid only a flat fee for their services. The iconic horn lines heard on recordings by R&B artists Wilson Pickett, Otis Redding, Sam and Dave, Aretha Franklin, James Brown, and a host of Motown artists from the 1960s and 1970s, stand as testaments to the central role of music arrangers in making a "hit" record. Some recordings depended on formal written arrangements, while others, particularly those made in the legendary Stax and Muscle Shoals studios, were more impromptu studio collaborations among the singers, musicians, and producers.[5]

In the world of Caribbean calypso, arrangers have received more attention than their North American counterparts. Since the period of Trinidad independence in the early 1960s, they have been recognized as vital to music production process, with skills that are distinct from those of the song writers and the calypso performers. Trinidad arrangers Frankie Francis and Bertram Innis were instrumental in shaping the modern calypso sound of the 1960s; Art de Coteau and Ed Watson were dominant in the 1970s; and the soca sound of the late 1970s and 1980s was forged in large part by arrangers Leston Paul, Pelham Goddard, Clive Bradley, and Frankie McIntosh. Most Caribbean calypso and soca music arrangers, unlike their American equals, were credited by name on the record or the liner notes, an indication of their essential contributions to the music. Surveying calypsonians and their recordings from the 1980s, Jocelyne Guilbault concluded: "arrangers often end up being as prominent as the calypsonians singing the songs . . . in the process they leave indelible marks of their own specific styles on calypso productions."[6] She notes that calypsonians tended to cede musical decisions to their arrangers, confirming Alston Becket Cyrus's observation that "we gave Frankie the words and melodies and he gave us the music." Such accolades need to be tempered by the reality that despite this recognition, calypso arrangers rarely received co-composition credit or royalties. In terms of the calypso music industry, they were considered simply labor for hire.

What exactly do calypso arrangers do? The previous chapter's description of Frankie's early work with Becket and Chalkdust reveals the typical division of labor between the calypsonian and the arranger. Calypsonians first composed a set of lyrics and a basic melody set in a verse/chorus structure. The arranger was then responsible for determining the proper key, the instrumentation (depending on the budget), the basic chordal structure and underlying bass line(s), and the appropriate horn lines for the introduction and band choruses that occur in between each verse/chorus vocal section and during the final tag (coda). The arranger might also write original bridges to connect sections, and call for instrumental solos and percussion breakdowns to break up the verse/chorus structure. The new material that arrangers were expected to write often blurred the line between arranging and composition, a distinction Frankie does not hesitate to challenge.

From the 1960s on most calypso arrangers depended on written scores. The charts they were paid to produce were used in several performance settings. They served as prescriptive scores for reading musicians, particularly the horn players, during initial recording sessions. The arranger was expected to have the scores complete and in order upon arrival at a recording studio where musicians were expected to sight read with minimal rehearsal (perhaps a single run-through). This was in order to save on studio time and costs, and producers operating on tight budgets discouraged too much rearranging during recording sessions. The resulting recordings, featuring the singer and the instrumental accompaniment, were broadcast on radio, especially during Carnival season, and sold commercially for play at home and by DJs at parties, fetes, or Carnival road marches. In addition, the recordings often served as sources for steelbands looking for catchy material for their Carnival Panorama entry. The instrumental introductions and band chorus interludes of a popular calypso were often well known to the public thanks to these multiple mediated sources.

Following the initial recording session, the calypsonian would retain the full set of charts for future live performances at dances, tents, and contests. This was important because most calypsonians did not work with a regular band. As a result, individual calypsonians were responsible for providing charts each time they performed in a new venue, most likely with a new group of unrehearsed musicians.[7] Because calypsonians were expected to sing new songs (with new accompaniments) every year, instrumental groups could not depend on published tune collections or standard fake books for their music.

Most contests and shows involved a number of singers who had minimal (if any) rehearsal time with the stage band, so musicians were expected to sight read the set of charts that was handed to them before each calypsonian went on stage. A full set of well-organized charts was essential for satisfactory performances at most calypso venues.

The first section of this chapter will recount the early training and musical influences that shaped Frankie's development as a calypso/soca arranger. The remainder will delve into his arranging philosophy and process, focusing on the specific methods he used to move from the skeletal melody he receives from a calypsonian to a full-blown arrangement ready for recording sessions with the rhythm section, horns, and vocals. The choices he made became the musical scaffolding that supported the vocal melody and lyrics. Equally important, the instrumental arrangements provided distinctive sonic markers or hooks—punchy horn lines, propulsive bass grooves, memorable guitar or synthesizer strums, or unexpected harmonic twists—that were easily recognizable by the listening public. Those markers, along with the overall form of the arrangement, set the mood, energy, and groove to support and accentuate the vocal performance. They were unquestionably essential to a song's success.

Frankie: On Early Training and Influences

RA: Did you ever have any formal instruction on how to go about arranging the music to accompany a calypso song?

FM: No! Nobody ever explained to me "this is how you arrange a calypso." Nor have I ever taken a class on calypso arranging—not in person, via correspondence, or online. My success as an arranger is a result of both my formal musical training and my lived experiences growing up in Saint Vincent and playing and listening to Caribbean music as well as Black American jazz and R&B.

RA: Fair enough. Now I would like you to talk about the more formal aspects of your craft because I suspect that most soca fans do not understand the role of written scores in the arranging process. How did you first encounter musical scores, and how did you learn the rudiments of orchestration that allowed you to score out your first charts?

FM: My earliest contact with written scores was the big band arrangements used by my father's dance band, where all the musicians were strong readers. Those scores gave me a model for arranging tunes for his band and my own group in Saint Vincent. In Antigua, although I scored Laviscount's arrangements on music manuscript, the parts were communicated to the players orally, since not all were fluent readers. While I was working there, I met jazz bassist Alex Lane who suggested a book by Gordon Delamont, *Modern Arranging: Modern Harmony Technique*.

I got a hold of it and immediately read it over three times—it was rich with information and gave me a solid foundation in the basics of musical form, harmony, and orchestration. I then acquired and read all the books by Delamont that I could find. In fact, when I arrived at Brooklyn College, the harmony and theory courses posed little challenge for me, largely due to what I'd absorbed from the Delamont books.

RA: Speaking of Brooklyn College, did you take courses in orchestration or arranging? Today the BC Conservatory offers classes in jazz arranging and composition, but I believe you said back when you started there were no courses focusing specifically on jazz.

FM: No, at Brooklyn I took no formal courses in jazz arranging, or any jazz for that matter. As we previously discussed, the classically trained professors simply did not respect jazz as serious music. As galling as that might seem today, I did not go to Brooklyn College to study jazz, but my arranging skills benefited immensely from the courses I took there in music theory, harmony, and orchestration. That sort of training, I would come to realize, was essential for any music arranger working with written scores, be it with an orchestra, a jazz big band, or a calypso ensemble. I recall that Professors Levarie and Starer were sticklers for notating music correctly in order to facilitate readings of your scores by performers. I am not sure I appreciated their obsession with detail at the time, but years later I participated in sessions where the arrangers' charts were so poorly written (often notwithstanding their brilliant ideas) that the musicians would be unable to make sense of them. The arranger would then have to resort to singing individual lines to the session guys, and so crawl through the recording process, while the producer watched the clock and wrung his hands. Learning how to notate clearly and thereby communicate my ideas effectively was a tremendous boon for me as an arranger.

RA: At Brooklyn College you were in a conservatory that focused on Western classical music. But you must have studied jazz arranging when you went to New York University, right?

FM: Correct. In fact, I had a course called "The Structure of Jazz" with Stanley Persky when I did an initial semester of graduate work at City College. At NYU I had two semesters of "Jazz Arranging" with Tom Boras, and received many valuable pointers from Jim McNeely, my piano teacher, who also was the arranger for the Thad Jones/Mel Lewis Orchestra. Jim explained how that band's unique horn voicings were constructed. There was one big advantage to the way the instruction was set up at NYU—I had the opportunity to have live musicians play the scores I was working on in my arranging classes. Boras would take my charts to the student jazz ensemble he conducted and they would play them for me. It was no longer just a case of notes on a page, now it was a real aural thing, an acoustic reality. And I could listen and make adjustments for next time. For example, a close voicing would have been more effective than an open one in a certain setting; or a bed of longer note values would better support the melody than would obtrusive counter-lines; or the bass would be more supportive of the horns by playing the root instead of the third of the chord. That trial-and-error process really helped me. You just do not get that from a book!

RA: It sounds like this academic training was important for you. What else?

FM: Absolutely, there is no substitute for formal study with internationally acclaimed music professionals. That said, my success as a calypso arranger was due in no small part to my experiences growing up in the Caribbean and being immersed in its music and culture. That is, I am sure a lot was absorbed informally. For example, I've always believed that the rhythmic cadences of speech had strong influences on the music of any given people. There is a certain lilt to West Indian speech that finds its way into much of our music, and having grown up speaking that way, I felt a deep, innate connection. I know those sorts of cultural factors influenced the way I put a song together, the rhythmic patterns and accents, the melodic and rhythmic flow to my solos and instrumental lines. Knowledge of music theory and harmony were helpful, even necessary, but that alone was not enough to make an individual a good calypso arranger. You had to be a culture person, what we call a "roots man," keeping your ears open to the local music around you at all times. You had to be conversant with all sorts of Caribbean music, especially the calypso of the past.

RA: All right. So formal training and firsthand experience were important; how about recordings? Were there certain bandleaders and arrangers you listened to that influenced you early on as a musician and arranger?

FM: Oh yes, I grew up listening to a good deal of vocal and instrumental calypso music from the 1960s and 1970s on records and the radio. I would say my most important influences came from the calypso dance bands that played primarily instrumental arrangements and rarely used singers. With those bands one could hear the real art of the arranger. They would compose memorable introductions, develop complex themes, inject colorful harmonies, call in solos where they pleased, write lengthy tags, and so forth. They could take a simple folk calypso and by dint of arrangement render it into a sophisticated, multi-theme composition. And their tastes were broad—in addition to calypsos they would rearrange big band jazz, pop standards, and even classical pieces with a calypso or Latin beat. Just about anything!

RA: Who were your favorite band arrangers from that early period?

FM: Bertram Innis (pianist and arranger for Sparrow), Ottmar de Vlugt (pianist and arranger for the Dutchy Brothers), Beverley Griffith (pianist and arranger for the Clarence Curvan Orchestra), Ron Berridge, and Cito Fermin. Musicianship was at a high point back then due to the challenging nature of the repertoires. And there were a number of brilliant soloists. A few that come to mind are saxophonist Harold "Vasso" Defrietas (on Sparrow's "Take Your Bundle and Go"); trumpeter Errol Ince (on Sparrow's "Ten to One is Murder"); and pianist Ottmar de Vlugt (on The Dutchy Brothers' "Caremelos").

My two biggest heroes from that bunch were pianists Bertram Innis and Ottmar De Vlugt. Bertram's piano style was reminiscent of that of George Shearing, a distinguished American jazz pianist of the time known for his generous use of color tones (the addition of major sixths, sevenths, and ninths to a basic triad), his smooth voice leading that connected one chord to another, and his skillful employment of locked hands technique (playing the melody with the right and left hands, an octave apart, with three or two notes interspersed between). Bertram demonstrated those approaches on Rupert Clemendore's early 1960s album *Jazz Primitif*, where his solos on "Princess Charming," "Bongo Bop," and "One Bass Hit" stand out as textbook examples of Caribbean jazz piano. Bertram's gift for harmonic complexity, voicing, and color, may also be heard in his own orchestra recordings from the period, such as "Sonny Boy" and "Harry and Mamma," and on his arrangements of the early Sparrow songs "Jean and Dinah" and "Man Like to Feel." I repeatedly listened to his records and tried to emulate his playing, especially the way he put his chords together.

Listening back from the present one might conclude that Betram Innis was ahead of his time, but to me he was more a product of that time—back in the 1950s and 1960s, before the music of the Anglophone Caribbean had become polarized into triadic soca and reggae. It was a time of musical variety and harmonic color when nearly all Caribbean musicians aspired toward jazz, and a time when the general public knew who Erroll Garner and Duke Ellington were. Of course, I was a youngster then, but through the influence of my dad, Bertram, and others, that time left a spiritual stamp on me and my music—fortunately so.

RA: I am familiar with Bertram Innis, but not Ottmar De Vlugt of the Dutchy Brothers. Why did he stand out to you?

FM: The Dutchy Brothers were a well-known dance band from San Fernando in Trinidad. They were acclaimed for the way in which they blended calypso and Latin rhythms, their creative introductions and montunos, and the distinctive solos of their flamboyant pianist Ottmar De Vlugt. They even ventured into the classical repertoire, of course with a Caribbean twist. Their renditions of Tchaikovsky's *Waltz of the Flowers* and the B section of Chopin's *Fantaisie-Impromptu* (which the Dutchys called *Piano Bolero*) were amazing! I admired Ottmar's incredible technique and the variety of styles he could play—Latin, calypso, classical, and jazz—all with a real flair.

RA: Why do you suppose we do not hear more about Innis, De Vlugt, and these other important figures from those calypso dance orchestras?

FM: Unfortunately, many of the talented arrangers and instrumentalists of the 1960s are no longer with us—Bertram Innis, Frankie Francis, Ottmar De Vlugt, and Beverly Griffith have all passed on. Sadly, those still alive, like Ed Watson, are only recognized today as a result of their association with singers, rather than for their work with instrumental bands. Many possessed knowledge of advanced music theory that far surpassed what they were required to write or play for calypsonians. As singers became increasingly the center of attention in the recording industry, instrumental arrangements and solos became subservient to the voice, with solos all but disappearing. As a musician and an arranger, I found that to be a regressive move, and tried to inject more of a balance between music and voice.

RA: How about the musicians you played with, did you learn much from them? Obviously, your dad was helpful when you were starting out, but who else?

FM: Sure, I acquired a great deal of music knowledge informally through countless conversations with my fellow musicians. Playing with Lio Smith's orchestra soon after I arrived in Brooklyn brought me in contact with all sorts of knowledgeable persons who talked about music at rehearsals and during breaks. Trumpeter Ray Copeland especially loved to sit around and dissect music with me. The same was true with jazz saxophonists Howard Kimbro, Jimmy Tyler, and Charlie Parker's bassist Tommy Potter, with whom I played in the 1970s before my calypso arranging career took off. That was really the sort of on-the-job training that you could not get in the classroom.

Getting Started

RA: You mentioned earlier that you needed to "find" the arrangement that was inherent in the song you were presented with. Can you explain that process without giving away too many of your secrets?

FM: Of course! Upon receiving a song from a calypsonian, typically in cassette format, I would first listen intently. Instead of imposing an arrangement immediately, I would do the reverse by allowing the melody itself to suggest the arrangement to me. When the material I received was stimulating, I knew the arrangement was there in the song; it would then be my task to find it.

Now that might require my extracting parts of the original vocal melody to construct band choruses and instrumental background lines, or perhaps composing entirely new lines and riffs, but ones that would be in keeping stylistically with what I was originally given. When I began to assemble these pieces, it was essential that the vocal, horn, bass, and synthesizer figures maintain their separate identities, yet sound as if they belong to the same arrangement. One could say unity in variety.

In terms of process, I would usually begin by charting out the basic chord progression and the overall form of the piece—where I wanted the verses, chorus, instrumental band sections, and tag to land. In the early days it was common for me to score an entire arrangement in one sitting. However, when some singers began changing their melodies in their initial studio session, I would have to wait until the next day to fill in the specific details of the horn lines for the band chorus, the bass line, and so forth. Eventually I realized it was best to allow a little time for the whole sense of the song to sink in.

RA: What kinds of specific things would you listen for in the original song melody and lyrics?

FM: I paid close attention to the rhyme scheme, repeated lines within a stanza, and the rhythm of the singer's melody that might engender possibilities for background instrumental hooks. Small vocal rhythmic and melodic cells often generated bigger ideas. In some instances, singers might present ideas for bass or horn lines. I was never dismissive of those, but would try to integrate them into the arrangement by modifying my concept and style to match theirs. You never wanted the final outcome to sound like two arrangers—the final product needed to sound like one seamless piece of cloth. Thankfully most of the calypsonians I worked with were flexible—either they trusted me to come up with all the music, or they were willing to work collaboratively to invent figures that we were both satisfied with. Whenever their ideas were unmusical, I would be frank in letting them know.

RA: I think of calypso and soca as primarily vocal musics for which the lyrics are central. Do a song's lyrics influence your arranging process?

FM: Oh yes! Listening carefully to the lyrics and to the vocal delivery to gauge the overall tone and mood that the calypsonian hoped to convey is fundamental. Is it a "jump and wave" dance/party or road march tune that demands a driving rhythmic groove, accentuated by bright horn riffs and hits? Or is it a more serious, text-dense "message song," perhaps for a calypso competition. In which case the tempo might be slower and I would need to be careful to keep the instrumental lines subordinate to the voice? The latter might have been less interesting to the dancers, but I needed to be mindful of the calypsonian's intention for the song. In consideration of all this, I found it more challenging and painstaking to arrange message songs than the dance/party pieces. Crowds sat and listened, judges assigned marks for arrangement, and a song that earned the contestant the title of "Calypso King" would become part of the nation's history. The arranger's skill was being judged and I felt there was a lot at stake! Also, a popular message song often enjoyed greater longevity than its evanescent dance counterpart.

Establishing the Key

RA: When a singer would show up at your house with a song, would he or she always know what key they should be in?

FM: No, not always. That was why the first thing I always tried to do when a singer arrived with a song was to determine the proper key, depending on their vocal range. If they didn't have a guitar I'd sit at the piano and try different keys until we found the one they were the most comfortable with. I also had to be careful to avoid certain keys like F♯, C♯, B that were not particularly friendly for horn players (F, B♭, E♭, and C were preferred). Many singers had limited range that would predetermine the key, and they would resist my trying to move things up or down even half a step. The initial establishment of the key was important, because I probably would not see the singers again until the recording session. At that point changing the key would mean transposing my scores, which could be done, but was a time-consuming process that was best avoided.

Establishing the Form

RA: To my ear, most of the calypso and soca songs from the late 1970s and 1980s followed a standard verse-chorus format, right?

FM: Yes, that is correct. Most followed a basic structural formula that was inherited from older calypsos, but don't forget about the introductions and band choruses, that was where the arranger and musicians got to shine. Now that overall form consisted typically but not exclusively of:

1) An eight-bar (measure) or sixteen-bar instrumental band chorus, played on the horns and synthesizer over the rhythm section. This was usually based on the singer's vocal chorus melody (hence the term "band chorus") and would establish the key and set the mood for the entrance of the verse.
2) An eight-bar or sixteen-bar vocal verse.
3) An eight-bar or sixteen-bar vocal chorus.
4) Repeat the eight-bar or sixteen-bar instrumental band chorus.
5) A series of two or three additional vocal verses, vocal choruses, and instrumental band choruses.
6) An open-ended tag (montuno) or jam section based on a two- or three-chord progression that was repeated over and over. New horn riffs, synthesizer lines, and horn solos are introduced, alternating with ad-lib lines that the singer felt moved to deliver.

On the written score I would label these sections A (band chorus), B (vocal verse), C (vocal chorus), and D (tag). Structurally the first three to four minutes of a song would be an ABC/ABC/ABC loop played by the musicians while the singer delivered as many verses and choruses as he/she chose. The final few minutes would be the tag (D), which was usually faded out by the engineer.

This ABC/ABC/ABC/ABCD structure was common practice, but exceptions abound. Occasionally a brief (maybe a four-bar) introduction would precede the first band chorus to perk listeners' interest. This might consist of a percussion roll, a distinctive guitar strum, or horn hits. When a profusion of lyrics resulted in the length of a song exceeding six minutes, several of the intervening band choruses would be omitted, resulting in something like an ABC/ABC/BC/BCD structure. Or I might decide to break things up by throwing in a short melodic interlude or a bridge based around a new chord progression. When a singer did not do much ad-libbing and I needed to extend the tag, I would call for more instrumental solos, or perhaps bring back the band chorus or a variation of it.

RA: I stand corrected. Clearly there was a lot more than just a verse and a chorus. Can you say more about the instrumental introductions and the initial band chorus? Why was that material so significant?

FM: A strong initial opening was extremely important, probably the most important thing I would write. Think of someone listening to a record, say in Straker's store; the introductory band chorus would be the first thing they heard. If the music during the first ten seconds was not catchy, they were likely to tell Straker, "take that off, let me hear something else!" That introduction had to be appealing to the customer or the record would not sell, a big factor to consider!

RA: OK, so how did you put those initial band choruses together? When it came to horn and synthesizer lines, did you use materials from the singer's original melody or did you write your own?

FM: I did both. You see, I used different strategies to construct a band chorus. If the tune of the vocal chorus made for a great sing-along, then that usually became the basis for my band chorus, perhaps with minor embellishments to avoid a verbatim repetition (for example, Short Shirt's "Push," described in chapter 5, and Chalkdust's "Ash Wednesday," described in chapter 6). I might use a little heterophony—playing around the main vocal melody without stating it verbatim. But you would still get a strong sense of the melodic and rhythmic relationships between what I wrote for the band chorus and the main vocal melody I was given. That was also a way of introducing the listener to the vocal melody that would follow the instrumental band chorus. A strong horn line could serve as a musical teaser for what would follow. Other times I would write new phrases or melodies, alluding to characteristic motives that jumped out at me from the original material (for example, Swallow's "Fire in the Back Seat," described in chapter 5, and Rose's "Sideman Sweet," described in chapter 6). I might use the melodic rhythm only, substituting my own pitches. Or perhaps I would extract the contour of the original melody and add new pitches and rhythms. But always I would keep in mind the overall feel of the song. Whether I was using hooks from the original melody, or creating new material, the introduction and band choruses had to relate musically to the vocal verse that would follow. The overarching goal was to achieve a natural flow from one section to another—the transitions from A to B to C and back to A needed to be seamless.

RA: Now tell me about the final tags. These often lasted two minutes or longer and were built around repetitive chordal vamps, right? I have heard that sort of vamping in Black gospel and R&B, and in salsa music. Why were they important?

FM: The tags (also referred to as jams or montunos) occurred in the latter part of songs, after the singer had delivered three or four verses interspersed with band choruses. Yes, the band would usually vamp—that is, play a simple chord pattern over and over again while the singer would improvise. During the final tag I might also introduce a new melodic theme on the horns and keyboard, often a variation on the original band chorus.

Occasionally I would call for a solo by a horn player or the guitarist. The tags served several purposes. First, they provided a platform for the singer, and sometimes the instrumentalists, to stretch out and improvise, to add their own unique stylistic mark to the piece. From my perspective as an arranger, tags offered space for fresh instrumental passages—yet one more instance where I was composing, generating new material, not just arranging. Tags also extended the length of the song, which was beneficial to DJs for radio airplay or at a live event if the dancers wanted to keep going. (Which reminds me—back in Saint Vincent, at a community dance, you would be frowned upon if did not play a hot montuno jam at the end of a popular calypso!) Of course, whether on the air or live, when time grew short, the tags could be easily faded out.

Orchestration

RA: Now let's talk about orchestration. What instruments did you ideally work with, and how did you use them?

FM: I almost always worked with a full rhythm section: drum kit (later augmented and at times replaced by a drum machine), conga drum and additional hand percussion, electric bass, electric guitar, and keyboards (usually a synthesizer, but occasionally acoustic or electric piano). The budget of the artist or producer would dictate how many horns I would have to work with. Occasionally one opted for simple rhythm section backing, omitting horns altogether, hoping to capture more of a reggae sound. Such details would be worked out up front, before I began scoring.

RA: Tell me more about the horns. Obviously, they play an essential role in calypso and soca arrangements.

FM: They do, a powerful horn line can make a song! Ideally, I would have a first and second trumpet, a tenor and alto saxophone, and a trombone. That would allow for four- or five-part harmony, close or open voicings, and a reasonable set of choices for timbral and textural contrast. For example, the trumpets might lead with saxes and trombones providing support; or the saxes might play alone but in unison; or the trumpets and saxes might alternate in call and response to one another; and so on and so forth. But Straker tended to be conservative, one might say frugal, so often I would have just two or at most three horns—at least one trumpet and one saxophone. That presented some voicing challenges: you cannot play a triad with two instruments!

RA: Right. Now it sounds like you sometimes used synthesizer lines to fill in horn parts.

FM: Yes, because one solution was using horn patches on the synthesizer for augmentation. At first, I saw the synth as an arranger's boon—a means of applying my formal training in big band arranging and orchestration. And the synthesizer had come on the American R&B scene in the 1970s, with Caribbean audiences in New York quickly embracing the new, modern sound. As a result, calypso and soca keyboardists jumped onboard.

RA: Honestly, I am not a real fan of synthesized horns, but I supposed there were pros and cons to using the synth patch in lieu of a live brass or reed instrument. What were the advantages?

FM: Well, let me begin by saying that I personally found the synthesizer attractive for several reasons. First, they were always in tune, unlike many of the acoustic pianos in some of the recording studios and in many of the dance halls. Musically, they expanded the palate of sounds, colors, and timbres available to me. They offered a variety of sonorities—from bass to flute and everything in between. When I only had two or three horns, the synthesizer helped fill things out, when mixed correctly, to create a fuller sound. I really preferred the early analogue synths, like the Oberheim Matrix and Prophet 5 (which I first played at Sound Heights Studio in Brooklyn), and of course the Arp Odyssey (which I used on Becket's "Wine Down Kingstown"). They had a full, fat sound that worked particularly well for solo work and for adding body to the horn mix, especially a unison section (despite drawbacks in blending mentioned below). The later digital machines, like the Yamaha DX7, were a little too clean and seemed thin to my ear compared to the older analogue models.

RA: But you never abandoned live horns. Now playing devil's advocate, using the synthesizer was cheaper and less of an organizational ordeal. So why bother with all the horns?

FM: Despite these advantages I generally preferred the sound of live horns. Notwithstanding how realistic the synthesizer sounded by itself, when combined with real horns, I was never convinced that the resultant sound was that of a true big band horn section (certainly not like that of Duke Ellington or Thad Jones/Mel Lewis). When synthesized horns replaced real horns on a track, they often sounded like cheap, synthetic imitations. If the synthesizer timbre dominated in the final mix (which unfortunately it occasionally did), the intonation of the live horns could be affected, making them sound slightly out of tune. Trumpeter Errol Ince was fond of reminding me that the synthesizer just did not sound like a real horn. I suppose as a horn player he was biased, but to my ear he had a point. That said, the public did not discriminate between the real deal and the imitation; they either liked the sound or not, and many of my hybrid combinations were favorably received. Considering that my artists and/or producers could rarely afford a full, big-band brass and reed section, I had to make do—I could not turn down a job because they could not hire five horns.

RA: Let's move on to the rhythm section starting with the bass, then on to the drums and guitars. Can you talk about the role of the bass guitar in the overall scheme of your arrangements?

FM: In older calypso arrangements, like the ones my dad's band played, the bass generally served as a timekeeper that established the beat and provided the harmonic foundation for everything else. It was root oriented, moved mostly in quarter notes, and generally remained within the instrument's lower register. Very early calypso bands used the acoustic bass exclusively.

RA: Understood. But that is not the case for soca, right?

FM: No, the bass graduated from the background to the foreground in many of the new soca arrangements, becoming more active and melodic. At times the bass would move in counterpoint to the voice and horns, or otherwise double them (an octave below) for emphasis, especially on the vocal hooks. By the time I began working for Straker in the late 1970s, acoustic double basses had fallen by the wayside and the electric bass had become the instrument of choice.

RA: What sorts of things did you take into consideration when coming up with a bass line?

FM: Writing a more active bass line was tricky. After all, the bass was still the instrument capable of playing the lowest notes in the band, and as such, needed to support the instruments above it by establishing the home key and outlining the chords that the guitar and keyboard were playing. Because the lead voice always had priority, my first concern in constructing a melodic type bassline was that it worked with the vocal and horn melodies rather than obtrude upon them. The bass might be in counterpoint to the lead vocal line, or used to answer the voice if there were noticeable gaps in the melody (for example, the bass and horns answer Scorcher's opening vocal verse lines in "Party Fever," discussed in chapter 5). And there were occasions when the bass line would double the vocal line for emphasis, often in a chorus situation (for example the B and C chorus sections for Sparrow's "Don't Back Back," described in chapter 6). When voice and bass were linear, I would relegate the horns to short accented figures. Too many independent, active voices could befuddle the listener, especially in the case of a message song where the lyrics needed to be foregrounded. But I generally aimed to keep the bass line consistent throughout the song, especially in terms of the overall rhythmic feel that it generated.

Keep in mind that the newer soca bass lines tended to employ more complicated, syncopated figures, often built around smaller note values like eighth and sixteenth notes (while the older calypso bass lines employed mostly quarter notes). On top of that, the tempos of the new soca songs were usually considerably faster, so you had to come up with lines that allowed the bass to maintain clarity while continuing to support the other instruments.

RA: Summing it up, what makes a good soca bass line?

RA: For soca, you wanted a bass line that would catch the listeners' attention, that they could dance to and even sing along to, but one that would be part of the whole musical tapestry. It was a challenge, but when the right combination was captured, a bassline could "make" a song and listeners would hum it before they hummed the singer's refrain or chorus.

RA: Moving on, were you involved in scoring out the specific patterns for the drum set and other percussion instruments?

Habanera rhythm notation.

FM: The drum set players I worked with early on—Elvis Rose, Wayne Wilson, and Anthony "Bugs" Niles—played a basic calypso beat that was some variation of the Caribbean four-beat *habanera* rhythmic pattern with the beats alternating between the bass drum and snare. Now, most of the drummers did not read music so there was no sense in scoring anything out for them. I would set the tempo, and occasionally ask them to add an accent like a snare hit or a cymbal crash, or even a roll, to highlight an important vocal line or brilliant passage on the horns. I might throw in a stop to break up the beat, or have them play along in rhythmic unison to a short horn or vocal phrase that needed emphasis. In that way the drummers were more than just timekeepers! They did keep the basic pulse going, but they contributed immensely to the subtle rhythmic and timbral nuances of the arrangement. Occasionally the drummer would take a solo on the tag, during a percussion break, especially on the earlier recordings with live drums.

RA: That brings us to the question of drum machines. Sorry to sound like such a Luddite, but mechanical drumbeats are not my favorite sound. In any case, when did they come into play?

FM: By the mid-1980s we were increasingly replacing live set drummers with drum machines. That was all to save money. You had to pay a kit drummer and an extra conga players and hand percussionists, and it would take up to an hour to get a good drum sound in the studio—tuning and miking the drums. That cost money for producers like Straker who opted to go with the cheaper mechanical beats. Studios started to purchase machines like the one made by Lynn (later Roland R-8 and Yamaha RX-15) and I quickly figured out how to program them myself.

RA: OK, I understand their practicality, but did you find the drum machines musically satisfactory, aesthetically speaking?

FM: Not really. What we gained with drum machines in saved time, we lost in terms of the variation in dynamics, the use of accents and dramatic rolls, and overall sense of rhythmic nuance and the human element. The early drum machines were capable of producing many different and fascinating sounds, but they were just fancy timekeepers, and I always preferred live drummers when the budget permitted. Sometimes I'd have a drummer like Niles to program the machine for a session, just to get him a little money, even if we couldn't afford to have him actually play live.

RA: Now, how did you work with the guitarists? Did you have scores for them?

FM: I generally provided a chord chart for the guitar and keyboard (which I was usually playing), not fully notated scores like I would produce for the horns. In our warmup session I would listen to the guitarist's feel for the song. If I was not satisfied, I might make suggestions—change the rhythm of the strum if it was not fitting with the bass line, or play an octave higher. Occasionally I would have to demonstrate the actual rhythm I wanted, but these players were real professionals who lived and breathed calypso, so they would usually come up with something that worked—honestly, it was cultural. Guys like Jeff Medina, Scipio Sargent, George Victory, and Larry Marsden knew what they were doing, and always came up with interesting rhythmic strums, fills, and ornamented lines. Sometimes I would write out short lines for one or more guitars to play underneath or during a bridge. If the line was difficult to read, I would sing or play the notes on the keyboard for them to and commit to memory. In all, the process involved both reading and playing by ear.

RA: You sometimes use the word "beat" when describing the output of a good rhythm section—what exactly do you mean by that?

FM: I have talked about the individual components of the rhythm section, but in reality, what many people today refer to as the "beat" of a song is really a composite of all the rhythms. A strong beat is the result of the interaction of the drums, bass, the guitar, and keyboard strums, and finally the way the horns on top interlock with the rest of the instruments. That beat, or groove as it is sometimes referred to, is essential to a soca song's appeal to the general public, especially the dancing public.

Harmonic Accompaniment and Voicing the Horns

RA: To my ear, one thing that distinguished many of your arrangements from other popular soca songs of the 1980s was your use of elaborate harmonies and chord progressions. In some ways this was a throwback to the calypsos of the 1950s and 1960s and arrangers like Bert Innis, John "Buddy" Williams," and Ron Berridge that you mentioned earlier. Can you talk about that?

FM: Yes, but let me begin with a story. Sometime back in the 1980s, when I was doing a session with Sparrow at Charlie's studio, a journalist who was there to do an interview asked him about the difference between soca and calypso. And Sparrow immediately piped up, "Well you know, a soca tune is really a calypso that failed to grow up." That was a good observation, because he was pointing out that many soca tunes were based entirely on the jam or the tag in a calypso without the harmonic and melodic variations typically heard in the verse and chorus. That is, the tag was basically a vamp section where two chords, say a I and a V (for example, a C chord and a G chord in the key of C), were repeated over and over again, while the singer and instrumentalists ad-libbed. When I was first playing with my dad's orchestra, that was the final part of a calypso tune where people would really let go dancing. But while the vamp might only have employed two or at most three chords, the main verse and chorus sections of a typical calypso song were built around more involved harmonies. This was especially true for the calypsos of the 1950s and 1960s when Sparrow was coming up—the arrangers for those earlier songs had learned a great deal from American big band and pop tunes. Sparrow's point was that the newer soca songs, like the tags of the older calypsos, were not too harmonically adventurous—they had "failed to grow up" as he put it—because they were built on only two or three chords looped over and over. Honestly, for some of us, a song that went on for six minutes with only two chords ran the risk of becoming boring. In fact, Chalkdust wrote a song, "Two Chords and Leston Paul" (1988), about just that! He used the piece to vent his resentment to the reduced harmonic vocabulary that had come to define soca (and still does). I will have more to say about that song in chapter 6, but the point is that Chalky's lyrics were something of a spoof, and despite the song's title, his melody called for numerous changes, not just "Two Chords," in his verses and choruses.

You could say that I have always been more of a harmony person, more akin to those older calypso arrangers. As a result, when I started out arranging with those early projects with Becket, I tried to get away from the basic I-IV-V progression of triadic chords that characterized many early soca arrangements. I created new introductions and built-in transitions and bridges. I also would use extended chords from my jazz piano playing. When I was harmonizing melodies, I wanted to create more variety and richer timbral color by adding sevenths, ninths, and thirteenths on the keyboard and guitar and on the horn voicings. For example, if a song called for a conventional I-VI-II-V chord progression (C-Am-Dm-G in the key of C major), I would play the initial C major triad, but then dress up the rest of the chords as follows: instead of an A minor triad (voiced a-c-e) I would use an Am7add9 chord (voiced a-c-e-g-b); instead of a D minor triad (voiced d-f-a) I would use a Dm7add9 chord (voiced d-f-a-c-e); and instead of the G major triad (voiced g-b-d) I would use a G7add9&13 chord (g-b-d-f-a-e). Now this all seemed very natural to me, not formulaic. I was not consciously thinking about formal jazz harmonizing theory or anything like that, these things were just what I was hearing. I believe I had internalized those voicings, textures, and sonorities from all the American music, the jazz, and R&B that I had been playing and listening too since arriving here in New York, and of course, back to my early days in my father's orchestra in Saint Vincent.

RA: It seems to me you were swimming against the tide back then, because many, perhaps most, of the early soca hits were built around two- and three-chord loops. How do you think your more complex harmonic approach went over with your Caribbean audiences?

FM: That is a good question and one I had to wrestle with. You see, many younger Caribbean people who had not lived through the Dutchy Brothers period, were not as familiar with fancier chords and jazzier voicings back then. I am not too sure that my more adventuresome efforts were always well received, especially after the advent of soca, where the three-chord, triadic approach became the cornerstone of the music. At first this irked me, but eventually I came to realize that if I wanted to continue to make a living doing this, I had to be mindful of the desires of the artists, the producer, and of course the Caribbean audiences that would buy the records. If I got too fancy with non-conventional harmonies, the singer or the producer might object. And if the record did not sell, the artist might not come back next year. In fact, I found that the songs with the simpler harmonies seemed to sell better than those where I employed more jazzy sounds. As time went on, I felt the pressure of the market—I had to find a balance between art and making a living. There were some calypsonians—Becket, Duke, and Shadow come immediately to mind—who appreciated my occasional harmonic excursions. But Straker and others wanted adherence to some permutation of a I-IV-V loop with triadic chords, so that is what I generally, and somewhat begrudgingly, gave them.

RA: Sounds like you felt constrained at times. That must have been frustrating, given your background in classical music and in jazz harmonization, no?

FM: Yes, I was certainly frustrated at times. But I should add that the strength of traditional calypsos has always been in the realm of melody and rhythm, rather than harmony. As a result, there was a good deal I could do when presented with a strong melody and the motives it might generate, even if limited to a simple underlying I-IV-V triadic progression. I was often able to find interesting ways to integrate the brass and reed instruments on the sections I discussed above—the introductions, band choruses, and the tags, as well as occasional bridges and transitional passages.

RA: Right. Now let's talk about the different techniques you used to voice the horns.

FM: Having all the brass and reeds play in unison was a very effective for sharp, cutting melodic phrases that I wanted to jump out, perhaps something recapitulating the main hook of the vocal chorus that I wanted listeners to really focus on. But of course, unison sounds best when contrasted with something else, like harmony, so someplace in the arrangement I would score the horns in either close voicings (where the different horns are playing notes close to each other) or occasionally in more expansive, open voicings (where the different horns are playing notes spaced further apart). You need variety and contrast within one song to keep things interesting for the listener—playing everything in unison would quite quickly become boring!

RA: Would you say a bit more about the close and open voicing approaches—when would you use one or the other?

FM: Close-voiced harmonies worked best for the faster tempo songs, where the notes were moving along quickly. I usually voiced the horns in close harmony (and at times in unison) on the introductions and band sections of driving dance pieces (for example, "I Don't Mind" by Winston Soso, discussed in chapter 5). In contrast, a slower calypso ballad or moderate-tempo message song might call for open, voicings underneath the lead vocal to evoke a more dramatic or contemplative mood. When the tempo was slow and you have longer note values, I might voice the instruments at larger (open) intervals from one another, thereby creating space. You needed at least four or maybe five horns to make this work effectively, to get a real spread, say between the low trombone, a mid-range tenor sax and a slightly higher alto sax, and one or more higher-register trumpets. I recall using open-voiced horns on several of my earlier arrangements, such as Becket's "Legalize the Grass." Unfortunately, it is difficult to hear them clearly on the recording mix due to competing synthesizer, string, and background vocal lines. In retrospect, open voicings were used sparingly, and close voicings were the norm, especially for the later, up-tempo soca songs.

RA: How did you think about the horn parts in relation to the voice?

FM: I would use the horns in a number of ways. Their main function was to introduce and support the voice with material drawn from or complementing the main vocal melody. This began in my introductory band chorus, where listeners first heard snippets of what was to come in the vocal sections of the song. After the voice entered, the horns might support the melody with short riffs and accents when appropriate. Sometimes they would answer the voice with short phrases, filling in the space to complete an incomplete vocal phrase, or to connect two vocal phrases in a verse (for example, the horns and synthesizer voiced together in response to the vocal verses in Explainer's "Celebration," discussed in chapter 6). When done correctly, the effect was seamless, with the calling vocals and responding horns feeling like a complete unit. This of course is related to the classic call-and-response structure you hear in so much African, Caribbean, and Black American music. The horns could also introduce new material that I composed for the tag—fresh melodic lines related to but not derived directly from the original vocal melody line (for example my descending brass lines during the tag sections of Duke's "Total Disorder," discussed in chapter 6).

RA: I am wondering, how much did you have to worry about the technical demands you were placing on your musicians as you scored out your arrangements? Did they ever complain?

FM: I certainly had to be aware of their instruments' limitations, especially for the horn players. Every wind instrument has a low and high pitch limit, but within that ambit lies a characteristic range where it sounds best, and within which players are most technically comfortable with tone production and fingering. I avoided taking the saxes and trumpets above written high C (the C two ledger lines above the treble staff). With a trumpeter like Errol Ince who could easily double high C (play it an octave higher), those reservations did not apply, but then Errol's musical gift is sui generis. Note values and tempo had to be jointly taken into account: at a brisk tempo, say 125 beats per minute in 4/4 time, rapid passages of sixteenth notes were avoided if considered too difficult to articulate. Conversely, long, unbroken whole notes held at slower tempos (around 70 beats per minute) could render the player breathless.

You see, there was no sense in writing instrumental music that was too difficult to play, especially since our rehearsing in the studio added to the producer's overhead costs. Producers always preferred musicians who could do the job in the least time. Fortunately, session musicians rarely complained about my charts, as challenging as they sometimes were. But a number of stage band musicians opined that they were too difficult, so I was occasionally obliged, for the benefit of the artists' employment opportunities, to simplify them. If the house band backing one of my singers complained about my charts, the promoter might not bring that singer back. It was another balancing act: make the parts complex enough to be interesting without making them so hard that the musicians couldn't play them.

RA: And how about improvised solos? When did you choose to use them, and what were the expectations?

FM: I might also call for an individual trumpet or saxophone to play a solo during the tag to break things up and give the singer a little rest while extending the piece. It was an effort to escape the repetitive humdrum of the voice, band chorus, voice, and so on. Here the approach was generally similar to a jazz arrangement where the soloist was expected to improvise over the chords of the tag.

RA: I am very interested in the various ways that musicians approach improvisation. Was there a difference between the way Caribbean players soloed, say as opposed to American jazz musicians who you worked with?

FM: Well, I do not think it was simply a matter of where you were from geographically speaking, it was more what sorts of music you were immersed in. Those who favored a more Caribbean style of soloing stayed closer to the original melody while adding flourishes of melodic embellishments and ornamentations, and subtle variations in their rhythmic phrasing. These were the types of solos you generally heard from the calypso dance bands and on early calypso vocal recordings. Other players, who more conversant with modern American jazz, might go for inventing new melodies using rapid bursts of notes, chromatic lines, and dissonant runs. Most were like me (on my keyboard solos), employing both approaches depending on the mood of the song. In the studio I usually did not need to offer much direction, perhaps remarking off the cuff, "Imagine yourself playing on the road Carnival Day or for a Carnival dance, or that you are John Coltrane playing calypso." I saw no reason for any of my musicians to limit themselves.

Fortunately, I had many choices given my New York jazz contacts. Trumpeters Shake Keane, Errol Ince, and Ray Maldonado, and saxophonists Sam Furnace, Gene Jefferson, Charles Dougherty, and Lio Smith were among the superb jazz players whom I recruited for recording sessions and could call on to solo at any time. Most were from the Caribbean, but were well versed in contemporary jazz techniques.

RA: So, you do not think of improvising in strictly American jazz terms?

FM: No, no! Improvising was not just a jazz thing for me or many of the folks I played with. We grew up with the idea back in the Caribbean, and later became conscious that improvising was part of the African artistic expression. You hear it in African drumming with one leader improvising above the support drums and then another taking over, and of course in jazz, and more recently in vocal rap. The idea was to allow an individual player or singer to make a statement, to say "this is me, this is who I am, this is what I have to say." That, rather than me just writing the exact lines out for them to play all the time the way a classical composer would (or at least used) to do. I knew the horn players might get bored just sitting and reading the charts all the time, so I wanted to give them the opportunity to play freely at some point. And I believe that many of the horn and guitar players looked forward to my sessions because they knew they might get a chance to solo. In retrospect, I wish I had done more of it, but time constraints and the market forces did not always allow for it.

RA: Let's end this section with your thoughts on arranging and composing. Where does one end and the other begin?

FM: I do not believe that the distinction is always that clear. I have composed very few calypso tunes from scratch, and I certainly do not consider myself a calypso songwriter. However, there have been instances when my musical contributions equaled or at times exceeded that of the so-called songwriter who brought forward the original melodic line and lyrics. For example, the song "Coming High," which I will discuss in the next chapter, is registered under Alston Becket Cyrus's name. But what Becket created was about four measures of music, while the introduction and bridge sections that I wrote were considerably longer. When you look at it, my musical contributions were significant enough that my whole creative process transcended arranging and got into something closer to composition. That happened a lot back then. The arranger would put his heart and soul into the music and just create parts without claiming coauthorship. I am certainly guilty and regret that now. The arrangements often had more musical substance than the raw melody verse and chorus melodies that the singer would bring to the table, and in many cases, the arrangement would really be what sold the song! It got to the point where the calypsonians expected the arrangers to compose new musical lines for their songs, but we were never offered a coauthorship credit. In retrospect I realize this, but back then, getting caught up in the whole creative process, I didn't think about business, copyright registration, or coauthorship.

I don't mean this to be a criticism of Becket, or for that matter any other individual calypsonian. That was the system we were all working in, and most of the singers had a difficult time making a living themselves. On the positive side, it was through the notoriety I acquired from working with Becket that my arranging career blossomed, and for this I am eternally grateful. He was a consummate gentleman and artist with a sense of morals and ethics not commonly found today, and over the years Becket became a virtual family member, my "brother from another mother" as the saying goes.

• • •

We hope this chapter has given readers a glimpse of what a calypso and soca arranger does. The choices that Frankie made regarding instrumentation, basic form, and harmonization were essential in shaping the sound of the calypso and early soca recordings of the late 1970s and 1980s. Now let's move on to see how those choices actually played out on a sampling of his most successful arrangements.

CHAPTER 5
ARRANGING WITH THE SMALL ISLAND CALYPSONIANS

Critical histories of calypso and soca have focused almost exclusively on the Trinidadian origins of the music and its diaspora to North America and Great Britain.[1] This is not surprising. The calypso songs that found their way onto early commercial recordings in the late 1920s and 1930s were performed primarily by Trinidadian singers who drew on a well-established calypso song tradition that had become central to the island's pre-Lent Carnival celebration. These Trinidadian roots acknowledged, it is important to recognize that calypso is a hybrid art form, with transnational ancestral roots in African drumming and ritual song, vernacular songs and dances from England and France, and folk song traditions from other nearby islands and coastal Venezuela and Guyana. We know that syncretic folk musics associated with Carnival developed on other English-speaking islands, and that inter-island migration hastened their spread, with Trinidad becoming a central cultural crossroads.[2] Dorbrene O'Marde, in his biography of Antiguan calypsonian Short Shirt, sums up: "The movement and sharing of music (across the Caribbean) suggest that calypso is but the most recent accommodation and fusion of different creole musics that evolved across the region, which found home in the larger population and better economy of Trinidad."[3]

By the time Frankie came along in the post–World War II years, Trinidadian-style calypso had established its hegemony in the Eastern Caribbean, due to a plethora of professional Trinidadian singers who toured the region and the circulation of their recordings that received ample airtime on local radio stations. As a result, little attention has been paid to "small island calypso," despite the fact that Carnival-related calypso scenes developed in Saint Vincent, Barbados, Tobago, Grenada, Antigua, and other English-speaking islands.[4]

In this chapter we will turn to Frankie's arrangements for six calypsonians from the islands of Saint Vincent and Antigua: Alston "Becket" Cyrus, Trevor Winston Soso Lockhart, Cyril "Scorcher" Thomas, MacLean Leroy "Short Shirt" Emanuel, Rupert "Swallow" Philo, and Paul "King Obstinate" Richards. These singers were chosen because of their impact in the Caribbean and in New York, much of which was due to working with Frankie. We have selected several tunes recorded by each calypsonian, based on their popularity in the Caribbean community and the stylistic elements they reveal about Frankie's arranging process. Listening outlines, timed to YouTube recordings of each song, are found in appendix 1. Chord charts and a sampling of notated scores are included for those interested in more formal music structure.

Alston "Becket" Cyrus

First River Records, 1978.

Today Alston "Becket" Cyrus (b. 1949) is recognized as a soca pioneer whose late-1970s recordings were pivotal in the emergence of the new sound. At the time, however, he did not receive the attention nor the credit he deserved, no doubt due to his stature as a Vincentian in a calypso world dominated by

Trinidadian singers. Becket began playing in a steelband as a youngster in his hometown of Layou, Saint Vincent. He did not start performing as a calypsonian until 1969, two years after Frankie had left for Antigua and the States. It would be years later when the two would connect in Brooklyn, although Becket recalled that as a teenager, he helped hire the Frankie McIntosh Orchestra for a fund-raising dance in Layou. Becket migrated to New York and then Washington in 1969. After attending a trade school, he served a two-year stint in the army to help obtain citizenship for himself and his mother. Following his discharge, Becket pursued his singing career more seriously. In 1975 he won the Saint Vincent calypso contest with an original tune "Mas at Victoria."

Next, Becket approached Granville Straker and Rawlston Charles, Brooklyn's top calypso record producers, but failed to get either to take him on. Undaunted, the following year he released a self-financed and -produced LP, *Raw Calypso*, which he recorded in Trinidad with arranger Art De Coteau. The album sold well in Saint Vincent and around the Caribbean, but Becket decided to go a different route for his next project. He took a new set of songs to Frankie, a fellow Vincentian with whom he had become acquainted the previous summer in Brooklyn when he needed help retranscribing several of his arrangements. As described in chapter 3, one of the songs they worked on, "Coming High," was picked up by the American label Casablanca Records, and released on the album *Disco Calypso* (1977). The musical innovations on *Disco Calypso* and its 1978 follow-up, *Coming Higher*, placed Becket and Frankie on the forefront of the soca revolution.

Following their collaborations *Disco Calypso* and *Coming Higher*, Becket and Frankie worked together on dozens of recordings, most of which were released on Becket's own Cocoa label. Becket maintained his US residence while performing around the world, but kept close ties to his homeland. In 2001 he was anointed as a Goodwill Ambassador by the government of Saint Vincent and the Grenadines, and in 2022 was awarded an honorary doctorate from the University of the West Indies.[5]

Frankie on Becket

"Coming High" (Casablanca Records, 1977)

RA: You reminisced about meeting Becket and how you got started on the *Disco Calypso* album in chapter 3, so let me get right into the music. "Coming High" was very popular in Brooklyn and back in the Caribbean when it was released in 1977—tell me how you came up with the arrangement.

FM: When Becket brought me the song, the first thing I observed was that there were just a few measures of melody built on two main ideas: one being the descending line "I coming high, high, high," the other the ascending tirade "Mary do you Wanna? Mary do you Wanna?" So, I knew I'd have to compose some music to fill things out, a challenge I welcomed. First, I wrote an introductory bass line that worked well under the cycling I-IV-V guitar chords, and then I added light horn lines under Becket's introductory rap, "Hey Mary, come here girl, I want to tell you something." Because the "Mary do you wanna" motive was really the punch line for the chorus, in fact the main hook for the whole song, I had the bass and horns double it in unison under Becket's vocal for extra umph.

RA: I notice there is some sort of key modulation around two minutes into the recording. Why did you deviate from the standard chord progression and make that addition?

FM: Yes, glad you brought that up. You see, back then I was not very tolerant of the three-chord, triadic progression that seemed to trap Becket's original song in an interminable loop. My ear grew quickly tired, so I composed a short piece with blues overtones and inserted it into the arrangement. After repeating the bluesy synthesizer line in the original key of B, the harmony modulated up a half-step to the key of C where that same synthesizer line was repeated. You can hear this clearly at the 1:57 mark of the recording. Next, the horns and bass riffed together against the synthesizer while a descending chord progression wends us back down to the original key of B. You know you are back home when the brass and reeds reestablish that familiar, tonal center of B major, setting up the second vocal verse that begins "Me head bad, bad, bad, bad, bad" at 2:30. That brief harmonic excursion added a bit of tonal variety, but it had to end up back in the original key where Becket was comfortable singing.

RA: There are several synth breaks in this one—how did that come about, was it your idea?

FM: Becket's combined vocal verse and chorus were so short, only about twenty seconds, it would have been monotonous to have the horns play the same instrumental band chorus at the end of each vocal segment. Instead, I folded in the first of several bluesy-sounding synthesizer figures right after his initial "Mary do you wanna" chorus." At that time, I was experimenting around with the synthesizer, so I ad-libbed those parts on the spot in the studio because I didn't own one myself. It ended up that those short synth solos turned out to be integral parts of the final arrangement—they gave the song a contemporary sound.

RA: Later in the piece there is a percussion break and a guitar solo. How come?

FM: Once all the fundamental instrumental themes and riffs had been introduced on the synthesizer, horns, and bass, it was percussion's turn in the sun. The percussion break afforded the listener's ear a brief reprieve from the foregoing thick textures, and of course dancers love pure rhythm. After about ten seconds of percussion playing alone under Becket's "Mary do you wanna" chant, I gradually rebuilt things. I brought back the bass, followed by the "coming high, high" vocal refrain, and finally new horn lines. Eventually I opted for a different instrumental sound by bringing in a bluesy-sounding guitar solo by Victor Collins that led to a final bridge. Victor's guitar gave the song a bit of a rock feel, and playing over the bridge and key modulation provided yet another textural surprise.

RA: "At the end of "Coming High" things speed up. Was that on purpose?

FM: Oh yes. Toward the end of the song, what we called to tag or coda, I decided to increase the tempo while Becket ad-libbed. This would not be that common today with the use of robotic drum machines, but we used live drummers back then. The texture thickened with the layering in of the guitar, synthesizer, horns, and vocal refrains while things continued to speed up (this happens around 7:50 on the recording). I call it a celebratory section, in the spirit of a "last lap" at a Caribbean dance (the last song of the night). It's as if the music was announcing "we going home," and the spirit prevails till the end of the song. The full running time, over eight minutes, was long for those days, but no one seemed to mind. Back then the Caribbean radio stations would play an eight-minute piece, or if they had to, they would just gently fade the song out after four or five minutes to introduce a commercial.

RA: We should remind readers that a complete listening outline of your arrangement for the original 1977 recording of "Coming High" is the first music example in appendix 1. Those who really want to dig into the music should take a listen to the youtube recording and follow along with the outline.

FM: Right, please listen to the recordings—all this discussion will make much more sense. Now let me add one more interesting point about my "Coming High" arrangement. The recording went smoothly, but later at live shows musicians complained it was too difficult to play with the complicated bridges and key modulations. It was fine to record in the studio where the engineer could rewind and fix errors along the way, but donning my sideman's hat as a band keyboardist I can sympathize with their concerns. The full arrangement as originally written would have taken up too much time in a rehearsal where you are trying to prepare ten artists (singing two songs each) for a show the following night. The fact that the song was pitched in the "not so horn friendly" key of B major and then modulated up to the key of C didn't help. For those reasons, I wrote a scaled-down version for Becket's live performances that was pitched in B-flat (which the horn players appreciated), with only three chords and no fancy bridge or key modulation.

RA: On the lyrics, do you think the allusions to drugs and sex were part of the song's allure?

FM: Funny you should ask that. Becket's licentious rap at the beginning of the song, where he keeps asking "Mary, do you wanna?," that was Buddy Scott's idea. He wanted to make it clear that Becket was not singing about "marijuana," but rather asking Mary if she wanted to, you know, get intimate so to speak. So, when we finished recording the song, we went back and edited in those vocal lines. I suppose Scott figured that way the song would have a better chance of being played on the radio—back then they weren't likely to play a record on air that might have been interpreted as promoting smoking weed. Amazing, an eight-minute song about seducing a woman was okay, as long as no marijuana was involved!

"Wine Down Kingstown" (First River Records, 1978)

RA: Now let's move on to two songs on Becket's next LP, *Coming Higher* (1978). One of the most popular tunes was "Wine Down Kingstown," which was also released as a single with an instrumental version on the flip side. The introduction is pretty wild, it sounds very jazzy to my ear. Tell me about that.

FM: Yes. I opened the arrangement with a choppy call-and-response line by the saxophones playing against the trombone and synthesizer, quickly giving way to the bass and the vocal chorus refrain "We gonna wine down Kingstown Lord, oh wine them down." Then, in order to add momentum, I backgrounded the horns and played a rapid ascending synthesizer line that led right into Becket's first vocal verse. This all happened in about twenty seconds at a frenetic pace, setting up a party mood to go with Becket's lyrics celebrating Carnival in Kingstown ("Wine down" referred to uninhibited Carnival dancing). The strong bass line was particularly important in holding things together and propelling the song forward so things did not fall apart.

RA: Listening back, do you hear other elements of jazz in the arrangement?

FM: Well, I used a rapid turn around at the end of the vocal chorus where Becket sings "Gonna wine, gonna wine, gonna wine, gonna wine, gonna wine Kingstown down" (0:57). Now that is something you would be more apt to hear in a jazz arrangement, not in modern calypso or soca. And there was a break by trumpeter Ray Maldonado. He was a Brooklynite, well versed in Latin and jazz music, so he was comfortable taking the solo. I had marked this on the chart beforehand, but Ray would not have known until he walked into the studio that I would be calling on him. It had to be spontaneously in the jazz tradition, there was not time to practice, he just did it on the spot.

RA: What about your synthesizer breaks, were they precomposed?

FM: No, no! The extended runs on the synthesizer just came up extemporaneously. They were rapid, even sixteenth notes, largely chromatic in approach. I'm not sure you would call them jazzy, but certainly improvised! Now I may have gotten a little carried away because I was using this new Arp synthesizer that I had rented from a friend, Darlington Brown. This was advanced technology back then, and I was fascinated with the capabilities of the Arp; it was full-bodied, and a great substitute for strings. I just started playing and these long ascending passages poured out—I'd never played a solo that long on the synth before, it lasted almost two minutes.

RA: The tag sounds fairly elaborate, and at the end includes these very dissonant chords. Can you explain further?

FM: For whatever reason, Becket chose not to do much ad-libbing on this tune, so I strung together instrumental solos interspersed around the female vocal chorus. I had plenty of room to work with, so in addition to the trumpet and synth solos, I brought in a percussion break to give the arrangement a real Carnival feel. Becket and the chorus returned and we went out with me trading more synthesizer licks with dissonant horn hits.

RA: Yes, I was a little surprised when I first heard the ending. Those final brash chords were common fare in jazz and Latin music, but generally not part of the calypso vocabulary back then.

FM: That's true. I suppose early on in my career I was more apt to experiment with different harmonies and textures. Technically they were dominant-seven-sharp-nine and thirteenth chords—very colorful, emotive, and dissonant compared to the previous horn figures. I wanted to go out with a punch!

RA: The score for the first eight measures (0:00–0:13) of "Wine Down Kingstown" is included in appendix 1 (Example 2). The different instruments appear vertically on the left margin, and the individual series of notes (the lines) each one plays moves from left to right. What should our readers take from that?

FM: Even if they do not read music, readers can visualize how the instruments interact. For example, the alto and tenor saxophones are playing by themselves and in unison on measures 2 and 4, creating a stark, thin sound, leaving the listener expecting that something bigger would follow. Then all instruments and backup vocals jump in for measures 5 through 8, producing a much thicker texture, as the different parts interweave and compete for the listener's attention. Another good example is my use of call-and-response voicings to create continuously flowing lines, such as the interaction of the two saxophones (call) against the trombone and synthesizer (response) in measures 1 through 4. Keep in mind that the entire score would be much longer (at least two hundred measures), but this snapshot demonstrates how I would organize a written chart. A timed listening outline for the recording is included with the score sample, so please take a look and have a listen to the Youtube recording.

"Tony" (First River Records, 1978)

RA: My other favorite piece on the *Coming Higher* LP is "Tony." What's that about?

FM: This one involved a double entendre that folks in the Caribbean would recognize. The lyrics were supposedly about how this woman loves Tony, perhaps poking fun at my brother Tony who was playing bass on the recording. But Tony could be heard as "Toti" (or "Toh-ty" or "Toe-Tee"), which in the Caribbean is slang for male genitalia. So, the song recounts how this woman loved so many different kinds of Tony or "Toti." This sort of risqué humor is typical of calypso lyrics.

RA: Thank you for that explanation! I doubt many listeners from outside the Caribbean would have caught the "Tony" reference. Now tell me about the music arrangement, how you came up with the various melodic lines for your instrumental band chorus? Were these your ideas or Becket's?

FM: Becket had some really interesting melodic motives in his vocal lines, so I decided to incorporate them into my instrumental sections. For instance, the opening seven-note piano figure was taken from the backing vocal line, "She gets all kinds of Tony." Then I doubled that phrase with piano and bass while the female vocalists entered singing "Tony, I want Tony." But I still felt that the introduction lacked something because it hadn't reached a climax before Becket came in. I decided to add in a brief section built around a crescendo on a fancy suspended chord that functioned to build up the tension that would be resolved with Becket entering with his first vocal verse, "Yea, male chauvinism is not for me / I got the deaconess, to christen my Tony." You can hear that suspended chord leading into his verse at 0:25 in the recording.

RA: So that suspended chord was your idea?

FM: Absolutely! And I came back to that opening phrase and suspended chord crescendo at the end of each instrumental band chorus to segue into each new vocal verse. Using those fancy chords to create suspense and expectations was definitely something that came out of my jazz background.

RA: The final tag has several solos, including a flute?

FM: Yes, to the solos, but it wasn't quite a flute. After Becket sang three verses and choruses, I added an extended tag with three instrumental solos, interspersed with Becket's ad-libbing about all the different kinds of "Tony" that his female protagonist wanted. The first was by trumpeter Ray Maldonado and the second by alto saxophonist Sam Furnace. The third was not actually a flute—it was me, using a flute patch on the synthesizer. We all were well versed in the bebop idiom—the music of Parker, Gillespie, Powell, and so on—which I am sure influenced our playing. Now I don't recall trying to limit the solos to something like sixteen or thirty-two bars—we each just took our turn and let loose. That accounts for the overall length of the song at just under seven minutes. It was unusually long for a calypso back then, but Becket had no problem with it. I sensed that he liked the fact that we were doing something different.

RA: These early Becket arrangements sound, to my ear, very jazz-influenced—some of your most innovative work, do you think so?

FM: Listening back, I am struck by just how adventuresome and at times unconventional those early Becket arrangements were. At that time, back in the 1970s, I was immersed in jazz with my steady gigging. Also, I was still early in my arranging career and feeling freer in my thinking. Perhaps I was being naive, but I really wasn't constrained by concerns for the market. That is, I didn't feel that I had to arrange songs using only standard triadic harmonies and simple variations of the I-IV-V chord progressions and loops—that was what was becoming the norm for the new soca sound that emphasized rhythmic groove over harmonic development. I was willing to use jazzy and bluesy voicings when and where I pleased, and dissonant harmonies here and there to spice things up. I didn't hesitate to bring in horn and guitar solos, and I was experimenting around with the new synthesizer possibilities. Maybe it was because Becket was his own producer, and while he wanted to score hits, he was truly committed to bringing new sounds and approaches into calypso. And there was no Granville Starker or Rawlston Charles worrying that if my arrangement strayed too far from the mainstream the audience might reject it and the record would not sell. Now I have to admit, as the years passed I would, at times, capitulate to those sorts of market concerns. I came to realize that there had to be a balance between my own creative desires and the wants of the Caribbean audiences for whom we were creating the music. But back then things felt much looser, and I believe you can hear it in the music.

Trevor Winston Soso Lockhart

Straker's Records, 1981.

Next to Alton "Becket" Cyrus, Winston Soso was Saint Vincent's most heralded calypsonian during the 1980s and 1990s. Trevor Winston Soso Lockhart (1952–2021) grew up around the Sion Hill neighborhood of Kingstown listening to Vincy calypsonians Becket, Scorcher, Sheller, and Toiler. As a youngster he excelled at football, eventually assuming the position of goal-keeper for the Saint Vincent national team. But his first love was singing, and by the time he was a teenager he was performing soul and R&B songs at Kingstown's downtown Lyric and Russell theaters. Soso eventually began fronting a local combo, Volume 5, which, following a series of personnel shuffles, was renamed Clymax. He was in and out of the group for several years, but in 1978 Soso traveled with Clymax to Barbados where they made their first recordings, "Carnival Boogie" and "Vincy Spree."

Based on the strength of those records and the popularity of Clymax at local Vincy fetes, promoter Bernard James brought Soso and the band to New York for a series of gigs at Brooklyn's 1979 Labor Day Carnival. Following the success of their first New York recording, "Soca Diane," Soso left Clymax to embark on a solo career with the help of fellow Vincentians Granville Straker and Frankie.

Over the next decade they would collaborate on the production of ten LPs and a series of singles that earned Soso legions of fans around the Caribbean, North America, and Europe. Along the way he turned out sensual soca romps such as "How Some Men Love Their Women" and "Ah Feel to Party Tonight," while maintaining the venerable calypso tradition of social commentary with offerings such as "Too Much Corruption" and "Out on the Edge." "I Don't Mind," his 1985 R&B-tinged hit, was perhaps his most enduring song. Soso was a remarkably versatile singer who could croon soul ballads, get funky with R&B, wax poetic with provocative calypsos, heat up with soca, and cool down with reggae.

Soso maintained a full-time residence in Brooklyn following his arrival in 1979, using New York as a base for touring and recording for the rest of his career. He kept close contact with his native homeland, often returning to perform at Vinci Carnival. In 2014 he was named a goodwill cultural ambassador by the government of Saint Vincent and the Grenadines.[6]

Frankie on Soso

RA: Working with Soso was one of your earliest projects with Granville Straker. Did you know Soso back in Saint Vincent?

FM: No, I never met him back in Saint Vincent, I believe he started singing just after I left for Antigua. It was Granville Straker who introduced us here in Brooklyn in 1979, after I agreed to oversee the recording of his song "Soca Diane" with the band Clymax (see chapter 3). Soon after that, Soso left Clymax and decided to go it on his own as a solo singer. When Straker sent him to my house with his songs a year later I was excited! Here was a fellow Vincentian with a gorgeous voice and fresh songs in need of arrangement. He was later dubbed "The Rolls Royce of Calypso" and listening to him you can hear why. He could sing songs in different genres. In addition to calypso, he was especially good at soulful R&B ballads, giving his voice appeal beyond the Caribbean audience.

"Too Much Corruption" (Straker's Records, 1981)

RA: Tell me about *Too Much Corruption*, the first LP you worked on with Soso. What was your routine with him?

FM: I remember he sang half a dozen songs to me while I sat at the piano. I asked him to give me everything he had—the lyrics, vocal melodies, and any ideas he might have for bass and horn lines. I would plunk around a bit to confirm the best key for his voice, make some preliminary notes, and sketch out a few possibilities. After he left, I would get serious, working out all possibilities for the chord structure, coming up with ideas for an introduction, for bass and horn lines, for bridges and transitions, and so forth.

RA: The title song, "Too Much Corruption" was one of the most popular tracks. What do you think made it so attractive to soca fans?

FM: Yes, "Too Much Corruption" was well received, catching the mood of the early 1980s, with so much government and business corruption, both in the Caribbean and here in America.

RA: It sounds to me as though the song is based on a standard I-IV-V harmonic loop that you hear on many soca songs. What did you do to spice it up?

FM: I wanted an assertive introduction to establish a heavy dance vibe, so my initial band chorus kicked off with bright, punctuated phrases played on the trumpets, which were immediately answered by the low brass. Those punchy brass riffs interlocked with the bass and strumming guitar to create a strong groove and to set up Soso's first vocal verse that began "Too much corruption, too much brutality." That call-and-response horn figure was very distinct and served as part of the song's hook—it was repeated in the subsequent band choruses that were sandwiched between his vocal verses and choruses. By the way, I wrote the bass and horn lines for the band chorus myself. Soso didn't have any input on this one, although he would on others.

RA: "Corruption" has a long tag, any reason?

FM: Well, Soso was very good at extemporizing, so after three vocal verse/chorus and band chorus sections the tag opened with him ad-libbing over a set of new horn riffs (4:00). That went on for almost two minutes. Then we continued alternating synth and horn lines—Straker liked to extend the recordings, and this one clocked in at just over seven minutes. Those new horn lines were melodically related but often a bit different from the lines I used in the introduction and band choruses. But they were important, because I aimed for variety in my tags, especially on the extended ones. Despite the long tag, "Corruption" ended on a sharply punctuated riff. For whatever reason Straker and his engineer decided not to fade out on this one—good decision to my ear!

"I Don't Mind" (Straker's Records, 1985)

RA: "I Don't Mind," Soso's biggest hit, was very popular all over the Caribbean and here in New York. Can you talk about your approach on that one?

FM: Soso was one of the singers who had some good ideas for bass and horn lines. I remember his singing something when he was warming up, and I thought that would be a good line for the introduction. It ended up being the opening line on the synthesizer. Then I brought the horns in playing a line that was basically taken from his vocal chorus—they served to brighten the timbral pallet. Those bright horn lines also produced a sense of acceleration as Soso commanded the band to "Push it" around the 0:20 mark of the introduction. That sort of thing excited the listeners and dancers! The initial ascending bass line worked well with the horn figures, holding things together and anchoring a very tight, well-balanced band chorus. I should add that Soso sang the original bass and horn lines to me. As it turned out, a number of Soso's ideas were incorporated into my final instrumental arrangement, and I want to give him credit.

RA: It sounds to me like you employed the horns in several different ways on this song.

FM: Right. This arrangement is a good example of how I used the horns to fill in and reinforce sections of the vocal verse and the vocal chorus. On the second half of each vocal verse, I brought in short ascending horn lines to complete the ideas introduced by the voice. That is, where he would leave off singing, I would continue the idea with the horns—a sort of call-and-response structure between the voice and the horns. You can hear one of these horn lines clearly after Soso sings "Just as we reach / she took off her costume and put on she robe," and again after his line "Have something to eat / have some of dis food, all the meat is yours." But on the vocal chorus I doubled the horns with the voice to reinforce the "I Don't Mind" hook. Yes, there are a number of ways that good horn lines could support the vocalist.

RA: I hear several instruments are working together to establish the groove; can you explain?

FM: Throughout the song I overdubbed one of my favorite synth patches that produced a staccato pick guitar sound. That pick guitar synth line interlocked tightly with the live guitar played by Scipio Sargent who was repeating this sliding, African high-life style lick (his guitar is prominent underneath the vocal choruses, and throughout the entire coda). The synthesizer, guitar, and bass lines meshed together to form the heavy groove underneath the vocals and horns. That groove, I believe, was part of the song's appeal.

RA: And the coda, another long one!

FM: Yes! Soso was very prolific with his vocal ad-libbing, he went on for nearly three minutes. That obviated the need for any instrumental solos. I did, however, add in a few new horn riffs and broke up his ad-libbing by bringing back the "I don't mind" vocal chorus several times. And I played around with some spacey synthesizer riffs. The purpose was to add variety as we stretched the song out, and to give listeners and dancers a few more chances to sing along with the catchy chorus hook.

Cyril "Scorcher" Thomas

Straker's Records, 1981.

Like Becket and Soso, Cyril "Scorcher" Thomas (b. 1947) established himself as a calypso singer only after migrating from Saint Vincent to Brooklyn. Raised in Sion Hill, Kingstown, he began singing calypsos in high school, much to the chagrin of his mother, who disparaged the music as "street" culture unbecoming of her son. He competed in the 1964 and 1968 Saint Vincent Calypso Monarch contests with little success, and in 1969 he decided to emigrate to the United States. Landing in Brooklyn with a student visa to study electronics, Scorcher quickly determined his best path forward to obtain citizenship was to join the military. Following two years of service, including ten months in Vietnam, he went to school on the GI Bill, earning a bachelor's degree in Political Science in 1975 and a masters in Urban Administration in 1981, both from Brooklyn College. That training led him to a position at the Jackie Robinson Intermediate School in Brooklyn, where he taught for eighteen years, before taking the post of Deputy Counsel General of Saint Vincent and the Grenadines to New York, where he served from 2001 until he retired in 2011.

Scorcher began singing seriously while still a student at Brooklyn College. In 1973 fellow Vincentian expatriate and cultural activist Mary Neverson Morris arranged for him to appear on a program on Saint Vincent music that she had organized at the Brooklyn Academy of Music. That show brought Scorcher to the attention of Brooklyn calypso fans, and eventually Alston Becket Cyrus steered him to Straker and Frankie. In 1978 Scorcher recorded "Deep Seated Conviction," which was followed by successful singles "East 95th Street" (1979) and his most popular, "Party Fever" (1981). "Fever" announced his enthusiastic return to Saint Vincent for a boisterous Carnival celebration, while "East 95th Street" chronicled the popular Saint Vincent basement social club located in Brooklyn's East Flatbush neighborhood. After recording his first full album, *The Hoper*, for Straker in 1982, Scorcher decided to go it on his own and self-produce his records. He left Straker, but not Frankie. Over the next decade Frankie arranged another half dozen albums and several singles for him on his own Scorcher Records label.

"Party Fever" was especially popular in Trinidad, and the strength of the record led to tours of the eastern United States as well as Saint Vincent, Trinidad, England, and Canada in the early 1980s. Unfortunately, profits from the tours and his early recordings were slim, leading Scorcher to pivot back to his college training and seek a fulltime teaching position. His work as teacher and later as a government diplomat provided him with a steady income from the mid-1980s on, allowing him to pursue his singing career as a more leisurely sideline activity.

Although Scorcher never rose to the star level of his fellow countrymen Becket and Soso, his recordings enjoyed moderate success in New York and the Caribbean. Saint Vincent welcomed back their native son, regularly inviting him to perform during their summer Carnival celebration, and in 2014 awarding him the honorary title of Cultural Ambassador of Saint Vincent and the Grenadines. In his seventies at the time of this writing, Scorcher is still held in high esteem by Vincentians at home and in Brooklyn for his innovative songs as well as his service as an educator and government administrator.[7]

Frankie on Scorcher

RA: Yet another Vincentian—did you know Scorcher back home?

FM: Not really—you see, we attended different secondary schools. I recall us passing each other on the street in Kingstown, but never engaging in any meaningful conversation. I believe it was Becket who introduced us up here in Brooklyn shortly after we had worked together on the *Coming Higher* LP. I was eager to help out a fellow Vincentian, so we decided to work on one of his songs called "Deep Seated Conviction" that told the story of an expatriate returning to Vincy Carnival. Scorcher paid my arranging fee and for the studio time, and after we had made the recording, he convinced Straker to put the record out. That was 1978.

RA: Was "Conviction" the first vocal arrangement recording you did with Straker?

FM: In retrospect yes, although I didn't know it at the time because Straker was not involved in the original production.

RA: Interesting. So how did that recording session go? Honestly the mix sounds a little muddy to me.

FM: Listening back I would have to agree. In fact, there was nothing remarkable about the arrangement. Scorcher didn't have a big budget so we only used two horns—that was limiting for me. Nor was it one of his better-mixed productions—fortunately that would improve in the future. It was my decision to end the song with a minute-and-a-half solo on acoustic piano which was unusual for a calypso or soca recording at that time. Eagle Sound Studio did not have a synthesizer at that point, which explains my use of the acoustic piano. I don't think I set out to do a jazzy sounding solo, but many listeners have described it as such.

RA: Well, I certainly agree; your piano solo sounds quite jazz-influenced to my ear. Now I assume Straker must have been satisfied because he brought Scorcher back for another recording session with new songs.

FM: Straker must have heard something he liked on the first record, and once he recorded an artist he usually wanted more. Remember, Straker was into volume when it came to the number of releases.

"East 95th Street" (Straker's Records, 1979)

RA: Let's turn to the recording "East 95th Street" that you and Scorcher made for Straker. I don't suppose he was referring to the Upper East Side of Manhattan, was he?

FM: Oh no, Scorcher was singing about a popular social club located on East 95th Street in East Flatbush, Brooklyn. It was run by this guy named Fire, and was a weekend hangout for Caribbean people, mostly for Brooklyn Vincentians. I guess Scorcher had been up here long enough to write a calypso about Vincentian life in Brooklyn. That was not uncommon back then.

RA: This sounds like a rowdy piece with a strong dance groove. Were you thinking about the scene at the social club when you put the arrangement together?

FM: Right. Scorcher's first verse described the site of the action: "Fire's party, was really grooving / East 95th Street, was sweet and salty." Obviously, this was meant to be a party and dance song, so I built the introduction around snappy call-and-response riffs between the low reeds and high brass. Once his verse began, I answered those initial vocal lines with a descending high brass riff to complete his short vocal lines. I didn't want to leave too much empty space, but rather create a continuous flow of sound to keep the groove going.

RA: On this one you used trumpet rather than piano or synthesizer for the tag solos. How come?

FM: I suspected that Scorcher would not ad-lib on the tag as long as Soso did, and that Straker would want to stretch the recording out for at least five minutes, so I needed something for the tag. Rather than write new parts, I decided to fill the space with an instrumental solo or two. I felt that a fiery trumpet solo might work in that context, and Ron Taylor, an extremely talented jazz player, was there at the horn recording session and eager to go. Ron played with a bright, brilliant style, and used lots of chromatic runs and rapid figures. He was out of the bebop school, very influenced by Dizzy Gillespie and players of that era and ilk. The solos were supported by the same chords I used for opening section of the band chorus and his vocal chorus, and partway through I brought in low horn riffs under the solo to change the texture and build up the energy. That was a common technique in American big band jazz arrangements. I was never sure how the public reacted to these sorts of voicings, but to my ear they really enhanced the overall merit of the arrangement.

"Party Fever" (Straker's Records, 1981)

RA: Scorcher's biggest hit was a song called "Party Fever." Is this one about Brooklyn or Saint Vincent Carnival?

FM: Definitely back home in Saint Vincent. He starts singing about walking through the streets of Kingstown during Carnival time drinking Ju-C, a soda that was very popular in Saint Vincent, before describing the wild party that is about to unfold. With that in mind I knew my arrangement had to have a lively Carnival vibe.

RA: Yes, "Party Fever" definitely had strong dance groove. How did you use the horns, synth, and bass toward that end?

FM: My opening band chorus was a simple synthesizer line, a slight variation of his vocal chorus melody, punctuated with responding horn riffs. By that time alternating synthesizer and horn lines had become an effective combination for many of my instrumental sections. As on "East 95th Street," Scorcher's verse lines tended to be short, so I used horn lines to fill in to give a sense of continuous melodic flow. I brought the horns and bass together in unison after he sang "Every year I come down to this party," and again after "I walking in town drinking "Ju-C." That brief horn/bass unison riff became one of the song's primary instrumental hooks.

RA: What's going on harmonically in the second half of the verse that leads into the chorus? It sounds like you are changing up the chord progression?

FM: Yes, I added a little twist to harmonize Scorcher's vocal melody and to connect the end of the verse with the chorus. I brought in a B minor chord to change the mood, then followed with a sequence of climbing chords (Bm-C-A/-D) as Scorcher sang "While they jumping, and they prancing / And the people, going wild." That built up the tension that was finally released when we reach the chorus, which is back to the original V-I (A-D) chord progression as he proclaimed "This year I go tear downtown / this year I go jump around." I did that to break things up, so the song moved from simple to more elaborate, back to a simpler harmonic feel. I tried to do that whenever I could, but I had to be careful to not be too obtrusive, because you wanted an arrangement that would get people to dance and sing along. It was a constant balancing act to maintain the requisite groove and simple chord sequence to please the audience while adding just enough of harmonic and textural variation to keep the arrangement fresh. The rest of the song followed the regular structure of band chorus, vocal verse, bridge, vocal chorus, and so forth. The tag featured Scorcher's vocal ad-libs over repeated cries of "Party" and "Fever" from the female chorus.

"I'm a Hoper" (Straker's Records, 1982)

RA: You mentioned that "I'm a Hoper" was one of your favorite Scorcher songs. Why so?

FM: "I'm a Hoper" was the title track to the first full album I did with Scorcher for Straker. I remember thinking the song was a bit unusual because it transcended the common I-IV-V calypso vocabulary. In fact, when Scorcher first sang me the song it didn't make much musical sense, because the melody just seemed to wander, to drift. There didn't seem to be any logic to the way the phases were connected. I thought he was just singing out of tune—he presented the song a cappella to me, with no guitar chord accompaniment. On top of that, his musical phrasing seemed uneven, each line he sang didn't necessarily fall neatly in a four-beat measure. Initially that threw me off because it made it difficult to figure out where to drop in the down beat. As a result, I put that song aside and worked on other material for him.

RA: So, what happened to change your mind?

FM: Eventually, when I listened to the melody more attentively, with a more analytical mind-set, I realized it was a masterpiece—not only my favorite Scorcher song, but one of my all-time favorite calypsos! The melody seemed to be moving through different key centers, and I could see a way of getting from one tonal area to another. I harmonized the song by beginning in the key of E for the first seven measures of his irregular vocal verse: "You hear in my calypso / on the radio / and everywhere they go. / In every party / in the ghetto / even in the disco." Then I transitioned to the key of B (at 0:41) as he sang "And now things I write make Grand Prix / they trying to label me / filthy rich / man with money living in luxury." While he sang that second line, I moved through a chord progression that landed back on the original key of E for the vocal chorus "But I'm a hoper, trying to get over" (at 0:56).

RA: How about the instrumental sections, did they involve any key modulations?

FM: No, the introductory and subsequent band choruses remained centered in the key of E. They were constructed around an A-B-A sequence, with the A section featuring a jangly-sounding synthesizer line answering the initial horn hits, and the B section emphasizing extended horn lines taken from his vocal chorus "I'm a hoper." Then a return to the A culminating with a bright horn/synth unison hit before his first vocal comes in. The introduction was meant to create an upbeat, optimistic mood for Scorcher to declare himself a "hoper."

RA: Do you still think you made the right choice going with "Hoper"?

FM: Oh yes. Looking back, I realize that what I had initially dismissed ended up being one of the most musically significant melodies I had worked with! Even up to today "The Hoper" really stands out to my ear. Scorcher didn't know much about music, he just trusted me. He just said, "Frankie, I'll leave it up to you, try and make this sound like music."

RA: Needless to say, "I'm a Hoper" was not one of Scorcher's bigger songs. Why not?

FM: Back in that period the more sophisticated musical productions, especially in terms of harmonic complexity, often got overlooked in favor of more dance-oriented pieces. I'm not sure the soca audience appreciated Scorcher's unconventional melody and my key changes, but the arrangement pleased me. And he had other songs like "East 95th Street" and "Party Fever" that were quite popular, so he could get away with a slightly more unorthodox number like "I'm a Hoper" once in a while.

MacLean Leroy "Short Shirt" Emanuel

B's Records, 1986.

MacLean Leroy "Short Shirt" Emanuel is arguably Antigua's most popular calypsonian of the modern era, winning the National Calypso King crown fifteen times and taking seven Road March titles between 1964 and 1992. Born in 1942, the last of nine children, he grew up in St. John's working-class Point neighborhood where he earned respect as an amateur boxer. He began singing in school, joined the Point Iron Steelband (predecessor of the acclaimed Hells Gate Steel Orchestra), and occasionally fronted Oscar Mason's Vibratones Orchestra. In 1960 he traveled to the US Virgin Islands, where he worked as a laborer while honing his skills as a calypso singer in local hotels and nightclubs.

In 1962 Short Shirt returned to Antigua and began competing in the national Calypso King contest, which he eventually won in 1964 with the tune aptly titled "No Place Like Home." He became a national favorite, taking four of the next six Antiguan Calypso King competitions and another half dozen in the 1970s with the help of his poet cousin Shelly Tobitt, who often penned his lyrics. In addition to his singing career, Emanuel proved to be a successful local entrepreneur, running his own club in Halcyon Cove where Frankie first met him while playing with the Laviscount Brass.

Short Shirt's initial LP, *Calypso Caribbean*, was recorded in 1970 in a local Antiguan ABS radio station. In hopes of broadening his audience, he traveled to Trinidad for his next two recordings, *Meet Raycan* (1971) and *Caribbean Charms* (1972). There he worked with arrangers Ed Watson and Earl Rodney, producing *Charms* on his own A&B record label. By the mid-1970s he was collaborating with Trinidad arranger Art De Coteau. His first two albums with De Coteau, *Jammin' Tight* (1975) and *Ghetto Vibes* (1976), were recorded in Trinidad but released and distributed on Brooklyn's Straker and Charlie's record labels, an arrangement that provided a more international audience for his music. Short Shirt's career received an additional boost when De Coteau helped him acquire a spot in the 1976–77 Trinidad calypso tent circuit. His energetic dance tune, "Tourist Leggo," proved to be extremely popular, leaving a number of critics questioning why the song did not win the Trinidad Road March title (Calypso Rose's "Tempo" was awarded the title that year). Calypso historian Gordon Rohlehr notes that in the wake of Short Shirt's success with "Tourist Leggo," the Trinidad Carnival Development Committee voted to ban all nonnational singers from competing in the Calypso Monarch or Road March competitions.[8]

Short Shirt reconnected with Frankie in 1981 when he began to travel to New York to take advantage of the city's advanced recording and mixing facilities. The two ended up working together on half a dozen albums that included Antiguan Road March–winning tunes "Push" (1982) and "J'Ouvert Rhythm" (1987), as well as Calypso King winners "World in Distress" (1986), "Han Kari" and "J'ouvert Rhythm" (1987), and "Fire After" (1988).

Unlike the Saint Vincent calypsonians covered in the first half of this chapter, Short Shirt never relocated to Brooklyn, preferring to occasionally journey north to record and participate in Brooklyn's Labor Day Carnival celebration. Antigua's robust tourist scene apparently provided him with adequate work opportunities, enabling him to maintain his permanent Caribbean residency. His contributions to the calypso world were recognized by the Antiguan government in 2003, when he was proclaimed "Sir MacLean Emanuel of The Point" and awarded the Knight Grand Cross of the Most Distinguished Order of the Nation.[9]

Frankie on Short Shirt

RA: I recall you ran into Short Shirt when you spent a year in Antigua, right?

FM: Yes. Shortly after arriving in 1967, I became aware of the island's thriving calypso scene, with passionate supporters rooting for their favorites. Short

Shirt and Obstinate, both of whom were Antiguan calypso crown winners, were among the most popular. Eventually Swallow would join their ranks to form the great triumvirate of Antiguan calypsonians.

I first met Short Shirt when I was playing keyboards with Laviscount. He was quite popular then, having already won the Antiguan Calypso Crown several times, and occasionally we would back him up on a calypso show. He also had this outdoor bar, a bamboo tent setup he called the Calabash, that I described in chapter 1. Laviscount often played there for the locals. Once in a while he would join us for an impromptu rendition of his latest calypso—we all knew his songs from hearing them on the radio so we just played by ear. After I left for Brooklyn my brother Tony played keyboards in a band that backed up Short Shirt.

RA: I've heard that Short Shirt had a bit of a reputation as a sort of tough guy, maybe a bit of a "Bad John" character in his earlier days?

FM: Ha! Well people said you never messed with Short Shirt—he was a boxer, and you knew the judges must have felt a bit of trepidation when they didn't award him first place in the Calypso Crown competition. But we always got along well together and I was excited to reconnect with him in Brooklyn years later. By then he was well known not only in Antigua but also in Trinidad. His song "Raycan," with arranger Ed Watson, was about this legendary Antiguan derelict named Raycan—that was big for him. And then there was "Tourist Leggo" with arranger Art De Coteau, that did very well in Trinidad.

RA: Now how did you get together with him up here in Brooklyn. Had he moved here like Soso and Scorcher?

FM: I don't believe Short Shirt ever lived in Brooklyn, but he had a sister in the Bronx with whom he would stay with when he came up. One year, around 1980 I think, he came to New York with a group of Antigua singers—Obstinate, Shelly Tobitt (who wrote a number of Short Shirt's songs), and a few others. He gave me a call and told me he wanted me to do the music for the whole group. I believe the project involved six singers, and was the first of a series of annual albums that were released for Antigua's August Carnival. They all came over to the house and I notated all their songs. They wanted to make one record with each singer allotted two songs, so we recorded the singers one at a time. Short Shirt was pleased with my work, and he came back to me over the next few years to arrange and to coordinate his recording sessions. In fact, I eventually worked with Obstinate and then Swallow, so I had all the three big calypsonians from Antigua.

RA: Tell me about that first LP you did with him, *Leroy* (1982).

FM: That was a reference to Short Shirt's middle name—MacLean Leroy Emanuel. We recorded the tracks at Sound Heights Studio here in Brooklyn, and I remember he had his producer/writer, Stanley Humphreys, with him. I should note that Short Shirt was quite innovative in the studio. On the final vocal he would often record his voice twice, that is he would overdub his vocal line over this initial take. He was always right on point, matching the two voices with precision, so when you played it back it got the desired effect—this one powerful voice really cutting through the mix. He could do this with amazing perfection due to his superb vocal control. He also tended to revamp the song lyrics on the spot—often with the help of his writers, Stanley Humphreys or Shelly Tobitt.

"Push" (A&B Records, 1982)

RA: I've heard that the songs "Alive and Kicking" and "Antigua" were popular back in Antigua. But I believe the song from the *Leroy* LP that got the most international attention was "Push." Herbie Mann, the well-known American jazz flutist, made a cover of it for Atlantic Records in 1983, right?

FM: Oh yes, he certainly did! In fact, the irregular meter and horn lines that Mann used were close copies to what we did on our original recording. Short Shirt, of course, received composition credit (and I assume royalties), while I received neither credit nor monetary compensation for my arrangement. But that's another story.

RA: Right. Now I do hear some sort of irregular phrasing when Short Shirt sings his verses. Can you explain?

FM: Yes, here is how that came about. I recall Short Shirt coming over to the house and working that song out in my basement. What struck me as a bit odd was that the first measure of each vocal verse was a six-beat figure, not the typical four or eight-beat pattern of most calypsos. The rest of the verse and the chorus, by comparison, consisted of a series of conventional four beat measures. I remember trying to get him to cut out a word or two so we could even it out. He would follow my initial suggestions, but then when we played the song again, he would revert to his original way of singing with a six-beat figure, what he was hearing. I realized that was coming natural to him, so I wasn't going to force him to do otherwise. Finally, I ended up writing out the arrangement to correspond to what he was singing: 6/4–4/4–4/4–4/4–4/4–4/4–4/4 for thirty beats and a final 4/4 on the horns for a total of thirty-four beats where a quarter note equals one beat (try counting along from 0:30 through 0:45 on the recording—his singing feels uneven but it adds up to thirty-four beats). Once it was written, the guys in the band had no problem, they could handle metric changes.

RA: Your arrangement of "Push" begins with an aggressive figure, a call and response between brass and reeds. Where did that come from?

FM: I liked Short Shirt's punchy "Push" vocal chorus, so that became the center of my instrumental band chorus. I began with a sharply accented hit on the high brass, followed by quick response on the saxophones—I was trying to create a sense of forward propulsion, a kind of "sonic push" if you will. I also doubled the horn lines and bass in response to each of his vocal verse phrases to fill in the space and to complete the melodic lines: "It was past midnight" (horn response) / "nobody around" (horn response) / "As I turned out the lights" (horn response) / "and I hear a sound."

RA: I take it your introduction and band choruses with the brash horns were meant to create a certain mood?

FM: Of course. I was hoping to capture the sensual but comical tone of the lyrics. In the song Short Shirt recounted hearing what he initially took to be a tawdry sexual encounter outside his window, but upon further investigation (verse 3) learned that a young woman's impassioned pleas to "push" were actually her innocent cries for assistance in moving a stalled car. The nuances of his double-entendre might have been easily lost during the female chorus's steamy refrain, "push it, push it for me" that continued throughout the tag.

I was surprised at first that "Push" was one of Short Shirt's biggest songs, because I heard some complain that it was confusing to dance to given the unusual rhythm. But it proved to be so popular in Antigua (it won the Road March that year) and elsewhere that audiences would immediately start to sing along with Short Shirt's six-beat phrasing, and the Caribbean musicians had no problem accompanying him live.

Champion (B's Records, 1986)

RA: One of Short Shirt's most popular songs was "The Champion" from the *Power Pack* LP you two made in 1986.

FM: Yes, "Champion" was Short Shirt's ode to his own prowess as a soca star. He was indeed a great singer, but modesty was never on the top of his list of personal attributes, at least not back then. This one was produced for B's Records and came with a budget, so I was able to hire a full band with two trumpets, two saxophones, and two trombones.

RA: Your band chorus has a catchy hook—how did you come up with that?

FM: After an eight-measure bluesy introduction on the synthesizer and guitar, the band chorus itself opened with the high brass playing a driving line derived from his "You are the Champion" vocal chorus. That was answered first by the saxophones, then by the synthesizer, and a final trumpet flurry just prior to his entry with the first verse. I was aiming for a variety of different voices and timbres. But you are right, the initial high brass riffs drove the introduction and gave listeners a taste of what was to come in the vocal chorus. Now if a song received ample radio air time, and the band chorus was catchy enough—and I agree this one was—the crowd would hopefully start singing along with the initial instrumental melody, even before his first verse. That was the sort of energy we hoped to create, especially for a song that might go before judges in a contest, and certainly before dancers!

RA: Sounds like you changed those horn lines a bit on the band chorus that followed the first vocal verse and chorus. Why did you do that?

FM: I wanted to keep things interesting without departing too far from that initial familiar melody, so on the second band chorus I used a slight variation on the trumpets for the first four measures—they played an ascending melodic line that offered contrast in terms of motion to the descending trumpet figure in the introduction (between 1:18 and 1:24). But they were melodically related, so there was nothing jarring to the listener's ear. I switched back and forth between these two band chorus variations to keep things from getting too repetitive. I also used sharp horn hits during his vocal verses to add punch. You can really hear them on the second verse (between 1:46 and 2:00), where Short Shirt sang "You gave such good performances / at home and abroad / people begging for repeats" and "You know how to shake an audience / take your trumpet call / you have them jumping out of their seats." Those accents were particularly effective with the big horn section I had at my disposal. Taken all together, those horn accents and variations were my way of trying to liven things up within the confines of the I-IV-V chordal vocabulary.

"World in Distress" (B's Records, 1986)

RA: Another song from the *Power Pack* LP that really grabs my ear is "World in Distress." That one was more of a message song than a wine and party tune, right? As an arranger, how did you approach that sort of piece, knowing that the message might be more important than a heavy dance groove?

FM: My approach was certainly different from what I was aiming for with "Push" or "Champion." You are correct that "Distress" was a message song, one that addressed numerous global conflicts, from Nicaragua to Afghanistan to

South Africa. The lyrics were important and the text was very wordy, so the arrangement demanded a moderately paced, lilting calypso beat that would allow for more precise vocal articulation. With the full band, thanks to the generous budget, I could write with a broader harmonic pallet. The overall sound was in a more traditional calypso vein, a bit reminiscent of an older Bertram Innis arrangement.

RA: Your band chorus sounds sectional, that is, it includes several distinct parts. Why did you take that approach?

FM: Yes, my band chorus was lengthy, and in three parts, combining lines I composed from scratch with those derived from Short Shirt's vocal melody. The A section opened with four measures of high brass and bass voiced together, followed by four measures of alternating saxophone, trumpet, and finally trombone lines. These were all my own creations. The B section featured eight measures of call and response between the brass and reeds, loosely based on his "The world in distress" vocal chorus. Again, the aim was to tantalize listeners with snippets of things to come. The final C section, a four-measure bridge on the saxophones, was a variation of the final measures of his vocal verse where he sang "Even in the Caribbean / we had peace and tranquility / Grenada opened our eyes to reality."

RA: Your introduction ends on a very dramatic chord—what is happening there?

FM: During the last two measures of the C section, the horns converge for a II-V-I turnaround, landing on a C♯Maj9 chord (at 0:40) that led into the first vocal verse, "Look around and tell me what you see." That last fancy chord really added color and sweetening to the otherwise major triadic feel of the accompaniment.

RA: Your accompaniment is relatively light on his verses, but the horns are more prominent on the chorus. Why so?

FM: Like I said, on this sort of song it's the lyrics, especially the words during the verse, that are crucial, so you don't want too much extra instrumentation to get in the way of the voice. But on the vocal choruses I decided to thicken the texture by bringing in a unison blend of brass, reeds, and bass in response to each of his "The world in distress" vocal lines. The goal was to add urgency to his message, you might say to stress the degree of distress he was singing about.

RA: Listening back to your arrangement from forty years ago, are you pleased?

FM: I have a hard time judging my own work, but I will say that "Distress" was one of Short Shirt's finest songs, and it's not a big surprise that it won the

1986 Antigua Calypso Crown. In those calypso competitions it was usually the craft and delivery of the lyrics by the singer, rather than the dance beat or horn hooks of the arranger, that held the day. At least that was the way it was back then. So yes, I am pleased that I came up with musical support for Short Shirt's vocal performance and helped him win that year.

Rupert "Swallow" Philo

Charlie's Records, 1988.

Most older Antiguans would agree that Short Shirt, with his unmatched record of Calypso King and Road March titles, is the island's most renowned calypsonian. But the Antiguan who gained the most international acclaim during the 1970s and 1980s was no doubt Rupert Philo, better known as King Swallow. Born in the small rural hamlet of Willikies in 1946, Swallow benefited from early piano lessons and school chorus before pursuing a career as a calypsonian. He began singing in the Antiguan Calypso King competition in the early 1960s, eventually taking the title four times between 1973 and 1985, often in pitched battle with his rivals Short Shirt and King Obstinate.

After winning the Antigua Road March competition in 1972 with the tune "Pow Pow," Swallow traveled to Trinidad in hopes of making a recording. With the help of Trinidadian producer Romey Abramson, he connected with Rawlston Charles in Brooklyn. Charles financed and released "March to Freedom," which won Swallow the 1973 Antiguan Calypso King Crown. Working with Trinidad arrangers Joey Lewis, Ed Watson, and Art De Coteau, Swallow went on to make a series of LPs for Charles in the late 1970s. One of his most popular songs "Don't Stop the Party" (1979), arranged by De Coteau, signaled his move from calypso to soca with its heavy melodic bass line, swirling synthesizer riffs, and lyrics exhorting listeners to dance all night. The recordings were made in Trinidad's K.H. Studio, but Swallow would carry the master tape north to Brooklyn where he and Charles would oversee the final mix.

In the early 1980s Swallow began traveling more regularly to Brooklyn to perform and record, spending monthlong stints and returning to Antigua for summer Carnival. Around that time, he was introduced to the young and relatively unknown soca arranger Leston Paul. Encouraged by Charles, the two worked on a series of recordings that yielded several of his biggest soca hits, including 'Subway Jam" (1981), "Party in Space" (1983), and "Satan Coming Down" (1984).

Swallow recalled meeting Frankie briefly in Antigua in the late 1960s, but it wasn't until 1982 that the two began their musical partnership. During one of his visits to Brooklyn, Charles reintroduced them and recruited Frankie to work with Swallow on several songs that appeared on the LP *Dance Any Way You Want*. Over the next decade, Swallow and Frankie would collaborate on seven more LPs, all recorded in Brooklyn and released on Charlie's Records. The most successful, *Swallow on the Streets of Brooklyn* (1988), included the hit "Fire in the Backseat." Winner of the 1989 Sunshine Award for "Best Calypso Arrangement," the song led one commentator to pronounce the work "a career defining masterpiece that elevated him [Swallow] from Antigua Calypso icon to Caribbean legend."[10]

Despite his international success, Swallow stayed true to his roots and maintained his Antiguan residency. A favored son, he won the island's Calypso Crown four times and the Road March title five times. In addition to his artistic prowess, he was a strong supporter of Antigua's local calypso scene, managing his own tent, the Calypso Pepper Pot, up until his passing in 2020. In recognition of his immense cultural contributions, the Government of Antigua and Barbuda awarded him the Order of Merit (Gold) and the Grand Cross of Princely Heritage, and in 2011 bestowed the title of Knighthood on Sir Rupert Philo.[11]

Frankie on Swallow

RA: Wasn't Swallow another of the calypsonians you first met back in Antigua?

FM: Right, we crossed paths while I was working with the Laviscount Brass and we were playing at an open-air dance venue called the Town House in downtown St. John's. The show that night featured Rupert Blaize, regarded locally as a "soul singer," and an up-and-coming young calypsonian who called himself the Mighty Swallow. I don't recall there being any rehearsal, since the band knew the songs that each artist intended to sing. The show was well attended and enthusiastically received, with both singers being recalled for encores. They were both sons of Antigua, and clearly quite popular with the locals. My conversation with Swallow was brief, more or less congratulatory. I had no idea the level of fame he would eventually acquire, or that we would meet again in Brooklyn more than a decade down the road to work together.

RA: And how did that come about, another Straker of Charles connection?

FM: I believe it was Rawlston Charles who approached me in Brooklyn about working with Swallow. I'd already had success working with Charlie on arrangements of Explainer's tunes for *Man from the Ghetto* (see next chapter), so when he needed someone to record with Swallow in Brooklyn I got the call. I arranged three songs for him that ended up on an LP, *Swallow: Dance Anyway You Want* (1982), which also included three tunes arranged by Leston Paul that had been previously recorded in Trinidad. Charlie would do that sort of thing, mix recordings from different sessions and different arrangers on one album.

RA: What was it like working with Swallow?

FM: It was very smooth. I recall Swallow coming to my house with a box guitar which he could play well enough to accompany himself while he sang. In contrast to Obstinate and Short Shirt, there was no need for me go through a series of different keys at the piano, because Swallow could play his songs on the guitar, moving between higher or lower keys as needed. If his melody required a supporting chord which he could not form on the guitar fretboard, or one that he did not hear, I would notate that in the provisional score. After I had a pretty clear idea what the melodic form would take, and the harmony I chose to accompany it (often deviating from what Swallow played), we would record a cassette demo with just voice and piano, no guitar. That demo would be my reference in creating the final arrangement. It was easy working with Swallow in the pre-studio phase because he wrote his own songs, memorized them, and could play enough guitar to provide a helpful guide.

"Find the Spot" (Charlie's Records, 1982)

RA: Let's talk about a few of Swallow's songs. How about, "Find the Spot," from the initial 1982 album? What a kicking dance groove, to say nothing of the humorously suggestive lyrics.

FM: "Find the Spot" was one of the first tunes we worked up. The lyrics played on a double entendre, with Swallow portraying himself as renowned guide who was only too happy to help his lovers locate treasure, or more specifically, their "treasure spot" of womanly pleasures. His vocal verses were in three parts (A/B/C), with the final four bars (C) leading into the female-driven chorus that exhorts Swallow to "find the spot, find the treasure spot." The mood was jovial and sensual, and his three-part verses and powerful chorus gave me plenty of melodic and rhythmic material to work with for the introduction and the band choruses.

RA: The opening really cooks, especially when you bring in the horns over that initial guitar riff. How did you put that together?

FM: The introduction to "Find the Spot" is a good example of the additive approach to an arrangement—starting out with one or two instruments and adding more to thicken the texture and establish the dance groove. I opened with a call-and-response figure between a melodic bass line and a guitar riff, all over a simple drum beat. Then I added a synthesizer line, and then a second. The idea was to interlock the guitar, the two synthesizers, the bass, and drums together to form the underlying beat, or the groove. Next, I brought in the horns in on top, playing a bright, five-note riff taken from Swallow's "find the treasure spot" vocal chorus. This all happened in the opening thirty seconds. Next, for contrast, I backed off the high horns and just let a single synthesizer sound against the low reeds, then brought the high brass back, and finally the single synthesizer once more before Swallow came in with his first verse. It was a complicated introduction, nearly a minute long. But it was effective in solidifying a groove, building up the energy, and introducing melodic material that listeners would soon hear in Swallow's vocals.

RA: Yes, I love the way all those guitar and synth parts interlock. This is one of your best introductions to my ear. Now, Swallow's vocal verses and choruses were sectional—how did you handle them?

FM: That sectional structure provided complexity and variation to the overall song that never strayed from the I-IV-V triadic major harmonies. The verse was built around an A/B/C structure. The first eight measures (A), beginning with the lyric "Sweet little Stephanie from Tobago," were sung smoothly over the guitar and synthesizer. In contrast, Swallow sang the next eight measures (B) using shorter phrases and a percussive delivery while the bass and horns doubled his vocals. This began with the line "She tells Becket not to ease up" (a reference to the popular Becket song "Don't Ease Up"). For the C section, the horns dropped out for the first three measures as he sang "Soon as I hit the target" and returned on the last measure to reinforce his dramatic descending vocal line, "I-yi-yi-yi" that led into the chorus. There was a lot going on in those verse sections. The variety and contrast, I believe, were a big part of the song's success.

The chorus structure was A/B/A. The first A section was built around Swallow and the powerful female voices singing "Boy you find the spot / Find the treasure spot." The B section was more relaxed with him singing "She jump up and ball," followed by a return of the A section, this time with the high brass reinforcing the vocal lines. With these three lengthy verses and choruses, combined with my intermittent band choruses, we did not need a coda. The engineer simply faded the song out around the six-minute mark following the final vocal chorus.

RA: All the albums you did with Swallow were for Rawlston Charles, is that right? Swallow never worked with Straker or other Brooklyn producers?

FM: As far as I know that's correct. I worked on a number of albums with Swallow during the 1980s, all of which were produced by Rawlston Charles and distributed on his label. Swallow and Charlie were really tight. You know, Swallow's loyalty to Charlie was unusual, because back then most singers did not have exclusive contracts with any one label, so they tended to move around quite a bit. For Charlie, Swallow was one of his most prized artists.

"Fire in the Backseat" (Charlie's Records, 1988)

RA: The most popular song you did with Swallow was "Fire in the Backseat" in 1988. Tell me about that.

FM: We recorded that one in Rawlston Studio on Fulton Street, above Charlie's record shop. That was a state-of-the-art facility! Charlie had all the latest equipment, including a thirty-two-track Neve mixing board. Now there is a funny story about how this song came about. Every year Swallow would call me when he was in town and we would get together to work up his new songs for the upcoming Carnival season. One year (1988) I hadn't heard from him, and I was driving down Fulton Street and saw him liming out on the street with some guys. I asked him if he was going to record that year, and he said yes, but first he had to get in the right "spirit." He went on to explain that he would first have to pray and read the Bible to get in the correct frame of mind to go into the studio to record his material. This would, he claimed, help inspire his lyrics. So, he called me about a week and a half later to announce that he was ready. He brought me the songs, and as I listened, I slowly realized that none of the lyrics had anything to do with the Bible, unless it was so subtle that I could not pick it up. The title alone, "Fire in the Backseat," was very suggestive that something sensual might be going on in the rear of a car. But perhaps Swallow did find inspiration in the Bible, not to write "Fire in the Backseat" necessarily, but simply to overcome writers' block and to induce an overall creative frame of mind? Only the Almighty knows for sure, but whatever spiritual introspection Swallow engaged in that year did result in a highly successful song, one of his most popular.

RA: Listening to it today, what do you think made it so appealing to audiences?

FM: That's a good question. Honestly, I was not that impressed with Swallow's original melody, and I worried that the tonic/dominant (I-V) chord loop might result in a monotonous accompaniment. In fact, the most interesting thing about his original song was the unevenness in the verses, his eighteen-beat verse structure divided among 4+4+2+4+4-beat phrases was rather uncommon in calypso (you can hear this in his first verse that begins at 0:40 with "Going down San Fernando / To put on a big show / I catchin' cold sweat / I frightened to death").

RA: How about the lyrics? "Fire" seems to be another tongue-and-cheek story about sexual escapades.

FM: Right. In retrospect I think it was the lyrics that really sold the song, the allure of what sort of "fire" was being generated in the backseat of Swallow's car. He employed a clever double entendre, in the first two verses suggesting that there was sensual "tumbling" and possible weed smoking going down in the back of the car, but in third verse he finally revealed that there was a literal "fire" resulting from a dropped match accidently igniting the woman's dress. Now sometimes the story that the singer is telling, in this case a humorous tale ripe with sexual overtones, can suggest musical possibilities for me as the arranger. It might give me ideas for my choices of timbral shadings. I might look for colors that would represent the female character, or the female voice, as opposed to the male voice. Strongly accented, aggressive horns, for example, might be suggestive of the male, while the higher-register, lighter responses by the synth or sax might connote female. What I'm getting at is that sometimes the lyrics can set up the tone of the arrangement—if you just listen to the a cappella song delivered in person or on cassette, a certain mood ensues, and you want to keep that in the arrangement.

RA: Interesting. Now with all the nonbinary issues being raised in discussions of gender politics these days, I wonder if some readers will find your male/female voicing theory outdated and perhaps objectionable?

FM: Perhaps, but the reality is that gender roles were quite strict in the Caribbean back then. Men and women were often depicted as being at odds with one another in calypso and soca songs, but the tone was usually humorous and the songs were often intended to mediate those tensions.

RA: Understood. Now, how did these gendered voices work with your instrumental band chorus for "Fire"?

FM: That band chorus was fairly simple, beginning with my synthesizer line doubled by the bass, built around a motivic variation of the "Fire in the Backseat" vocal line from the chorus. Next came contrasting lines by the full and assertive brass section (perhaps heard as masculine) riffing on another variation of the "Fire in the backseat" hook, followed by a lighter/sweeter, more lyrical saxophones/synthesizer response (perhaps heard as feminine), playing a motive derived from the "Oy, that heat in me tummy / Oy, is burning me plenty" vocal line of the chorus.

RA: Do you really think your audiences back then would have heard the aggressive brass as masculine and the more lyrical reeds as feminine?

FM: Well, maybe not consciously, but I suspect there were probably some gender associations. This would have been especially true for the brass—there were very few if any female trumpeters or trombone players back in the 1980s. Those instruments were considered male-appropriate, and thus sounded male, especially when played forcefully, as in "Fire."

RA: We will return to this discussion of the dearth of women horn players in chapter 7. But for now, let's get back to your band chorus for "Fire."

FM: Although this introductory band chorus was not as complex as the opening of "Find the Spot," it did succeed in introducing listeners to the melodic and rhythmic ideas that form the basis for the ensuing vocal verses and choruses. The I-V chord progression and rhythmic groove were maintained throughout, but I wrote a new set of melodic lines for the horns on the second band chorus to break up things up a bit. These new lines were variations, but of course preserve the character of what previously occurred in order to maintain a sense of continuity.

RA: "Fire" has a lengthy tag that includes a trumpet solo. How did that come about?

FM: The tag was actually more elaborate, alternating my synthesizer lines with the chorus and Swallow's ad-libbing. The tag's groove and sexual energy were accentuated by aggressive, macho horn hits over the sensual "fire" and "oy" cries of the female chorus. That's another example of the sort of male/

female voicing contrasts I sometimes employed. I decided to close the tag section with a trumpet solo by Errol Ince—that was a bit unusual for a soca song in the late 1980s, but I knew we would need a solo to extend the song and I immediately had Errol in mind. He was deep into Dizzy Gillespie and Miles Davis, and you can hear the ornamentations and turns characteristic of the great modern bebop players. I had Errol play the solo during the horn studio recording session, hoping that neither Swallow nor Charlie would object and put something over it in the final mix. Fortunately, they didn't, a wise decision! Errol's solo floats above this dense texture of the rhythm section led by the bass, and accentuated by horn stabs, a female chorus of "ohs," and whistles and sirens. A very creative mix by Charlie! In retrospect, all those things contributed to the song's success.

Paul "King Obstinate" Richards

Green Bay Records, 1982.

Next to Shirt and Swallow, Antigua's most popular calypsonian of the 1980s was Paul Richards, known to his fans as King Obstinate. He was born in 1941 in the small town of Green Bay, situated a few miles south of the capital St. John's. He sang in school competitions, and eventually acquired a banjo to accompany himself while singing for tips around town. As a teenager Obstinate performed in a calypso tent located in the capitol's Princess Elizabeth Hall, and in 1958, at the age of seventeen, he won the second annual Antigua Calypso Crown contest with the song "Dance, Dance, Dance." With his $100 prize money he bought a Stella guitar and soon after traveled to St. Thomas, US Virgin Islands, a destination with a growing tourist industry. There he eked out a living as a janitor, dishwasher, and waiter, before landing singing gigs at the Gram Boco and Caribbean Beach hotels.

Obstinate's singing career received a boost when, during a trip to New York City, an agent helped him gain an invitation to perform at the Caribbean Pavilion of the 1964 World's Fair. For the next decade and a half, he shuttled between St. Thomas, New York, and Washington, DC, working as a singer and club manager, and occasionally appearing on larger calypso programs that headlined stars like Sparrow and Lord Nelson. In 1968 he worked with Trinidad arranger Frankie Francis, recording his first LP, *In a Calypso Groove*, which he released on his own Green Bay Records. In the late 1970s he resettled in St. Thomas and eventually returned to Antigua.

Although he relocated back to the Caribbean, Obstinate continued to travel to the States to perform and record. Sometime around 1980 he was introduced to Frankie by Short Shirt, who had arranged for a group of Antiguan singers to visit and record in Brooklyn. Throughout the 1980s, Obstinate and Frankie worked together, producing half a dozen LPs, all released on Green Bay Records. Their collaboration yielded a number of Antiguan Calypso Crown–winning songs: "Antiguan Independence" and "Fat Man Dance" in 1981; "Coming Down to Talk to You" and "Elephant Walk" in 1982; and "Antigua's True Heroes" and "Children Melee" in 1983. In addition to his patriotic and message songs, Obstinate released a number of popular dance pieces including "Got A Little Something for You" (1982), "Shine Eyes" (1985), and "Hungry" (1985).

Admired for his prowess as a singer, Obstinate was also known for his flamboyant apparel and theatrical antics. He would don a fat suit to perform "Fat Man Dance" and an elephant costume for the comical "Elephant Walk." He once jumped out of a coffin on stage to sing "Resurrection," a song boasting his return to the Antiguan calypso stage. A witty entertainer, Obstinate occasionally worked as an emcee and deejay.

After moving back to Antigua, Obstinate continued to sing and manage his own open-air bar in downtown St. John's. In 1994 the Antigua government awarded him the Gold Order of Honor Grand Cross for his contributions to national culture. He was dubbed Knight Commander in 2006.[12]

Frankie on Obstinate

RA: Like Swallow, I assume you initially met Obstinate when you were living and working in Antigua?

FM: Exactly, we crossed paths while I was playing with Laviscount Brass. "Obsti" (as he was known to his most devoted fans and friends) was living in Saint Thomas in the later 1960s, but I had heard of him from his hit calypso "L.B.J. for the USA." Fortunately, shortly after I arrived, a local promoter flew him to Antigua to headline a big calypso show, and Laviscount was hired as the backing band. I remember his entrance on stage that night was majestic: immaculately dressed in a three-piece suit, and he delivered a performance to match. He was revered in Antigua as a real son of the soil.

RA: Was it Short Shirt who reunited you two in Brooklyn?

FM: Yes, that was years later, sometime around 1980. Obsti was part of the previously mentioned group of Antigua calypsonians that Short Shirt brought up to Brooklyn to record. In retrospect he might have regretted that move. You see, Short Shirt and Obsti would become arch rivals, and when Short Shirt was out of earshot, Obsti pulled me aside and expressed his desire to work with me as arranger on his own next album. We had a verbal deal then and there. But as a result, for a time I was arranging for both of them in the same year, which was somewhat awkward, as both were pressuring me for an arrangement that would win the Antiguan Calypso Crown. On every meeting Obsti tried diligently to convince me that he and I were a team with the express objective of overcoming all contenders for the Calypso Crown that year. He would say things like, "Frankie, we gotta bang dey ras this year you know!!" I always assured him "we" would win, but admittedly I extended this same assurance to his competitors who expected the same from me. Fortunately, I did manage to deliver winning arrangements for both, but of course not in the same year! I remember that Obsti wouldn't record with the same engineer or in the same studio that Short Shirt used. He usually recorded at Platinum Factory, so Obstinate demanded Sound Heights. And Swallow, the other Antiguan who often vied for the Crown, would usually record at Rawlston and Crystal Sounds studios. They were very competitive, but mostly in a friendly way.

RA: Well, I hope Short Shirt didn't pull out his boxing gloves for Obstinate or you. In any case, let's talk about how you two began collaborating.

FM: Obstinate started to bring his material to me a year or so later—the first album we worked on together was *Calypso, Soca, Reggae*, which came out in 1981. At that time, I don't think he was living in Brooklyn. I believe he had gone back to the Caribbean. He would call me up in advance from St. Thomas or Antigua, before he'd come up, to reserve some time to work with me. When he arrived at my home, he usually would present a song a cappella. I would tinker at the piano trying to find a basic key. I then shifted up or down in half steps during several iterations of his melody until his "best key" was agreed upon by both of us.

I should mention that Obsti's voice was commanding. He possessed a deep, resonant baritone, and always enunciated his lyrics with immaculate clarity. His melodic lines were particularly well developed, they were easy to remember and sing along to. But I don't think the lyrics were all his—I'm quite sure that another calypsonian named Reality wrote some of his material, perhaps most of it. When we were in the studio, he might call Reality to check on a verse. A native of Montserrat, Reality once told me that he wrote many of Obsti's hits, including "Children's Melee" and "Shiny Eyes."

When it came to business, Obsti was always true to whatever financial arrangements we had settled upon. At Sound Heights Studio, where most of his recording took place, Obsti would retire to a back room and parcel out on a table the appropriate cash amounts for each musician on the session that day. He called it his "buffet." Sometime this would take place before the recording session began, which was very unusual! Back then musicians were rarely paid in advance for recording sessions or life performances. The going rate at that time was $40 per track, therefore for an eight-track album, every sideman, regardless of instrument, received $320. That was a rewarding day's pay in the 1980s!

RA: I've gathered that Obstinate was quite a showman, was that your impression?

FM: Absolutely, many of his songs were geared toward a live, theatrical performance. On "Fat Man Dance," from that first LP, he did this thing where he'd stuff his suit with foam rubber to look like a big fat man. The song "Elephant Walk," from our *So Calypso* LP (1982), was written with stage entertainment in mind. He developed this funny elephant walk dance that he would do on stage, and I think that's what won him the Antiguan Calypso Crown one year. I remember when he brought the song to me, he explained he already had this elephant suit, so I figured out a heavy, wah-wah bass line on synthesizer to emulate a plodding elephant lumbering along (you can hear it clearly in the first fifteen seconds of the recording). It worked and audiences really loved it!

When we met in Antigua he came off as a larger-than-life character, always well dressed and speaking in an exaggerated, highfalutin way, like he was putting on more of a fancy American accent. But in New York he was just the opposite, a really down to earth Antiguan, with Antiguan lingo and all. I guess when he went back home he put on this different persona. In any case he was a singer, a comedian, a performer, and a guy who really knew how to promote himself.

"Shiny Eyes" (Green Bay Records, 1985)

RA: I understand that "Shiny Eyes" was one of, if not the, most popular Obstinate song. It doesn't have much going on harmonically, but it really kicks with a great dance groove. What was your approach to arranging that one?

FM: Well, the title itself suggests something bright, and I think I tried to reflect that in the high brass lines in the introduction and band choruses. The whole mood of the song is upbeat, you think of a festive occasion with people dancing. After opening with a funky guitar riff, I added a synth line and eventually the horns in order to thicken up the texture. That all led into the first vocal verse, "I met this girl in St. Lucia / She had, shiny eyes." I thought it was an effective introduction so I brought those figures back as the band chorus—I was aiming for strong contrast between swirly synthesizer lines and the bright, sharp horn lines. You mentioned the original groove—that guitar figure that settled in after the first ten seconds was the real foundation, and continued throughout the song, unifying the whole arrangement that never deviated from the original I-IV, two-chord structure. I knew that people liked it, because sometimes you would hear them singing that background line during the band chorus when the vocalist took a break. I'm quite sure those opening licks contributed to the song's appeal.

RA: And it sounds like another sectionalized vocal chorus. What's going on there?

FM: The vocal chorus was somewhat unusual with its tripartite organization. Obstinate began the first eight-bar section (A) with the "Come back and love me" line followed immediately by horn hits and the female chorus responding "Shiny Eyes." That sequence was repeated twice before he crooned a legato, four-bar hook (B), "Oh-h-h, shiny eyes." Next, he switched to a rapid-fire vocal rap (C): "Soon as I mention / glitter and shine / says she'll come back / and see me some t-i-i-i-i-me," which was answered by a sharp, syncopated horn line. The (B) "Oh-h-h, shiny eyes" hook returned followed by a shorter (C) rap that leads into the band section that is similar to the instrumental introduction. One thing that made that A/B/C/B/C vocal structure particularly effective was the contrast between the smooth "shiny eyes" refrains (A and B) the rhythmic rapping sections (C).

Obsti's vocal chorus and my instrumental band sections had to have multiple parts because the chordal accompaniment was a repetitive two-chord loop that otherwise could have become boring for listeners. But I think we put in enough variety to keep it fresh. The song had a strong dance groove and sold well in Brooklyn and back in the Caribbean.

"Antigua Independence" (Green Bay Records, 1981)

RA: Let's switch to something more in the message vein. I think "Antiguan Independence" is a real gem. I believe Obstinate wrote it in honor of Antigua's formal severance from Great Britain in 1981. How did you approach that one?

FM: Well, I knew he intended the song for that year's calypso competition, so the lyrics needed to be foregrounded, especially given the impassioned lines recounting the evils of slavery and the travails of colonialism. With this in mind I decided to arrange the song in the style of an older calypso, with a moderate, lilting tempo. I wanted to convey an anthem-like feel, so I had the bass play on the beat, outlining the chords without syncopation. The introduction employed triadic, open-voiced harmonies befitting a national anthem. The song opened with a bold, ascending line on the high brass, which was followed by an immediate response on the low reeds. Next, all the instruments join in a dramatic crescendo, landing on a big tonic chord that ended with a series of staccato hits before Obsti's verse began. That final horn crescendo was meant to ramp up the drama and to announce that something important was about to be said, or sung in this case. Obsti's first verse got right to the point: "Oh land of peace, haven of rest / Antigua, your shores are blessed / with the sweat of those who toiled / in bondage, to till the soil. / From Black hands, sweet sugar flowed / many died with each pay load."

RA: Wow, very intense. Your introduction and the opening verse and chorus really sound like a national anthem, at least in the European sense of the genre.

FM: Ha! Yes, you might say that the melodramatic use of those harmonies gave a certain European-colonial feel to the piece, which was of course ironic, because the lyrical message was an indictment of slavery and British colonial rule. One thing I was sure of was that the pomp and splendor of the song's introduction would be in keeping with Obsti's persona. And for what it's worth, Antigua already had a European-style national anthem, "Fair Antigua, We Salute Thee." Beautiful melody, but no reference to slavery or colonial rule.

RA: No surprise there. Tell me more about your musical strategy for the rest of the song.

FM: The accompaniment on his vocal verses was more subdued, aimed to support but not overwhelm the lyrics. The guitar and organ played a steady progression that included a minor VI chord (Fm) in both the A and B sections, and a minor II chord (B♭m) in the B section, all to temper the otherwise major voicings. The song was meant to be celebratory, but also contemplative, given what the Antiguan people had been through. In addition, I wove in a synthesized flute figure in the background to provide a light, airy feel to the vocal accompaniment. The wooden flute was an instrument that was used in different genres of Caribbean folk music, so that sound evoked a sense of history to complement Obstinate's narrative of Antigua's 400 years of struggle.

RA: And how about the chorus, very powerful!

FM: Yes, the chorus was meant to be the climactic celebration of the song. It opened with the dramatic line "But my people fought on, for four hundred years." I used bold, arpeggiated major triads on the high brass to complete his vocal phrases and convey splendor. A brief I-III7-VIm (A♭-C7-Fm) turnaround chord progression (at 1:14) added harmonic color and landed back on the tonic A♭ chord just as the chorus swelled to its dramatic climax, "Antigua, Freedom Forever."

RA: The tag has a spoken word section which is unusual for calypso and soca songs of that era, no?

FM: Well, I wouldn't even call it a tag. After running through the vocal verse, vocal chorus, and chorus format three times, I reprised the band chorus while Obsti recited a passionate verse honoring those who died in the struggle for freedom. This was followed by a final vocal chorus and a return to the original brass crescendo and staccato hits in order to go out on a dramatic note. Apparently, my arrangement struck the right mood to complement Obsti's patriotic message, because "Antiguan Independence" won the Antiguan Calypso Crown with it 1981.

• • •

FM: Let me close this chapter by saying how thankful I am for the opportunity to have worked with these singers from Saint Vincent and Antigua, as well as with artists from Grenada, Dominica, Barbados, and the other so-called "small islands." Many, probably most, people associate calypso and soca exclusively with Trinidad, but there were other voices that needed to be heard. As a small islander myself I am proud to have been part of the process of bringing them forward. And thanks to Straker and Charlie for helping that to happen.

With that tip of the hat to my small island brethren, let's move on to Trinidad and the best-known calypso/soca stars.

CHAPTER 6

ARRANGING WITH THE TRINIDAD STARS

Throughout the 1970s, Trinidad's top calypsonians visited New York with increased frequency. They sought to take advantage of the city's advanced recording studios and mixing facilities, as well as new performance opportunities in Brooklyn's bourgeoning West Indian community with its annual Labor Day Carnival festivities. Three of the singers discussed in this chapter—Rose, Duke, and Sparrow—made New York their home base of operations. The other four—Chalkdust, Explainer, Shadow, and Kitchener—cycled in and out of the city to record and perform, but maintained their primary residency in Trinidad. They all moved freely between the Caribbean, New York, Toronto, and London, which by the 1980s had become the primary nodes of an expanding transnational Carnival network. When the Trinidad calypsonians landed in New York, Frankie and the Brooklyn-based record companies were ready to serve them.

Hollis Chalkdust Liverpool

Straker's Records, 1978/1979.

Dr. Hollis "Chalkdust" Liverpool is the most acclaimed calypso bard of his generation when it comes to social commentary and political satire. Born in the Trinidad village of Chaguaramas in 1941 and reared in Tobago, Chalkdust excelled as a student, earning certificates from St. Mary's College and the Government Teacher's College in Port of Spain, and a bachelor's degree from the University of the West Indies. With these credentials he embarked on a career as a public-school teacher at the Nelson Street Boys RC School. Along the way he had developed a keen interest in Trinidad's steelband and calypso music, and began writing calypsos while still a student at St. Mary's. In 1968 he made his debut as the singing schoolteacher (hence the sobriquet "Chalkdust") in Port of Spain's Calypso Theater tent. His first song, "Brain Drain," expressed his passionate support for national culture, urging young, educated Trinidadians not to abandon their homeland, and for the inclusion of steelband and calypso in school curriculums. He won his first Calypso Monarch competition in 1976 with "No Smut for Me," a satirical piece chastising his fellow calypsonians for their emphasis on licentious lyrics while ignoring pressing social issues. He would go on to win nine Calypso Monarch titles, his latest in 2017.

Chalkdust began recording in the late 1960s for a Trinidad-based subsidiary of RCA, but quickly grew dissatisfied with the financial arrangements. In 1972 Granville Straker, on a trip to Trinidad, heard Liverpool singing at a Carnival tent, and recruited him for his new record label. The following year Straker released Liverpool's first full album, *First Time Around*, arranged by Art De Coteau and recorded in Port of Spain's Semp Studios.

Chalkdust worked with De Coteau on half a dozen albums in the 1970s before being introduced to Frankie while on a visit to Brooklyn in 1978. Straker brought them together to record *Origins*, the first full album production Frankie would do for the Straker label. Chalkdust appreciated Frankie's innovative arrangements and egalitarian style, and the two of them went on to collaborate on more than a dozen albums in the 1980s and 1990s. Their efforts yielded two Calypso Monarch–winning songs, "Chauffeur Wanted" (1989) and "Kaiso in the Hospital" (1993).

In addition to his international success as a calypsonian, Chalkdust has enjoyed an esteemed career as a scholar, educator, and cultural activist. After earning a PhD in history and ethnomusicology from the University of Michigan, he returned to Trinidad where he assumed the post of Director of Culture in the Ministry of Culture and Community Development. He went on to teach at the University of the Virgin Islands, and at the time of this writing is Professor of Carnival Arts at the University of Trinidad and Tobago. He is author of a number of books on Carnival music and culture, including *Rituals of Power and Rebellion: Carnival Tradition in Trinidad and Tobago 1763–1962* (Research Associates School Times, 2001) and *Thoughts Along the Kaiso Road* (Juba Publications, 2017).[1]

Frankie on Chalkdust

RA: What was it like meeting Chalkdust for the first time? He was a big-time calypsonian by the late 1970s, and you were relatively unknown as an arranger. How did that come about?

FM: I was a big fan of Chalkdust long before I met him. When I was growing up back in Saint Vincent, he was a very famous calypsonian, known for his social and political commentary. Years later up in Brooklyn, when Straker asked me to arrange and record an entire album of his songs, I was of course elated! Now meeting a famous person like Chalky could be a bit intimidating, because you imagined him walking off the ground, high above the rest of us. But it turned out he was a humble, down-to-earth person, very much focused with no attitude. And smart! His grandfather was from Saint Vincent, and all the Liverpools were well educated and successful, including several doctors. It did not surprise me that Chalky had studied to become a teacher, then got a PhD, and went on to write all those books.

RA: Before we get into specific examples, what can you say broadly about Chalkdust's calypsos and the way he sang them? What made them so distinct?

FM: When I first heard his songs, I sensed that he had been brought up in church, because many of his melodies evinced a hymn-like quality. They tended to move diatonically, in smooth, conjunct fashion—that is from one small scale step to the next, without jumping around. His rhythmic delivery and the way he would scoop up his notes were reminiscent of what one might hear in church. Chalky's melodies resonated with the largely Christian Caribbean audiences, and I believe that is what set him apart from most calypsonians,

On top of the hymn-like feel of his melodies, Chalky's mode of delivery was almost sermon-like. When you add his topical lyrical content and set it to a driving calypso accompaniment, success was inevitable. His songs resonated with his target audience, which was mostly Trinidadian, because they knew what he was singing about. As a Vincentian living outside the Caribbean, I myself had to read up on certain Trinidad political issues to figure out what and who some of his songs were referring to. But that was fine, and like many, I admired him as an erudite composer of powerful calypso message songs.

RA: What was it like working with him on arrangements?

FM: Oh, Chalky was always a pleasure to work with—and I certainly can't say that for all calypsonians! He wrote his own songs, and although they were usually quite lyrically complex, he had them memorized and ready to go when he came to my house. He also played the guitar and usually had figured out the right key to pitch each song. If he got to a certain point where there was a chord that he could not form on the guitar, I could fill it in because I could hear what he was really aiming for. When I wrote out the arrangement, I added the new chords and he never minded. Chalky trusted me—I just wrote out the music and he would sing.

RA: Okay, let's talk about the first album you did with Chalky, the *Origins* LP. Was that the first full LP you did for Straker, back in 1978?

FM: That's correct. Straker set things up for us to record in Studio 21 on Madison Avenue in midtown Manhattan. I called on my calypso contacts to assemble a band that included Lio Smith and Gene Jefferson on saxophones and Ron Taylor on first trumpet. I also brought in Eddie Payne, a bass player who was a friend of my father's back in Saint Vincent. Eddie had become something of a surrogate dad, advising me on the right steps to take here in

New York. I brought him into the studio that night but somehow he forgot his glasses so he couldn't read the charts. Things started going awry, and Straker wanted to get in and out of the studio as quickly as possible. I was thinking oh boy, we're wasting time here on my first big session with him. But then the engineer suggested we use a Moog synthesizer that was capable of producing a suitable bass sound on its lower octaves. Now I'd never done that before, but given the situation I decided to take him up on the idea, and throughout that whole album I played the bass on the synthesizer with my left hand. I'm not sure if anyone had ever done that before, at least on a calypso album as far as I know. Fortunately, Starker was satisfied!

RA: I hear the *Origins* album as classic Chalkdust—message songs with unabashed social commentary, and more in line with the older calypsos as opposed to the emerging soca sound. Am I right?

FM: Definitely. Several of his songs were aimed specifically at Trinidad society and politics, such as "De Spirit Gone," his rebuke of the commercialization of Trinidad Carnival. Others, addressed more universal issues. "Black Inventions," for instance, was about all the great discoveries by Black people that had been written out of the white history books. And yes, stylistically they certainly had more of a calypso feel than say the arrangements I'd done for Becket during that early period. Not surprisingly, Chalky wanted the songs rendered at relatively slow to medium tempos, say around 90–95 BPM. He favored rhythms that were reminiscent of the older calypso style that emphasized the lyrical narrative and the message. In fact, he wasn't wild about soca at first because he felt that the younger singers weren't really telling stories, they were just stringing together hooks and one-liners, and rarely did they address social issues. One of the songs I arranged for him, "Two Chords and Leston Paul," satirized the repetitive monotony of the new music.

RA: Agreed, but one question. What about your use of the synthesizer on *Origins*? That's something I associate with the new soca, not the older calypso, right?

FM: You see, during the *Origins* recording sessions I was still trying to figure out how to integrate the new synthesizers into my arrangements. In fact, at first, I didn't even know how to program them! I had to have the engineer at Studio 21 play around with the settings until I heard a sound I liked. On the Becket recording I had used the polyphonic Arp machine, which was capable of sounding multiple notes and chords at one time. But the Moog at Studio 21 was monophonic, which meant that it could only play one note at a time, no chords. I was able to play the bass lines I'd written without a problem. The sound was solid but just a little robotic and synthetic in terms of the decay, and I decided going forward that I would use a live electric string bass whenever possible. More to my liking were the dubbed-in high, flute-sounding fills behind his vocals on "De Spirit is Gone," and a fuzz bass patch on the introduction to "Tantie Merle." These synthesizer embellishments foreshadowed the coming of new electronic sounds that would be prominent in soca music.

Now, the synthesizer did give Chalky's songs a slightly modern flavor, but the overall form and feel of most were closer to that of traditional calypsos—that is a short, simple instrumental band chorus, followed by vocal verse and chorus, then return to the beginning and repeat the sections depending on how many verses the song contained. In retrospect, my arrangements on *Origins*, like those for the early Becket recordings, were transitional, at a time when I was beginning to incorporate more contemporary elements into the conventional calypso style I had grown up with.

RA: Yes, I can hear that. And the mid- to late 1970s was the time when the synthesizer was starting to make serious inroads into American popular rock and soul music. Now let's talk about a few specific songs.

"Black Inventions" (Straker's Records, 1978/79)

FM: My favorite track on *Origins* is still "Black Inventions," Chalky's recounting of African people's unrecognized contributions to the world. Now the band chorus was short but lively, propelled by a bright, full horn figure that was derived from the second half of his vocal chorus ("Today when you watch the electric light / remember a Black man Latimer had the foresight / he used carbon to make bulbs burn bright / A Black man invented that"). A rhythmically active bass line gave the introduction an additional push. The format was quite standard for a calypso—Chalky sang four sixteen-measure verses, each followed by a ten-measure chorus and my short, eight-measure band chorus. The end of the song was a long tag where he recited an exhaustive list of accomplishments over the chorus refrain "A Black man invented that!" Like I said, Chalky always had a lot to say, so there was little room for instrumental breaks or tags.

RA: So, what was going on harmonically? It's not just a simple I-IV-V triad progression—don't I hear some big band jazz voicings?

FM: That's right. I took Chalky's basic chords and embellished the harmonies by adding what we call extensions—that is additional raised fifths and ninths to the original major or minor triad. And I expanded the standard I-IV-V progression with the addition of passing chords, so the underlying harmonies changed quickly. That all provided variety in tonal color and a sense of motion and swing, together giving the arrangement a slightly jazzy feel.

RA: Tell me again how you used the synthesizer on "Black Inventions."

FM: I kept the horns backgrounded during his verses and added high, flute-sounding synthesizer fills. I wanted to suggest the sounds of the wind or a bird flying in between the trees, perhaps to evoke the sense of the Caribbean or even Africa. Those figures provided listeners with another layer of sound, floating lightly on top of his voice, the horns, and the bass. During the lengthy tag I improvised more freely with the synthesizer fills, but Chalky's list of Black inventions, the theme of the song, was of primary importance. The creations went on and on, leaving no room for a more developed instrumental solo by me or one of the horn players. That high, warbling sound on the synth did not intrude on his singing, so you could hear the interplay of the voice, the synthesizer, and the horns. The singing was repetitive but the texture was rich and provided a sweet way to fade out.

"Ash Wednesday Jail" (Straker's Records, 1983)

RA: One of my favorite Chalkdust Songs is "Ash Wednesday Jail." That one was more in the soca vein, right?

FM: That is correct. In fact, "Ash Wednesday Jail" was not exactly representative of his style, it was more of a dance piece than a message song. The story is about partying on Carnival Tuesday, but with the humorous twist as the protagonist warns his sweetheart not to provoke him into too much wild revelry or she would have to bail him out of jail the following (Ash Wednesday) morning. It was one of the few up-tempo songs he did, and it took a little prodding to get him to sing that fast—we finally got him up to around 120 BPS. I remember he was reluctant at first, but I believe he was pleased with the results.

RA: Okay. In addition to upping the tempo, how did your approach to "Ash Wednesday" differ from that of a message song such as "Black Inventions"?

FM: I wanted the song to start with a kick, so my band chorus opened with a drum roll followed by a full horn line and bass voiced in unison on the bouncy melodic motive drawn from the first line of his vocal chorus—"Marylyn girl, do you want me to make a jail?" That line became the sing-along hook for the song. I answered that brass with an immediate synthesizer line, then played a second motive on the reeds followed by synthesizer response. Those call-and-response figures between the horns and my synth structured the band chorus, providing variety and forward motion. I had the Prophet 5 synthesizer set on a steel pan-sounding patch, and took an eight-measure solo about halfway through the song. I was trying to catch the ambiance of street Carnival, because pan was an essential component of the celebration. Chalky went on to sing three more verses and choruses, interspersed with the introductory band chorus. The vocal chorus and full horn lines really gave the song a sense of drive and vigor—it was a good road march tune, although it didn't win that year, perhaps because Chalky wasn't known for road marches.

RA: Why did you elect to go with a pan-patch on the synthesizer, rather than bringing in a live pan player? I suspect that some folks in the steel pan community were not pleased with your choice.

FM: That is a fair enough question, and over the years I have received criticism from some people who did not appreciate my use of synthesized pan on this and other recordings. You see, one of the advantages of the synthesizer is that you can create all these colors. If you are open to this way of thinking it works as part of the whole tapestry of sound. You don't have to accept it as a natural, pure instrument if you imagine it as a color. But pan players have said, "This guy Frankie is using a pan that's not a pan!" I think their main concern was that the synthesizer and I were putting them out of work! They probably wondered, "why didn't he hire us?" But I knew the overall feel and the specific lines that I was looking for, and back then I didn't know any pannists in Brooklyn who would play exactly the way I wanted (This was before I met Garvin Blake; more on him in chapter 7). That would demand someone who could ad-lib a solo but also who could read music, learn the chords, and would know when to lay out and not to step on the voice or step on the horns. Bringing a nonreading pan player (which most of them were at that time) into the studio and having to teach by singing the parts to him or her would have been cumbersome and might well have lost all the spontaneity. And it would have racked up a lot of time that Straker would have had to pay for. I just preferred to play it myself because I knew what I wanted. And people seemed happy with the sound. "Ash Wednesday" was a big hit!

"Two Chords and Leston Paul" (Straker's Records, 1988)

RA: Interesting that Chalkdust, despite his objections to soca, was willing to indulge in the style with the right arrangement. Tell me about "Two Chords and Leston Paul," which you mentioned earlier in our conversations. What was he trying to say about soca, and especially about soca harmonies?

FM: Yes, that song expressed Chalky's chagrin at calypso (more specifically soca) composers who were writing such simple melodies that they only required the arranger to come up with two chords. They were expecting the arrangers like Leston (or me) to make music out of their uninspiring melodies, to spin gold out of straw you might say. I recall when he first brought the song to me we talked about his overall dissatisfaction with the direction that soca music was taking. You see Chalky comes from the older calypso school, like Kitchener, Melody, and Sparrow, where there was a lot more interest in traditional harmony. They favored more complicated chord progressions, not just a two-chord loop. Chalky lamented the loss of those rich harmonies, and thought that was a disservice to calypso.

RA: The lyrics, as I understand them, involve Chalky having this imaginary conversation with the calypsonian Relator who is encouraging him to forget his traditional sweet melodies and to just concentrate on two-chord songs.

FM: Right. Chalky proclaims he would do this, and then demonstrates the results in the second half of his chorus that rocks back and forth between a B♭7 (V) and an E♭ (I) chord while the chorus sings the monotonous lines "dance / dance / dance / dance / dance," prance / prance / prance / prance / prance," and "wine / wine / wine / wine / wine." Now this is all in done with a degree of mocking irony, because his verse and the first part of the chorus move through multiple chords that you would associate with older calypsos. For example, the initial lines of the verse are sung over a I-III-VI-II-V-I (E♭-G7-C-Fm-B♭-E♭) chord sequence, something familiar to calypso but that you would not hear in too many soca arrangements. Chalky's melody demanded those chord changes, while the two-chord refrain was clearly a spoof.

RA: Yes, Chalky was and still is a master of satire, and your arrangement helped make it work musically!

FM: Chalky and I are on the same page when it comes to appreciating harmony. Let me add that working with Chalky was a real honor for all those years. I was disappointed when our collaboration came to a close in the 1990s, but that was not Chalky's choice or mine. It had to do with some breakdown in business arrangements between him and Straker, rendering it necessary for him to record in Trinidad rather than New York.

Linda "Calypso Rose" McArthur Sandy Lewis

Straker's Records, 1986.

Linda McArthur Sandy Lewis, aka Calypso Rose, is known by fans around the world as the Queen of Calypso. Her pioneering efforts paved the way for Singing Sandra, Lady B, Denyse Plummer, and a host of younger calypso and soca women singers. Born in Tobago (1940) into a family of eleven with a Spiritual Baptist preacher for a father, Rose was brought to Trinidad to live with her uncle's family at the age of nine. Like many young West Indian girls, her earliest singing experiences were at church and in school choirs. At the time calypso was frowned upon by many religious Trinidadians, and was certainly not considered appropriate for girls and young women. Over her family's objections, however, Rose began writing her own calypso songs. As a teenager she made her first public appearances in Port of Spain's Roving Brigade Tent with Mighty Spoiler, and in 1964 moved to the prestigious Young Brigade Tent headlined by the Mighty Sparrow. After touring the Caribbean and winning the 1963 Virgin Islands Calypso competition, her career took off in 1966 with the release of her provocative hit "Fire in Me Wire." Many felt the song should have won the Trinidad Carnival Road March in 1967, but at that time there was no precedent for a song by a woman singer taking the prize. Not surprisingly, that year the song "Sixty-Seven," performed by an old favorite patriarch Lord Kitchener, was the winner.

In 1969 African American promoter Earl Harris brought Rose to perform in a calypso extravaganza at New York's Madison Square Garden, and subsequently set up tours in other US cities. She traveled back and forth between Trinidad and New York, and in 1973 released the LP *Splish Splash* with arranger Art De Coteau, the first of a number of LPs she would record for Granville Straker. Rose's biggest success came in 1977 when she recorded "Give Me Tempo" with arranger Pelham Goddard. Released on the Brooklyn-based Charlie's Records label, the song celebrated Carnival revelry in the Trinidad city of San Fernando, but was actually written while riding on a New York subway. "Tempo" finally won her the prestigious Trinidad Road March in 1977, and the following year "Come Le We Jam" brought her a second consecutive Road March win. That same year her songs "Her Royal Majesty" and "I Thank Thee" earned her the Trinidad Calypso Monarch crown, marking the first time a woman had taken the title.

Despite these accomplishments, Rose grew increasingly frustrated with the sexism of the Trinidad Carnival tent and competition scenes and decided to withdraw from the formal contests following her victories in 1978. Several years prior she had relocated to New York, using the city as a base for recording and for touring North America, Europe, the Caribbean, and Africa. Rose was one of the few calypsonians of her generation to enjoy success outside the Caribbean and its immigrant communities in North America and England (Kitchener and Sparrow being the most notable others). Throughout her long career she has been an outspoken advocate for women in calypso and soca.

Rose made a number of recordings with Pelham Goddard for Rawlston Charles's Brooklyn label in the late 1970s, but by the 1980s was working primarily with Granville Straker with Frankie as her arranger. Together they produced eight albums and a number of singles between 1981 and 1989. Rose continued to record and tour internationally for decades, writing over 800 songs and recording two dozen albums.

In 2016, at the age of seventy-six, Rose's career was rejuvenated with the release of her album *Far from Home* with French singer Manu Chao. The recording won the World Music Album of the Year award from the Victoire de la Musique, the French equivalent of an American Grammy. In 2019 she released "Young Boy" with Trinidad star Machel Montano, and that year became the first calypsonian, and the oldest artist, to perform at California's celebrated Coachella Music Festival. Lewis has won numerous awards for her art and cultural advocacy, including the 2013 lifetime achievement award from the Consulate General of Trinidad and Tobago in New York.[2]

Frankie on Calypso Rose

RA: It's safe to say that Calypso Rose was the greatest female calypsonian of her generation, probably the greatest of all time. When did you first meet her?

FM: Believe it or not, I first heard Rose sing when I was around twelve years old. My family was at a music festival on Union Island (one of the Grenadines, just south of Saint Vincent) where my father was the District Officer at the time. He put together a little pick-up band with guitars and drums to accompany her. I recall it was outdoors, we were all sitting on the grass in front of a small stage. There was no sound system or amplification of any kind, just these guitars and Rose singing. It was so natural, so beautiful! Rose's voice could really carry. I was impressed with how effortlessly she established rapport with the audience—everyone sang along because they knew her songs.

RA: Sounds like she left quite an impression on you as a youngster. How did you finally connect with her?

FM: Years later in Brooklyn I was introduced to Rose through Straker. He called me up, said he wanted me to do some arranging for Calypso Rose, and he would be sending her by the house. I recall that on occasion she would come by with her guitar and sing for me. Other times she would just drop off a cassette of her new songs.

RA: What was so special about Rose, from your perspective as an arranger?

FM: First of all, Rose wrote all her own songs, unlike some of the calypsonians I worked with. She always knew which key she wanted and was very congenial and accommodating. Most of her melodies were built around the basic triadic I-IV-V chords, but occasionally I was able to expand the harmonic vocabulary. She had a very strong, clear voice in the mid to higher registers, and she could really project, both live and in the studio. In the final mixing sessions, no instruments ever intruded on her voice, it was never lost, she was clear as a bell.

RA: You and Rose worked on eight albums for Straker during the 1980s. Tell me about a few of your favorite arrangements.

"No Mister" (Straker's Records, 1986)

FM: One Rose song that really stands out for me, and one of her most popular, was "No Mister," from the *Stepping Out* LP. The story line was about this sweet-talking East Indian taxi driver who tries to pick her up and allegedly take her home to meet his family—his Mammy, Pappi, Tantie, and all. But Rose would have none of it, suspecting that he had other things in mind, and rebuffed him with the choral refrain "No mister, no mister." A number of Rose's songs dealt with these sorts of male/female tensions, the battle of the sexes you might say. Her strong female protagonists usually gained the upper hand and persevered. I believe that was part of Rose's appeal: she provided a counterpoint to the boasting, macho-male calypsonians by singing the story from a woman's perspective.

RA: Your arrangement brings in some unusual chords and scales—that is, not the sort of sounds one would expect from a standard calypso or soca song. What inspired that?

FM: The band chorus to "No Mister" is particularly interesting because I attempted to incorporate East Indian–sounding elements into the arrangement. That was something I rarely did, despite my own Indo-Asian heritage, but in this case, it seemed particularly appropriate, given the characters in the story. Now, I hadn't listened to too much Indian music, but I thought that using a big glissando on the synthesizer might create the fitting effect—you get that by running your hand up the keyboard before landing on the main note (you can hear this at 0:16 and again at 0:31 on the recording). The horns join in at the end with a sharp attack on the final target note that the glissando is headed for. The main horn line was taken from the melody of her vocal chorus refrain, "No mister, no mister." When you put it all together its sounds very dramatic, and I think I had heard something like this in an Indian song somewhere. In addition to the glissando, I used the notes of a harmonic minor scale on my synthesizer fills (3:45) and a final solo (5:58). Many Western listeners associate the harmonic minor with Oriental or Asian music, and it provided quite a contrast to the major scales and chords heard throughout the rest of the piece. There was nothing in Rose's melody that was noticeably East Indian, and, I should point out that I was simply trying to catch the overall spirit of that music. I wasn't necessarily using genuine ragas or anything like that.

RA: In addition to the glissando runs, your synth and horn lines are very distinct. Where did they come from, and how did you envision them fitting into the whole arrangement?

FM: I ended up composing two synthesizer lines (labelled A and B) with "No mister" horn responses and then repeating everything, so the introductory band chorus had an ABAB structure. That band chorus would appear three more times, followed by a tag that included my harmonic minor improvisations. Rose didn't ad-lib on the tag, which gave me room to throw in that Indian-flavored synthesizer solo.

RA: Yes, those harmonic minor synth parts do stand out, but also the horns figure prominently in your arrangement.

FM: The whole song cycled around the I-V chords, so in order to distinguish the vocal chorus from the verse I added several sharp horn hits behind her voice in the opening measures of the chorus. Then I brought the horns back in hard to double her voice on the song's "No mister, no mister" hook. That added another layer of sound and an energetic push to the chorus. And of course, it hammered home Rose's point: no thanks mister—leave me alone! Interestingly this was some thirty years before the "Me Too" movement, so Rose was definitely ahead of things.

"Side Man Sweet" (Straker's Records, 1987)

RA: Rose certainly dealt head on with themes about the battle of the sexes, that's for sure. Nor did she shy away from controversial themes such as female sexual infidelity. I'm thinking about her popular song "Side Man Sweet." What can you say about that one?

FM: "Side Man" was a humorous warning to men to not neglect their wives lest they get lonely and look for favors from another man. My arrangement had a more traditional calypso feel, taken at a moderate tempo with a full horn section employing extended chords for lots of color. The basic chord progression for the instrumental band chorus was another II-V-I-VI (Bbm-Eb-Ab-Fm7 in the key of Ab major) variation of the standard I-VI-II-V progression with substitutions.

RA: Yes, this one has a more swinging, jazzy feel. The saxophone line is very cool and sensual. What was going on musically?

FM: Glad you mentioned the saxophone—that was Jean Jefferson, playing a line he came up with in the studio. He was Panamanian, and well versed in jazz and Latin music as well as calypso. The opening band chorus was built around a four-measure riff by the full horn section, followed by four measures of his smooth, melancholy saxophone. The band chorus culminated with a sharp horn stab that set up Rose's vocal entry. She sang a series of four verses and choruses, listing a litany of the side man's talents ("Who sit in your chair and drinking your beer? Side man! / Who dipping his pen in the ink? Side man! / Who feed the pussy cat milk? Side man!"), each followed by the original band chorus.

RA: Again, the supporting horns really add to the arrangement. Can you explain?

FM: On this arrangement I used the horns on the chorus for two different effects. They doubled the vocal chorus "Side Man" (0:45 and 0:49; again at 1:41 and 1:45), giving weight and emphasizing the vocal hook, the response to Rose's rhetorical questions about who could best satisfy a women's needs. Then the horns responded to the final refrains "Side Man Sweet" with short figures (0:56, 0:59; again at 1:52, 1:54) to fill in empty space and evoke a sense of connectedness between the vocal and instrumental lines.

RA: Jean Jefferson's sax comes back near the end on the tag, was that planned?

FM: Not really. For some reason Rose did not ad-lib in the tag, so I set up a chord sequence conducive to jazz-styled soloing and then brought in Jean's alto sax to fill out the last minute and a half of the recording. It's a wonderful solo, effortlessly laid back, fitting perfectly with the mood of the song. It was a bit unusual to include such a lengthy solo and I'm grateful that Straker left it in the final mix. As for Rose, she was very open-minded, and seemed to appreciate the instrumental solos I brought to some of our arrangements.

RA: Rose is known for her Carnival party and male/female themed songs, but she also had a keen sense of history and heritage.

FM: Absolutely! "Leh We Punta," for example, was a song she wrote in honor of the Garifuna. That one resonated with me, because the Garifuna, the mixed-race Carib/African people, had been in Saint Vincent for a period before they were exiled to Central America in the late 1700s by the British and eventually settled in what today is Belize. After she brought the song to me, I contacted Felix Miranda, President of New York's Garifuna Chapter, and he shared a 1970s video of a Garifuna dance in Belize. That was when I realized that the beat to the punta drum-dance was quite similar to that of soca. I incorporated a few of the punta rhythms into song's percussion break (2:20–2:50), playing them myself on a Linn drum machine of all things!

"Back to Africa" (Straker's Records, 1983)

RA: How about "Back to Africa," from your LP *Rose Goes Soca Unlimited*. That one was certainly in the heritage and ancestry vein.

FM: Good example. Rose's lyrics proclaim her allegiance to Africa and her desire to return to "me country . . . the rightful land of the Black mother." That was a growing sentiment among many musicians back then.

RA: Interesting. Now, while "No Mister" was pure soca and "Side Man Sweet" was more of a traditional calypso, "Back to Africa" had a distinctive Jamaican reggae feel, am I right?

FM: Yes, Rose and other calypsonians occasionally dabbled in reggae influenced songs. "Back to Africa" was slow, with a heavy bass line interlocking with the off-beat reggae guitar accents, rocking back and forth between the tonic and the flat seven major chords (D-C-D-C). I was aiming for a classic, cool reggae vibe, although I'm not sure now authentic Jamaican listeners might have found it.

RA: The chorus is quite sweet, even majestic.

FM: Yes, on the chorus Rose extended her vocal phrases, giving the song a Negro spiritual sort of quality, as Bob Marley was apt to do on his best songs. I held off on the horns during the introduction and vocal verse to maintain the reggae feel, but on the chorus, I used three fanfare-like horn figures for drama between her first three lines: "I want to go" / horn fanfare (0:48) / "but the land too far" / horn fanfare (0:50 / "I want to go" / horn fanfare (0:53). A series of punchy, six-beat synthesizer/bass hits, a common reggae riff, signaled the end of the chorus as Rose intoned "I want to go" / synth-bass hits / "Back to Africa" / synth-bass hits (1:06).

RA: This one includes several instrumental solos. What was your thinking there?

FM: As I said, Rose was usually supportive of my desire to break things up with instrumental interludes in addition to the band chorus and repetitive vocal refrains, especially in the tag. With that in mind I called for a tenor sax break in between Rose's second and third verses. The final tag included a muted trombone solo and a trumpet solo and a brief return of the saxophone, all while Rose ad-libbed. Those plaintive solos, sounding over the rocking tonic and flatted seven chords, evoked a feeling of longing that was, to my ear, in keeping with the singer's lament over being stranded far away from her homeland.

Rose moved on to work with other arrangers in the 1990s and beyond. Her recent work with Manu Chao and Machel Montano has brought her, and calypso, some serious recognition outside the Caribbean. She's always been an international ambassador for the music, and I was honored to work with her.

Kevin "Mighty Duke" Pope

Lem's Records, 1987.

Kelvin "Mighty Duke" Pope occupies a special place in Trinidad's pantheon of esteemed calypsonians. Duke possessed a distinctive voice, a charismatic stage presence, and an ability to compose sophisticated songs that blended humor, love, and politics. In his eulogy to Duke's passing in 2009, Chalkdust eloquently described the singer as "a noble soul who lived, ate, and slept calypso daily, and who within the seventy-six years he spent on this earth contributed immensely to the world of calypso and calypso music."

Duke was born in 1932 in Point Fortin, an industrial town located in the heart of south Trinidad's oil industry. Two years after his birth, his parents returned the family to their native Saint Vincent, where he spent his childhood. As a teenager he moved back to south Trinidad, finished school, served as a pupil-teacher, and eventually took a job with the Shell Oil Company. But his love of calypso drew him to the Southern Brigade Calypso Tent in San Fernando and to victories in the Calypso South Crown competitions of 1959 and 1960. He left his job with Shell to pursue a full-time career as a calypso singer and composer, moving to Port of Spain in 1964 to perform in Sparrow's Original Young Brigade tent. In 1968 he captured his first Calypso Monarch

Crown with "What is Calypso?," a tribute to the music that he described as "a feeling that comes from deep within / a tale of joy or one of suffering / an editorial of a song of the life that we undergo / that, and only that I know, is true calypso." He went on to take the Calypso Monarch crown in 1969, 1970, and 1971, distinguishing himself as the only singer to win four consecutive titles. Duke carved out a successful touring career in the 1970s and 1980s, singing throughout the Caribbean, North America, Europe, and Africa. He relocated to Brooklyn for a period during the 1980s, where he recorded and began his long association with Frankie.

Known for his sharp wit and biting social commentary, Duke's most poignant calypsos dove deep into Black consciousness and the struggles of African people around the world. The names of some of his most successful compositions reflect his steadfast commitment to music and activism: "Black is Beautiful," "Brotherhood of Man," "Teach the Children," "Martin Luther King Day," "Apartheid," "South Africa Must Be Free," "Tribal Wars," and "How Many More Must Die?" The last won the Sunshine Award for Best Social Commentary Calypso in 1989.

Later in his career, Duke embraced the new soca sound, showing his versatility by penning wine and dance songs including the popular "Is Thunder," "Total Disorder," and "Soca Have Meh Tu Tul Bey." "Thunder," arranged by Frankie, won the 1987 Trinidad Road March. A highly skilled songwriter, Duke occasionally composed calypsos for Lord Nelson, Lord Shorty, and others.

During his fifty-year career Duke recorded more than two dozen albums and scores of singles. His earliest releases were on Trinidad-based labels, working with arrangers Clive Bradley, Ed Watson, Ron Berridge, and Art De Coteau. By the late 1970s he was cycling in and out of New York where he recorded for Camille Hodges's Camille Records, and eventually for Straker's, Charlie's, Lem's, B's, and J&W Records. Although he jumped from label to label in the 1980s and 1990s, Frankie was clearly his preferred arranger during that period. Together they produced more than a dozen LPs, beginning with *Carnival Anniversary* (Straker's Records, 1983) and continuing up through a series of CDs they recorded for Eddy Grant's Ice label from 1994 through 1999.

In addition to his Calypso Monarch and Road March awards, Duke received the Silver Hummingbird Medal in 1970 for his contributions to calypso. In 2006 he was inducted into the Sunshine Hall of Fame in honor of his lifetime accomplishments in promoting Caribbean culture.[3]

Frankie on Duke

RA: How did you hook up with Duke? I know he was born in Trinidad, but didn't he grow up in Saint Vincent?

FM: Indeed, he did. You see his parents were Vincentian, and had moved to Trinidad, where he was born. Then his family moved back to Saint Vincent when he was only two, and he grew up there until he returned to Trinidad as a teenager. In fact, that would later cause some controversy. After he won the Trinidad calypso crown four years in a row, his Vincentian parentage was revealed in the Trinidad papers, and I believe that worked against him in future contests.

RA: Did you finally meet him up here in Brooklyn for the first time?

FM: Yes, and not surprisingly it was Straker who brought us together. He loved making those Saint Vincent/Brooklyn connections. By the time I started working with Duke in the early 1980s, he was already quite famous, known especially for his political message songs.

RA: What were your first impressions?

FM: Duke was a tall, handsome, imposing figure on stage, and fans really responded to his live performances. Duke had a very distinct voice—he sang in a resonate, warm baritone that was sweet, smooth, and soulful. The melodies Duke wrote tended to be very lyrical and flowing, but there was sometimes an unevenness in his vocal phrasing—on occasion he instinctively added extra beats to the standard eight- or sixteen-bar structure of a verse or chorus.

RA: Do you think that was on purpose? Can you give an example?

FM: Sure, listen to our arrangement of "Tribal Wars"; he added two extra beats to the second phrase of the chorus ("we still fighting tribal wars"), which resulted in an eighteen-beat structure (4-6-4-4), rather than the conventional sixteen beats (4-4-4-4). In some cases, I was able to get him to cut off the extra two beats so everything would be in 4/4, common time. But I was not always successful. For "Tribal Wars" I tried to make an adjustment to sixteen beats, but Duke would always revert back to the original, so I finally went with his eighteen-beat chorus, because that seemed comfortable to him.

RA: How did you feel about that, trying (and failing) to get Duke to conform to a sixteen-beat standard?

FM: You know, sometimes I felt guilty with singers like Duke, trying to force their songs into some sort of a duple-meter box. I believe there may have been something deeper going on, possibly going back to our African and Caribbean rhythms and speech. The way we phrase things is not so cut and dry, not always in straight four- or eight-measure phrases, so you need to make allowances for those extra beats and accents. Employing what we might call "uneven beats" by European standards is sometimes an African way of doing things, because African musicians use all sorts of multiple rhythms and meters. So, this might have been something deep in Duke, some ancestral thing, that was coming out as these extra notes, and I tried to respect and accommodate that in my arrangements when I could.

RA: Duke could sing in a number of styles, including R&B. That was part of his appeal, don't you think?

FM: Of course. Duke was a versatile singer and composer. He could write down-home calypsos, but he also had the talent to compose what you might call crossover type songs that had potential outside the Caribbean. "Love Me All Over," one of the first songs I arranged with him for Straker in 1983, was a love song with a pronounced two/four accented beat and a crooning, R&B feel to the chorus—it was certainly not a standard Carnival song. On "DJ Honeyneedle," also from that first album, he vocally mimicked that repetitive cutting technique of a DJ dropping the needle over and over again on a single phrase ("gimmie, gimmie, gimmie . . ."). In addition to his traditional calypso and pop songs, he was starting to transition to soca when I met him in the early 1980s. Our recordings of "Is Thunder" and "Total Disorder" became classic soca hits.

RA: And how about his message songs? He seemed deeply committed to social justice for African people on a global scale.

FM: Oh yes, Duke was very conscious of the Black condition and his African heritage. We worked on the songs "MLK Day," "Apartheid," "How Many More Must Die," and "South Africa Must be Free." The ones referencing South Africa were particularly powerful, given the situation in the 1980s when musicians were becoming increasingly active in the anti-apartheid movement. In fact, when apartheid fell and Mandela came into power, the African National Congress invited Duke to South Africa to sing for the celebrations, based on his years of support for the movement over the years.

"How Many More Must Die" (Straker's Records, 1986)

RA: Now tell me about "How Many More Must Die." You arranged that song with him for Straker in 1986.

FM: That was one of his most popular South African songs. The chorus, "How many more must die, before they set South Africa free?" really rang out like an anthem that invited listeners to sing along and join the movement. I harmonized his melody with elementary I-IV-V triads—nothing jazzy, I wanted it to sound more like a hymn. My band chorus opened with a forceful, full horn theme taken right from the vocal chorus, giving listeners a preview of the song's main hook. I used the horns sparingly throughout the verses, adding short figures to complete his vocal lines. The vocal chorus repeatedly delivered the lyrical message and could stand on its own without additional instrumental embellishment, but on the final "How Many More Must Die" refrain I decided to bring back the horns for extra impact. On top of that was another sax improvisation by Jean Jefferson, but unfortunately you only hear a few measures of it because the engineer faded the mix at that point.

RA: Now Duke eventually left Straker, and around that time was really starting to embrace the soca style. What happened?

FM: I arranged four albums for Duke on Straker's label, but for some reason in 1987 he decided to switch over to another Brooklyn label, Lem's Records. I imagine it was financial, because this fellow Lemon, who also happened to be a Vincentian, paid artists top dollar. One year I remember he chartered a plane and flew a bunch of singers and musicians to Saint Vincent for Carnival—he paid all the travel and accommodation expenses. It was wonderful for the artists but it must have cost him a fortune! In fact, his label didn't last long because he wasn't the best businessman, but that's another story. The point is Duke was very loyal to me. Over the years he recorded for Starker, Charlie, Lem's, J&W, and Ice Records, but he always wanted me as his arranger.

"Is Thunder" (Lem's Records, 1987)

RA: Let's talk about his 1987 recording "Is Thunder" for Lem's Records. That was your most popular song with him, winning the Trinidad 1987 Road March.

FM: "Thunder" was a classic male bravado song, with Duke boasting how he would deliver "thunder" to his sweetheart for the "whole night." With that in mind I was aiming for a raucous feel to the arrangement with a strong, dance-friendly beat. The song was built around a simple V-IV-I major chord sequence (D-C-G in the key of G). The band chorus was a series of call and responses between the brass and reeds followed by all the horns coming together for a series of final riffs to set up the first vocal verse.

RA: Duke's verses are a little irregular on "Thunder," right? I guess this was another case of him not conforming to the standard thirty-two-beat structure. And the vocal chorus was sectional?

FM: Right on both counts. His verse was a little unusual because it was organized into an irregular, thirty-beat structure (for example between 0:32–0:43), rather than the conventional eight measure, thirty-two-beat verse structure. The vocal chorus took on an A/B/A form, with and A section anchored by a "Whole night" refrain; a B section with an "Is thunder, I giving you thunder" refrain; and finally returning to the "Whole night" A refrain. We used the sectionalized verse and chorus to break up the monotonous chord loop. Duke did that often—he liked to vary things, and as long as the parts fit together (which they almost always did), it made his songs more interesting and artistic to my ear.

Speaking of variation, I inserted several brief synthesizer improvs to break up the vocal and instrumental sections. The final tag combined more synth improvs, vocal refrains, Duke's ad-libs, and a closing horn line. Again, the underlying chords were simple and repetitive, but I aimed to create variety with the superimposed horn figures and synth solos.

"Total Disorder" (JW Productions, 1989)

RA: Another popular song you did with Duke, and one of my favorites, was "Total Disorder." It's got some quirky-sounding synthesizer and an incredible hook for dancing. How did that come about?

FM: We recorded at Platinum Factory for JW Productions. I remember that they had a D-50 Roland synthesizer that had a heavy decay and an "orchestra hit" patch that fit into the arrangement. "Disorder" was a classic Carnival jump up, a real wild dance piece. In the tag Duke and the female chorus command listeners to "jump, jump, jump, jump / jump, jump, jump, jump."

"Disorder" opened with Duke yelling "Boyyay" over a bouncy unison synth/bass figure. The synthesizer patch produced an exotic pan-pipe sound with a decay effect. The band chorus consisted of a series of short riffs by the brass, synth, and reeds, culminating with a synth line followed by a full brass/reed response. As in "Thunder," Duke broke up the simple I-V chord progression, this time with a "Is total disorder / with the social order" vocal line built on a rising melodic phrase that he tagged onto both the verse (at 1:08) and the chorus (at 1:30). This necessitated an ascending chord progression (E♭-Fm-Gm-A♭), creating a sense of expectation and building toward the climactic "Blow your brains out" chorus.

RA: The tag really cooks. What did you do there?

FM: I broke up the verse/chorus structure with an initial tag/interlude that began with Duke ad-libbing over the female chorus refrain "Party like you're mad," followed by a full horn line ending on a descending major scale.

That simple but distinctive line really drove the song and I would return to it later. The final tag began with a percussion break under the female chorus "Let me see you getting down." The energy built as the chorus switched to the "Jump up! / Jump up!" and then "jump jump jump jump / jump jump jump jump" refrain following the earlier descending horn figures. After one more synth interlude and horn line, the "Jump up" refrain with descending horns returned for a final reprise and fade out.

RA: That "Jump up" horn and vocal section was a powerful figure that served as a memorable hook. Can you explain in more detail what was going on?

FM: It was a four-measure figure. The first two measures (eight beats) consisted of a quick, ascending chromatic hit (Jump-up/rest/rest/rest at 5:22) that were repeated (Jump-up/rest/rest/rest), followed by two measures (eight beats) of a descending major scale (at 5:25) with "jump jump jump jump / jump jump jump jump" vocals. The horns and voices were in unison for maximum strength, and the ascending and descending movement of the lines created a sense of balance.

RA: Did you or Duke come up with those catchy "Jump up" vocal lines?

FM: Ha, the way that came about is a great example of arrangers creating things and not receiving ample credit. I composed that line specifically for the horns and we recorded it at the horn session. Then, at the next vocal recording session, the singers came in, heard that horn line, and put the "Jump Up / jump, jump" lyrics to the instrumental line. I don't know specifically whose idea it was, but it was either Duke or one of the backup singers at the vocal session. It was spontaneous and that sort of thing happened often—singers would add words to the horn lines I wrote and I didn't know about it until the record came out! But yes, it turned out to be a very effective hook.

RA: Now you did some sessions for Eddy Grant's Ice label in the 1990s. How did that come about?

FM: Well, Eddy was successful with big hits in the UK, and he bought this beautiful old colonial compound in Barbados. He built a state-of-the-art studio on site where a lot of the top calypso and soca singers recorded in the 1990s. Eddy wanted to arrange Duke's music himself, but Duke insisted on using me, so I was flown in for several sessions. He brought in Roy Cape's horn section, so I had a band of Trinidad's top players to work with. But I didn't think that Eddy's production ideas worked very well with Duke—his final mixes lacked some essential element that animated Caribbean audiences. I think he was aiming for a more pop sound, and failed to capture the drive and spirit of what Duke's music was about. The first CD we did, *Mask*, had some good material, but yielded no hits for Duke. But those were memorable sessions for me, playing and communing with Duke, Roy Cape, and those other musicians at Eddy's place in a beautiful Caribbean setting. I should add that I admired the fact that Eddy Grant, a Black Caribbean artist, felt the need to reinvigorate our culture. Rose, Sparrow, Kitchener, Lion, Super Blue, and others were on his label in the 1990s. Although Duke didn't fare well with hits, others on his ICE label did.

Mighty Explainer

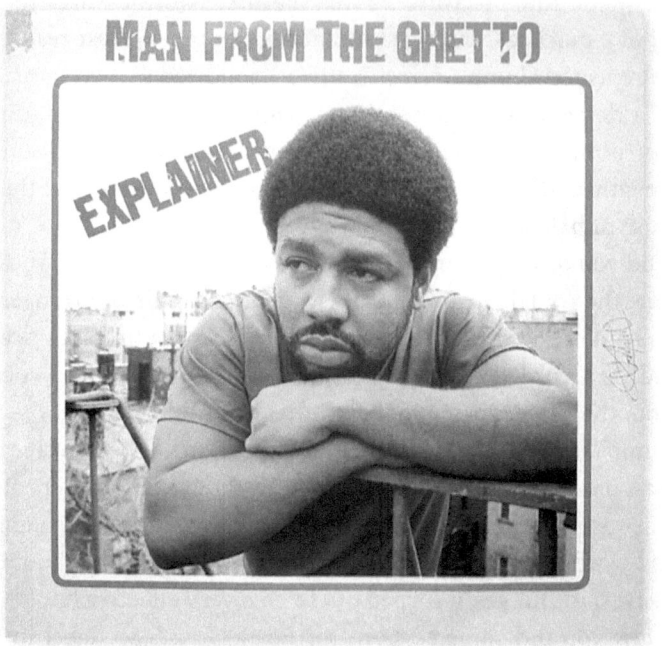

Charlie's Records, 1981.

The Mighty Explainer (1947–2022) was one of Trinidad's best-known calypsonians of the 1980s and 1990s. Born Winston Henry in the East Dry River section of Port of Spain, he attended Calvary Roman Catholic School and worked as a welder with the Public Transport Service Corporation for eight years. He began composing calypso songs at age sixteen, and at the prompting of two older calypsonians, Valentio and Prowler, he decided to leave the welding business and pursue a career in music. At their suggestion he took the stage name Explainer, and in 1970 he made his professional singing debut in Lord Kitchener's Review. He went on to perform in the Original Young Brigade tent around 1975, and eventually toured the Caribbean as part of

Sparrow's entourage. Explainer began recording for local Trinidad labels with arrangers Ed Watson and Earl Rodney, and in 1979 released the LP *Positive Vibrations* with arranger Godwin Bowen for the UK company Semp Records.

In 1980 Explainer's career got a boost when he traveled to New York and began recording for Rawlston Charles in Brooklyn. His first release for Charles, the LP *One Day*, included the popular "Ras Mas," a song that took him to the 1981 Calypso Monarch finals and that placed third in the Road March competition. That year he met Frankie, and over the next decade the two would collaborate on ten albums for Charlie's and B's Records. Their first LP, *Man from the Ghetto* (1981), included his biggest hit, "Lorraine." The song, recounting Explainer's longing to return to Trinidad for Carnival but regretting leaving his sweetheart in New York, was tremendously popular in Trinidad and Brooklyn, and rose to the #48 spot on the UK national pop singles charts that year. "Lorraine" demonstrated Explainer's stylistic flexibility, which allowed him to comfortably fuse calypso and soca with elements of rock and pop music.

Although he never won a Road March or Calypso Monarch title, Explainer was extremely popular in Trinidad, placing among the leaders of the Calypso Monarch competition throughout the 1980s and early 1990s ("Lorraine" came in a close second in 1982, just behind Scrunter's "The Will"). Like many calypsonians of that era, he was a transnational artist, splitting his time between New York and Trinidad and touring frequently in the UK. Throughout the 1980s he spent six months of the year living with his cousin in St. Albans, Queens. He recorded with Frankie, and with the help of Rawlston Charles was able to book shows in Brooklyn and Manhattan, while occasionally traveling to Boston, Baltimore, and Washington, DC, to perform. He would return to Trinidad for an extended Carnival season to sing in the tents and to compete in the Monarch competition. Explainer's passing in October 2022 was mourned by fans around the calypso world.[4]

Frankie on Explainer

RA: Explainer had been working with the arranger Godwin Bowen in the late 1970s. How did you get hooked up with him?

FM: Rawlston Charles was the one who first introduced me to Explainer. He needed someone to arrange a batch of new songs for his next album, what would become the *Man from the Ghetto* LP. I believe that was sometime in 1981. Yes, Explainer had been working with Godwin Bowen, an arranger who also who played piano in Sparrow's Troubadour band. He was a talented musician and his arrangements of "Strings" and "Monarchy" for Explainer are two of my all-time favorites. Explainer and Godwin had a big hit with "Ras Mas" from an earlier album with Charlie, so by the time I got together with him he already had a name in Trinidad and New York. I suppose Explainer's choice to leave Bowen and work with me was due in part to his desire to do his recordings here in New York, a decision no doubt prompted by Charlie. By that time Explainer was spending a good deal of time up here, staying with family in Queens, while Bowen still resided in Trinidad. This was part of a trend, as big-name calypsonians were coming to New York to record back in the early 1980s. In any case, working with a Brooklyn-based arranger was more convenient for Explainer and Charlie, and it certainly worked out for me.

RA: Explainer was a versatile singer. Did he write all his own material?

FM: Well, certainly not all of it. I believe Explainer got most of his songs from other sources, from other songwriters. He once admitted to me that the calypsonian Joker wrote some of them, and there were no doubt others. As a result of these multiple writers, his styles were quite diverse—some of the songs sounded more pop, some in a dance soca vein, and a few in a more traditional calypso style. Even within those broad categories there was a good deal of diversity, which posed a challenge for me as an arranger. Sometimes it felt like I was working with five different artists on a single album, each with his own style, and I had to figure out the right musical accompaniment for each. But I understood, because his versatility was part of his appeal.

"Lorraine" (Charlie's Records, 1981)

RA: Let's talk about his most important song, "Lorraine." How much did you have to do with that one?

FM: After I agreed to take on the project, Explainer came to my house with about ten songs and we had to whittle the number down to seven or eight. He wasn't wild about the one called "Lorraine" at first, and it initially got placed on the chopping block. But when I started to listen to it closely, I realized its potential, and advised him to keep it and let me work it up. He agreed, and it turned out that "Lorraine" was his biggest hit in New York, Trinidad, London, and all over.

RA: What was the recording session with Explainer like? This was one of your first ventures with Charlie. Did he bring in the musicians or was that up to you?

FM: For the *Man from the Ghetto* session, I called on many of the Equitables musicians I'd worked with for Straker. It was a pretty international cast, with Trinidad expatriates Jeff Medina and JR. Wharwood on guitars, Dennis Wilkinson and Jude Bethel on saxophones, along with trumpeters Ray Maldonado from Puerto Rico and Stanton Davis, a native New Yorker. I believe the Trinidadian calypsonian Defosto played trombone on that session. That gave me five horns for a full sound.

I remember a strange thing happened when we went into the Platinum Studios to record Explainer's songs. As we got ready to play, all of the musicians discovered they had oil on their hands. It turned out that Explainer believed in the traditional African Shango religious spirits, and he had this special oil that he wanted us all to wear to ensure we would play at our best and the songs would all be hits. So, he put the oil on his hand and shook with each of us before we started. When we realized what was going on we said it wasn't cool, because oil was slippery and it made it harder to play. He said he understood, so the next year he didn't shake hands but instead put oil on the studio doorknob. That was Explainer!

RA: Well, I guess he trusted in the Shango spirits. Now tell me about your arrangement for "Lorraine."

FM: I decided to try a slightly different chord sequence for the accompaniment to give the song a bit more dramatic depth. I went with a I-V-♭VII-IV chord sequence, something you might expect to hear in an American or British pop song rather than a calypso. The initial move from the I (C) down to the V (G), and then from the ♭VII (B♭) down to the IV (F), created a sense of descending motion, which in turn evoked an unresolved tension in keeping with the singer's dilemma of yearning to return home but not wanting to leave his lover. The horn lines that first appear under Explainer's cry for a taxi followed that basic harmonic structure. The figures were built around a call and response between the low reeds doubled with bass, voiced against the full horn section with heavy brass. These were all my inventions; they did not come from Explainer's original verse or chorus melodies. As a matter of fact, Explainer always encouraged me to write new horn lines, especially in the tag, and sometimes he would put lyrics to them and sing them, or have the background vocalists sing them, as if he had written them himself.

I held off on the horns during the verses in order to foreground his vocals, but brought in sharp, five-note horn riffs to introduce each phrase of the vocal chorus. Those brief horn riffs really energized the chorus and pushed the song forward. In order to break up the monotony of continuous chord loop, I interspersed his vocal sections with several instrumental band choruses and synthesizer interludes. At the end of the song the female chorus chanted the names of the legendary steelbands "All Stars" and "Despers," infusing the song with the spirit of Trinidad Carnival.

RA: Why do you think "Lorraine" did so well? It even hit the pop charts in the UK.

FM: Well, even though the lyrics referenced the singer leaving Brooklyn for Trinidad Carnival, the broader theme of two lovers reluctantly parting probably appealed to wider, non-Caribbean audiences. That I-V-♭VII-IV chord progression gave the whole song a bit of a pop feel, and Explainer could articulate his words with great clarity. Those factors, along with the soulful timbre of his voice, probably explains why "Lorraine" made it to the UK pop charts. That was fairly unusual for a calypso song at that time, and spoke to Explainer's crossover potential for rock and pop audiences.

RA: Yes, I can see, or hear, that is, why British and possibly American audiences might respond well to the song. Explainer really conveyed the genuine sense of pain that lovers feel at that moment of pending separation—a deep sadness, almost in a Caribbean blues sort of way.

"Heroes" (Charlie's Records, 1982)

RA: How about "Heroes," from your *Nature* LP. That had a very different sound, almost like a patriotic anthem, but with a bit of bluesy guitar, yes?

FM: You could say that. In "Heroes" Explainer scolded Trinidadians for not paying more homage to their national heroes. It was meant for listening, not dancing, and thus was paced at a moderate tempo. The guitar on the introduction, played by Junior Wharwood, had a bluesy and mournful sound that seemed to fit the melancholy mood of the song. The whole piece was built around a basic I-IV-V chord progression with four beats per chord on the vocal verse and two beats per chord on the vocal and band choruses. Changing the pacing of the chords on the chorus added a certain urgency to the song's main message about the mistreatment of Trinidad's heroes.

RA: The introductory band chorus is quite striking, how did you come up with those figures?

FM: I opened the instrumental section on an assertive ascending line with the horns voiced in unison followed by a call-and-response figure between the lower reed and trombone voiced against the upper-register trumpets. The guitar continued to riff under the horn lines, providing an edgy contrast to the horns. Together they built up the drama for Explainer to enter with his first verse: "Trinidad is radiant / Trinidad is nice / When it comes to our heroes / we got to think twice." The female background vocalists provided a soothing layer on the vocal verses, so the horns were backgrounded for the first eight-measure section. To add a bit more textural differentiation between the vocals and the instruments, I brought the horns in more forcefully during the second eight bars (0:38), this time with a high trumpet figure followed by a low reed response. An unusual element occurred at the end of the vocal chorus, where instead of segueing directly into the instrumental band chorus, there is an elided cadence that unexpectedly extends his vocal melody, as he sang "No, no-no-no / We shouldn't treat our heroes so" (1:14). That extension added depth to his message, his plea to for recognition of Trinidad's heroes.

"Celebration" (Charlie's Records, 1989)

RA: As you said, Explainer had different types of songs—"Lorraine" had a pop feel and "Heroes" was anthem-like. But he could also do wine and wave soca songs, like "Celebration." I see that you have a coauthor credit on that one.

FM: Yes, "Celebration" was one of the few tunes that I wrote the full melody for. I came up with it one day while I was fooling around with a simple I-V progression and thinking about writing a melody that a calypsonian would like. I was considering giving it to Becket, but when I played it for Explainer he liked it, recorded it on his cassette machine, and came back a few days later with lyrics. So, we put it together.

RA: Talk about the musical arrangement if you will. The song opens with a dramatic glissando on the synthesizer followed by a punchy brass/synthesizer riff.

FM: That was to catch people's attention, to announce that something was about to happen. After running through the chords, I brought in a chugging, mambo-sounding line on the low reeds. That was to get things cooking as Explainer was ready to enter with his first verse.

RA: It sounds like the vocal verses are sectionalized. Can you explain?

FM: Each verse was sectionalized into four divisions of four measures each (AABC). During the first four measures (A), Explainer sang the initial phrase "All my friends keep telling me." That occasioned a response from the synthesizer, horns, and bass voiced together in unison. During the next four measures Explainer returned with the line "We want to see something more jumpy" (A), which was followed by a second synth/bass/horn response. Next, Explainer and the chorus sang "Celebration time" for four measures

(B), followed by a final four-measure solo vocal line, "So we can wine down" (C) that segued into the first vocal chorus. Those instrumental responses really sewed the verse together, filling in the space between his vocal lines and serving as a literal response to the lyrical request for "something more jumpy." And they gave listeners another distinct melodic line to sing (or hum) along to.

RA: How about the vocal chorus; don't I hear that mambo-sounding riff again?

FM: Right. We livened things up by bringing back the mambo figure from the instrumental introduction, but now sung by Explainer and the female chorus: "Carve it up, rope it up / with your sexy action. / Jump it up, wine your waist / with the pace of the rhythm section." He further commands his partner to "Rock, rock around the clock." Exhorting listeners to dance, and even telling them how to dance, is a common theme in soca songs, but in this instance, Explainer invoked a classic American rock and roll line from Bill Haley and the Comets.

One way I broke things up was with some new material in the second band chorus. I began with the low mambo theme on the reeds, followed by Explainer ad-libbing about taking the party to the streets. Then I introduced a set of new, rapidly descending horn lines (at 2:38). They were punchy, meant to stir things up a little. The final tag was a real mix, beginning with a percussion break, then moving to a return of the vocal chorus, and finally Explainer ad-libbing over the female chorus and horn lines.

RA: "Celebration" was not a big hit, but it has a heavy dance groove. I wonder if you were satisfied with the final arrangement?

FM: Listening back, I believe the mambo figure gave the song that strong dance groove, and the sectionalized vocal verses and choruses, along with the modifications in the band choruses, provided enough variety to counter the monotony of the two-chord loop. So, there you go Chalky and Leston Paul, "Two Chords and Frankie McIntosh." But seriously, I know I'm biased because I coauthored the tune, so I'll let listeners be the final judge.

I will say I was happy to collaborate with Explainer, and in retrospect wish I had done more with him and other calypsonians. It was gratifying to finally have coauthorship on some of the music I wrote.

Winston "Shadow" Bailey

Straker's Records, 1988.

"Shadow" is an apt moniker for the eccentric calypsonian Winston Bailey (1941–2018). In the modern Carnival world of flashy, colorful costuming, he stood out in his black cloak and wide brimmed hat, reminiscent of a traditional midnight robber character who boasted with impunity of his malevolent deeds. While songs of sensual celebration increasingly dominated the calypso stage and road contests, he wrote dark and introspective lyrics.

Born in the Belmont neighborhood of Port of Spain, Shadow was brought up by his grandparents on a farm in Tobago where his grandfather, a choir master, provided his initial singing instruction. He taught himself to play guitar, began to compose calypso songs, and at age sixteen moved back to Port of Spain. His first professional gig came as a backup singer in the famed Young Brigade calypso tent, and in 1971 he was given a slot to perform his own songs in Lord Blakie's Victory tent.

Shadow's big breakthrough came when his song "Bass Man" took Trinidad's 1974 Road March title. The quirky lyrics described the torment of a "bass man in meh head" who literally drove him into a trance—apparently a familiar experience for some of his listeners. Shadow's percussive vocal delivery, along with arranger Art De Coteau's pumped-up melodic bass and plucky electric guitar lines, were harbingers of the new soca style looming on the horizon. Granville Straker, upon hearing Shadow sing "Bass Man" in his shop, immediately recorded him, a move that propelled both Shadow's career and Straker's Brooklyn record label.

Shadow recorded for several Trinidad companies, including his own SR Records. He visited Brooklyn often to record for Straker's, Charlie's, and B's records, and was a regular at the annual Labor Day Dimanche Gras concert. During his early career he worked primarily with arranger Art De Coteau. Following the famed arranger's passing in 1987, Shadow teamed up with Frankie to produce four albums for Straker's Records. "Tension" and "Columbus Lied" were among the popular tunes they collaborated on, the latter a scathing rebuke of history's claim that the Italian explorer "discovered" America.

By the time of his passing in 2018, Shadow had recorded more than two dozen LPs in addition to over fifty singles. Despite his immense popularity in the Caribbean and New York, he only won the Trinidad Road March twice (in 1974 with "Bass Man," and in 2001 with "Stranger") and the Calypso Monarch crown once (in 2000 with "What's Wrong with Me?" and "Scratch my Back"). Over the years critics and fans have surmised that his idiosyncratic persona may have been off-putting to the judges. Fortunately, his enduring contributions to the calypso and soca world were acknowledged through the awarding of the Trinidad Hummingbird Medal for cultural achievement (2003) and an honorary doctorate from the University of the West Indies (2018).[5]

Frankie on Shadow

RA: Shadow was associated with the arranger Art De Coteau in the 1970s, and it wasn't until the late 1980s that you started working with him. Was that Straker's doing?

FM: Yes, Straker was the one who invited me to arrange for Shadow. He had the reputation for being a bit quirky, but it was Shadow, so how could I say no? Now Shadow had been working with De Coteau in Trinidad for some time, but I guess he wanted to do more recording up here so Straker suggested me. I recall that one of the first things Shadow mentioned when he came to my house was that De Coteau had told him that "if you are going to record in New York don't use anyone else than Frankie McIntosh." I certainly felt good about that, because a recommendation from Art De Coteau really meant something back then, especially when delivered by such a heralded calypsonian as Shadow.

RA: You said Shadow was a bit quirky. What was it like working with him?

FM: When Shadow arrived at my house we headed for the basement and my old acoustic piano. He was very philosophical about things—we would sit around for a while talking about life and our experiences, and then he would sing me a song or two. I would make some notes, and then we'd shoot the breeze some more. I remember he told me he once sat on a beach in Tobago, watching the sun set, and he commanded the sun not to move—and it stayed right there, or so he said. I figured okay, I should expect some deep songs here. Eventually I realized that he had a very different approach to his music, that he seemed to hear things that other calypsonians did not.

RA: Shadow has a very distinctive voice, wouldn't you agree?

FM: Absolutely. He had a rougher, more rootsy sound then most of the Trinidadian calypsonians who came up in cities like Port of Spain or Arima. Shadow attributed his personal style to growing up in Tobago, where he planted peas on a farm and listened to ritual Shango music and folk-dance songs. He also told me that he was fond of visiting mental institutions in Trinidad where he led percussion jams with the residents. Those experiences, he claimed, inspired him to write more enigmatic, introspective songs, stuff that you would just not hear from more conventional calypsonians.

"Tension" (Straker's Records, 1988)

RA: Tell me about "Tension," one of the most popular songs you arranged for him, back in 1988. I hear lots of synthesizer, but maybe no horns? That is a bit odd for a soca song from that time, no?

FM: There is an interesting story there. I came to the Platinum Studio with charts, but when Shadow started singing, there was such a vibe, such electricity, that I realized right away that my horn lines just were not going to work. They didn't live up to the presence or liveliness of what he was doing. So, I just forgot about the horn parts I had written and I used the Mirage sampler machine that had a distinctive horn patch that had previously caught my ear. As I mentioned earlier, I usually preferred live over synthesized horns, but there was something about the particular timbre of that Mirage horn patch that seemed to fit the mood of the song—the sound was a little unsettling, invoking a feeling of tension. And I could play more complicated keyboard lines with the Mirage that horn players couldn't reproduce. Shadow went into the booth, and as he was singing, I just started improvising, playing whatever came into my mind at that moment. Then we changed the ordering of the way we lay down the instrumental tracks—the Mirage-horns were done first while he was singing, and then I put down the basic keyboards and rhythm. Shadow and I were happy with the final arrangement and recording, but the only problem came afterwards. You see he had a hard time finding horn players at his shows who could perform the parts I had originally played on the Mirage. Those lines were difficult for your average horn player, sometimes they went higher or lower than the possible range of their instruments. He told me that at one gig, when he pulled out the charts for "Tension," the horn players and the keyboardist yelled "Go get Frankie to play this!"

RA: Well, I'm not surprised to hear that. Tell me about the introduction to "Tension"; there are a bunch of instrumental lines interlocking during the first thirty seconds. Were they all synthesizer generated?

FM: One guitar part, the rest were synth patches. That introduction was constructed around the additive principle. Following two measures of percussion I brought in a simple guitar line and synthesizer response that was repeated four times (a). Next, I layered in a rhythmic clavinet keyboard line (b), and then a series of brash, pentatonic (five-note) synthesizer-horn figures on the Mirage (c). I was trying to echo the feel of his pentatonic vocal lines with my instrumental responses. Then I backed off the high synthesizer phrases, repeating the earlier synthesizer/guitar figure (b) and finished with a second, jagged synthesizer-horn line on top that was derived from his vocal verse melody (d). The idea was to establish the groove, then to thicken the texture and build up the excitement before his vocal was introduced.

RA: Got it. Now, what was happening during the vocal verses?

FM: Shadow's verses were in two sections. The first was a series of four short, rhythmic, pentatonic-like vocal motives, beginning with "What's wrong with the controllers / the soca controllers?" Each vocal phrase was followed by four beats of a synthesizer fill. This was repeated four times over eight measures. The second section consisted of four more connected, lyrical phrases, starting with "I've spent restless days / and sleepless nights" over eight measures to complete the sixteen-measure vocal verse. There was a real difference in character between the way he phrased those two vocal verse sections.

RA: The chorus also sounds sectional.

FM: Yes, the vocal chorus was even more sectional with an ABCB structure. The first (A) was built around a rhythmic "Tension" vocal refrain reinforced by synthesizer/horn hits and the female chorus; the second (B) revolved around a staccato "Ease the tension" refrain by Shadow and the chorus; on the third (C) Shadow sang alone, with a more lyrical delivery, "The tension keeps rising / reaching for me head." Finally, the "Ease the tension" (B) refrain reappeared. The structure was similar to the verse—short, staccato vocalizations interrupted by longer vocal phrasings in order to create contrast.

RA: Why do you think "Tension" was popular back then? Was there something about Shadow's voice? Or was it the instrumentation, perhaps the peculiar Mirage synth sounds or the pentatonic melody?

FM: Listening again today, I think the song won so much acclaim for those reasons and more. One was the timbre of Shadow's voice—he delivered his lyrics with such a genuine sense of concern and desperation that it seemed he was on the verge of succumbing to the very tension he was singing about. Another was the variety and contrasts of vocal and instrumental elements that somehow came together in a unified manner. I'm thinking back about Shadow's initial choppy vocal lines that were followed by more legato phrases in the verse, or the contrast between his staccato "Ease the Tension" refrain (B) and his smoother delivery of the "The tension keeps rising / reaching for me head" (C) line in the vocal chorus. On my side, the jagged, pentatonic, Mirage-horn figures felt divergent from the steady groove of the introductory synthesizer, guitar, and clavinet lines that were centered in triadic harmony. That pentatonic-like scale, with all its gaps, was the foundation of much of the song's vocal melody, horn lines, and bass figures. That scale was the glue that held things together.

RA: Yes, "Tension" was a very sophisticated composition with a satisfying arrangement. I'm assuming Shadow was open to new and possibly unorthodox approaches to the music?

FM: You could get away with some more adventuresome ideas with Shadow than you could with many calypsonians. He loved what would be considered dissonant by the relatively conservative Caribbean audiences. I guess you could say it went with his persona.

RA: Can you give an example?

FM: I'm thinking about one of my wilder band choruses that appeared about halfway through his recording of the song "Tempo" (1991). The first two band choruses were tonal and partially taken from his vocal melodies. But for the third one I wrote a sharp call-and-response figure between the brass and reeds, followed by four dissonant raised-ninth horn stabs, and finally by a wavey synthesizer response, all over four measures. You can hear this at 2:39 and again at 3:55 on the recording. I wrote another set of dissonant horn lines and synthesizer runs for the tag that you can hear briefly at the end before the recording is faded out. Those were the kinds of sounds that Shadow appreciated, and thankfully Straker kept it in the final mix.

"Music Turns Me On" (Straker's Records, 1989)

RA: Tell me about "Music Turns Me On." That has to be one of the more adventuresome arrangements that you did with Shadow, or anyone for that matter. I hear a very unusual introduction and an even more unconventional band chorus toward the end of the piece.

FM: Yes, unusual and unconventional are good terms to describe the arrangement. The song was pitched in the key of E major, but instead of opening with a horn riff over a standard E major (tonic) chord progression, I decided to lead with the synthesizer and bass doubling on a descending, pentatonic figure over a C♯ minor chord (the relative minor to E). The synthesizer patch had a heavy decay that produced a slightly eerie sound, a bit like a distorted pan pipe. Then, twelve measures in, things abruptly flipped from a minor to a major (back to the key of E major) with the horns entering. You can hear this clearly at the 0:30 mark of the recording. The full-sounding live horns, voiced in major harmony, totally changed the complexion of things, providing contrast to the introductory, minor-voiced figure that emphasized the decayed timbre of the synthesizer. Finally, the live horns and synthesizer joined together for the final four measures of the introduction that led into Shadow's first vocal verse.

RA: Yes, a lot going on there. The move between major and minor was not something I would expect in a soca song from that era.

FM: That segue from minor to major was a bit jarring, but in keeping with Shadow's approach to disrupting things, it was a device to upend the listener's expectations. As an arranger that was part of my job, to provide surprises for the listeners, at least within reason. Now, those minor/major shifts were my ideas but Shadow definitely approved, in fact he never questioned any of my musical suggestions. I think we were on the same page when it came to the way my instrumental accompaniments should support the mood of his songs.

RA: How about the instrumental section that starts around four minutes in? I am not sure I would label it a band chorus—it sounds more like a chaotic jam where things became dissonant, almost atonal. What was happening?

FM: At that point I decided to try something really different with the Mirage synth. Shadow gave a yelp as the dominant major harmony turned minor and dissonant on the synthesizer (beginning around 4:10). The bass established a steady C♯ minor pedal while I superimposed a series of figures on the keyboards that resulted in a dense texture. All those figures came from the Mirage sampler, because I realized I could not get the desired sound or balance from a live horn section. I actually overdubbed three keyboard parts.

The first contributed an atmospheric ambience while sustaining the C♯ minor harmonic foundation with the bass. A second ventured in and out of that C♯ minor harmonic bed, wandering around and playing chords and figures that occasionally clashed with the bass and first keyboard. A third keyboard really took things out, playing the dissonant, synthesized horn-sounding lines, improvising around chromatically without a logical road map or apparent tonal center. I got into a zone where I wasn't sure what would happen, but always trying to create new sonorities and textures that were not tied to a single tonality. I just kept pushing until I felt things had gone far enough. Then after about forty seconds of chaos I had the harmony abruptly return to the E major tonic (4:51), while the steady rhythmic groove, anchored in triadic synthesizer lines, reemerged. I suppose I might have extended this section, but I figured I'd wandered around far enough and had better get back to the comfortable, home tonality. I needed space to get Shadow back in for his final verse that was supported by the original E-major tonal progression.

RA: So, Shadow approved?

FM: I knew that Shadow would be quite amenable to my little experiment. He was probably smoking a "spliff" and digging it the whole time I'm coming up with these synthesizer parts and trying to figure out how to dub them together. But I couldn't do that with everybody, and I realized that too much disorder and dissonance might not sit well with the Caribbean calypso and soca audiences. I knew that I had to be careful to stay within the confines of what the singers and the public would tolerate, and that sort of pressure placed constraints on my creativity, which of course was frustrating. I would have liked to do more of that sort of experimenting, but most calypsonians were not as open to such things as was Shadow. That was one of the great things about my experience working with Shadow, I wish there had been more like him!

RA: Upon further listening I think "Music Turns Me On" is one of your most experimental arrangements Do you agree?

FM: Well, I like to think of it as an example of what I mean when I speak about what calypso could be, how you can express different musical ideas under the heading of calypso. Purists might say, "Frankie's crazy, putting all those harsh sounds in there, that's not really calypso." But I'd answer, that's my calypso, and dissonance can be emotionally engaging, even beautiful, in the right context. Sometimes you have to experiment, even make mistakes, because that's the only way you'll ever progress forward to make new music. I was coming to realize that by mixing calypso with jazz I might be able to do more creative things, because a listening-jazz audience was generally more receptive to new ideas than was the dancing-soca crowd we were aiming those records at. I will talk about my pivot back to jazz in the next chapter, but as for Shadow, he certainly was not afraid to use new sounds to turn his listeners on!

RA: Your last album with Shadow was *Keep on Dancing*, in 1991. Why didn't you do more? He seemed to appreciate your more daring arrangements more than many singers did.

FM: I believe Shadow and Straker had some sort of falling out around then, and as a result he did the rest of his recording back in Trinidad. I regretted that, because he was such a brilliant and unique songwriter, and as I said, he appreciated my occasional musical excursions outside the norms of calypso arrangements. Now many people think of Shadow as this sort of madman, because of the offbeat nature of his songs and his erratic stage presence. But I knew him as a thoughtful, respectful, gentle person. I will never forget one time, it must have been the year after we made our final recording together, that I was playing keyboards with the band at a Brooklyn Museum Dimanche Gras show. And after he sang, Shadow approached me and pulled some money from his pocket and tried to give it to me. He said, "you know Frankie, the album we just did down in Trinidad this year, we used a lot of your ideas, and I just thought you should have this." I told him to put the money back in his pocket, I couldn't take a cent from him. His words of appreciation were worth so much more to me, knowing that he respected my work that much. That was the sort of deeply humane person he was, and I mourned his passing a few years ago.

One more recollection of Shadow. He made it a point to catch up with me on my subsequent visits to Trinidad. On one occasion he took me to a mountain spring where he claimed to receive his "blessings." But that account would require its own chapter.

Aldwyn "Lord Kitchener" Roberts

Charlie's Records, 1988.

Aldwyn Roberts (1922–2000), known to the calypso world as Lord Kitchener, was arguably Trinidad's most revered calypsonian of the postwar era. His influence predated the arrival of Sparrow, and his overall impact on the evolution and international popularization of Trinidadian calypso during the 1950s and 1960s was immense.

Kitchener, the son of a blacksmith, was born in the central Trinidad municipality of Arima. He taught himself guitar and began winning local Arima calypso competitions while still a teenager. In 1943 he moved to Port of Spain, where he sang at the popular Victory and House of Lords calypso tents. He eventually joined Lord Melody and Spoiler in the "Young Brigade," a group of singers who pushed to modernize calypso with jazzy, horn-driven arrangements, Latin rhythms, and an emphasis on humorous lyrics. In 1946 Roberts won the first of his eleven Road March titles with his original song "Jump in the Line."

In late 1947 Kitchener joined a wave of West Indian migrants who set sail for the United Kingdom. He stayed in England for fifteen years, carving out a successful recording career with the Melodisc and Lyragon labels and opening his own club in Manchester. In 1963 he returned to Trinidad where he dominated the Road March competition, taking ten titles between 1963 and 1976. His 1975 offering, "Tribute to Spree Simon," won the Road March and Calypso King competitions, while an arrangement of the tune by the Hatters Steelband placed first in the Panorama contest that year. Kitchener's tunes proved well suited for steelband interpretation, winning an unprecedented eighteen Panoramas between 1964 and 1997. His 1987 "Pan in A Minor," a collaboration with arranger Leston Paul and pan virtuoso Boogsie Sharpe, placed second in the 1988 Panorama, and remains one of his most beloved odes to Trinidad's steelbands.

Upon returning to Trinidad, Kitchener continued to record for the UK-based Melodisc label while entering into an arrangement with RCA records (joining Sparrow, Duke, Melody, and Belafonte on the RCA calypso roster). He released five albums and a number of singles for the US label between 1964 and 1967, further expanding his international reach.

Throughout his career, Kitchener worked with numerous Trinidad arrangers including Earl Rodney, Ron Berridge, Ed Watson, Clive Bradley, Art De Coteau, and in later years Leston Paul. Frankie arranged only one album for Kitchener. Released in 1988 on Charlie's Records under the title *The Master and the Grandmaster*, the album featured a picture of Frankie, seated and grinning at the piano, and Kitchener, the Grandmaster, singing exuberantly to the camera. The album yielded no competition winners, but "Two to Go," Kitchener's account of a pan yard rehearsal in anticipation of Panorama, was popular in Trinidad and Brooklyn.

Kitchener believed that calypso was by nature an evolving style, and he unapologetically embraced American jazz arrangements and Latin rhythms early on in his career. Singing in a warm baritone voice, he was known for his rhythmic intricacies, skillfully landing off the beat and dragging his phrases over the bar line. The jazz influence was undeniable, and he occasionally played the bass at jazz sessions in English clubs. Equally significant was his embrace of the new soca sound. His 1976 song "Sugar Bum Bum," released on Charlie's Records with an arrangement by Ed Watson, featured a catchy melodic bass pattern, airy synthesizer lines, and laid-back horns that together formed the song's primary hook. "Sugar Bum Bum" was Kitchener's best-selling song to date, and helped legitimize the emerging soca style for the calypso world in the mid-1970s (Sparrow, Rose, Melody, Duke, and other established calypsonians would soon follow his lead and pivot toward soca).

Kitchener, unlike his competitors Sparrow, Rose, and Duke, never relocated to New York, choosing rather to remain in Trinidad after his return from the UK. But his influence in the West Indian diaspora was strong. He was a frequent visitor to Brooklyn, helping to establish the popularity of the Labor Day Dimanche Gras concerts with his appearances throughout the 1970s, and recording for Charlie's, B's, and J&W Records. He also became a featured guest at the Madison Square Garden Mother's Day calypso program, and in 1971 chronicled the festivities with the calypso "Mas in Madison Square Garden," with an arrangement by Art De Coteau. The song was tremendously popular in New York and back in Trinidad, where it won the 1971 Road March.

In 1969, Kitchener was awarded Trinidad and Tobago's Humming Bird Medal for his service to the nation. In the early 1990s, fans lobbied the government to award him the Trinity Cross, the highest civilian honor. But when the officials offered him the lesser Chaconia medal he turned it down. The University of Trinidad and Tobago conferred a posthumous honorary doctorate on Roberts at their 2017 graduation ceremony.[6]

Frankie on Kitchener

RA: Was it Straker or Charlie who first hooked you up with Kitchener?

FM: I got together with Kitchener through Rawlston Charles. Kitchener was living in Trinidad at the time, but traveled regularly to New York to record and perform. I had backed him on live shows as a keyboardist, but never arranged anything for him until Charlie brought me on board. Kitchener was an amazing songwriter, to me a truly artistic composer who approached his craft in a very studied manner. I remember the first day he came to the house and sang with his guitar while I sat at the piano and plunked along. In between songs we started chatting about his time in England and how he had taken up playing the double bass at jazz jam sessions. After a while I started fooling around with this jazz standard on the piano, "How High the Moon," and sure enough, Kitchener began accompanying me on the bottom four strings of his guitar, which are tuned like an upright bass. I realized then that he had extensive experience as a jazz bassist and he knew all the chord changes.

RA: So, Kitchener was conversant in jazz?

FM: Very much so. That may have come from his time in London, where he was immersed in the worlds of calypso and jazz, playing in clubs with Caribbean jazz musicians like trumpeters Shake Keane and Harry Beckett, guitarist Fitzroy Coleman, and arranger Rupert Nurse. And that explained a lot about why his melodies were different and so much more sophisticated from those of many other calypsonians I'd worked with. He could hear notes outside the typical I-IV-V harmonic vocabulary, and wrote melodies that lent themselves to more complex chord progressions. Kitchener welcomed my efforts to sweeten the sound with colorful chords, and never tried to intervene. That was quite the opposite of Sparrow, who always was injecting ideas, but, in the end, preferred simpler, folk-like sonorities.

"Two to Go" (Charlie's Records, 1988)

RA: How did that play out in your arrangement for Kitchener's "Two to Go"?

FM: First of all, you need to understand that "Two to Go" was a real calypso, not like the simpler wine and wave soca tunes that were becoming popular by the late 1980s. Just listen to the lyrics that recounted the intensity of a steelband rehearsal two days before the big Panorama contest. Kitchener was aiming the song at older calypso and steelband folks, not necessarily a soca dancing crowd. As calypso fans know, he was highly respected in the steelband community, and many of his songs were picked up by the great pan arrangers and ended up as Panorama winners. That's probably why he decided to use a live steel pan on the recording, but I'll get to that shortly.

Kitchener's melody on "Two to Go" was quite sophisticated and adaptable to a variety of arranging possibilities. I wanted a thicker, richer horn blend, a real big band feel that called for additional horns. Fortunately, Charlie had the budget so I could hire three trumpets, a trombone, and one tenor and two alto saxophones. Part of what prompted those choices were Kitchener's earlier recordings in London where Rupert Nurse was his arranger. Nurse was quite talented at getting a big band horn sound.

RA: Seems as if you wanted a slightly older calypso, pre-soca sound for your arrangement. So how did you proceed?

FM: To kick the song off I used two keyboard figures, one on electric piano and one on a funky-sounding clavinet, interlocked with the bass and drum machine. That was to establish a groove around a simple I (D) and V (A7) chord sequence. Then I began the introductory band chorus with a series of short, bright horn riffs followed by a more lyrical figure led by the low reeds. For the end of the introduction, I wrote a three-measure transition passage (0:37–0:42) that began with the synthesizer, bass, and reeds in unison. They were joined by the high brass for a dramatic rising figure that led into Kitchener's initial verse: "Two days to go / before Panorama / When we should know / pan take over." I was consciously thinking about a figure that a panorama arranger might like for the competition when I came up with that one. In any case, the final horn-heavy transition gave the introduction a touch of a big-band feel, befitting of a Kitchener song.

RA: How did you handle the vocal verses and the chorus?

FM: The verses were in two sections. The first eight measures were major, sung over a I-IIm7-V7-I (D-Em7-A7-D) progression common to jazz and pop tunes. The second eight measures were introduced with a minor harmony (Bminor) for contrast, a testament to Kitchener's sense of balance. The rapidly changing chords on the last four measures (1:07) accelerated the harmonic pace and heightened the tension as Kitchener approached the line, "That's why you hearing the sweet, sweet pan, jammin' all over." That led to the vocal chorus and with the powerful female refrain "I jam up, I getting the pan fever / I'm feeling to ja-a-a-m up / ma-a-a-sh up."

The vocal chorus was divided into four sections. The first four measures were taken by the female chorus as outlined above, followed by Kitchener's four-bar response, "Is mas, when you be there rehearsing for the crown . . . ," sung over a descending chord progression. The initial move in that sequence, a half-step drop from the D chord down to the C♯7 chord (at 1:24 on the words "rehearsing for the crown") was highly unusual, almost unimaginable for most calypso writers, but Kitchener's melody invited that move and it worked. Meanwhile, the last four chords, sounded under him singing "prang, parang, parang, parang," were played at a pace of one beat each (at 1:28), accelerating the harmonic rhythm to energize and push the song forward. Next the female chorus returned over horn riffs for four measures. Kitchener completed the chorus by singing "And when the bass pans join me, this is how they sound," followed by a scat figure mimicking the sound of a bass steel pan run (1:44).

So, you see, Kitchener's original melody really lent itself to the sort of sophisticated harmonic accompaniment that harkens back to his earlier material, and that you rarely heard in the soca of the 1980s. But this is not surprising, because Kitchener, at heart, was really a calypso singer.

RA: You brought in a steel pan later in the arrangement. Was that you on a synth patch, or a live pan player?

FM: Well, after I had laid down the rhythm and horn tracks, Charlie set about his "producing." On my third band chorus he brought in a live steel pan for the eight opening measures. That steel pan was called back to solo for the entire tag section, beginning at just after the five-minute mark and continuing for the final three minutes of the piece—for some reason Kitchener was not brought back to ad-lib on the tag. Now the decision to use a real pan player instead of me playing a synthesized pan break was no doubt Kitchener's, and seconded by Charlie. For Kitch to use a synthesized pan in a song about a steelband rehearsal would not be well received by the Trinidad pan fraternity. I suspect in the earlier sessions we had laid down one or more solos on the synthesizer or on one of the horns as part of the tag. But Charlie took them out in the final mix and added in the live steel pan. I have to admit that acoustic pan over my funky synthesizer ostinato actually worked well—the sound was both traditional and contemporary. I'm not sure that was our intention back then, but that's how it comes across today, thirty-plus years later.

RA: I love the arrangement; it really does harken back to some of the older calypso recordings. But you mentioned you were not totally satisfied with the final mix?

FM: The problem was that all my efforts to get the proper balance for a large horn section were somewhat undermined in the final mix, which unfortunately I did not attend. The engineer had no experience mixing a horn ensemble of that size. I intended for them to blend smoothly, with the first trumpet standing out on top, the second and third trumpets at a supporting level, and a trombone on the bottom. They were too preoccupied with the sound of the bass and rhythm, and tended to overemphasize the synthesizer at the expense of the horns. I can blame myself for not being there, but having the arranger present for the final mix wasn't Charlie's modus operandi. He thought he knew his market and audience, and how to mix to get his people to dance. As I said, to my ear this wasn't your typical "bass in your face" dance song.

My disappointments regarding the mix aside, overall I was pleased with the original arrangement, certainly on paper. I was aiming for something befitting of the wonderful song Kitchener gave me, an arrangement with a big band flavor that Rupert Nurse would have approved.

RA: Any idea why you only arranged one album for Kitchener?

FM: The connection came through Charlie, and for reasons I'm not privy to, Kitchener moved on to other labels after we finished *The Master and the Grandmaster* LP. He'd been doing quite a lot of work with Ed Watson and Leston Paul prior to our project, and I think he had Leston arrange a number of his final albums in the 1990s. Both he and Leston were based in Trinidad at that point, and Leston was certainly deserving. But for me it was disappointing, because I enjoyed working with such a sophisticated songwriter.

Slinger "Mighty Sparrow" Francisco

B's Records, 1984.

Today the name Mighty Sparrow is synonymous with calypso music around the world. During his seven-decade career he recorded scores of albums, several hundred singles, won the Trinidad Calypso King Monarch title eight times, and captured the Road March seven times. Beginning in the early 1960s and continuing throughout the 1990s, Sparrow toured the globe as the leading ambassador of Caribbean calypso music.

Born Slinger Francisco in Grenada in 1935, he and his family moved to Trinidad when he was twenty-two months old, settling in the St. James neighborhood of Port of Spain. He attended Newton Boys Catholic School, where he sang in the choir. His professional career as a calypsonian began in 1954 when he appeared as "Little Sparrow" in the famed Old Brigade Tent. The following year he moved to the popular Young Brigade Tent where he performed alongside calypso luminaries Lord Melody and Growling Tiger. In 1956 he won the Road March and Calypso King title with "Jean and Dinah" (originally titled "Yankees Gone"), a jubilant song announcing the long-awaited departure of American troops from Trinidad.

Sparrow's first recordings were with the local Trinidad label Kay CRS. But it was in the late 1950s that his recording career took off when he traveled to New York and began working with RCA Records. The move broadened his international reach through the production of ten albums and several dozen singles between 1961 and 1964. Meanwhile, back in Trinidad, he helped launch the National Records Company, a label that released dozens of his songs from 1963 through 1967.

Sparrow recognized the advantages of using New York as a base for recording and international touring, and by the mid-1960s moved his operation and family to Jamaica, Queens. He retained his home in Diego Martin and remained active in Trinidad Carnival during his international tours. He became a fixture in Brooklyn's Labor Day Carnival, regularly appearing at the big Dimanche Gras show at the Brooklyn Museum. In 1969 he headlined what would become an annual Mother's Day Calypso Festival at Madison Square Garden.

One of Sparrow's performances was recorded live at Brooklyn's Blue Cornet club by Granville Straker. Released in 1970 under the title *The Best of the Mighty Sparrow*, the LP sold well and helped launch Straker's Brooklyn-based label. He would go on to record for Brooklyn labels Charlie's and B's Records. *Mighty Sparrow—25th Anniversary*, his 1980 double-album release with arranger Art De Coteau on Charlie's Records, signaled a stylistic shift from calypso to the new soca sound with heavy dance rhythms, pumped-up bass figures, and prominent synthesizer lines. In addition to his satirical calypsos addressing local Trinidad happenings and universal themes of social justice, Sparrow wrote about life in New York, bookended by his 1969 classic "Mas in Brooklyn" and his provocative 1992 "Crown Heights Justice." In "Mas" he recounted Brooklyn's early neighborhood Carnival celebrations, famously announcing "Brooklyn is Meh Home" for the newly arrived wave of West Indian immigrants. "Justice" was a plea for peace between Brooklyn's Jewish and West Indian residents following the 1991 Crown Heights riots stemming from the deaths of Gavin Cato, a Guyanese youth, and Hasidic scholar Yankel Rosenbaum.

Over the years Sparrow worked with many of Trinidad's top arrangers, including Frankie Francis, Bertram Inniss, Earl Rodney, Ed Watson, Art De Coteau, Errol Ince, and Pelham Goddard. For reasons he will explain, Frankie only recorded one LP with Sparrow, *King of the World*. Released on B's Records in 1984, the album included Sparrow's seventh and final Road March winner, "Don't Back Back."

Sparrow has received numerous awards for his work with calypso and Caribbean culture, including a 1987 Honorary Doctorate of Letters from the University of the West Indies and a 2013 lifetime achievement award from the

Consulate General of the Republic of Trinidad and Tobago in New York. In 2014 he was initiated into the Order of Trinidad and Tobago and in 2015 he was confirmed to the Order of the British Empire. But for his admirers in the Caribbean and around the world, he is simply the King of Calypso.[7]

Frankie on Sparrow

RA: Let's finish this chapter with Kitchener's main rival, the Mighty Sparrow. You only worked with him once, but with memorable results.

FM: Sparrow was one of my idols growing up. When he came to Saint Vincent, I would do anything to sneak into his show, just to witness this man on stage! If I heard a new Sparrow tune on the radio, I would run home and try to figure it out on the piano. And I loved Bertram Inniss's arrangements and piano style on those early Sparrow songs—he employed such rich sonorities and called on terrific horn players and guitarists for solos.

RA: Sparrow is something of a larger-than-life figure; what was he like to work with?

FM: I had great respect for Sparrow and still do, but I must admit he was, at times, difficult to work with. Doing anything with Sparrow was very time consuming, because he was so creative and his profusion of musical ideas were in a constant state of flux. I remember when he first came to my house and pulled these sheets of notated music and lyrics from a brief case and asked me what I thought. I inquired who had written them and did not get a satisfactory answer. Eventually he sang a few lines to me and I went to work on the arrangements as usual. But then he would call me a few days later and say "well let's try this," and then we'd get into the studio and he would want something else. So, I had to keep writing and rewriting. And when we finally got settled in the studio and ready to play, the arrangement had little bearing on what we had discussed in our first meeting.

RA: How was he in the studio?

FM: Let's just say he could be mercurial. I remember in one studio session that we were all tuned up and had a great horn sound, when suddenly Sparrow decided that the horns were out of tune. He believed he possessed such an impeccable ear that he could tell when something was sharp or flat, when no one else could. So, he ran out and got this electronic tuner, and had each musician play a note, and claimed the tuner proved he was right. But the horns didn't need to be in perfect tune according to the gradations on that sort of device. The collective ears of those highly experienced session players were far more reliable than any sort of electric tuner, at least for achieving the desired calypso and soca sound. And there was Sparrow, telling these professional players like Shake Keane that they were out of tune! He had to show that he had input on everything, so when they began playing, he immediately started to suggest changes to his own horn lines. Finally, as I recall, trumpeter Ray Maldonado intimated that Sparrow might have to use a different horn section if he could not make up his mind, since the guys didn't have all night to be subjected to his whims. Sparrow finally got the gist and he backed off a bit. And I agreed with Maldonado. After weeks of revisions, the fact that changes were still being demanded in the studio seemed to fall more in the realm of subjective indecisiveness than in creativity. Over the years I found that the best adjustments to musical arrangements usually took some sort of rational, linear path, but Sparrow's changes tended to be circular.

"Don't Back Back" (B's Records, 1987)

RA: Please back up, how did the *King of the World* album come about?

FM: Michael Gould of B's Records made the initial contact, then Sparrow called me and we set up an appointment to come over to the house.

RA: "Don't Back Back" was the most successful song on the album, winning the Trinidad Road March in 1987. Tell me about that one.

FM: "Back Back" went under constant transformation with all Sparrow's ideas. And it wasn't just the horn lines I mentioned above. I remember he was finishing up the vocal background session, something I would not normally be present at. He called me and asked if I could come in to the studio and make "one small change on this one little synthesizer line." Now, that was at 5:00 p.m. on Christmas Eve, if you can believe it! So, I took the train into Manhattan and we spent the whole night working on it. You see that "one small change" produced a multitude of ideas from Sparrow's fertile imagination. We ended up working on it all night and I did not get home until 6:00 a.m. Christmas morning. And the backup singers went through hell; he kept telling them that they were singing out of tune. That kind of attitude was pervasive throughout the whole recording project. Often his suggestions did not make much sense musically to me, but in the end the song made Road March so maybe Sparrow was right.

RA: Tell me about the music. It had a great groove and swinging horn lines. Were those yours or Sparrow's?

FM: Let's start with the lyrics. "Back Back" was a humorous song in which Sparrow, tongue-in-cheek, begs his partner not to tempt him with her sensual dancing. The song clearly demanded a strong dance beat. I opened up with a galloping band chorus with a full-horn, four-measure figure. The unison was intended as a powerful introductory statement designed to get listeners' attention. Next came a similar line on the synthesizer, followed by another horn line and synth phrase. The exchange between the horns and the synthesizer provided a change in timbre, in color. In answer to your question, most of these horn lines actually came from Sparrow, he sang them to me and listening back today I think they were effective.

RA: The chord progression was basically a simple triadic I-V loop, right? What did you and Sparrow do to liven things up?

FM: One thing was that call and response between the horns and synthesizer in the introductory band chorus to start things off with a bang. And the vocal chorus was particularly interesting, because it had four separate sections that resulted in an ABCABD form. During the first four measures, Sparrow and the chorus repeated the phrase "Don't do that" four times, each time followed by a synthesizer line to complete the melodic phrase (A). Then they sang "Don't back back on me, don't back back" twice with the voices doubled by the bass for emphasis to the vocal line (B). Sparrow specifically asked for that and it worked. Next Sparrow sang three measures alone, "Dancing with you, man you only, jammin' down se Bam Bam," again doubled by the bass (C). That was followed by a repeat of the A ("Don't do that") and B ("Don't back back") sections. During the final six-measure section of the chorus, Sparrow sang the ascending vocal line "You look so pretty / really sexy / boom-boom look so heavy jamming on mey purposely," while the underlying chords outlined a rising progression (D). That final section built up the intensity with Sparrow and his chorus finally pleading "Darling, don't do that to me." The band chorus reentered, and hopefully by that point everyone in the audience was dancing and singing along.

RA: Now you added a few synth breaks into the mix, but nothing too jazzy to my ear.

FM: First I took a short synthesizer solo to break things up toward the middle of the song. For some reason Sparrow did not ad-lib on the final tag, so I stretched out on another synthesizer improvisation over the "Don't do that" vocal riff. I tried to keep this break simple, no chromatic jazz runs or substitute chords or anything—quite a contrast to the synthesizer solos I did on the early Becket recordings! Here I was basically playing variations on Sparrow's original melody with slight ornamentations, but always sticking to the basic I-V harmonies. That was more or less in keeping with a more folk-oriented Caribbean approach to improvising, or embellishing a melody, and felt right in the musical context of the original song. Sparrow and the engineer evidently liked it and they kept it in the final mix.

RA: It sounds like doing the LP with Sparrow was stressful, despite the good outcome with "Back Back."

FM: Well, let me say this. Doing that album with Sparrow was an experience I do not regret. But there was a limit to how much I could tolerate, and afterwards I told Errol Ince, "You have more patience than I do, so you do Sparrow's arrangements and just let me play the keyboards." The next year, when Sparrow called me, I had to dream up an excuse that I could not arrange his new set of songs. But it eventually worked out. Errol Ince took over as arranger, and I played keyboards on several of Sparrow's albums going forward. I was happy with that situation, just being a sideman, getting paid, and going home. I should add that I really enjoyed playing on live gigs with Sparrow and his musicians, who were all top artists. On several occasions I had a chance to travel internationally with them—we toured to London, Ghana, Nigeria, Australia, and Japan.

Flying High with Sparrow in Ghana

RA: Tell me about your tour to Ghana. What was it like going "back to Africa" for you?

FM: Yes, that trip was especially memorable. I remember the day Sparrow called me and said "Frankie, we are going to Africa," and I said "count me in!" That was in February 2000, and the whole band departed together from New York. I recall there was Sunshine Diaz on bass, Jimmy Brown on guitar, Anthony "Bugs" Niles on drums, Charles Dougherty and Dennis Wilkinson on saxophones, Errol Ince on trumpet, and Wayne Walker on trombone. These were the top Caribbean players in New York at the time, and they'd all played with one another and backed up Sparrow beforehand, so there was really no rehearsal necessary. Sparrow had charts, so the musical end of things was easy.

We flew into Accra, Ghana, and when we emerged from customs there was this crowd of people who greeted us with a chorus of "Welcome home Brothers." Honestly, I really did feel at home, the color of the earth, and the smells, and of course lots of Black people—it felt familiar, tropical, with me coming from the Caribbean. We stayed at the Ravico Hotel in Accra.

Sparrow was not the only artist on the trip. We were all part of a tour that Mike Howard, a New York–based jazz promoter, arranged with the help of some Trinidad diplomats in Ghana. There was a jazz trio led by the

Panamanian saxophonist Carlos Garnett, and another group led by Hamiet Bluiett from the World Sax Quartet. He really played some wild stuff that was way out there, but the people responded positively to him. The whole thing was probably originally envisioned as a jazz tour, but I think the package included Sparrow at the request of the Trinidad embassy in Ghana. That gave the show a vocal component, and the people there loved him—they gave Sparrow an African name, something like "Oma-Walli."

We performed at a few theaters and hotels, mostly around Accra. We also played at an outdoor event across from the tomb of the famous African American activist W. E. B. Du Bois. That was special because we shared the stage with African groups. I remember another venue was this community hall where things turned into a jazz jam session. I sat in on piano with Carlos Garnett and some of the other musicians.

Another memorable event was when I attended a funeral wake for one of the hotel worker's grandfathers who was an eminent tribal leader. There was a band there playing African highlife music, and I could really relate to it right away, probably because it felt a bit like our calypso. When they learned there were American musicians at the gathering, they invited me to sit in with them on piano for a few songs. I picked up on the rhythm right away and felt very comfortable playing with them, even though I'd never heard those songs before. I also got a chance to play the djembe drum with a group of drummers who played outside our hotel. That was so interesting because we Caribbean musicians seemed to adapt to their polyrhythms, but the Africans had some trouble with our Caribbean *tresillo* beats.

One other thing that sticks in my memory was when Charles Dougherty and I went to the infamous Elmina Slave Castle, which was located in the fishing village of Elmina, just west of Accra. Even before we got there, I was struck by the construction of some of the mud houses in the countryside. They reminded me of things I'd seen back home. They were oval-shaped houses made of sticks and plastered over with mud. I remember seeing similar houses in the rural parts of Saint Vincent, on the windward side of the island approaching Kingstown, where they used mud and cow dung as plaster. They must have been based on African models, hundreds of years later! That was African architecture, like African music, surviving in the Caribbean. Of course!

When we reached the Slave Castle there was drumming going on way down the beach—it was this very sad, mournful sound, and one of the fellows at the castle explained it was a funeral in progress. We toured around the castle, and saw the room where they chained the kidnapped Africans who were being shipped off to the Americas, and there was the final gate they had to

Frankie with Djembe drum in Ghana (circa 2000).

pass through, called "the gate of no return." That was an intense feeling, knowing that at some point in the past, some ancestor of mine might well have passed through that gate! My Ancestry report says that much of my DNA comes from Ghana and Nigeria, so it was a real connection. And the emotion was so strong, so moving, transporting your mind back hundreds of years, to imagine what might have happened, right at that spot. I will be forever grateful to Sparrow for giving me the opportunity to go back to Africa.

CHAPTER 7

JAZZING UP CALYPSO IN THE NEW MILLENNIUM

On Thursday, 21 April 2016, Frankie's old alma mater, the Brooklyn College Conservatory of Music, hosted "An Evening of Calypso Jazz." An enthusiastic audience of students and members of the local Caribbean community crowded into the college's Whitman Hall, a popular venue for calypso shows thanks to its location in one of Brooklyn's largest West Indian neighborhoods. The program notes reminded guests of the "centuries old, ongoing dialogue between musicians from the English-speaking Caribbean and their North American counterparts," laying the foundation for "this evening's exploration of the blending of West Indian calypso and steelband music with African American jazz." In keeping with that goal, the program began with a preconcert talk, moderated by Ray, with Frankie in conversation with steel panist Garvin Blake, bassist David "Happy" Williams, and trumpeter Etienne Charles.[1] The issue of what exactly constituted "calypso jazz" was bandied about and left hanging, suggesting that perhaps that question was best answered by the music that would follow.

The Brooklyn College Conservatory Big Band, under the directorship of Arturo O'Farrill, opened the program with a hot Latin jazz piece by Dafnis Prieto. Frankie then took the stage to introduce the first calypso jazz piece of the night, his big band arrangement of Alston "Becket" Cyrus's popular calypso "Teaser." This was followed by Etienne Charles playing selections from his critically acclaimed *Culture Shock* CD, and back to Frankie's lively arrangement of "That's the Culture," a classic by Trinidadian pianist Raf Robertson.[2] The second component of the program featured a sextet led by Frankie and panist Garvin Blake, who were joined by Charles, Williams, saxophonist Charles Daugherty, and drummer Damon DueWhite. They improvised on Sparrow's classic calypso "Rose," added a calypso beat to the American pop song "For All We Know," and treated the audience to "One for Boogsie," Frankie's ode to steel pan virtuoso Lennox "Boogsie" Sharpe.[3]

The featured artists and their selections represent varied musical currents that flow together under the broad banner of "calypso jazz."[4] Frankie's aforementioned big band arrangements of calypso tunes by Becket and Robertson harkened back to the venerable calypso dance band tradition of his father's Melotones Orchestra as well as ensembles led by Bertram Inniss, John "Buddy" Williams, Frankie Francis, Ron Berridge, Syd Joe, and Lio Smith. Those bandleaders, like Frankie, borrowed freely from American big band swing in their arrangements of calypso instrumentals. Frankie's individual keyboard work in the small ensemble was in the tradition of Caribbean pianists Clive "Zanda" Alexander, Raf Robertson, and Monty Alexander, while reflecting the influences of Black American jazz greats John Lewis and McCoy Tyner. Blake's integration of the steel pan into a small jazz ensemble format can be traced to the "pan jazz" movement popularized by Rudy Smith, Boogsie Sharpe, Ray Holman, and Andy Narell. For decades Williams's lilting bass rhythms anchored dozens of American jazz ensembles looking for a little Caribbean tinge, and more recently his own calypso-flavored songs danced over jazzy voicings. Charles's efforts to resynthesize Caribbean rhythms and Carnival folk idioms with elements of modern jazz to create multi-sectional suites placed him at the forefront of a new generation of island musicians who sought to reimagine what calypso jazz might be. Worth noting is that all four were Caribbean expatriates who wrote and performed in the United States (Frankie, Blake, and Williams in New York, Charles in Florida and Michigan), underscoring the transnational dimensions of calypso jazz and the importance of Caribbean musicians working in the diaspora.

The 2016 Calypso Jazz concert is historically significant on several counts. The acceptance of jazz and world music at Brooklyn College reflects a broader trend in American higher education to recognize the value of musical traditions falling outside the realm of European art music. Indeed, such an event, sponsored under the auspicious of the Brooklyn College Conservatory of Music, would have been unimaginable back in the late 1960s when Frankie and his fellow students had to hide out in the basement of Gershwin Hall to play jazz. In retrospect, the concert was a high-water mark for global jazz at Brooklyn College, for budget cuts and faculty disagreements over curricular priorities have hampered the growth of the jazz program over the ensuing years.[5]

Brooklyn College 2016 "Calypso Jazz" Concert—Frankie, Garvin Blake, David "Happy" Williams, and Charles Daugherty. Photo by Jeff Grannum.

For our story, the 2016 concert provides a useful vantage point to view the arc of Frankie's musical career. Nearly fifty years prior, Brooklyn College was the sight of his initial formal music training. Although jazz was not officially taught there, he found kindred spirits to jam with while immersing himself in New York's thriving jazz scene and eventually undertaking formal jazz studies at NYU. After spending two decades working as Brooklyn's most prolific soca music arranger, he found himself gravitating back toward jazz, and particularly the Caribbean-tinged jazz that he had never totally abandoned. How and why did this happen? Shifts in musical style, along with certain technological developments, led to a slowdown in soca production in Brooklyn during the 1990s, and with it the diminishing need for his arranging services. These developments presented him with both challenges as well as opportunities.

Frankie—From Arranging to Teaching

RA: I understand your work as a soca arranger began to dry up in the early to mid-1990. Why do you think that was?

FM: From my perspective there were several reasons. A big one was the transition from vinyl to CD. When it became easy to burn pirate copies, sales of original copies went down, and that really hurt the small record labels run by Granville Straker and Rawlston Charles. That, combined with the establishment of more recording facilities in the Caribbean, like Eddie Grant's Ice Studio in Barbados, led to a real decline in recording activity in Brooklyn.

Eventually new computer software allowed musicians to make quality recordings at home and studio sessions became less necessary. At the same time increased availability of drum machines, synthesizers, and computers did away with the need for live drummers and horn players. Some artists had the notion that synthesizers and drum machines made the music sound more "modern," which is no surprise, given what was going on in the American R&B and pop music at the time. I'm sure I contributed to that situation, because early on I was willing to use multi-tracked synthesizer lines in the place of live horns, and I didn't challenge Granville Straker when he wanted to save money by using a drum machine on our recordings.

RA: So, your services as an arranger were no longer in steady demand?

FM: You see, musicians with basic piano skills could figure out synthesized horn lines on their own and record and mix them without the need for a sound engineer, horn players, or musical arrangers like me. As a result, a few of my clients shifted to other arrangers who were going all tech, not because the musical product was better but because it cost so much less! On top of all that, younger calypsonians were increasingly willing to perform on stage backed by prerecorded, synthesizer-heavy tracks. That diminished the need for brass bands that in the past would have required my written scores to accompany calypsonians at live performances. Now all this didn't happen overnight, I still had occasional arranging projects. It was a gradual process, but I could see the writing on the wall.

RA: That must have had some serious ramifications for your career and your income. Did you ever consider forming your own band, you know, reconstitute the Frankie McIntosh Orchestra for calypso dances and soca shows in New York?

FM: There were several reasons why I chose not to go the band route. Most importantly, I was never totally comfortable as a bandleader—that takes a certain temperament and character, and I don't see myself that way. There was a lot of responsibility in seeing that everyone got paid. Too many times I saw the bandleader call musicians for a gig, but the dance "went bust" as they say, and the promoter couldn't pay up. So that then fell to the bandleader, because the musicians demanded to be paid. I just didn't want to go through that, I preferred to be just a side man. Let the bandleader and manager assume the responsibility—just let me play and get paid and go home. There was also the issue of creativity. You see, the calypso bands I played in, like the ones led by Lio Smith and Syd Joe, had regular personnel and a relatively fixed repertoire of pieces that they played over and over again. I never wanted to run a band like that, to me it would have become boring. I liked playing a variety of styles as a sideman—one night it was jazz, another R&B, and then a calypso/soca gig.

RA: Sounds like you were returning to your earlier experiences as a performer, rather than a studio musician, yes?

FM: Well, I continued to gig as a sideman, but those jobs were sporadic and I needed a steadier source of income with the loss of the regular arranging work. And by that point I was getting older and didn't want to do a lot of touring and being away from Patsy and my family.

RA: What about teaching? You once had notions of that as a career path, right?

FM: Exactly. At that point I remembered my college degrees that were gathering dust in some drawer and decided to pull them out and look into teaching—that was one of the reasons I pursued those formal studies years ago before my arranging career took off. One of my friends, the singer Glenda Efill, arranged a substitute gig for me in a public school in the Bronx. Unfortunately, the kids were so undisciplined and the commute was so long that I just couldn't take it.

RA: Sounds as if your first foray into teaching might have been your last.

FM: I certainly thought so at the time. But about a year later, I think it was in 2000, a gentleman named Mitra Lutchman gave me a call. I knew him as a calypso fan who frequented Charlie's record shop and who had relatives in Saint Vincent. Now Charlie and others in that group called him "Teach," because he taught at the elementary school PS 270 on DeKalb Avenue in Bedford Stuyvesant. But what I didn't realize was that he was actually the principal at 270. Lutchman invited me in to help put together the music for a graduation ceremony. The program went well, and I liked the faculty and students at the school. I guess they liked me, because he offered me a part-time job as the director of the school's music program.

RA: What sorts of things did you do with the kids?

FM: I brought in the music, played the piano, and helped the teachers who could sing work up choral arrangements with the students. I remember one teacher, Ms. Charmine Wells, had perfect pitch and was very helpful. I also organized a recorder class in which the students learned the fundamentals of reading music, but putting together a full ensemble with band instruments proved too logistically difficult. Fortunately, most of the children, many of whom were from Caribbean families, loved to sing—we did mostly Broadway pop tunes and gospel numbers, and occasionally a calypso. Once in a while they would ask to do a rap song, but the lyrics were usually so bawdy that I wouldn't allow it.

RA: How long did you teach at PS 270, and what were your overall feelings about the experience?

FM: I stayed until around 2012. Lutchman was retiring that year, and I was not sure if his replacement would be as supportive of my music program. By then I was over sixty-five and ready to ease up on the work schedule. I have to say that I loved teaching the kids and found the whole experience quite rewarding, and of course the steady income helped until I was at the point where my social security kicked in. I should add that teaching at PS 270 really gave me insight into the inner-city Black experiences and the obstacles so many of these students faced—the struggles of a single parent on a fixed welfare income, students living with a grandparent or placed in foster care, that sort of thing. Yet most of the children came to school smiling, and many were brilliant academically. So many of them loved music, so I felt our little program was a very positive force in their lives.

Raf Robertson and Revisiting Jazz

RA: In addition to your teaching activities, you began revisiting jazz more seriously. How did that happen?

FM: That's true, but remember there was always a jazz side to me, I never totally gave it up, even at the height of my soca arranging career. As I mentioned earlier, I occasionally gigged as a sideman with small jazz ensembles. Saxophonists Jean Jefferson and Lio Smith, trumpeter Errol Ince, and others I used in recording sessions were also working jazz musicians who occasionally called me when they needed a keyboardist. And I performed sporadically with Jimmy Tyler, Don Maynard, Eddie Payne, Howard Kimbro, and Tommy Potter (he was Charlie Parker's bassist), so I was able to keep up my jazz chops. Playing with these folks was rewarding because it offered the opportunity to be more creative musically than I could be in the average soca recording session. As the soca arranging work began to dwindle, there was more time for jazz projects.

RA: Before we get to the musicians you have been playing with recently, tell me about your relationship with Raf Robertson. He was probably Trinidad's most well-known jazz pianist in the 1990s and 2000s, right?

FM: That Raf was, and he really helped me connect with other Caribbean musicians who were into the jazz scenes in Brooklyn and Trinidad. I first met Raf sometime in the mid-1970s when he came to New York working with a group that was backing up Lord Shorty. I think it was Eddy Quarless who brought Raf over to my house. Eddy was a saxophonist and arranger, originally from Trinidad, with a strong interest in jazz, and he used to come over with his saxophone and work things out with me at my old apartment at 1299 St. Marks. When Raf sat at the piano and played "Strange Meadow Lark" by Dave Brubeck, I said to myself, "yes, he is one of the fraternity!" Even though we were both pianists there was no competitive tension, we became friends and often exchanged musical ideas. In fact, Raf was extremely genial to me. He introduced me to Boogsie Sharpe, Garvin Blake, and a number of other musicians from the islands who were interested in jazz. He recommended me for a gig teaching at the at Birdsong Academy in Trinidad, which I will talk about shortly. In 2007 he produced a program in tribute to Lord Kitchener he called "Return of the Hat." He could not find a bass player who could play with the feel he wanted, so he asked me to come down to Trinidad to play synthesizer-bass while he played the piano, which I was honored to do.

RA: I've heard of the Birdsong Academy. What was your involvement with it?

FM: Well, sometime in the mid-1990s, at Raf's behest, I was invited down to Trinidad. The academy was a music school started by members of the Birdsong steelband, and they eventually had some association with the University of the West Indies (the St. Augustine Campus), a relationship that was fostered by the steelband's manager Dennis Phillips, who worked in the UWI administration. The students were young, ranging in age between ten and eighteen. Raf taught keyboards at Birdsong, and he suggested that I come down to work with the program. In addition to pan and piano instruction, there were children learning band instruments including flutes, saxophones, trumpets, and trombones. They had police band musicians like Ritchie Quarless (Eddie Quarless's brother) who offered the children individual lessons to get them up and running. And all this took place on the premises of the Birdsong pan yard.

RA: Birdsong is famous for its steelband. Did the school also have a brass and woodwind band that you were able to work with?

FM: Yes, and other things too. You see, by the time I arrived the students were already working in ensembles, small pan-sides as well as a band with conventional brass and woodwind instruments. I was there to teach piano, harmony, and to arrange and conduct rehearsals for their big band. What I wrote for them were more-or-less jazz arrangements of popular calypsos. I could have done anything that I chose, but they just wanted something in a jazz vein and I was only too happy to accommodate them. My reasoning was that since the children would be familiar with the melodies of Kitchener and Sparrow songs, it would be easy for them to learn the full arrangement, because they would already have had the melody down and an idea of what the song sounded like. I would reharmonize the rudimentary chords in order to familiarize them with elementary jazz voicings, encourage them to take solos, and try to embellish basic melodies. I also threw in a few American jazz standards for variety. They kept inviting me back, I went down maybe five or six times during the 1990s and early 2000s. We did concerts at the Birdsong pan yard, at the Royal Bank Auditorium at Queen's Hall, and at the Napa Auditorium (dedicated to Kitchener), all in Port of Spain.

RA: I'm curious, were there both boys and girls in those brass band ensembles you were arranging for?

FM: Yes, when I taught at Birdsong there were plenty of young women in their brass bands, and in their steelbands too.

RA: I ask because, while there have been significant numbers of girls and women in steelbands for some time, you don't see many playing instruments in brass bands. In fact, none of the musicians you worked with in the Equitables or any of your sessions were women—they were all men, right? Why do you think that was?

FM: Well, I simply was not aware of any women saxophonists, or trumpeters, or trombonists, or drummers to call for sessions here in New York, at least not back in the 1970s and 1980s. That was true for jazz as well as Caribbean music back then—there were a few famous pianists, like Mary Lou Williams and Alice Coltrane, but very few horn players. The women I worked with were mostly singers such as Calypso Rose and Singing Francine, and backup singers like Glenda Ifill. And of course, there was the well-known pianist and calypso-band leader Daphne Weeks here in Brooklyn. I think the lack of women horn players had a lot to do with training opportunities. When I was coming up, young girls in the Caribbean were either encouraged to sing or play piano, the latter learned through private lessons for those who could afford it. There were no bands or orchestras in the schools, so youngsters either joined community steelbands (at little expense) or had to seek out private lessons for piano or orchestral instruments (which could be expensive). For whatever reasons, only boys were directed to take lessons on brass and reed instruments and drums. In addition to private lessons, training on brass and reed instruments often happened in police marching bands, but the Caribbean police departments (and their bands) were primarily populated by men. I am sure that has changed, but that was the way it was back then.

Now, back to your question of why there were not more women in my sessions—I just did not know of any women horn players with experience in Caribbean music and who could play at the necessary level. If I had been aware of such musicians, I certainly would have hired them! I should add that I enjoyed teaching the young women students in the Birdsong ensembles, and hope that experience encouraged them to stay with the instruments.

RA: Well, we know that historically brass marching and dance bands in the Caribbean and in the US have been heavily male dominated, and the same can be said for most early American jazz. But women have certainly infiltrated the steelband world that was once the exclusive province of men, so it will be interesting to see what happens with contemporary brass bands. In any case it sounds as though you have fond memories of your time at the Birdsong Academy.

FM: Absolutely! I really enjoyed those visits and working with those kids. They were extremely respectful, and I appreciated their enthusiasm for learning and practicing. I really felt at home culturally, even though it was Trinidad and not Saint Vincent. Raf, Dennis, and the rest of the faculty were all terrific—everyone was so deeply into the arts and culture, it was really refreshing. And on those trips, I met other kindred spirits with strong interests in jazz, musicians like Boogsie Sharpe.

Boogsie Sharpe and Pan Jazz

RA: Boogsie Sharpe is no doubt Trinidad's most renowned pan arranger and soloist of his generation. How did you meet him?

FM: Raf introduced me to Boogsie one evening while I was in Trinidad working for the Birdsong Academy. He took me to a rehearsal Boogsie was running at the Phase II panyard. Now I had heard recordings that Boogsie had made and was eager to make the connection. Here was one of the few steel pan players who understood jazz, who understood how to improvise within a context of a harmonic scheme. Most of the other pan players I heard back then—except for Rudy Smith, Othello Molineaux, and a few other professionals—would just play a pentatonic or blues scale over the chords. But Boogsie was conversant with all sorts of chord progressions, and his improvisations were geared to suit that harmonic content. He had a great feel for phrasing, he never just played a string of notes. He could articulate, and he knew when to rest, which was important in jazz. Boogsie made good use of silence.

RA: How did you connect with him up here in New York?

FM: Shortly after we met in Trinidad, Boogsie was visiting New York to perform and he called me to sit in with him. That was the summer of 1993, at the Brooklyn African Street Festival at Boys and Girls High School, not far from where I lived. It was a big outdoor summer event, featuring all things African related—food, crafts, music, and so forth. I recall that the legendary South African trumpeter Hugh Masekela was on the program. The promoters decided they wanted something with a Caribbean flavor, specifically with a steel pan, but in more of a jazz ensemble format than a conventional steel panside. With that in mind they booked Boogsie, and he put the band together. We had a rehearsal at the home of Talib Kibwe (aka TK Blue), a jazz saxophonist who played and arranged for the famed Brooklyn pianist Randy Weston. He was born in Brooklyn but I later found out that he was of Trinidad and Jamaican parentage. Boogsie also hired jazz bassist Marcus McLaurine, who had recorded with South African pianist Abdullah Ibrahim, and drummer Greg Buford. It was really a top-notch ensemble of experienced American jazz players and Boogsie and myself from the islands.

RA: Now several recordings have survived from that festival, and they might be worth a listen as we ponder the question of what, if anything, is calypso jazz?

FM: Absolutely! But before we begin, let me reiterate, there is no easy answer to that question.

"Blue Bossa"

RA: Understood. Now, one tune you played back then with Boogsie and the ensemble was "Blue Bossa." That was written by American trumpeter and composer Kenny Dorham, and made popular by the American jazz saxophonist Joe Henderson in a 1963 recording on the Blue Note label. It's become something of a jazz standard here in the US, right? So how did that translate into Caribbean jazz, or pan jazz, with Boogsie?

FM: We weren't consciously thinking. "Hey, let's play some calypso jazz." Our rendition of "Blue Bossa" took the form of a typical modern jazz piece for small ensemble—that is, the melodic instruments open with the main theme (often referred to as the "head"), followed by a series of solos. First by the saxophone, then the steel pan, the piano, the bass, and finally the drums. The piece comes to a close with the whole ensemble restating the head. And we should remind readers that "Blue Bossa" and all the pieces we will be talking about in this chapter have full listening guides in appendix 3.

RA: Yes, appendix 3, and do not forget the YouTube channel for all the recordings. Now, was there anything Caribbean or calypso about your rendition of "Blue Bossa"? If this was a case of Caribbean musicians playing an American jazz standard your own way, can you articulate what that way was?

FM: The main melody has a bit of a syncopated lilt common to much Caribbean and Latin music, but honestly the most obvious thing that would lead listeners to associate our performance with calypso jazz was the prominence of Boogsie's steel pan. He was the bandleader who played the main theme, a lengthy improvised solo several minutes into the piece (parts of which he sang along with—amazing!), and a minute-long, unaccompanied coda at the end of the tune. But if you kept Boogsie's melodies and improvisatory runs and replaced the steel pan with another instrument, say a trumpet, I don't think many folks would have called this calypso jazz, or Caribbean jazz, or Latin jazz. In fact, it would have just been heard as jazz. Interestingly, our performance was faster than the original Henderson Blue Note recording—that one is played at a moderate tempo with a slight Latin beat, which I assume the composer Dorham called for.

RA: That sounds right. Dorham was American, but evidently had visited Brazil prior to writing the piece, and given the name "Blue Bossa," you would have to guess that he was announcing some sort of Brazilian influence.

FM: No doubt. And of course, there have been songs from Brazil, like "Girl from Ipanema," that have become jazz standards here in the United States. All these styles were mixing around between North America, the Caribbean, and Latin America. In any case, having Boogsie's steel pan out front no doubt marked our performance, at least in a stereotypical sense, as calypso jazz, or perhaps as pan jazz. I should add that many attending the festival were West Indians who knew Boogsie well, and a few no doubt knew me, so they probably came to our performance with the expectation of a calypso vibe.

"St. Thomas"

RA: A second tune you performed was Sonny Rollins's classic "St. Thomas," a piece that has become synonymous with Caribbean jazz for many Americans. Rollins was born in Harlem, not the Caribbean. Most jazz aficionados and critics know him as giant among modern jazz saxophonists, a leader in the hard bop style of the 1950s and 1960s.

FM: That's true, but don't forget that he was always up front about his Caribbean roots—his parents were from the US Virgin Islands, and "St. Thomas" was clearly a nod towards his family heritage. He claimed that the original tune was a Bahamian folk song that his mother sang to him as a lullaby, and he transformed the song into a modern jazz piece that he recorded in 1956 with a quartet that included drummer Max Roach (himself of strong Bajan heritage). That recording employed standard jazz instrumentation and format—the sax and piano introduced the main theme over the bass and drums, followed by a string of improvised solos, and a restatement of the main theme, or head.

RA: Were there any distinguishable Caribbean or West Indian elements to the Rollins original?

FM: To me there were. What eventually became a standard American jazz piece was actually built around a Caribbean-feeling melody. When I played "St. Thomas" I understood it was a composition by Sonny Rollins, an iconic jazz figure, but I also heard all these rhythms that I associated with vocal calypso. Sonny Rollins intended to write a calypso and he did. The rhythms were inherent in the bouncy, syncopated melody of the tune's head, and I naturally identified with those calypso rhythms and subconsciously improvised accordingly. I suspect that Boogsie and Talib did too.

RA: Speaking of improvising, tell me a little about your piano solo on "St. Thomas." Do you think your approach was different from that of an American jazz pianist, say like Tommy Flanagan, who played on the original Rollins recording?

FM: Well, I won't compare myself to Flanagan, one of the great jazz pianists of his generation. Regarding my solo, first off you can hear that I was more relaxed on "St. Thomas" than I was earlier in the set. We were playing outdoors, it was a chilly evening, and my hands were cold when we opened up so I wasn't as adventuresome on "Blue Bossa" as I would have liked. But all my fingers were warmed up by the time we got to "St. Thomas" and there was more fluency in my playing. As I said, the rhythmic character of the melody set up the way I would improvise. I was riffing off the Caribbean rhythms inherent in Rollins's original tune—you can hear a variation of the tresillo rhythm on his introductory head, and that no doubt subconsciously influenced where I placed my accents during my solo. There was no planning beforehand; when it was my turn, I would simply start improvising, stirred by the rhythms and mindful of the underlying chord changes. Whatever came out at that moment, well that was it. I was no doubt inspired by Boogsie and the other musicians, and of course by the Caribbean audience and the whole ambiance of the African festival. I'm quite sure I would have played my solo differently with American jazz players in a club setting.

RA: So, you agree that your performance with Boogsie of "St. Thomas" constitutes authentic calypso jazz?

FM: Well, I tend to resist labels, and I am not terribly comfortable with that term, but I will say this. Looking back, we performed this piece in a standard jazz format, but the rhythms of the melodic themes and solos, along with the prominence of Boogsie's steel pan, were definitive Caribbean markers, especially for those Caribbean people attending the festival in Brooklyn. Let me add that as a musician I really enjoy playing this piece and I'm quite sure Boogsie would agree, judging from his superb solos on the piece. My only reservation is when an audience, particularly an American audience, is overly demanding to hear "St. Thomas," as if no other jazz-influenced pieces ever came out of the Caribbean. Like "Girl from Ipanema," "St. Thomas" runs the risk of becoming a musical and cultural cliché. I fear it may already have.

I performed with Boogsie a few more times, including a wonderful gig at the Barbados Jazz Festival, and another with just the two of us at the Carnegie Recital Hall. I would have liked to do more with him, but he curtailed his visits to New York, and since I rarely traveled to Trinidad our paths seldom crossed. Boogsie was a complex character, but to me he was quite affable and always treated me as a musical brother. He was aware that those of us from the Caribbean who were well versed in jazz were somewhat on the sidelines. But as a group we had a musical bond, and that translated into a social bond.

The Jazz-tinged Calypsos of David "Happy" Williams

RA: I know you did some playing and recording with Trinidadian jazz bassist Happy Williams. How did you and Happy get hooked up?

FM: I first ran across Happy Williams sometime in the early 1970s, not too long after he arrived in Brooklyn. I was a great admirer of his father, the renowned Trinidad dance bandleader John "Buddy" Williams, and Happy had heard about me through Shake Keane and some of the other musicians in London, where he had been living and playing for several years. I believe our first meeting was in a small park in Bed Stuy at a Jazz Mobile concert where I joined the band impromptu because the regular pianist hadn't shown up. Naturally we hit it off. I was excited to meet another young Caribbean musician interested in jazz and I soon learned what a superb bass player Happy was.

You might say Happy and I were musically bilingual—that is we both spoke both calypso and jazz, and were able to speak them simultaneously. In fact, Happy was one of the few musicians I'd met in Brooklyn who really understood the relationship between jazz and Caribbean music. When he played you could feel that calypso influence that enhanced the straight-ahead 4/4 of bebop. You might say he brought the Caribbean sunshine to jazz, and that's why he was so sought after by so many musicians in New York.

RA: Did you two play together often, on stage or in the recording studio?

FM: During the 1980s and 1990s Happy and I worked together sporadically. A few of the more notable gigs were at Sweet Basil in the Village with Garvin Blake, at a midtown jazz club called Smoke with saxophonist Vincent Herring, at an auditorium in Hartford with the famous saxophonist Jackie Mclean, and a big show in Lincoln Center with saxophonists Vincent Herring and Yosvany Terry. But we didn't play together regularly, because Happy was in such demand for jazz gigs and I never used acoustic bass for my calypso and soca arrangements. While I was busy arranging all those sessions for Granville Straker, Happy was playing with jazz greats like Freddie Hubbard, Elvin Jones, and Jackie McLean. And he had a steady gig with the noted bop pianist Cedar Walton thorough out the 1980s and 1990s. You could say we were in two different worlds, despite our shared interests. But we stayed in touch until he started reaching out to me more often as he ventured out on his own as a bandleader, and when he started recording more of his original calypso-inspired songs. Raf Robertson and I were his two go-to pianists for those projects, because we knew Caribbean music and understood the sound he was looking for.

RA: You mentioned that you played with Happy at a steel pan festival at the Queens Royal College (QRC) in Trinidad, right?

FM: Yes, that was one of the more memorable shows we did together. The Pan Royale Festival at QRC was an annual event organized by pan arranger and producer Ainsley Mark. Happy was recruited to perform there a number of times, and 2003 he put together a quartet with me on piano. As I recall we did mostly American jazz standards and a few calypsos. We had a female violinist named Marlene Rice, but no steel pan. With that sort of small ensemble setup I didn't have to do any horn arrangements. Happy had the charts with the basic chord changes, and I could concentrate on my own soloing. It was a joy performing with him and other high-quality players; it allowed me to exercise my jazz alter ego.

RA: Now tell me about your recording project with Happy.

FM: I believe Happy's initial venture into recording his own calypso songs was the CD *Rhythm of the Street* (1999) that he did with Raf Robertson. The following year, when he brought his next batch of songs to me, I was honored! Something resonated that went beyond the lead sheet with the chords and melodies—there was a deeper understanding, a real cultural connection.

I should add that his songs were so well crafted that all I had to do was to add my own interpretations. Our first recording collaboration resulted in the CD *Ping Pan Obsession* (2000), which included four of his songs plus one of mine and one of Raf's. In terms of process, we first got together at Happy's apartment and he would sing me the songs. I would play along on this little four-octave keyboard he had, and we would figure out the chords and how we wanted to set each song up. We worked out appropriate lines for the keyboard and I would fill out the voicings. The pan parts were key elements that I put together later in the studio with a synth-pan patch. Next, we went into the Asinto studio in Brooklyn and recorded the rhythm section and guide vocal. I went home with a cassette copy of that session and wrote the horn parts that we recorded at a subsequent session.

RA: Was there anything about Happy's songs that made them distinct, that made them different from most of the he calypso and soca songs you had previously worked with?

FM: You can hear that the songs on *Ping Pong Obsession* were written by a jazz musician. They certainly capture the spirit of the Trinidadian calypso music he grew up with, but the melodies and harmonies are more progressive and jazz influenced. These are not the sort of simple triadic chords that you would hear in your average contemporary calypso or soca song. His vocal melodies, for example, incorporated things I am sure he absorbed from his immersion in jazz. That meant that I could use more colorful voicings in my piano accompaniments that would be in keeping with the melody he was singing.

RA: Can you give me a specific example?

"I Love the Pan"–*Ping Pong Obsession* CD (2000)

FM: Sure, take his song "I Love the Pan." Happy's smooth vocals floated over my piano and horn accompaniment. The three-part verse used several jazzy chord sequences, most prominently the I-III7-IV7-♭VII7+9 progression (D-F♯7-G7-C7+9 at 0:30) where Happy sings "They say they want me bass man / they call me jazz man / and now you're writing for steel band." That ascending chord progression ends with a lush dominant C7+9 chord (at 0:33) that is common in jazz. Here it sets up a tension that is resolved when Happy finally sings "My love is steelband," back on the home tonic chord D.

RA: How about the instrumental introduction, did you write that?

FM: It was a collaboration. I wrote the horn lines, but they were derived from his vocal line, "My love is steelband, I love the pan." The pan introduction and band chorus interludes that I played on the pan/synth patch were Happy's creations. In fact, most of the musical ideas on this one came from Happy, the jazz man!

RA: So, the result was a calypso with a jazzy flare?

FM: Well, the whole instrumental arrangement was built around elaborate harmonies often associated with jazz, but there was a definite calypso vibe with the steel pan figure and horns riffs over the iron-driven percussion common to steelband accompaniments. And think about the lyrics—in the first verse Happy swore allegiance to steel pan and Carnival, even though some might call him a "jazz man." I think he was affirming dual identity as calypsonian and jazz man.

"That's the Culture"–*Ping Pong Obsession* CD (2000)

RA: Why don't we move on to another song on the CD, Happy and your rendition of Raf Robertson's "That's the Culture."

FM: Yes, that one really captured the Caribbean spirit with a melody rooted in the older calypsos of Sparrow and Kitchener. But Raf was a musician well steeped in jazz, and like Happy's songs, his melody lent itself to more complex progressions and substitute chords that you don't normally find in calypso or soca. My opening instrumental band section used close voicing on the horns under a colorful II-V-IIIm7-VI7 chord progression (Cm-F7-Dm7-G7 in the key of B♭). Later I added a descending progression that moves through a cycle of fourths in the middle of his verse—you can hear this where Happy sings "no Panorama, no Sharpe to play your mellow way" (between 0:21 and 0:25). Those harmonic choices worked with Raf's original melody and complemented Happy's smooth vocal delivery. Halfway through the song I modulated the key up from B♭ to B major (at 2:28), aiming to create a sense of uplift and energy for the final verses. Those sorts of key modulations were common in gospel and R&B, and seemed to work with this song that was about celebration.

"Ping Pong Obsession"–*Ping Pong Obsession* CD (2000)

RA: Interesting. How about the title track, "Ping Pong Obsession"? That had a very different vibe, there is something more traditional about it to my ear.

FM: Yes. The song was pitched in the key of D minor, giving it the feel of an older lavway folk calypso, like the songs of Atilla, Tiger, and Lion, that were often sung in minor. Happy would have been familiar with those songs, because his father, "Buddy" Williams, would have been playing old records around the house. What is striking about this song is the switch from the minor to major key—it's like two different spirits, or two varied musical complexions. The first section had a minor feel, rocking back and forth the between D minor and A7 figures on the piano. Then there is an abrupt switch to the key of F major around a minute into the song, which produced a brighter mood. The pacing of his chords increased under Happy's vocal as the melody ascended and he began the chorus "I had to wuk with the steelband / I had to wuk with the pan man." Finally, I added a brief turn around at the end of his final line "clear the way / for steelband music to play" (at 1:09) to get back to the original D minor key for the traditional "Ah-ya-ya-ya-ya" chorus. I had a flute and saxophone double on the main melody in the instrumental interlude that followed to evoke a sound that was associated with the older folk calypsos. Overall, "Ping Pong" combined the minor feel of an early calypso with major harmonies and a chord progression associated with more contemporary styles. It was one of Happy's best, I believe.

RA: I agree. For me, "Ping Pong Obsession" really evokes and celebrates that older calypso feel. But I do not think I hear an acoustic bass anywhere on the *Ping Pong* CD. What happened?

FM: Happy did not play his acoustic bass on any of the songs on the album—those low register lines heard throughout are me playing-synth bass. I encouraged him to play, but he wanted a more contemporary sound. The acoustic bass was not used in any of the soca music from the late 1970s on, and I think he was afraid it wouldn't cut though and provide the depth and punch of an electric or synthesized bass. I suspect that Happy wanted to convey the persona of a modern vocal calypsonian that was distinct from his work as a jazz bassist. You know, he even performed in the calypso tents in Trinidad for a few years in the early 2000s—singing, not playing bass.

RA: Let me ask once more, how would you categorize Happy's songs—do they fall under the so-called calypso jazz umbrella?

FM: Listening back twenty years later, I would say that they were certainly in a calypso vein, given their lyrical themes, rhythmic lilt, and use of the steel pan fills and interludes. In terms of form, melodic structure, and harmony, they were more elaborate than the typical calypso and soca songs of the day, and it is fair to attribute that to the jazz backgrounds that Happy and I shared. But unlike most music that is considered jazz, these compositions contained no noticeable improvised instrumental solos. That was in part because Happy's songs were so packed with verses that I, as the arranger, had no room for anything more than several brief instrumental interludes lead by the flute and my synthesized steel pan. But there was no real improvisation, and Happy did not push for any. Perhaps "jazz-tinged calypsos" would be the most accurate description? One thing is for certain, Happy's grounding in the older calypso, and his experience playing with so many of the great American jazz masters, made him more highly qualified than most to compose music that blends calypso and jazz.

Cool Pan Jazz with Garvin Blake

RA: Much of your playing in recent years has been with panist Garvin Blake. He was originally from Trinidad, immigrating to Brooklyn with his family as a youngster in the early 1970s a few years after you arrived. Eventually he came under the wing of Clive Bradley, the renowned pan arranger for Trinidad's legendary Desperados steelband and for the Metro and Depsers USA steelbands here in Brooklyn. How did you guys get together?

FM: Yes, Garvin and I have been playing together for over twenty-five years now, and I consider him to be my musical brother. We met sometime in the late 1990s when Garvin was fronting a group with Raf Robertson on keyboards; they were playing at this catering establishment called the Africa House in East Flatbush. One night I got called in as part of a trio that was backing up the Jamaican guitarist Ernie Ranglin. We were all together at the venue, and I believe it was then that Raf introduced me to Garvin.

Some time elapsed, maybe a year, when Garvin called me and proposed I play on the CD project he was putting together. He already had recorded several tracks with the South African accordionist and keyboardist Tony Cedras, but wanted a different sound for the rest of the project. He was familiar with my arrangements for Becket, and must have been impressed with what he heard me play at African House. I was certainly struck with what I heard from him! Garvin was one of those panists whose interpretation of jazz standards and Caribbean tunes stood out from the rest, because he had an especially wide jazz repertoire, a sophisticated knowledge of chord construction, and a well-developed sense of voice leading. Based on what I knew of his playing, I took him up on his offer and was not disappointed.

RA: The CD was called *Bella Eau Road Blues*, released in 2000. I believe the title was a reference to a street in the Belmont neighborhood of Port of Spain, right?

FM: Yes. But we recorded the music at Basement Recordings, a Brooklyn studio run by Trevor John. He is a real aficionado of calypso and steel pan music and the founder of the "When Steel Talks" website—that is a great source for information on steelband and calypso music.

Garvin Blake, Brooklyn, 2023. Photo by Ray Allen.

"Pan Romance"–*Bella Eau Road Blues* CD (2000)

RA: Let's start with the track "Pan Romance." What a beautiful tribute to the pan, and that's David Rudder singing, right?

FM: Indeed, it was Rudder on vocals. Garvin's "Pan Romance" was an original piece he composed as an instrumental tune for the Despers USA steel orchestra in 1991. He and his wife Phoebe later put lyrics to it, and he convinced Rudder to sing it for the recording. Rudder's smooth delivery was perfect for the song extolling the magical allure of pan music, and you can tell he is sincere about his own love for the instrument. Garvin gave me a cassette recording of the song and I came up with the charts before we went into the studio. My role was basically supportive, playing and embellishing the chords to enhance David's vocals and Garvin's pan solos. I used an electric piano, because there was not an acoustic at the studio.

RA: Can you be more specific about the harmonic setting you came up with for this one?

FM: I wanted to play in the style that Garvin had conceived, one with colorful chords and extensions reminiscent of the older instrumental calypso tradition but still with a modern feel. With that in mind, I ended Garvin's introduction by cadencing up half a step from G7 to a deceptive A♭major7 (at 0:12). That move created a little tension before landing on the C chord for David to begin the first verse, "Sweet pan, the voice of an island / in the Caribbean Sea."

RA: Now what's going on during the percussion break? Suddenly Rudder took off on what sounds like ritual chanting.

FM: Yes, that was typical David. Following two vocal verses and Garvin's pan solo came a break by Brazilian percussionist Cyro Baptista. David spontaneously began ad-libbing over the percussion in the style of a rhythmic Spiritual Baptist chant, I suspect his nod toward a Trinidad religious folk tradition. He'd done that sort of improvising on several of his own songs, like "Bahia Girls." I think that the modern chord movements juxtaposed against the traditional percussion and vocal chanting were part of the appeal of "Pan Romance" for some listeners.

RA: I agree, beautiful stuff! Now tell me about the two more popular calypsos on the CD, Kitchener's "Pan in A Minor" and Sparrow's "Jane." How did you handle them?

FM: Well, another way we approached the merger of calypso and jazz was to rearrange popular calypsos with substitute chord progressions and to bring in improvised instrumental solos. The original Kitchener and Sparrow melodies lent themselves to that sort of treatment. I should add that revamping popular vocal calypsos for instrumental groups was a long-standing tradition in the Caribbean, dating back to the calypso dance bands of the 1940s and 1950s like my Dad's Melotones, and continuing right up through the modern calypso jazz ensembles. The idea paralleled the American penchant for rearranging American popular songs by jazz artists—think of Coltrane's version of "My Favorite Things," or the Miles Davis/Gil Evans arrangement of "Summertime."

"Pan in A Minor"–*Bella Eau Road Blues* CD (2000)

RA: Good point. Let's talk about your arrangement of Kitchener's "Pan in A Minor." The original came out in 1986, arranged by Leston Paul. The tune was very popular with the Trinidad steelbands, a number of whom rearranged it for the big Panorama contest. Kitchener had a knack for writing melodies that appealed to pan players.

FM: Definitely! The original "Pan in A Minor" featured Leston's bluesy pan lines played by Boogsie Sharpe and Kitchener's haunting, minor-pitched vocal melody. There were even a few diminished chords thrown in among the minor harmonies, so there was plenty of interesting material to work with. Following an opening free-meter vamp around an A minor9 chord on piano and pan, we played something close to Kitchener's original introductory riff because that was a real marker of the song. Garvin played the basic melody that Kitchener sang for the verse and "beat pan" chorus, while I dropped in additional extended chords. The rest of the piece was basically a platform for Garvin's pan improvisations, first over a calypso/Latin beat (at 1:49) and then over a straight-ahead, 4/4 swing feel (at 3:04). That ended up being an effective combination. By the way, these were some of Garvin's best solos, built around ethereal passages meticulously rendered with the shimmering sonorities that only a steel pan can sound. We ended with a percussion/bass coda in recognition of the steel band's percussion section, fondly known as the "engine room."

"Jane"–*Bella Eau Road Blues* CD (2000)

RA: How about your treatment of Sparrow's "Jane," a classic calypso from the late 1960s? But that wasn't how you two played it.

FM: Not at all! My job on "Pan Romance" and "Pan in A Minor" was to support Garvin's improvisations. But on Sparrow's "Jane" I had a chance to step up and do some soloing myself. I selected a warm, synth/piano patch in consideration of the free, sustained accompaniment I had in mind. Sparrow's original "Jane" was a bouncy, up-tempo calypso, and Garvin had worked with Clive Bradley on a pan arrangement of the tune for the Despers USA steelband in 1992. I went in another direction, slowing the tempo in order to introduce a number of chord substitutions that were not there in the original Sparrow song. I recall doing this arrangement on the spot with Garvin in the studio—we decided to do it as pan/piano duet with no additional rhythm section. It was his idea, and we had not played the song before as far as I can remember, so it was all spontaneous. Garvin had such a remarkable ear and was able to adjust to my reharmonizations on the spot. He just played his lines while I provided the foundational harmonies and added in additional chords between spaces where the melody permitted.

RA: I hear you moving between rhythmically free and more conventional 4/4 metered sections. The introduction, for example is extremely cool and dreamy, not what I would expect from a Sparrow calypso.

FM: I am not surprised at your reaction. We opened "Jane" with an atmospheric, free-meter pan improvisation by Garvin over my sustained chords. I tried to lay back and let Gavin lead with the pan, which was difficult when you didn't have a steady beat. We were in the key of F but I was not trying to think in terms of any tonal home base at that point. I was trying to play more freely, just spontaneously dropping in chords that I thought might sound right. Next, we moved into a moderate 4/4 section where Garvin played something close to the original melody (at 1:20). That section wasn't as free, and I stayed closer to the root chord progressions on the Sparrow arrangement. Having stated the melody familiar to Sparrow fans and set the mood for our interpretation, we traded solos between the pan and piano, bouncing back and forth between free and steady meters for the rest of the piece. Our aim was to place Sparrow's original in a new harmonic context with gently interweaving the pan and piano lines.

RA: I certainly think you succeeded in evoking that mood. But listening back today, are you satisfied with your performance?

FM: Well, I was not 100 percent pleased with the final outcome, because I felt there were certain places where I was going too fast for the pan, not waiting long enough for him to hit a certain note. I was sort of anticipating. And I wasn't happy when I first heard my piano solo track played back, because of some of the gaps—I wasn't sure if I'd come up with enough new ideas to match Garvin's superb playing. But listening to it again today, as you suggest, I can appreciate those gaps a little more, you need some space to let things settle in. On the positive side Raf Robertson loved it, he was always speaking about how much he liked our interpretation of "Jane." His opinion means a lot to me.

RA: What came next with you and Garvin?

FM: After we made the *Bella Eau Road Blues* recordings, we started playing regularly at the Sugarcane, a small restaurant on Flatbush Avenue. It was a quartet with Damond DueWhite on drums and Calvin Jones on bass. We played there regularly, every Sunday for a while and later once a month, and we developed a solid repertoire of tunes including interpretations of American jazz standards and more calypso-oriented numbers. We did occasional other gigs together, including a big Steel Pan Jazz festival in Lincoln Center in 2004 and again in 2008. Garvin added Tony Cedras on accordion and Tony "Bugs" Niles on percussion for the first one. I recall that Andy Narell and Liam Teague were both on that program, each fronting excellent small pan jazz ensembles. Emmanuel "Jack" Riley, one of the earliest solo pan players, was honored. On the second program I played acoustic piano with the great Rudy "Two Left" Smith. It was very satisfying to see all those talented steel pan players doing a jazz program devoted to pan jazz on the stage of Alice Tully Hall in Lincoln Center. That was some serious validation of Caribbean music and pan-centered jazz.

RA: Yes, those Lincoln Center Pan Jazz programs brought real attention to pan in what some critics would consider to be a "serious" setting. Let's move on to your second recording project with Garvin, the CD *Parallel Overtones*. That came out in 2015, fifteen years later. What happened in between those two recordings?

FM: By the time we recorded *Parallel Overtones* we had playing together for a long time, and we chose tunes we had we had worked up at the Sugar Cane. We decided to record them as a quartet with Garvin on pan, me on piano, Calvin Jones on bass, and a rotating cast of drummers.

"One for Boogsie"–*Parallel Overtones* CD (2015)

FM: My contribution to *Overtones* was "One for Boogsie," an original tune intended as a tribute to the great panist whom we listened to earlier. I wanted to write something that would capture the spirit and energy of Panorama, where Boogsie had been such a force over the years as a pan arranger, so the piece opened with a strong calypso beat, what you would expect from the engine room of a big Panorama steelband. Also, I wanted something that would do justice to his abilities and genius as a player, something that he might someday enjoy performing to demonstrate his incredible dexterity and improvisatory skills on the pan.

RA: "One for Boogsie" is a fairly complicated tune, harmonically speaking. Can you explain your approach to that one?

FM: Let me try. I began the introduction with a IIdim-V-Im-VIdim progression in the key of C minor (Ddim7-G7-Cm-Adim), spiced up with diminished and extended chords for coloring. Next, Garvin joined me on a unison ensemble line, something one might associate with bebop. At that point we modulated up from the key of C minor to the key of E♭ major (0:32) as the pan took over with a more lyrical melodic line that served as the head. I closed the head with an accented, rhythmic figure that moved chromatically from a D7+13 to D♭7+13 chord (at 1:00), followed by my piano solo, back in the original key of Cm. The rest of the composition was in a standard jazz format with a series of solos: pan, drums, bass, and finally a return to the introductory unison line and reprieving the head with the piano and pan in unison. We flipped back and forth between the C minor tonal center and its relative major, E♭, in order to provide tonal variation and a bit of contrast. That was my compositional choice in an attempt to convey Boogsie's complex personality. Once again Garvin showed his superb lyrical playing, weaving together intricate lines in and around my piano chords.

"Pan in Harmony"–*Parallel Overtones* CD (2015)

RA: Yes, impressive solos from both you and Garvin. Now let's move on your rendition of another Kitchener song, "Pan in Harmony." Surprisingly you set this one in waltz time, yes? How did you come up with that idea?

FM: Well, this was a popular Kitchener song that we had been experimenting around with at our Sugar Cane gigs. Kitchener wrote a number of calypsos honoring Trinidad's steelbands, and often those bands would rearrange his tunes for the Panorama contest. Our arrangement was for jazz quartet with pan, as you note, moving from his original 4/4 to a 6/8 meter. That was my idea, I wanted to show how calypso songs were adaptable to meters other than the standard 4/4. You know, Frankie Francis rearranged "Yellow Bird" and Sparrow's "May May" in 3/4 waltz meter, what we called "Castilian style." Of course, the reverse also occurred where groups such as the Dutchy Brothers took Tchaikovsky's "Waltz of the Flowers" and placed it in a 4/4 calypso rhythm. In our case, Kitchener's original melody was so elegant that I could imagine it being played in a ballroom with ladies in long gowns floating around. With that in mind I tried a moderate tempo, 6/8 treatment, and we ended up with a jazz waltz! I also realized that the original Kitchener melody could be reharmonized in interesting ways. For example, I began with a piano introduction in the key of A major, and then modulated to the key of C major (at 0:15) for the first half of the verse, and then to the key of E♭ (at 0:24) for the second half of the verse. Finally, I pivoted back to the key of C for the chorus (at 0:49). Now, of course this was not something that the younger dance crowd would necessarily be much interested in, but more sensitive listeners who loved older calypso appreciated the arrangement—it showed the potential that calypso melodies could have in a new setting.

RA: I think Garvin and you laid down some of your more convincing solos on this track. Listening back, do you have any thoughts on that?

FM: Garvin's solo was a testament to his musical ear. What he played was a brilliant interpretation of the harmonic outline I gave him on the lead sheet. And he executed with a subtle, gentle touch that really captured the regal mood I was after.

As for my own solo, let me say it was not something I planned out or precomposed; in the jazz tradition, it was spontaneous. But listening back, I can hear some of the techniques I was using. Generally speaking, my approach was lyrical and melodic, I didn't want to get too busy. Much of the improvising was built around embellished motives from Kitchener's original melody, but I would occasionally interrupt them with more rapid melodic runs—you can hear this between 2:58 and 3:02, for example. I also used rhythmic variations by switching the accents in a few spots. The drums kept a steady 3/4 ground beat, what we would call "playing in three" with the accent on the first beat. I tended to follow along in three, but sporadically played heavy accents to create the impression of a duple meter (1–2–1–2) on top of the drummer's underlying triple meter (1–2–3–1–2–3) pulse—a ratio of 2:3. That move served to break up the steady rhythmic flow—you can hear it at 2:54 and again at 3:12. Playing two beats over three (or the reverse) is often called a hemiola rhythmic relation in Western music, and in West Africa it is referred to as a cross-rhythm (which is the rhythmic foundation of much African Music). I don't know where I got the impulse from, Europe or Africa, maybe both? In any case, it just came out naturally. My overall goal for the solo was to present a variety of well-executed ideas—motif embellishments, melodic runs, using accents to create hemiola/cross rhythm effects—in order to keep the listener engaged.

RA: You turned Kitchener's "Pan in Harmony" into a jazz waltz so to speak. What about the other two classic calypsos on the CD, Sparrow's "Ah Fraid" and "No Money No Love"?

FM: Our approach to those two was quite different. For "Ah Fraid" we decided to keep the conventional 4/4 calypso rhythm, which was the way we had been playing it at the Sugar Cane.

I added an introduction, and spiced up the harmonies from the original Sparrow version.

"No Money No Love"–*Parallel Overtones* CD (2015)

FM: Now, on "No Money No Love" I really did some serious reharmonization. The original Sparrow recording was in the key of A♭ throughout and was built around a standard I-VI-II-V chord sequence. But on my arrangement, the opening section jumped around unexpectedly among a series of different tonal centers, moving from F to D to G♭ to E♭ to C and finally back to F (0:14–1:01). In between those main tonal centers are rapidly changing chords that serve as secondary tonal centers that make the arrangement harmonically rich.

RA: Yes, that initial section sounds very sophisticated and avant-garde to me, something I would expect from John Coltrane or the Modern Jazz Quartet. Was that what you were hoping for?

FM: Well, you are aware of my aversion to labels, but let me say we were aiming for something slightly unconventional with our treatment of "No Money No Love." Garvin and I decided to take liberties with the original Sparrow melody and chords, moving rapidly through the tonal centers in an unpredictable fashion, thwarting listener's expectations, hoping to make people think outside the box. You know, that's what any good art should do! Interesting you should mention Coltrane, because I consciously applied his approach to dividing the octave into major thirds as he did in his introduction to "Giant Steps." You can hear this clearly on my short bridge (between 0:31–0:37). Following the introduction, the rhythm section broke into a straight-ahead 4/4 meter (at 1:02) with the main beat carried on the ride cymbal while a walking bass outlined the chords. Garvin and I jammed around with phrases of the original Sparrow melody, interrupting things with occasional stop-time figures and extended chords over a constant pedal (also a nod to Coltrane).

RA: I agree, the whole first half of the piece sounds like modern jazz to my ear—with the straight-ahead rhythms, key changes, fancy chords, and edgy stop-time and pedal interludes. In fact, I suspect that listeners who weren't familiar with the original Sparrow piece might not make any calypso connection. But then, things changed quite abruptly . . .

FM: Yes, yes! About halfway through we switched to a calypso beat (at 3:18) and jammed on a simpler I-VI-II-V progression (C-Am-Dm-G in the key of C) for what turned out to be an extended tag with Garvin stretching out over the loop of chord changes. The goal was to give calypso fans who were not so familiar with jazz something that they could identify with—a solid calypso dance beat and triadic harmonies that were essentially similar to the ones in the Sparrow original. We hoped they might forgive us for distorting Sparrow's melody and perhaps begin to appreciate that jazz and calypso can be blended together in new and exciting ways.

RA: Now why did you and Garvin choose these particular Kitchener and Sparrow songs?

FM: Here's the thing about jazzing up a calypso. If you are playing for Caribbean audiences, you need to keep enough of the melody for them to recognize the tune. If you play an unfamiliar piece with elaborate harmonies and dissonant improvisations, you already have two strikes against you—play it at a fast jazz tempo and you are out! But by maintaining some semblance of the recognizable melody and an identifiable calypso rhythm, we tried to make our arrangement more accessible to a broader calypso crowd who might not normally listen to jazz. Fortunately, both Sparrow and Kitchener wrote strong, flowing melodies that were familiar to our Caribbean listeners and that lent themselves to reharmonization. That's why we chose them!

RA: Yes, makes sense. You always need to be aware of your audience expectations, and the limitations of what they will tolerate.

Jazzing Up Calypsos

RA: You and Garvin have played together for some time, so I took the liberty of asking him about what constitutes calypso jazz. Like you, Garvin tends to be skeptical of labels, but for the purposes of this project I pushed him a little, and here is how he responded:

What is "calypso jazz"? Well, let me start by noting that musical styles are fluid, hence elusive and difficult to codify. Genres initially reflect the times and geography of their conception, then are shaped by internal and external trends. Very few styles, if any, are pure or static, because musicians have been borrowing from other cultures for centuries. Calypso and jazz are both good examples of this borrowing or fusion. Each taken on their own is difficult to define, and harder still is describing the fusion of the fusions, the mixing of calypso and jazz. That acknowledged, each idiom does have distinguishing qualities. Jazz puts a premium on instrumental improvisation, the blues, swing, and extended harmonies. Calypso is primarily a vocal style that speaks to social and political issues, but it has unique qualities that go beyond lyrics. It uses syncopated phrases that reflects the various Caribbean dialects. I call it "lavway swing." There is a lilting 2/2, 2/4, or 4/4 rhythmic underpinning that gives the music its forward motion or "calypso beat." This pulse can be felt at any tempo. And of course, the calypsonians are expected to improvise by employing unique melodic and rhythmic vocal phrasings (just as good jazz singers are expected to do).

I would contend any music that fuses some salient features of both idioms could be termed "calypso jazz." For example, a traditional calypso reharmonized using extended chords and improvisation would fit the label—that's what we were trying to do with our reinterpretations of Kitchener's "Pan in A Minor" and Sparrow's "Ah Fraid." An American jazz standard played with a calypso beat (or lavway swing) that highlights solo passages would also qualify. Original compositions that integrate elements of calypso and jazz, such as Frankie's "One for Boogsie" or my "Pan Romance," are other candidates.

Another way to approach the question is not to think in terms of genre or label, but rather to begin with the idea of process. My liner notes to the *Parallel Overtones* CD summed up my thoughts at that time. The project "explores the synergy between pan, calypso, and jazz. This is a journey in search of common ground, amongst kindred art forms. The borders dividing the genres are simultaneously blurred and crystallized, creating another interesting perspective on Caribbean music."[6]

FM: Garvin is a talented and thoughtful musician, and I value his opinions. I agree, we are two Caribbean musicians, presenting our instrumental interpretations of calypso songs, or original pieces inspired by calypso songs, employing calypso rhythms, foregrounding the steel pan, making generous use of colorful jazz harmonies, and engaging in jazz-influenced improvisation. But I still have strong reservations about the use of labels like "calypso jazz," because I'm not convinced that it constitutes its own distinct genre at this point in history, say the way bebop or Latin jazz have developed. I do agree with Garvin that process is a good way to think about this. That is, I'm more comfortable referring to the process of "jazzing up calypso" than I am the product or label "calypso jazz." But I understand that promoters, critics, and music historians (like you, Ray) demand categories, so there you have it.

New Directions with Etienne Charles

RA: Thank you for that explanation, and my apologies for continuing to harp on the question of musical labels—that is a part of my formal training I can't quite let go of. We will come back to this discussion in the next chapter. The other musician you played with at the 2016 Brooklyn College concert was the young Trinidadian trumpeter Etienne Charles. Where does he fit into this Caribbean musical puzzle?

FM: The music I played with Boogsie, Happy, and Garvin all highlighted the steel pan (or me playing steel pan synth), which has become the most prominent hallmark of so-called "calypso jazz" over the past few decades. The brass and reeds only appeared on Happy's songs, and there in a supporting, rather than a soloing, capacity. But one person who has brought back the instrumental band sound is Etienne Charles. The Brooklyn College concert was the first (and only) time I played with Etienne, but it was an eye-opening experience. I saw him as something of a Caribbean Wynton Marsalis, reviving and revitalizing instrumental calypso and Carnival folk music, as Wynton has done with the traditional music of New Orleans.

RA: Do you mean Etienne was trying to bring together a sort of Caribbean repertory band, to recreate the sounds of the great Caribbean bandleaders?

FM: Not exactly—let me put it this way. Etienne's arrangements and trumpet style were clearly influenced by the older calypso dance bands. That acknowledged, he could not avoid interpreting the music from his present position as a young jazz player. His music sounds rooted in the past but still contemporary, a fresh nod to heritage! For someone who didn't grow up in

Frankie and Etienne Charles Backstage at Brooklyn College, 2016. Photo by Jeff Grannum.

the 1950s or 1960s, Etienne has really done a convincing job of capturing the sound and spirit of the older calypso dance bands. One of the tunes he played at our concert that impressed me was "Old School," a tribute to the great calypso instrumentalists. He put the brass instruments right out front, not only to play riffs and themes, but to take extended solos, the way the old calypso dance bands used to do but you rarely hear today. You can really detect the influence of Errol Ince and Frank Joseph, the great Trinidad trumpeters who preceded him. Etienne can play with that bright, rhythmic swing you associate with those older calypso soloists. But he also draws on modern jazz—listen to the harmonizations on solos on "Culture Shock," another tune he played that night at Brooklyn College. It's a little like Miles Davis or Dizzy Gillespie meeting Trinidad Orisha drumming. Very powerful music!

RA: Do you think Etienne represents a new chapter in the story of jazz and Caribbean music?

FM: Good question. I suppose time will tell. In terms of history, Etienne arrived on the Caribbean music scene when the rich tradition of instrumental band music in Trinidad and Tobago was on the wane. Music of the conventional dance bands led by Frankie Francis, Ron Berridge, Clarence Curvan, and John "Buddy" Williams had pretty much shrunk into oblivion. Younger musicians were more inclined toward computer-generated music, and the majority of aspiring instrumentalists chose pan. Steel orchestras were the main (some surmise the only) defenders of the instrumental fort. Thanks in part to Etienne's effort, there has been renewed interest in brass bands playing on the road for Trinidad's Carnival parades, and Brassoramas (competition between bands employing brass and reed instruments) are regaining public recognition and support. I applaud his efforts, and the pride in his Trinidadian heritage that his music reflects. It is gratifying to see a talented, young Caribbean artist introduce his jazz-influenced interpretations of calypso to new audiences here in North America, and to old fans back in the Islands. Hopefully he will inspire more younger players to rediscover our rich instrumental calypso tradition and take it in new directions.

EPILOGUE
OUR CALYPSO TAGS

As the last threads of this manuscript are being stitched together, seventy-seven-year-old Frankie McIntosh finds himself busier than ever. Considering the arc of his musical life, it occurs to us that the past few years may well be the "tag" of his venerable career. We are by no means intimating that the end is near, but rather that Frankie continues to roll on in new and unpredictable directions. A tag in calypso, as we have discussed, is the final section of the song where the singer and instrumentalists stretch out, improvising on melodic motifs and rhythms from earlier verses and choral refrains. New riffs emerge, built on previous ideas, as the performance unfolds and propels forward until the singer, musicians, and dancers are finally satiated and run out of steam (or, in the case of a studio session, until the producer and engineer decide to fade out the recording). The intrigue is that no one knows what will happen during a good tag, how long it will last, or how it will end. And so, it currently appears to be with Frankie and his music.

While the outbreak of COVID slowed life down for over a year, by the fall of 2021 Frankie's playing and arranging activities were ramping up. Over the past two years he has prepared charts and coordinated recording sessions for calypsonians Short Shirt (Antigua), Slinger (Anguilla), Creeper (Trinidad), Edmund "Bunny" Nurse (Trinidad), Tellison "Tillo" Forde, (Trinidad), Mighty Sando (Tobago), Ajamu (Grenada), and for Jamaican gospel singer Sister Downer and reggae artist King Webb. He participated in the music for a joyful Christmas program at Brooklyn's Epiphany Lutheran School, and sadly has played at too many funerals.

In the spring of 2021, with COVID restrictions beginning to ease, Frankie joined a new quartet with his longtime collaborators, sax player Charles Dougherty and bassist Max Gouveia. They began performing regularly at the

Frankie and Short Shirt in the Studio, 2023. Photo by Ray Allen.

Frankie with Charles Daugherty on saxophone, Max Gouveia on bass, and Daisuke on drums, Queens, NY, 2022. Photo by Ray Allen.

Jamaican Center for Arts and Learning in Queens, and outdoor events including the Tribute to the Ancestors at Coney Island.

In the fall of that year the ensemble's bassist, Max Gouveia, released the *Major Matters* CD, featuring original material he had composed over the years. Unlike Frankie's previous jazz projects, *Major Matters* was primarily modern jazz with minimal calypso influence, even though all the players were West Indian.

In the summer of 2022, Frankie resumed performing in public with Garvin Blake at Bar Bayeux, a small club located on Nostrand Avenue in Brooklyn's Crown Heights neighborhood. In the spring of 2023 they began playing for pan brunches at the Sugar'd restaurant on Newkirk Avenue in East Flatbush.

This bustle of musical activity all took place amidst the ongoing flow of daily family life at his St. Marks Avenue home in Brooklyn, where he chauffeured his grandson Jaiden to and from school and his daughter Jamilah to work, and on many evenings helped the youngster with his school projects. Through it all he somehow has managed to maintain his old nocturnal schedule for arranging and composing, catching sleep in the early morning hours and during midday naps.

• • •

We will close with our own tags, reflecting upon some of the big ideas we ruminated over during the previous three years. Ray first.

In a world marked by increased racism, xenophobia, and authoritarian nationalism, Frankie McIntosh's life story offers a glimmer of hope for a

nkie and Max Gouveia, Brooklyn, 22. Photo by Ray Allen.

Frankie with Garvin Blake and Max Gouveia, Brooklyn, 2023. Photo by Ray Allen.

globalism grounded in the transnational diaspora of people and culture. On first glance it appears to be the classic American tale of an immigrant who arrived with little more than a suitcase and a dream. Through hard work, perseverance, and a good deal of talent, he was able to realize his aspirations. But a deeper look reveals his success would not have been possible without the support of the local West Indian community that made him welcome, providing a familiar and safe cultural space and a network of connections to New York's bourgeoning Caribbean music scene. In addition, public backing via a free CUNY college education and the private sector's willingness to provide a low-interest home loan and an affordable graduate education at NYU, were essential pillars of his success. Indeed, it took a village.

Frankie's story is even more remarkable considering that he made it as musician, a profession fraught with unsteady work, low wages, the grind of touring, and the ever-present temptations of drugs and alcohol. These tribulations were (and still are) exacerbated for musicians of color operating in the unpredictable worlds of jazz and popular music. But somehow Frankie navigated those rough waters as student, performer, arranger, and teacher. Throughout it all he remained a steadfast family man, still with his wife Patsy, the young woman he met over fifty years ago on the day he arrived in Brooklyn, and with whom he bought a house and raised four children while helping to support their parents and nine grandchildren. Working musicians with that sort of lifelong family résumé are a rarity anywhere in the entertainment world.

His talent and hard work notwithstanding, Frankie was fortunate to land in the right place at the right time. Brooklyn's Caribbean community was rapidly expanding in the late 1960s, with the music sector about to take off thanks to the soon-to-be established Labor Day Carnival and the independent record companies run by Granville Straker, Rawlston Charles, and Michael Gould. Frankie came on the scene precisely at the moment when the winds of musical change were picking up and Brooklyn was emerging as a major production center of the new soca music. His advanced musical skills, eclectic tastes, and openness to experimentation positioned him well to help usher in the soca revolution.

Frankie's contributions to the soca sound of the late 1970s and 1980s were immense—today he is recognized as a member of the esteemed pantheon of arrangers including Art De Coteau, Ed Watson, Errol Ince, Leston Paul, Pelham Goddard, and Clive Bradley, who were responsible for the musical transition from calypso to soca. Frankie's music spans the older calypso style of the 1960s that shaped the early arrangements of De Coteau, Watson, and Ince, to the modern soca sound associated with the younger arrangers Paul, Goddard, and Bradley who came into their own in the 1980s. Each of the pioneering soca arrangers had their trademark style—Paul was famous for his driving horn lines and technological innovations, Bradley for his funky bass, synthesizer, and guitar licks, and Goddard for the cohesive band sound that he developed with Charlie's Roots. Within the early soca world, Frankie was most known for his musicality, his deep knowledge of classical and jazz harmonic theory, and his unmatched keyboard skills. "Frankie really knew how to move harmonies!" Pelham Goddard told me. "And everybody wanted to play synthesizer like Frankie, but few could."[1] Goddard attributed Frankie's advanced arranging and performing skills to his formal university training and extensive performing experience with jazz and R&B artists in New York. Likewise, Leston Paul recalled that Frankie was like a "breath of fresh air" when he came on the scene with his early Becket recordings. "You could hear the calypso, but also the jazz and blues influence, and the extended chords in his orchestrations—I thought his music had a real international touch and would be attractive to ears outside the Caribbean."[2] To my outsider ear, Frankie was unique in his ability to reach back to the big band arrangements and colorful chords of 1960s calypsos, to create funky grooves to anchor wave and wine soca songs, and to occasionally push the music out of its pop comfort zone with snatches of modern jazz and experimental music.

Unlike other calypso and soca arrangers who shuttled back and forth between the Caribbean and New York during the 1970s and 1980s, Frankie's relocation was permanent, facilitating his rise to prominence as Brooklyn's top, in-house arranger. He was there, available for New York–based and touring calypsonians alike who wanted to take advantage of the city's influential independent record labels and advanced recording and mixing facilities. In addition to serving the Trinidad stars, he became a champion of small island singers Becket, Short Shirt, Swallow, and many others, bringing much deserved attention to their local calypso scenes. He and fellow Vincentian Granville Straker used their New York location to expand the transnational reach of calypso and soca.

While Frankie often gigged with African American musicians and called on local jazz players to fill out his horn sections for studio sessions, the bulk of his performing and nearly all his arranging activity took place within a Caribbean musical orbit. He clearly enjoyed working with American R&B singers Charlie and Yvonne Brown, and with New York jazz stalwarts Jimmy Tyler, Don Maynard, and Howard Kimbro. But first and foremost, he was a Caribbean musician who played with, and for, other Caribbean folk. The depth and diversity of New York's post-1965 Caribbean community, and the ease of movement between New York and the islands, made that possibility a reality. Frankie was comfortable within New York's burgeoning Caribbean diaspora that provided him with an ample livelihood as an artist, something that would not have been possible had he chosen to remain in his Saint Vincent homeland. Whether he would have done better financially or been granted more creative freedom if he had moved outside the safe Caribbean sphere as a fulltime jazz pianist or a pop music arranger is uncertain. He chose the more familiar path, and the soca world has been the beneficiary.

In a 1977 exposé on Alston Becket Cyrus that appeared in the *Amsterdam News*, critic Dawad Philip identified Frankie as the artist with the "talent and musical wizardry" behind Becket's groundbreaking *Calypso Disco* and *Coming Higher* LPs.[3] Fourteen years and hundreds of arrangements later, journalist Leslie Slater proclaimed Frankie, along with Leston Paul, as "first among equals in the business of arranging calypso music," while praising Frankie for being "in the vanguard of the efforts to establish the calypso world's new soca order."[4] Another fourteen years down the road, the *Trinidad and Tobago Guardian* lauded Frankie's accomplishments for arranging over 2,500 songs and leading recording sessions "with almost every important calypsonian and soca artist in the Caribbean."[5] For a Vincentian, small island outsider to gain such recognition and prestige as an arranger in the Trinidad-dominated world of calypso was, and remains, unprecedented. Herman Hall, a longtime Brooklyn Carnival observer and founding editor of *Everybody's* magazine, put it this way:

> Because he was from the East Caribbean, I believe Frankie could relate to singers from different islands, not just Trinidad. He understood and appreciated

them more than others did. Take Becket who also was from Saint Vincent—his song "Coming High" had a big impact in the late 1970s and might have won the Trinidad Road March if they hadn't changed the rules so only Trini nationals could compete. But that was Frankie's arrangement—a real breakthrough, and he became highly respected in Trinidad! When you listen to Becket's singing and Frankie's music you realize they went hand in hand. So, who made who?[6]

Frankie was highly respected by the singers, musicians, and producers he worked with, who often referred to him as "Sir Frankie" and "The Maestro."[7] Rawlston Charles declared that "Frankie had music all over him, look at the family he came from. He knew how to coordinate the singers and musicians to find a way to make the lyrics, melody, and musical accompaniments hug and kiss each other." Trumpeter and arranger Errol Ince attributed Frankie's unique arranging style to his formal music training, the fact that he was a "degreed musician who went to university to study classical music and jazz." Ince noted that Frankie was known for his advanced harmonic language: "the way he voiced his instruments by using substitute and extended chords was very sophisticated. You could hear ideas from jazz and different styles. That's what set him apart." Calypso Rose effused that Frankie's arrangements were "inspirational, they made my songs sound more powerful. He used these beautiful chords, and he had a great sense of rhythm that often sounded quite African to me." Rose was not alone in praising Frankie's ability to transform skeletal melodies into fully formed compositions. Becket, Explainer, Short Shirt, and Scorcher all lauded Frankie's talent for expanding their seed melodies into complete songs with compelling accompaniments that made them hits. "Sometimes I gave him ideas for a band chorus," recalled Short Shirt, "and sometimes he would come up with lines that were totally different than what I first envisioned. But I never questioned him, he knew music, and I was always satisfied with the final product!" The calypsonians he worked with clearly entrusted their songs to Frankie. As Becket put it: "We gave him the words and the melody, and he gave us super arrangements! To me he was, and still is, nothing short of a musical genius."[8]

Frankie was also admired for his honesty and modest demeanor, as an individual who never put himself above his bandmates, even though his knowledge and skills often surpassed theirs. His recording sessions were well-organized, and he was always ready to accept input that might enhance an arrangement. Chalkdust told me that Frankie's sessions were much freer and more relaxed than those of the older arrangers like Art De Coteau with whom he had worked. "Frankie would really listen to his singers and musicians,

Saint Vincent Postal Stamp, 1997.

and was willing to improvise and modify his original arrangements on the spot. There was a great deal of respect all around." Rawlston Charles praised Frankie's calm, quiet personality that set an easygoing atmosphere in the studio, and his willingness to give any reasonable suggestion a serious try. Herman Hall called him the "gentleman of calypso, someone who always modest and down to earth, an attribute his musicians appreciated."[9]

The shower of accolades from government and cultural organizations has been ongoing for decades. These include Arranger of the Year awards from the Caribbean Music Grammys (1990) and *Everybody's* magazine (1992); the Annual Award for Musical Excellence from the Brooklyn-based Trinidad and Tobago Folk Arts Institute (1993); a commemorative postage stamp (1997) and diplomatic passport (2010) from the Government of Saint Vincent and the Grenadines; the Sunshine Hall of Fame Award for outstanding contributions to Caribbean Culture (2015); numerous citations from the City of New York and the Borough of Brooklyn for community service; and most recently, an honorary doctorate from the University of the West Indies (2020).

Despite Frankie's many accomplishments, his musical career has not been without its frustrations. His close music partners Garvin Blake and Charles Daugherty remarked that the pressures of the commercial soca market too often compelled Frankie to rein in his more innovative inclinations. During a number of our conversations Frankie expressed his discontent over too often being imprisoned by the monotonous two or three-chord soca loop with its limited triadic harmonies. He occasionally resisted when calypsonians Rose, Chalkdust, Sparrow, Shadow, and Kitchener brought him melodies that lent themselves to the addition of more complex chord progressions and colorful harmonies. Perhaps his most innovative work was with the forward-thinking Alston Becket Cyrus, especially in their self-produced albums such *Coming Higher* LP (1978), where no commercial producer was standing over their shoulders. Frankie's arrangement of "Wine Down Kingstown," with its edgy sax and frenetic synthesizer lines, bebop-inflected trumpet solo, and closing dissonant horn blasts stands as a testament to the young arranger's vision for what the new calypso might be.

For better (economically) or worse (creatively), the commercial market forces tended to hold sway, limiting the output of Frankie's more daring arrangements. It was clearly an age-old dilemma—the juggling act of balancing art and commerce. The calypsonian Becket summed it up this way:

> You see, Frankie was a humble person who aimed to please his singers and musicians, but also the producers like Granville Straker and Rawlston Charles. Honestly, they were businessmen who were more concerned with the market than with making groundbreaking music. They went in with economics on their mind, come into the studio fast and get out fast, save money. Frankie generally gave them what they wanted, but I believe sometimes they limited his creativity. But you know he had to put food on the table, so that's what he did. It has never been easy to make a decent living in the calypso world, and I'll never forget this famous Frankie quote: "The worst thing in life is to be famous and poor."[10]

The world of the soca recording studio also placed constraints on Frankie as a keyboardist. His role at recording sessions was generally one of ensemble directing and contributing musical support on keyboards, not to stand out as a virtuosic soloist. The synthesizer he helped establish as a vital component of the new soca sound was adequate for melodic introductions, interludes, and fills, but was not well-suited for the high level of improvisation that he could engender on an acoustic piano, especially in a more jazz-oriented context. Indeed, his sophisticated harmonic palette, his impressive abilities as a keyboard soloist, and his fledgling efforts as a composer took center stage in his later jazz projects, especially his *Parallel Overtones* collaboration with Garvin Blake. Frankie's original "One for Boogsie," his elegant jazz-waltz setting for Kitchener's "Pan in Harmony," and his adventurous rearrangement of Sparrow's "No Money No Love" set high standards for the future blending of jazz and calypso.

Worth noting was our lack of agreement on a satisfactory term for that particular musical admixture. This was a sticky point that persisted throughout our conversations, and despite my nudging, Frankie remained uncomfortable with the terms "calypso jazz," "Caribbean jazz," or "pan jazz" to describe the music he and Garvin have been playing together in small ensembles over the past two decades. Garvin expressed similar qualms, and Happy Williams simply chose not to respond to my "What is calypso jazz?" query. All three view themselves as Caribbean musicians who play within the jazz idiom, but who resist naming the music they produce as a specific style or substyle of jazz. Their lived experiences as practicing musicians left them skeptical of labels originating from the music industry or from scholars and critics like me. Rather, as Garvin noted in the previous chapter, they prefer to look beyond categories to the process of synergy that has resulted in the formation of diverse musical expressions across the Caribbean and its diaspora, and indeed in the emergence of jazz itself. This may explain why Frankie likes to refer to the exercise of "jazzing up a calypso," rather than the label "calypso jazz" as end product. There is a lesson here for those of us who study and write about music—as ethnomusicologist and bandleader Christopher Washburne cautions, we need to temper our "idealized projections" of tightly defined generic categories.[11] Thanks for clarifying this, Frankie and Garvin—I finally get it!

One final observation: Frankie never thought of himself as a soca composer, but he certainly wrote a great deal of music. He almost always received arranging credit, but never coauthorship, save his "Celebration" collaboration with Explainer. In retrospect there are a number of instances where this seemed blatantly unfair. Consider, for instance, that he wrote at least half the music for pieces like Becket's "Coming High" and "Wind Down Kingstown," and for Shadow's "Tension" and "Music Turns Me On" (to name but a few). Arguably his original horn lines and hook-driven introductions were responsible for the popularity of numerous hits from Rose's "No Mister," Duke's "Total Disorder," and Explainer's "Lorraine" to Sparrow's "Don't Back Back," Swallow's "Fire in the Backseat," and Scorcher's "Party Fever." The system of awarding full legal authorship (and royalties) to the calypsonian who ostensibly wrote the lyrics and melody of a song has long frustrated Frankie and his fellow arrangers, who feel they did not receive ample creative recognition or financial compensation for their contributions. Chalkdust, always a shrewd observer of art and politics, has noted this dilemma, and chided his fellow calypsonians for assuming that arrangers would transform their skeletal melodies and snatches of lyrics into a hit by crafting all of the music.[12]

Turning to Frankie's more recent jazz projects, "One for Boogsie" was one of the few pieces he took full compositional credit for. But his treatment of Sparrow's "Jane" and "No Money No Love" and Kitchener's "Pan in Harmony" were such radical transformations that only a calypso aficionado would recognize the original tune in the new setting. Legally those songs were copyrighted by Sparrow and Kitchener, but in Frankie's hands they became new creations, thereby further blurring the boundary between arranger and composer. Going forward, will he continue to reinterpret the older calypsos in innovative ways? Or will he move more into the realm of composition, perhaps creating original material that pays homage to the sounds and styles of the past? Arranger, composer, or both?

In closing, as I ponder the past and look to the future, I cannot help but wonder how the evolution of soca might have taken a different path if the market forces had not pushed Frankie to limit the unconventional and jazz-influenced impulses that shaped his early Becket arrangements, and that occasionally resurfaced in his work with Rose, Shadow, and Kitchener? (The same question could be posed to Leston Paul, Pelham Goddard, Clive Bradley, and the other soca revolutionaries who, while lacking Frankie's formal training in classical music and jazz, no doubt wrestled with how much jazz and rock their Caribbean audiences would tolerate.) In a related vein, what might have happened if Frankie had focused more of his energies on some sort of calypso/jazz fusion earlier in his career as an arranger and performer? By his own admission he did not have the temperament to be a big bandleader, but what if he had established a small jazz ensemble in which he could regularly stretch out as a player, arranger, and composer? Might that have influenced the fusion of jazz and calypso back in the 1980s and 1990s? Obviously, these are unknowns that will remain unknowable, but his recent work with Garvin and Max may portend more fresh things to come. One thing that is knowable at the time of this writing, Frankie McIntosh's musical tag is not over yet. On that note I turn it back to him for a final word.

When Ray approached me in the summer of 2019 about a book focusing on my career as a soca arranger, I was flattered but uncertain. Such a thing was nowhere in my thoughts! I had never been very comfortable talking about my own music, preferring to leave analysis and evaluation to others. But here was someone proposing we spend hours dissecting my old arrangements! And how could I possibly find time for such an undertaking?

Ironically, the COVID shutdown proved fortuitous for our project. Live gigs and in-person studio appearances had been acutely reduced; but this facilitated weekly Zoom sessions, which provided a satisfactory platform for extended conversations and listening to music together. Relating my life's story was quite pleasurable, save the occasional moments of recalling family and musical friends who had passed on. Discussing my own work was more difficult, though: Forty years prior it had simply flowed "off the cuff," as naturally as speaking. Now I was being asked to analyze, explain, critique, and sometimes meta-critique it. Wow! Ray's queries were demanding, and quite often my tacit reactions were "why is this even important?"—at least until proffering an answer led me to realize how nuanced the questions were. The exercise turned out to be largely one of self-discovery, of "getting into my own head" as it were, and at times it proved frustrating. In retrospect my efforts to regress to the 1970s and 1980s in order to assess my original musical choices often fell short—a reminder that philosopher Martin Heidegger was right in that our interpretation and understanding of the past can only be derived from our position in the existential present. My comments throughout this book represent current reactions as I listen back, and not necessarily my thinking or intentions when I originally arranged the songs.

As I reflect on my experience with Ray, and our efforts to recall my musical past, one thing that strikes me is how deeply I lament the decline of purely instrumental calypso music performed by Caribbean dance bands. There was a time when in bars or on the street, music lovers would engage in conversation about the merits of Beverly Griffith's "Tropical," Ottmar De Vlugt's "Waltz of the Flowers," and Ron Berridge's "Paris Burning," all instrumental arrangements of preexisting pieces. I am aware that from its inception, calypso has been primarily a vocal tradition, with most commercial recordings emphasizing the calypsonian, at the expense of the band and its arranger. But there was a flowering of instrumental calypso from the 1950s through the early 1980s thanks to great arrangers like Frankie Francis, Beverly Griffith, Cito Fermin, and Ron Berridge, whose bands were fronted by talented soloists Harold Vasso Defreitas, Errol Ince, Ottmar De Vlugt, and others.

Those musicians, and most of the others cited in this book, are from Trinidad and are more widely known owing to the circulation of their recordings. However, similar situations existed on other islands—I am thinking of the Blue Rhythm Orchestra of Saint Vincent, led by alto sax virtuoso Syl McIntosh, and featuring the brilliant pianist Carver James and drummer Arnold McIntosh; the Latinaires, also of Saint Vincent, with star tenor saxophonist Julian McIntosh; the Big Six Combo of St. Lucia with "Pan" on keys; the Swinging Stars of Dominica; and the Maestros of Grenada with Bing Morriset on piano. That sort of instrumental music with four or five horns stating a melody in harmony is rarely heard in the Anglophone Caribbean today, save for a group like the Roy Cape Allstars. I think this is a huge loss. On the brighter side, I am encouraged that the instrumental calypso tradition has survived and flourished in the sophisticated Panorama arrangements for steelbands, and in small pan-jazz ensembles. I am confident that Garvin Blake, Boogsie Sharpe, Rudy Smith, Saeed Bowman, Rodney Small, Othello Molineaux, Vanessa Headley, Duvonne Stuart, and others will continue to champion improvised pan music. Meanwhile I am hopeful that younger players Etienne Charles, Jesse Ryan, Daniel Ryan, Ming Low Chew Tung, Luther Francois, Ricardo "Ricky" McIntosh, and Theron Shaw will continue to rejuvenate the instrumental calypso tradition and take it in new directions.

My music, like those instrumental bands, evinces a strong jazz influence, and why not? I was born in Saint Vincent and the Grenadines at a time when many musicians and residents embraced jazz. At age ten, as pianist in my father's band, I was introduced to such jazz standards as "One O'Clock Jump," "Star Eyes," and "Body and Soul." In Antigua, Laviscount's hotel repertoire included "Meme," "I Can't Get Started," and "Misty"—all from the American jazz canon. Although I never considered myself strictly a jazz musician, jazz-influenced improvisation had become part of my skill set. On migrating to New York, a bastion of jazz where I have lived close to three quarters of my life, how could I be impervious to it? Today, playing with Garvin, Max, and Charles is my modest contribution to keeping that wing of the instrumental calypso tradition alive, as long as I don't have to call it calypso jazz. Yes, "jazzing up a calypso" is a much better way to think about it.

Now back to soca arranging. Looking over our conversations, I may have been too harsh in my critique of the simple harmonic language that started taking hold in soca around the time I was beginning my career as an arranger. After all, there is so much more to music than Western tonal harmony. Africans did not arrive in the New World singing the major scale or strumming triads on guitars; they came with their own musical traditions. In the United States, African Americans transformed classical harmony, adapting it to their own musical practices as they forged the blues, jazz, and the spirituals. Most of the new soca music, however, embraced the European model in its most elementary form: triads built on the first, fourth, and fifth degrees of the major or minor European diatonic scale while ignoring the progressive, African-based innovations of jazz. I quickly noticed that the success of my jazz-tinged arrangements was falling short of those based on the conventional three-chord progression. Many Caribbean record buyers at Straker's shop would refuse to purchase a song that was "too jazzy."

Without warning, that rich calypso vocabulary was being reduced to a static model in which events recurred with predictable regularity. There was vertical and horizontal attrition of harmony while repetitive "one-liner hooks" replaced the stories of Sparrow and Lord Melody. Since the soca melodies themselves were generated from triadic chords they demanded basic triadic chordal accompaniment. Thus I, as arranger, was faced with Hobson's choice: conform or starve. Well, here I am writing about it forty years later.

I tried to break up the monotony by adding an expanded harmonic progression where possible, writing an occasional bridge or modulation, and sneaking in a jazzy instrumental solo or two. Those interventions were shaped in part by my prior experiences with classical, jazz, and R&B music, and can be heard in many of the songs we discussed in chapters 5 and 6. But listening back I have come to realize that music of the folk is influenced by factors beyond my ability to explain. Calypso and soca songwriters are often described as the "barometers" who are the first to sense a change in the direction of cultural winds, and then to express those changes in their compositions. Hence, the soca arranger must remain guided by whatever material the singer presents, even when it means adhering to a repetitive chord sequence and the curtailment of progressive voicings. A good arranger must be keenly aware of the original song's inherent melodic and rhythmic nuances, much of which I believe are derived from the expressive features of Caribbean English and serve as sonic markers of the Anglo-Caribbean experience. Being able to translate those basic linguistic features into strong rhythmic grooves, rich textures, and horn lines that complement and augment the vocal is at the heart of successful soca arranging. That was what Leston, Pelham, Clive, and I (among others) were up to back then—the challenge of making something interesting when a soca singer presented us with only a simple melody. I might add that those folk melodies and rudimentary harmonies are our Caribbean cultural inheritance, a mirror of our complex history of slavery, colonialism, independence, and ongoing cultural creolization. They should be respected as such, in the same manner that blues, jazz, spirituals, and other forms of Black American music are.

A few more observations: As Ray rightly points out, my arranging career never strayed far from the West Indian calypso world. This, despite the fact that I always enjoyed playing with American jazz musicians, was quite conversant with the R&B music of the era, and certainly possessed the skills to arrange that music. Other than the experience with Becket's first LP on the Casablanca label, the opportunity to arrange for bigger American music companies did not readily present itself, and I never actively pursued it. Honestly, I was comfortable with my calypsonians and our island culture, maybe because it reminded me of home—it was like living in the Caribbean but being right here in New York. In the end, things really did work out for me. I had my music, my socializing, a steady income that took care of my financial obligations, and I could stay home, close to my family. I never felt the strong temptation to move into uncharted waters and give up the security I had worked to establish. Today I have no reason to regret that choice.

Now in response to the question of doing more playing in a small, jazz-oriented ensemble. That is something I am really enjoying at this point in my life, but I just don't see how I could have done that full-time and made a reasonable living earlier in my career. Full-time gigging is a hard life. You have to really work to keep up your playing skills, and you have to be out there for some time in the right professional loops in order to get regular calls for jobs. And you must be willing to travel at the drop of a hat. It would have been simply impossible for me to be a performer and an arranger at the same time. Finally, it came down to time and money: there was no question that arranging was more lucrative and convenient, so that was the path I chose.

Do I have any regrets? Well, in retrospect I might have paid more attention to the business side of things, especially when it came to agreements over authorship. As we discussed earlier, the line between arranging and composing is often a blurry one. When I occasionally hear songs like "Lorraine," "Coming High," or "Is Thunder" on the radio I can't help but think, hey, that's my music! And then I remember that I did not get any coauthorship credit for it back then, or now, because I did not push for some share of the legal copyright. Yes, a few royalties would certainly help in retirement, and maybe give me something to leave for my kids and grandchildren. Now I do not hold any ill will toward the artists—that was the way things were done back then. But hopefully those ways are changing as we who arrange, rearrange, and compose the music begin to assert our rights to coauthorship with the songwriters.

Another thing I might have done differently if I had it to do over would be to attend more of the mix sessions in order to have had more input in the sound of the final product. After all, it was music that I had written, and I knew how I wanted it to sound in correspondence to my original vision in the score—particularly regarding the right balance of the instruments and where prominent parts should be featured. And I suppose I could have pushed more aggressively for live drums and more horns. But again, time and money too often intervened. Remember, I was not paid to come to the final mix, and those were hours that I could have spent doing more arranging or taking care of family business. On top of that, many producers did not welcome arrangers at mix sessions. They thought they understood the market and what sort of sound would sell best, and they were not interested in other opinions. But as an artist listening back to those early recordings, some of their decisions give me pause.

So, what of the future? I certainly intend to continue to play with Garvin and Max as long as my fingers and mind hold up. We want to see where we can go with our small ensembles that "jazz up calypsos." I also plan to work with calypsonians when the occasional opportunity arises. I recently worked up an arrangement for a new song by my old friend Short Shirt. He is still going strong, and collaborating with him has been pleasantly reminiscent of the old days. Maybe we can come up with one more hit for Antigua!

In terms of new compositions, I have in mind some more adventurous projects. I hope to explore new music that is less chordal-based, is more atonal and dissonant (perhaps built around tone clusters), and that employs multiple meters. That music will also remain based on the rhythmic contours of Caribbean speech, employ African call-and-response exchanges, and make generous use of improvisation. That is just what I am hearing in my head these days, in my inner musical consciousness. I played around with a bit of that with Shadow on "Tempo" and "Music Turns Me On," and on my piano solo on "Delicate Planet" from Max's *Major Matters* CD. I'm also thinking about more extended, sectional compositions that might capture different moods. We flirted with those forms on "No Money No Love" from *Parallel Overtones*, but I am imagining taking it further out. I believe artists can continue to evolve, and I hope that's what is still happening with me.

Working on this current book project has also made me consider writing more about my own observations regarding Caribbean music, perhaps from a more analytical perspective. I am very interested in exploring the changes that occurred in the music from the 1950s calypso band period up through the 1960s and into the soca era of the 1970s and 1980s. We have talked about some of that in passing with respect to my own musical trajectory, but I would like to look more closely into the works of the great Caribbean bandleaders, instrumentalists, and arrangers. I have also thought about putting together a methods book, a guide to playing jazz for steel panists, because they are the ones who are currently the most serious about carrying on the instrumental calypso tradition.

Now, two more things on my "to do" list—more frequent visits to Saint Vincent and eat more mangos! Those may go together.

A parting thought. By now readers should be well aware that this has not been a "how to" manual for calypso or soca arranging. Nor did we delve as

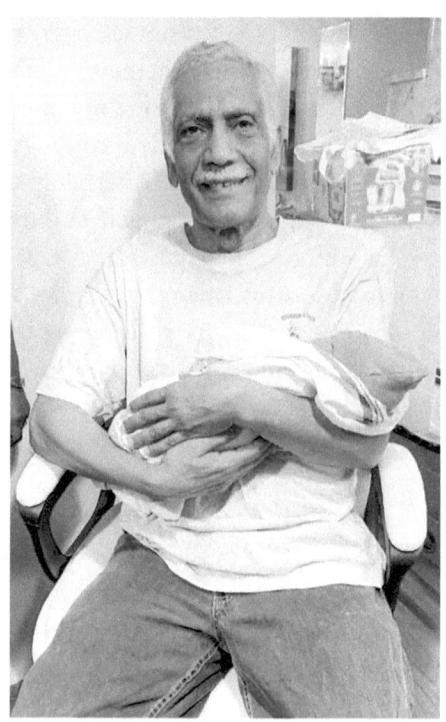

Frankie with Kymani McIntosh, grandchild no. 9, August 2023.

deep into the musical analysis of harmony, melody, and rhythm as some music theorists might wish. Those are projects for the future. For now, I hope that in addition to my life story, our discussions of the music underpinning the songs will prove informative to readers, including those not trained in the formal aspects of music. My final plea: please listen to the music on our "Art of the Soca Arranger" YouTube channel, consult the listening guides, and enjoy. This music was, and remains, my sustenance and my joy, the means by which I provided for my family and discovered my artistic self. It is also the reason that this book has been written.

APPENDIX 1

SMALL ISLAND CALYPSOS AND SOCA SONGS

1) "Coming High" by Alston "Becket" Cyrus (Casablanca Records, 1977)

https://www.youtube.com/watch?v=pwD2TXeBW5s&list=PLcldY-KYUdTwM_4E-rEroIUnjWi1vaMYG&index=1

0:00 – introduction with percussion, cycling guitar chords, and bass
0:10 – Becket enters with vocal rap to Mary
0:20 – horns enter under Becket's vocal rap
0:53 – "Mary do you wanna" vocal chorus
0:58 – "I coming high, high, high" vocal chorus
1:08 – "Mary do you wanna?" vocal chorus (doubled on bass and low horns)
1:18 – bluesy synthesizer figure
1:26 – vocal verse 1 – "Music sweet, sweet, sweet"
1:36 – "Mary do you wanna?" vocal chorus (doubled on bass and low horns)
1:46 – repeat bluesy synthesizer figure in original key of B
Bridge
1:57 – key modulation from B to C major and repeat bluesy synthesizer figure
2:07 – call and response between double-voiced horns/bass and synthesizer over descending chord turnaround
2:20 – modulate back to original key of B with call and response brass and reeds
2:30 – vocal verse 2 – "Me head bad, bad, bad"
2:40 – "Mary do you wanna?" vocal chorus (doubled on bass and low horns)
2:49 – variation on bluesy synthesizer figure
2:58 – vocal verse 3 – "Becket dred, dred, dred"

3:08 – "Mary do you wanna?" vocal chorus (doubled on bass and low horns)
3:18 – bluesy synthesizer figure
3:27 – percussion break with "Mary do you wanna" vocal
3:36 – bass reintroduced
3:46 – "coming high, high" vocal refrain reintroduced
4:04 – brass/reed call and response band chorus
4:32 – bluesy synthesizer variation

Bridge

4:40 – key modulation from B to C major while synthesizer continues bluesy variation
4:450 – call and response between double-voiced horns/bass and synthesizer over descending chord formation
5:04 – modulate back to original key of B with bluesy synthesizer variation
5:14 – light horn riffs
5:41 – bluesy guitar solo over key modulation and bridge
6:23 – brass/reed call and response band chorus
6:50 – bluesy synthesizer variation

Bridge

6:59 – key modulation from B to C major while synthesizer continues bluesy variation
7:08 – call and response between double-voiced horns/bass and synthesizer over descending chord formation
7:22 – modulate back to original key of B with call and response brass and reeds

Tag (coda)

7:32 – Becket begins ad-libbing over percussion
7:41 – bass reenters and the tempo increases (7:50) as the guitar, synthesizer, horns, and vocal refrain are layered in over Becket's ad-libs, followed by fade (8:15)

"Coming High" basic chord progressions (key of B)

Instrumental Intro/Verse/Chorus:

```
B   /  E   /  B   /  F#  / repeat
////   ////   ////   ////   ////
```

Six-measure, descending turnaround to move from bridge-modulated key of C back to original key of B:

```
F7  /  F7  /  Eb7 /  Eb7 /  D7  / Db7-C7 /  (2:07)
////   ////   ////   ////   ////   //  //
```

Listening Highlights

- Key modulation from key of B to key of C, synthesizer solo, and turn around sequence back to original key of C (1:57–2:21; 4:40–5:04; 6:59–7:22)
- Victor Collins bluesy/rock guitar solo (5:41)
- Percussion break followed by layered reentry of bass, guitar, synthesizer, horns, and vocals (7:32 to end)

2) "Wine Down Kingstown" by Alston Becket Cyrus (First River Records, 1978)

https://www.youtube.com/watch?v=icSbVMwovYQ&list=PLcldY-KYUdTwM_4E-rEroIUnjWi1vaMYG&index=2

0:00 – introduction with reeds and brass alternating choppy, bluesy phrases
0:06 – bass, percussion, and backing vocals enter with "Wine Down Kingstown Park" chorus
0:14 – ascending synthesizer lines over rhythm section
0:20 – vocal verse 1
0:40 – vocal chorus
0:50 – cycle of fourths chord progression leading back to tonic chord (F♯) and band chorus
0:54 – band chorus built around opening bluesy phrases played by reeds alternating with brass
1:08 – vocal verse 2
1:28 – vocal chorus
1:42 – band chorus built around opening bluesy phrases played by reeds alternating with brass
1:56 – vocal verse 3
2:17 – vocal chorus
2:30 – variation on band chorus with low reeds playing bluesy, syncopated riffs
2:58 – trumpet solo by Ray Maldonado
3:19 – syncopated horn riffs answered by ascending synthesizer figures
3:42 – vocal refrain in softly below horn riffs and synthesizer figures
4:48 – vocal refrain returns more forcefully under horn riffs and synthesizer figures
5:18 – percussion break

"Wine Down Kingstown" by Alston Becket Cyrus, music arranged by Frankie McIntosh.

5:47 – backing vocals and Becket return followed by full rhythm section
6:30 – vocals drop out, synthesizer figures alternating with dissonant horn hits
6:56 – vocals return over synthesizer figures alternating with dissonant horn hits
7:29 – vocals drop out, synthesizer figures alternating with original bluesy phrases on horns

"Wine Down Kingstown" basic chord progressions (Key of F#)

Instrumental introduction:

B-G#7/ C#7-F#7 / repeat
// //   // //

Vocal Verse:

C#7 / F#+6 / C#7 / F#+6 / repeat
////   ////   ////   ////

B / F# / G#m-C#7 / F#7
//// ////   //   //   ////

Vocal Chorus

B/ G#7 / C#7 / F#7 / repeat
// //   //   //

Listening Highlights

- Opening, choppy call (saxophones) and response (trombone and synthesizer) lines
- Two-measure turn-around progression at 0:50 leading back to tonic key of B (0:55):
  Cm7-F7-B♭m7-E♭7 / G♯+9-C♯-F♯-rest /
  /   /   /   /   /   /   /   /
- Jazz-flavored trumpet solo (2:58)
- Syncopated horn riffs answered by ascending improvised synthesizer figures (3:19)
- Final dissonant horns playing F♯7+♯9 voicing (starting at 6:30). (F♯dominant 7-♯9)

3) "Tony" by Becket (First River Records, 1978)

https://www.youtube.com/watch?v=Ksy9p_Rby4U

0:00 – percussive grove on drums and conga
0:08 – opening seven-note figure on piano, joined in unison by bass and then background vocals singing "Tony, I want Tony"
0:25 – dramatic crescendo on suspended chord
0:29 – music resolves to tonic chord as Becket enters with vocal verse 1
0:48 – vocal chorus ("She wants Tony")
1:00 – Becket ad-libs on different varieties of "Tony"
1:10 – return to opening piano/bass phrase, background vocals, and final suspended chord, now serving as the band chorus
1:30 – vocal verse 2
1:48 – vocal chorus
2:00 – Becket ad-libs second time on different varieties of "Tony"
2:11 – band chorus ending on suspended chord
2:31 – vocal verse 3
2:50 – vocal chorus
3:02 – Becket ad-libs third time on different varieties of "Tony"
3:12 – repeat opening piano phrase of band chorus
3:20 – Becket ad-libs fourth time on different varieties of "Tony"
3:42 – trumpet solo (Ray Maldonado)
4:30 – Becket ad-libs fourth time on different varieties of "Tony"

4:43 – alto sax solo (Sam Furnace)
5:12 – Becket final ad-lib on different varieties of "Tony"
5:30 – flute patch synthesizer solo
6:29 – opening phrase of band chorus and vocals return
6:44 – final dramatic suspend chord resolves to tonic

"Tony" basic chord progressions (key of D♭)

Intro:

D♭-A♭7/Dm-A♭7 / repeat
// //   // //

G♭maj7 with A♭ bass (horns outline notes in upper part of chord)
////   ////

Vocal Verse:

D♭-B♭m / E♭m-A♭7 / repeat three times
// //   // //

Fm7-B7 / C7-Fm / B♭m-E♭m / A♭7-D♭ /
// //   // //   // //   // //

Vocal Chorus:

D♭m-A♭7 / A♭7-D♭m /
// //   // //

Listening Highlights

- Crescendo on colorful suspended chord (G♭maj7 with an A♭ bass pedal) with synth-voice patch on top (0:25)
- Jazzy solos on trumpet (3:42), alto saxophone (4:33), and synthesizer with flute patch (5:30)

4) "Too Much Corruption" by Winston Soso (Straker's Records, 1981)

https://www.youtube.com/watch?v=N7vlT5bHYN0

0:00 – introduction with sharp, staccato horn lines over active bass
0:15 – vocal verse 1

0:38 – vocal chorus
0:55 – band chorus with horn lines from introduction
1:10 – vocal verse 2
1:33 – vocal chorus
1:49 – band chorus with horn lines from introduction
2:04 – vocal verse 3
2:28 – vocal chorus
2:44 – band chorus with horn lines from introduction
2:58 – vocal verse 4
3:22 – vocal chorus
3:38 – band chorus with horn lines from introduction
Tag
4:00 – Soso ad-libs over occasional horn and synthesizer riffs
5:02 – descending legato synthesizer line introduced
5:10 – horns play staccato intro/band theme riffs over synthesizer
6:12 – horns drop out and synthesizer improvises more actively
6:28 – horns return over synthesizer
7:04 – song ends on sharply punctuated horn riff

"Too Much Corruption" basic chord progressions (key of C♯)

Band Chorus, Vocal Verse, Vocal Chorus:

G♯-F♯ / C♯ / G♯-F♯ / C♯ /
// // //// // // ////

Listening Highlights

- Band chorus built around call-and-response between sharp, staccato trumpets (0:00) and low horns (0:04)
- Extended tag with vocal improvisation interspersed over new horn and synthesizer lines (4:00 to end)

5) "I Don't Mind" by Winston Soso (Straker's Records, 1985)

https://www.youtube.com/watch?v=nqRRxSR77n8

0:00 – introduction by percussion
0:04 – synthesizer and bass introduce theme A
0:19 – horns introduce bright theme B

0:35 – vocal verse 1
1:05 – "I don't mind" vocal chorus
1:20 – band chorus with A & B themes
1:51 – vocal verse 2
2:21 – "I don't mind" vocal chorus
2:37 – band chorus with A & B themes
3:08 – vocal verse 3
3:38 – "I don't mind" vocal chorus
3:53 – new variation on earlier synthesizer theme A
4:08 – "I don't mind" vocal chorus

Tag

4:24 – Soso ad-libs over rhythm section and new punctuated horn lines
4:58 – "I don't mind" vocal chorus returns
5:30 – Soso ad-libs
5:44 – "I don't mind" vocal chorus returns
6:15 – Soso ad-libs over rhythm section and punctuated horn lines
6:37 – "I don't mind" vocal chorus returns and fade

"I Don't Mind" basic chord progressions (key of B)

Band Chorus:

(Theme A): B / F# / B / F# /
            ////   ////   ////   ////

(Theme B): B / E-F# / B / F# /
            ////   // //   ////   ////

Vocal Verse:

B / F#-E / B /
////   // //   ////

Vocal Chorus:

B / E-F# / B / E-F# /
////   // //   ////   // //

Listening Highlights

- Synthesizer, guitar, and bass lines create heavy groove underneath the vocals and horns throughout

- Sectional band chorus (A/B). Note rate of harmonic change in B section, where the B major chord is held for four beats and the E and F♯ major chords are held for only two beats each (0:19–0:34), creating a sense of acceleration, reinforced with Soso's command to "push it" (0:20)
- Horns respond to vocal phrases during verse (0:55 and 1:02) and then double voice in "I don't mind" chorus (1:05 and 1:13)

6) "East 95th Street" by Scorcher (Starker's Records, 1979)

https://www.youtube.com/watch?v=h2Rf-TE8coI

0:00 – introduction with low reeds phrase followed by high brass
0:16 – vocal verse 1, punctuated by descending high brass phrases (0:21, again at 0:28)
0:48 – vocal chorus
1:04 – band chorus similar to introduction, built around call and response between low reeds and high brass
1:19 – vocal verse 2
1:50 – vocal chorus
2:05 – band chorus built around call and response between low reeds and high brass
2:21 – vocal verse 3
2:53 – vocal chorus
Tag
3:08 – Scorcher begins vocal ad-libs against vocal chorus
3:38 – first trumpet solo by Ron Taylor
4:08 – Scorcher returns with vocal ad-libs
4:40 – second trumpet solo by Ron Taylor
5:12 – Scorcher returns with final vocal ad-libs to fade

"East 95th Street" basic chord progressions (key of F♯)

Band Chorus:

C♯ / F♯ / C♯-B / F♯ /
////   ////   // //   ////

Vocal Verse:

C♯-B / F♯ /C♯-B / F♯ /
// // //// // // ////

Vocal Chorus:

C♯ / F♯ / C♯-B / F♯ /
//// //// // // ////

Listening Highlights

- Call and response between sung vocal verse phrases and descending high brass phrases (0:21 and again at 0:28)
- Bebop-flavored jazzy solos by Ron Taylor during tag (3:38 and 4:40)

7) "Party Fever" by Scorcher (Straker's Records, 1981)

https://www.youtube.com/watch?v=mR05A7aS_nw

0:00 – introduction on synthesizer with horn responses (0:05 and 0:13)
0:31 – vocal verse 1
0:46 – bridge on ascending (Bm-C-A-D) chord progression
1:00 – vocal chorus
1:20 – band chorus
1:54 – vocal verse 2
2:10 – bridge on ascending (Bm-C-A-D) chord progression
2:23 – vocal chorus
2:44 – band chorus
3:17 – vocal verse 3
3:30 – bridge on ascending (Bm-C-A-D) chord progression
3:46 – vocal chorus
3:54 – tag with Scorcher ad-libbing over "Party" and "Fever" chants from the female chorus

"Party Fever" basic chord progressions (key of D)

Band Chorus:

```
A   /   D   /   A   /   D   /   repeat
////    ////    ////    ////
```

Vocal Verse:

```
A-G   /   D   /   A   /   D   /
// //     ////    ////    ////
```

```
Bm  /  Bm  /  C  /  C  /  A  /  A  /  D  /
////   ////   ////  ////  ////  ////  ////
```

Vocal Chorus:

```
A   /   D   /   A   /   D   /   repeat
////    ////    ////    ////
```

Listening Highlights

- Horns and bass unison response to short vocal verse lines to produce melodic continuity (0:35, 0:42).
- Ascending bridge to at end of vocal verse (0:46) to build tension that is released with the vocal chorus built around the original A/D chord sequence (1:00).

8) "I'm a Hoper" by Scorcher (Straker's Records, 1982)

https://www.youtube.com/watch?v=3u9gtVz2Spc&list=PLcldY-KYUdTwM_4E-rEroIUnjWi1vaMYG&index=5

Introduction
0:05 – synthesizer line with brass response (A)
0:12 – brass lines from vocal chorus (B)
0:20 – back to synthesizer responding to initial brass (A)
0:28 – vocal verse 1 (modulate from key of E to key of B at 0:41 and then back to key of E at 0:53 to set up vocal chorus)

0:56 – vocal chorus
1:12 – band chorus (A-B-A)
1:35 – vocal verse 2
2:04 – vocal chorus
2:19 – band chorus (A-B-A)
2:43 – vocal verse 3
3:08 – vocal chorus (extended)
3:53 – repeat short band chorus
4:02 – tag with Scorcher ad-libbing

"I'm A Hoper" basic chord progressions (key of E, then modulates to key of B halfway through the vocal verse and then back to E for the final two measures of the vocal verse and the vocal chorus)

Band Chorus:

B / E / B / E /
////   ////   ////   ////

Vocal Verse:

E / B / D / A / repeat
//   ////   ////   ////

F#7 / F#7 / B / G#m / G#m-G#7 / C#m / A-B / E /
//// //// //// ////   // //   ////   // // ////

Vocal Chorus:

B / E / B / E /
////   ////   ////   ////

Listening Highlights

- Modulations in vocal verses from key of E to key of B at 0:41 (the F#7 chord above) and back to key of E at 0:53 (the A chord above) to set up vocal chorus in home key of E at 0:56

9) "Push" by Short Shirt (A&B Records, 1982)

https://www.youtube.com/watch?v=lSToeQS-z_U

0:00 – introduction with sharp, staccato trumpets with saxophone response
0:30 – vocal verse 1 (six beat phrases)
1:00 – vocal chorus ("Push")
1:30 – band chorus
2:00 – vocal verse 2 (six beat phrases)
2:30 – vocal chorus
3:00 – band chorus
3:30 – vocal verse 3 (six beat phrases)
4:00 – vocal chorus
4:30 – band chorus
Tag
5:00 – "Push it, push for me" female chorus
6:00 – band chorus
6:28 – "Push it, push for me" female chorus returns

"Push" basic chord progressions (key of C♯)

Band Chorus:

C♯	/	C♯	/	G♯	/	G♯	/	G♯	/	G♯	/	C♯	/	C♯	/
////		////		////		////		////		////		////		////	

Vocal Verse:

C♯	/	C♯	/	C♯	/	C♯	/	C♯	/	C♯	/	C♯	/	C♯	/
newline															

F♯	/	B♭m	/	F♯	/	B♭m	/
////		////		////		////	

F♯	/	B♭m	/	F♯	/	G♯	/
////		////		////		////	

Vocal Chorus:

C♯	/	C♯	/	G♯	/	G♯	/	G♯	/	G♯	/	C♯	/	C♯	/
////		////		////		////		////		////		////		////	

Listening Highlights

- Sharp, staccato horn lines of band chorus propel the music forward during introduction

- Irregular vocal verse with the first measure in 6/4, and the remaining seven measures in 4/4 for a total of 34 beats between 0:30 through 0:45

10) "The Champion" by Short Shirt (B's Records, 1986)

https://www.youtube.com/watch?v=SosoxtSh_bQ&t=7s

0:00 – eight-measure bluesy introduction on synthesizer with guitar response
0:15 – band chorus 1 leading with bright trumpets followed by saxophones (0:21), then by the synthesizer (0:28), and ending with high trumpet riffs (0:33)
0:35 – vocal verse 1
1:04 – vocal chorus "You are the Champion"
1:18 – band chorus 2 with variation on opening trumpet line
1:46 – vocal verse 2
2:15 – vocal chorus "You are the Champion"
2:29 – angelic female chorus sings "Oh, oh, the Champion"
2:44 – band chorus 1
3:05 – vocal verse 3
3:33 – vocal chorus "You are the Champion"
Tag
3:55 – vocal chant ("Come to making song / You're the champion")
4:15 – band chorus 2
4:30 – more vocal chorus
4:44 – variation on band chorus with saxophones leading and trombones responding
4:58 – more vocal chorus and fade

"The Champion" basic chord progressions (key of G)

Band Chorus:

```
C   /  G   /  D   /  G   / repeat
////   ////   ////   ////

D   /  G   /  D   /  G   / repeat
////   ////   ////   ////
```

```
C   / G-Em /   G   / D-G /
////   // //    ////   // //
```

Vocal Verse:

```
D   /   G   /   D   /   G   / repeat
////    ////    ////    ////
```

```
C-D / G-Em / C-D /   G   / repeat
// //   // //   // //    ////
```

Vocal Chorus:

```
D   /   G   /   D   /   G   / repeat
////    ////    ////    ////
```

```
C   / G-Em /   G   / D-G /
////   // //    ////   // //
```

Listening Highlight

- Eight-measure bluesy introduction on the synthesizer and guitar contrasts to the high, bright brass lines that drive the band chorus (0:15) and the vocal chorus (1:04)
- Variation in lead trumpet lines on band chorus 1 (0:15) and band chorus 2 (1:18)

11) "World in Distress" by Short Shirt (B's Records, 1986)

https://www.youtube.com/watch?v=uXic4-nHVwo&list=PLcldY-KYUdTwM_4E-rEroIUnjWi1vaMYG&index=11

Introductory Band Chorus
0:01 – section A, trumpets followed by alternating saxophone, trumpet, and trombone lines
0:17 – section B, call and response between the brass and reeds
0:34 – section C, saxophones, followed by all horns converging on a bright, C#+9 chord
0:42 – vocal verse 1
1:24 – vocal chorus
1:58 – band chorus (ABC)
2:40 – vocal verse 2

3:22 – vocal chorus
3:56 – band chorus (ABC)
4:37 – vocal verse 3
5:19 – vocal chorus
5:53 – band chorus (ABC)
6:16 – final open-voiced chord

"World in Distress" basic chord progressions (key of C♯)

Band Chorus:

```
G♯  /   G♯  /   C♯  /   C♯  / repeat (A)
////    ////    ////    ////

G♯  /   G♯  /   C♯  /   C♯  / repeat (B)
////    ////    ////    ////

C♯  /   F♯  /   E♭m7-G♯7 /  C♯+9  /        (C)
////    ////    //  //      ////
```

Vocal Verse:

```
G♯ /  C♯ /  G♯ /  C♯ /  G♯ /  C♯ /  D♯ /  G♯ /
////  ////  ////  ////  ////  ////  ////  ////

G♯ /  G♯ /  C♯ /  C♯ /  G♯ /  G♯ /  C♯ /  C♯ /
////  ////  ////  ////  ////  ////  ////  ////

C♯ / F♯  / E♭m7-G♯7 / C♯+9 /
////  ////   //   //    ////
```

Vocal Chorus:

```
G♯ / G♯ / C♯ / C♯ / repeat twice
////  ////  ////  ////

C♯ /  F♯  / E♭m7-G♯7 / C♯+9 /
////  ////   //   //    ////
```

Listening Highlight

- A/B/C sectional band chorus (0:01–0:41)
- During the last two measures of the band chorus the horns converge for a II-V-I turnaround, moving quickly through an E♭m7

to an G#7 and finally landing on a bright, C#+9 chord (0:40–0:42) leading into the first vocal verse
- Unison blend of brass, reeds, and bass in response to each of the "The world in distress" vocal lines (1:25, 1:28, 1:33)

12) "Find the Spot" by Swallow (Charlie's Records, 1982)

https://www.youtube.com/watch?v=zHlToasJocI

Intro Band Chorus
0:02 – melodic bass line followed by guitar response
0:09 – first synthesizer line added
0:15 – second synthesizer line added
0:24 – high brass and reeds in unison on "Find the Spot" vocal chorus riff
0:32 – synthesizer line followed by low reed response
0:46 – high brass and reeds in unison on "Find the Spot" vocal chorus riff
0:54 – synthesizer line leading into vocals
1:01 – vocal verse 1(A)
1:15 – vocal verse 1(B)
1:30 – vocal verse 1(C)
1:38 – vocal chorus 1(A)
1:44 – vocal chorus 1(B)
1:59 – vocal chorus 1(A)
band chorus 1
2:06 – first synthesizer line
2:21 – high brass riffs
2:28 – synth line returns
2:35 – vocal verse 2 (A/B/C)
3:12 – vocal chorus (A/B/A)
band chorus 2
3:42 – low reeds figure
3:48 – call and response between brass and reeds on new riff
4:04 – call and response between low brass/reeds and high brass on new riff
4:18 – high brass and reeds in unison on "Find the Spot" vocal chorus riff
4:25 – synthesizer line
4:40 – high brass and reeds in unison on "Find the Spot" vocal chorus riff
4:47 – synthesizer line leading into vocals
4:54 – vocal verse 3 (A/B/C)
5:31 – vocal chorus (A/B/A) and fade

"Find the Spot" basic chord progression (key of E)

Intro Band Chorus:

```
B   /  E   /  B   /  E    / repeat
////   ////   ////   ////

A   /  E   /  B   /  E-E7 / repeat
////   ////   ////   // //
```

Vocal Verse:

```
A   /  E   /  B   /  E    / repeat
////   ////   ////   ////

B   /  E   /  B   /  E    / repeat
////   ////   ////   ////

A   /  E   /  B   /  E-E7 /
////   ////   ////   // //
```

Vocal Chorus:

```
B   /  E   /  B   /  E    / repeat
////   ////   ////   ////

A   /  E   /  B   /  E-E7 / repeat
///    ////   ////   // //
```

Listening Highlights

- Interlock between the guitar, the two synthesizers, the bass, and drums together to form the underlying beat, or groove, during the introduction and throughout the piece
- Introduction demonstrates the additive approach to building up texture as each instrument is added one at a time, beginning with the melodic bass line and adding the guitar, synthesizers, and horns (0:02–0:31)
- Sectional A/B/C structured verses (1:01) and choruses (1:38)
- Band chorus 2 presents new horn lines (3:42)

13) "Fire in the Backseat" by Swallow (Charlie's Records, 1988)

https://www.youtube.com/watch?v=6YOvjkL7sGI

0:00 – percussion sets tempo; whistle sounds
Intro Band Chorus
0:09 – synthesizer doubles and bass line
0:17 – full, assertive horn riffs from vocal chorus
0:25 – lighter, lyrical sax/synthesizer lines
0:32 – synthesizer lines punctuated by horn hits
0:40 – vocal verse 1
1:07 – vocal chorus
1:30 – band chorus begins with bright, staccato horn riffs from vocal chorus
1:38 – low sax lines
1:46 – synthesizer lines punctuated by horn hits
1:54 – vocal verse 2
2:20 – vocal chorus
2:44 – band chorus begins with low sax lines
2:51 – sax lines punctuated by high brass riffs
3:00 – synthesizer line
3:07 – synthesizer line punctuated with horn hits
3:15 – vocal verse 3
3:41 – vocal chorus
4:08 – tag begins with synthesizer lines, followed by "oy" and "fire" chorus vocals
5:00 – Swallow ad-libs over rhythm section, "oy" and "fire" refrains return
5:40 – trumpet solo by Errol Ince

"Fire in the Backseat" basic chord progression (key of F)

Band Chorus:

```
F    /  C7   /  F    /  C7   /  repeat
////    ////    ////    ////
```

Vocal Verse:

```
F  /  F  /  F  /  C  /  F  /  repeat
////  ////  //    ////  ////
```

Bb	F	C	C7	C7
////	////	////	////	////

Vocal Chorus:

F	C7	F	C7	repeat
////	////	////	////	

Listening Highlights

- Contrasting lines by the assertive brass section (0:17) riffing on a variation of the "Fire in the backseat" hook, followed by a lighter/sweeter, more lyrical saxophones/synthesizer response (0:25)
- Uneven eighteen-beat verse structure (4+4+2+4+4; at 0:40)
- Bebop-flavored trumpet solo by Errol Ince during tag (5:40)

14) "Shiny Eyes" by Obstinate (Green Bay Records, 1985)

https://www.youtube.com/watch?v=ZlFOcswPuNE

Intro Band Section
0:00 – sliding guitar/synthesizer strum over syncopated bass line and drum
0:10 – second synth line enters over the established rhythm groove
0:17 – high horns enter
0:25 – second synth line reappears
0:33 – high horns reappear
0:41 – vocal verse 1
Vocal Chorus
1:04 – "Come back and love me" (A)
1:20 – "Oh shiny eyes" (B)
1:28 – rhythmic rap (C)
1:44 – "Oh shiny eyes" (B)
1:51 – rhythmic rap (C)
1:59 – band chorus
2:23 – vocal verse 2
2:46 – vocal chorus
3:41 – band chorus
4:05 – vocal verse 3
4:27 – vocal chorus

5:34 – tag with vocal ad-libs, female vocal refrain, and horn lines

"Shiny Eyes" basic chord progression (key of B♭)

B♭ / E♭ / B♭ / E♭ / repeat
////   ////   ////   ////

Listening highlights

- Funky guitar riff in introduction forms foundation of groove throughout song
- Sectionalized vocal chorus (A/B/C) provide contrast and variety over repeated chord loop

15) "Antiguan Independence" by Obstinate (Green Bay Records, 1981)

https://www.youtube.com/watch?v=qO0aHemnTGA

Introduction
0:00 – ascending high brass line
0:11 – response on the low reeds
0:15 – brass and reeds join on dramatic crescendo line
0:20 – all horns play sharp staccato hits on tonic chord, followed by abrupt stop
0:25 – vocal verse 1 – A/A/B
1:00 – vocal chorus
1:20 – band chorus repeats
1:45 – vocal verse 2 – A/A/B
2:20 – vocal chorus
2:42 – band chorus repeats
3:05 – vocal verse 3 – A/A/B
3:40 – vocal chorus
4:02 – band chorus repeats
4:26 – spoken verse
5:00 – final vocal chorus
5:20 – final band chorus with spoken voice
5:40 – final dramatic brass crescendo and staccato hits

"Antiguan Independence" basic chord progressions (key of A♭)

Band Chorus:

A♭ / A♭ / A♭ / E♭ /
//// //// //// ////

D♭-E♭ / A♭-C7-Fm / A♭-E♭ / A♭ /
// //   /   /   //   // //   ////

Vocal Verse:

A♭-D♭ / C7-Fm / Fm-D♭ / E♭ / repeat
// //   // //   // //   ////

D♭-E♭ / A♭-Fm / D♭-A♭ / B♭m-C7 /
// //   // //   // //   // //

A♭ / E♭7-A♭ /
////   //   //

Vocal Chorus:

A♭ / A♭ / A♭ / E♭ /
//// //// //// ////

D♭-E♭ / A♭-C7-Fm / A♭-E♭ / A♭ /
// //   /   /   //   // //   ////

Listening Highlights

- Introduction conveys an anthem-like feel with dramatic, open-voiced harmonies that end with an ascending horn line (0:15) and staccato hits (0:20) on tonic A♭ chord
- Synthesized flute figure to suggest feel of Caribbean folk music and evoke a sense of history (0:26 and throughout verses)

APPENDIX 2
THE TRINIDAD CALYPSOS AND SOCA SONGS

1) "Black Inventions" by Chalkdust (Straker's Records, 1978/79)

https://www.youtube.com/watch?v=01MuLwW9ISM&list=PLcldY-KYUdTwM_4E-rEroIUnjWi1vaMYG&index=2

0:00 – opening band chorus
0:10 – vocal verse 1
0:47 – vocal chorus
1:10 – repeat band chorus
1:20 – vocal verse 2
1:57 – vocal chorus
2:20 – repeat band chorus
2:29 – vocal verse 3
3:06 – vocal chorus
3:28 – repeat band chorus
3:38 – vocal verse 4
4:14 – vocal chorus
4:32 – tag with Chalkdust's reciting a lengthy list of Black accomplishments over chorus refrain "A Black man invented that," and high synthesizer improvised fillers

"Black Inventions" basic chord progressions (key of F#)

Band Chorus:

F#-F#7   / B-G#m7   / C#-C#7   / F#-C#-F#-C#7+5 /
// //   // //   // //   / / / /

Vocal Verse:

F♯   /   B♭7   /   B-G♯m   /   F♯-D♯m   /
////   ////   // //   // //

G♯minor-C♯7th   /   F♯major-D♯minor   /   G♯7th   /   C♯7th-C♯7th+5   /
      //   //   //   //   ////   //   //

Vocal Chorus:

F♯   /   C♯   /   C♯-C♯7   /   F♯   /
////   ////   // //   ////

F♯-F♯7   /   B-G♯m7   /   C♯-C♯7   /   F♯-C♯-F♯-C♯7+5   /
 // //   // //   // //   /   /   /   /

Listening Highlights

- Lilting rhythm, rapidly changing chords, and use of minor, minor7, and extended chords create a traditional calypso sound with a big band flavor
- Lengthy tag with improvised synthesizer fills (4:42 to end)

2) "Ash Wednesday Jail" by Chalkdust (Straker's Records, 1983)

https://www.youtube.com/watch?v=AG2UP_RACXU

0:00: drum roll
Intro Band Chorus
0:02 – full horns and bass answered by synthesizer
0:10 – reeds answered by synthesizer
0:17 – full horns answered by reeds
0:25 – all horns and bass join together followed by synthesizer
0:33 – vocal verse 1
0:48 – vocal chorus
1:19 – repeat band chorus
1:50 – vocal verse 2
2:05 – vocal chorus
2:36 – repeat band chorus
3:07 – synthesizer patch steel pan solo

3:23 – vocal chorus with synthesizer fills
3:54 – repeat band chorus
4:25 – vocal verse 3
4:40 – vocal chorus with synthesizer fills
5:11 – repeat band chorus
5:42 – vocal chorus with synthesizer fills
6:13 – repeat band chorus
6:44 – vocal chorus with synthesizer fills
7:15 – final band chorus and fade out

"Ash Wednesday Jail" basic chord progressions (key of E)

Band Chorus:

```
E  /  E  /  E  /  B7  /  F#m  /  F#m  /  B  /  B7  /
////  ////  ////  ////   ////    ////   ////  ////

E  /  E  /  E7  /  A  /  A-F#m  /  E-C#  /  F#m  /  B7-E  /
////  ////  ////  ////   // //     // //    ////    // //
```

VocalVerse:

```
E  /  E  /  E  /  B  /  F#m  /  E  /  B  /  E  /
////  ////  ////  ////  ////  ////  ////  ////
```

VocalChorus:

```
E  /  E  /  E  /  B7  /  F#m  /  F#m  /  B  /  B7  /
////  ////  ////  ////   ////    ////   ////  ////

E  /  E  /  E7  /  A  /  A-F#m  /  E-C#m  /  F#m  /  B7-E  /
////  ////  ////  ////   // //      // //    ////    // //
```

Listening Highlights

- Full horn line and bass voiced in unison create an energetic introduction
- Rapid soca tempo throughout (120 bps)
- Synthesizer patch steel pan solo (3:07)

3) "Two Chords and Leston Paul" by Chalkdust (Straker's Records, 1988)

https://www.youtube.com/watch?v=iKlVFcK39cQ

Opening Band Chorus
0:04 – synthesizer line over spoken dedication to arranger Art De Coteau (eight bars)
0:19 – sharp, staccato lines on horns (eight bars)
Vocal Verse 1
0:35 – A
0:51 – B
Vocal Chorus
1:07 – C
1:38 – D
2:10 – band chorus—horns and synthesizer
2:27 – vocal verse 2 (A & B)
2:58 – vocal chorus C
3:28 – vocal chorus D
4:01 – band chorus–horns and synthesizer
4:17 – vocal verse 3 (A & B)
4:48 – vocal chorus C
5:19 – vocal chorus D
5:52 – band chorus—new horn line and synthesizer
6:06 – tag with vocal chorus, horns return at 6:31

"Two Chords and Leston Paul" basic chord progressions (key of E♭)

Band Chorus:

```
B♭7  /  B♭7  /  E♭  /  E♭  /  B♭7  /  B♭  /  E♭  /  E♭  / repeat
////    ////    ////   ////   ////    ////   ////   ////
```

Vocal Verse (A/B):

```
E♭-G7  /  C-Fm  /  B♭  /  E♭  / repeat (A)
// //     // //    ////   ////
```

```
B♭ / B♭ / E♭ / E♭ / E♭7 / A♭ / E♭-B♭ / E♭ / (B)
////  ////  ////  ////  ////   ////   // //    ////
```

Vocal Chorus (C)

E♭ / B♭ / B♭ / E♭ / C / Fm / F / B♭ /
//// //// //// //// //// //// //// ////

E♭ / B♭ / B♭ / G7-C7 / A♭-B♭ / E♭-Cm / A♭-B♭ / E♭ /
//// //// //// // // // // // // // // ////

Vocal Chorus (D)

B♭7 / B♭7 / E♭ / E♭ / repeat
//// //// //// ////

Listening Highlights

- Changing chords on sectional vocal verses A and B and vocal chorus C (calypso style)
- Static I-V chord loop on band chorus and vocal chorus D (soca style)

4) "No Mister" by Calypso Rose (Straker's Records, 1986)

https://www.youtube.com/watch?v=9JH3YF9Xz8g

0:00 – drum beat introduction
Intro Band Chorus
0:08 – low horn theme
0:16 – (A) synthesizer glissando repeated three times followed by horn response
0:23 – (B) synthesizer figure and horn response
0:31 – (A) synthesizer glissando repeated three times followed by horn response
0:38 – (B) synthesizer figure and horn response
0:46 – vocal verse 1
1:02 – vocal chorus
1:25 – band chorus (ABAB)
1:57 – vocal verse 2
2:12 – vocal chorus
2:36 – band chorus (ABAB)
3:07 – vocal verse 3
3:22 – vocal chorus

3:45 – synthesizer harmonic minor line
3:54 – band chorus (ABAB)
4:25 – vocal verse 4
4:40 – vocal chorus

Tag

5:05 – tag begins with light synthesizer chords under "no mister, no mister" vocal refrain
5:42 – short band chorus (AB) reappears
5:58 – harmonic minor synthesizer solo
6:29 – original staccato reed line
6:37 – fade out on A section of band chorus

"No Mister" basic chord progressions (key of B♭)

Band chorus:

B♭ / B♭ / F / B♭ / repeat
//// //// //// ////

Vocal Verse:

B♭-E♭ / B♭ / F / B♭ / repeat
// // //// //// ////

Vocal Chorus:

B♭ / B♭ / F / B♭ / repeat
//// //// //// ////

Listening Highlights

- Synthesizer glissandos to suggest East Indian mood in introductory band chorus (0:16)
- Harmonic minor synthesizer fills (3:45) and final solo (5:58) to evoke "exotic" "Oriental" flavor (for Western listeners)

5) "Side Man Sweet" by Calypso Rose (Straker's Records, 1987)

https://www.youtube.com/watch?v=PCAZLpoBoiA

0:00 – beat established on drum machine
Band Chorus
0:08 – full horn figure voiced with extended chords (four bars)
0:17 – melancholy sax theme (four bars)
0:25 – sharp horn stab sets up Rose's vocal entry
0:26 – vocal verse 1
0:42 – vocal chorus
1:04 – band chorus with horns followed by solo sax
1:22 – vocal verse 2
1:38 – vocal chorus
1:04 – band chorus with full horns followed by solo sax
2:17 – vocal verse 3
2:34 – vocal chorus
2:56 – band chorus with full horns followed by solo sax
3:13 – vocal verse 4
3:30 – vocal chorus
Tag
3:54 – keyboard, guitar, and bass return to original band chorus chord progression to set up solo
4:28 – sax solo to fade

"Side Man Sweet" basic chord progressions (key of A♭)

Band Chorus:

B♭m-E♭7 / A♭-Fm7 / B♭m-E♭7 / E♭m7-A♭7 /
//   //   //   //   //   //   //   //

D♭-D♭m / Cm7-F7 / B♭m7-E♭7 / A♭-Fm7 /
//   //   //   //   //   //   //   //

Vocal Verse:

E♭-D♭ / A♭-Fm / E♭-D♭ / A♭ /
// //   // //   // //   ////

D♭ / Cm-Fm / B♭m-E7 / A♭-F7 /
////   // //   // //   // //

Vocal Chorus:

Bbm7-Eb7 / Ab-Fm / Bb7-Eb7 / Ab-Fm /
//   //   //   //   //   //   //   //

Eb-Db / Cm-Fm / Bbm7-Eb7 / Cm-Fm /
//   //   //   //   //   //   //   //

Bbm7-Eb7 / Ab-F7 /
//   //   // //

Subsite Chords in Band Chorus:

All Horns (initial four measures, 0:08):

Bbm11-Ebdom13 / Abm9-Fm7 /
//   //   //   //

Bbm11-Ebdom13 / Ebm11-Ab13 /
//   //   //   //

Chords Under Saxophone Theme (second four measures, 0:17):

Db9-Gb9 / Cm7-F7flat9 /
//   //   //   //

Bbm7-Ebdom13 / Ab6-F7flat9 /
//   //   //   //

Listening Highlights

- Colorful, substitute chords in band chorus and moderate tempo evoke older calypso style
- Rapidly changing chords (two per measure) add harmonic variety and color
- Bluesy saxophone lines (0:17) and alto saxophone solo (4:28)

6) "Back to Africa" by Calypso Rose (Straker's Records, 1983)

https://www.youtube.com/watch?v=tv8Xmk-1Kfs

0:00 – cool groove established by guitar, bass, and drums while Rose gives shout out to Jamaican drummer and radio DJ Ken Williams, "Mister Prime Minister of Reggae"

0:20 – sharp staccato horn stabs announce Rose's first verse
0:23 – vocal verse 1
0:46 – vocal chorus
1:06 – six-beat synthesizer/bass hits interspersed between "I want to go/back to Africa" refrain
1:26 – vocal verse 2
1:52 – six-beat synthesizer/bass hits interspersed between "Back to Africa" refrain
2:05 – tenor sax solo
2:23 – vocal verse 3
2:45 – vocal chorus
3:05 – six-beat synthesizer/bass hits interspersed between "I want to go/back to Africa" refrain
3:25 – vocal verse 4
3:51 – six-beat synthesizer/bass hits interspersed between "Back to Africa" refrain
Tag
4:05 – Rose ad-libs over light organ
4:24 – muted trombone solo
5:00 – trumpet solo
5:48 – sax solo to fade

"Back to Africa" basic chord progressions (key of D)

Instrumental Introduction:

```
D-C   /   D-C   /   repeat
// //       // //
```

Vocal Verse:

```
D   /   D-C   /   D   /   A   /
////     // /     ////     ////

D-D7  /   G   /   D-A  /   D-A  /
// //     ////     // //      // //
```

Vocal Chorus:

```
D   /   D   /   D   /   D-A  /
////     ////     ////     // //
```

```
D-D7  /  G-D  /  A-D  /
// //     // //    // //
```

Listening Highlights

- Slow reggae beat throughout song
- Hymnlike feel to chorus with open triadic harmonies accentuated by dramatic horn fanfares (0:47–0:54)
- Trombone (4:24), trumpet (5:00), and sax (5:48) solos on tag

7) "How Many More Must Die" by the Mighty Duke (Straker's Records, 1986)

https://www.youtube.com/watch?v=Gt58Znw8g6g

Band Chorus:
0:00 – forceful full horn figure (from vocal chorus)
0:11 – synthesizer line
0:15 – full horn line response
0:20 – vocal verse 1
0:54 – vocal chorus
1:35 – band chorus
1:53 – vocal verse 2
2:31 – vocal chorus
3:08 – band chorus
3:27 – vocal verse 3
4:04 – vocal chorus
4:41 – band chorus
5:00 – vocal verse 4
5:37 – vocal chorus
6:15 – repeat vocal chorus with horns in unison with vocals
6:34 – alto sax solo over repeated vocal chorus to fade

"How Many More Must Die" basic chord progressions (Key of F):

Band Chorus:

```
F  /  C  /  C  /  F-F7  /  B♭  /  Gm  /  C  /  F  /
////   ////   ////   // //    ////    ////    ////   ////
```

Vocal Verse:

F / F / C / C / C / F / C / C / repeat
//// //// //// //// //// //// //// ////

Vocal Chorus:

F / C / C / F-F7 / B♭ / Gm/ C / F /
//// //// //// // // //// //// //// ////

Listening Highlights

- Forceful full-horn introduction to evoke anthem-like feel
- Short horn lines to complete vocal phrases on verses (0:22, 0:27, 0:42, 0:47)
- Snippet of alto sax solo (6:34)

8) "Is Thunder" by the Mighty Duke (Lem's Records, 1987)

https://www.youtube.com/watch?v=IizX-cnOV_Q&t=32s

Band Chorus
0:05 – sliding guitar, synthesizer, and bass establish 3-chord groove
0:11 – brass enter
0:14 – low reeds respond
0:16 – brass figure repeated
0:19 – low reed figure repeated
0:20 – slightly higher brass figure
0:22 – low reed response
0:24 – highest brass figure
0:28 – brass and reeds join for final riffs setting up vocal section
0:32 – vocal verse 1
Vocal Chorus
0:47 – "Whole night" (A)
0:56 – "Is thunder, I giving you thunder" (B)
1:13 – "Whole night" (A)
1:23 – band chorus
1:40 – vocal verse 2
1:56 – vocal chorus (A, B, A)

2:31 – synthesizer break
2:59 – vocal verse 3
3:14 – vocal chorus (ABA)
3:51 – synthesizer break
3:58 – horns back with band chorus
4:16 – vocal verse 3
4:32 – vocal chorus (ABA)
Tag
5:07 – synthesizer break
5:26 – "Thunder, I giving you thunder" vocal refrain under vocal ad-lib
5:42 – more synthesizer and guitar improv
5:58 – "Whole Night" refrain under vocal ad-lib
6:15 – final horn line and fade

"Is Thunder" basic chord progressions (key of G)

Band Chorus:

```
D-C  /  G  /  D-C  /  G  /  repeat
// //   ////   // //   ////
```

Vocal Verse:

```
D7   /  D7  /  G  /  G  /  D-C  /  Bm-Am  /  D7  /  G  /
////    ////   ////  ////  // //   // //     //    ////
```

Vocal Chorus:

```
D-C  /  D-C  /  repeat (A)
// //   // //
```

```
D-C  /  G  /repeat (B)
// //   ////
```

Listening Highlights

- Introductory call-and-response brass and reed figures over sliding guitar riff (0:05–0:28)
- Irregular thirty-beat verse (0:32–0:43)
- Synthesizer solos (5:07; 5:42)

9) "Total Disorder" by Duke (JW Productions, 1989)

https://www.youtube.com/watch?v=S6h7D_KeURQ

0:07 – Duke yells "Boyyay" over syncopated introductory synthesizer/bass figure (four bars)

Band Chorus

0:15 – bright, full horn figure and synthesizer response
0:37 – short brass riff with reed response
0:45 – synth phrase with full horn response over ascending chord sequence
0:52 – vocal verse 1
1:15 – "Blow your brains" vocal chorus
1:37 – band chorus
2:15 – vocal verse 2
2:37 – vocal chorus

Tag 1

3:00 – "Party like your mad" refrain under vocal ad-lib
3:22 – full horn riff ending in dramatic, descending horn lines
3:37 – synth interlude
3:52 – variation of full horn riffs
4:06 – vocal verse 3
4:30 – vocal chorus
4:52 – synthesizer bridge

Tag 2

5:00 – percussion break over refrain "Let me see you getting down"
5:22 – "Jump Up! Jump up! Jump/Jump/Jimp/Jump/Jump/Jump/Jump/Jump" vocal refrain with descending horns
5:37 – synthesizer interlude
5:52 – variation on full horn riff
6:22 – "Jump Up! Jump up! Jump/Jump/Jimp/Jump/Jump/Jump/Jump/Jump" vocal refrain with descending horns to fade

"Total Disorder" basic chord progressions (key of E♭)

Synthesizer Introduction:

```
E♭-B♭  /  A♭-E♭  /  A♭-B♭  /  E♭
// //     // //     // //     ////
```

Band Chorus:

B♭7 / B♭7 / E♭ / E♭ / B♭7 / B♭7 / E♭ / E♭ / repeat
//// //// //// //// //// //// //// ////

E♭-Fm / Gm-A♭ / E♭-B♭ / E♭ /
// // // // // // ////

Vocal Verse:

B♭7 / B♭7 / E♭ / E♭ / B♭7 / B♭7 / E♭ / E♭ /
//// //// //// //// //// //// //// ////

E♭-Fm / Gm-A♭ / E♭-B♭ / E♭
// // // // // // ////

Vocal Chorus:

B♭7 / B♭7 / E♭ / E♭ / B♭7 / B♭7 / E♭ / E♭ / repeat
//// //// //// //// //// //// //// ////

E♭-Fm / Gm-A♭ / E♭-B♭ / E♭ /
// // // // // // ////

Listening Highlights

- Syncopated synthesizer/bass introductory figure with heavy synthesizer-decay effect (0:07)
- Ascending chord sequence (E♭-Fm/Gm-A♭) to break V-I loop and connect each section (0:45, 1:07, 10:30)
- Strong horn riff ending in dramatic descending line (3:22)
- Elaborate second tag with percussion break over refrain "Let me see you getting down" (5:00) leading into "Jump Up! Jump, jump, jump, jump" refrain with descending horns (5:22)

10) "Lorraine" by Explainer (Charlie's Records, 1981)

https://www.youtube.com/watch?v=aijYM34KZc4

0:00 – introduction with rhythm section and synthesizer line
0:16 – Explainer shouts "taxi, taxi" while band chorus enters (low reeds/bass against full horn section)

0:32 – vocal verse 1
1:02 – vocal chorus punctuated by sharp horn riffs
1:18 – band chorus returns
1:33 – vocal verse 2
2:04 – vocal chorus punctuated by sharp horn riffs
2:19 – band chorus returns
2:35 – vocal verse 3
3:06 – vocal chorus punctuated by sharp horn riffs
Extended Tag
3:22 – band chorus with horn line variations
3:37 – vocal chorus punctuated by sharp horn riffs (over the band chorus)
3:52 – synthesizer line interlude (outlining triadic chords)
4:08 – vocal chorus punctuated by sharp horn riffs
4:24 – band chorus returns
4:39 – vocal chorus punctuated by sharp horn riffs
4:54 – synthesizer line interlude
5:10 – vocal chorus punctuated by sharp horn riffs
5:25 – band chorus with horn line variations
5:40 – vocal chorus punctuated by sharp horn riffs
5:56 – band chorus returns
6:11 – vocal chorus punctuated by sharp horn riffs
6:26 – band chorus return
6:34 – vocal chorus chants "All Stars" and "Despers"

"Lorraine" basic chord progressions (key of B):

B / F♯ / A / E / repeat throughout
////   ////   ////   ////

Listening Highlights

- I-V-VII-IV chord progression evoke a pop feel to song
- Extended tag at 3:22 lasting for duration of song
- Soulful articulation of lead vocal

11) "Heroes" by Explainer (Charlie's Records, 1982)

https://www.youtube.com/watch?v=QMFNOSdU19o

Introductory Band Chorus

0:00 – bluesy guitar fills over horns (A) and Explainer dedication (0:03)

0:10 – call and response horn riffs (trombones and sax low/trumpets high) (B)

0:19 – vocal verse 1

0:56 – vocal chorus with "No, no, no/We shouldn't treat our heroes s" extension at 1:14

1:24 – band chorus (A/B)

1:42 – vocal verse 2

2:18 – vocal chorus

2:47 – band chorus (A/B)

3:05 – vocal verse 3

3:42 – vocal chorus

Tag

4:00 – repeat "We shouldn't treat our heroes so" chorus under Explainer ad-libs, band chorus horn lines, and bluesy guitar fills

"Heroes" basic chord progressions (key of F):

Band Chorus:

```
F-C  /  Bb  /  repeat
// //    ////
```

Vocal Verse:

```
F   /   C   /   Bb   /   F-C   /   repeat
////    ////    ////     // //
```

Vocal Chorus:

```
F-C  /  Bb-F  /  Bb-F  /  Bb-C  /
// //    // //    // //    // //

F-C  /  Bb-F  /  Bb-F  /  Bb-C-F  /
// //    // //    // //    / / //
```

Listening Highlights

- Bluesy guitar fills and staccato horn lines on introduction evoke pop/rock feel to song

- Chords change slowly on vocal verse (four beats/chord) and faster on vocal chorus (two beats/chord).

12) "Celebration" by Explainer and Frankie McIntosh (Charlie's Records 1989)

https://www.youtube.com/watch?v=GzmmUVdmQME

Introductory Band Chorus
0:09 – synthesizer glissando followed by synth/brass lines
0:16 – synthesizer chords
0:25 – mambo-style low reed figure
Vocal Verse 1
0:32 – "All my friends keep telling me" (A)
0:36 – response by horns/synthesizer
0:40 – "We want to see something more jumpy" (A)
0:44 – response by horns/synthesizer
0:47 – "Celebration time" (B)
0:56 – "So we can wine down" (C)
1:04 – vocal chorus over mambo-style rhythm
Band Chorus 1
1:20 – synthesizer figure based on chorus
1:27 – second synthesizer/horn figure
1:36 – vocal verse 2 (A-A-B-C sections)
2:07 – vocal chorus
Band Chorus 2
2:22 – low mambo reed theme
2:30 – Explainer ad-libs
2:38 – new descending horn line
2:54 – synthesizer chords
3:02 – repeat new descending horn line
3:10 – vocal verse 3 (A-A-B-C sections)
3:42 – vocal chorus
Band Chorus 1
3:57 – synthesizer figure based on chorus
4:05 – second synthesizer/horn figure
Tag
4:13 – percussion break over vocal chorus and Explainer ad-lib

4:29 – synthesizer glissando followed by synth/brass lines
4:38 – "Party party" chorus
4:45 – vocal chorus
5:00 – Explainer ad-libs over vocal chorus and horn lines

"Celebration" basic chord progression (key of F):

C7   /   F   /   C7   /   F   /   repeat throughout
////   ////   ////   ////

Listening Highlights

- Dramatic opening with synthesizer glissando followed by synthesizer/brass lines (0:09)
- Syncopated mambo riff on low horns (0:25) and repeated on each vocal chorus (1:04)
- Call and response between voice and horns on opening of each vocal verse (0:32, 1:36, 3:10)
- Percussion break and vocal ad-libs to open tag (4:13)

13) "Tension" by Shadow (Straker's Records, 1988)

https://www.youtube.com/watch?v=mURxpHlnXWw

Introduction
0:09 – simple guitar riff followed by synthesizer response (a)
0:17 – repeat with addition of clavinet figure over guitar and synthesizer response (b)
0:25 – add synthesized/horn on descending pentatonic figure (c)
0:34 – repeat original synthesizer/guitar response with synthesizer bass (b)
0:42 – add synthesized/horn a jagged figure based on vocal verse (d)
Vocal Verse 1
0:50 – four, short vocal phrased lines, each followed by synthesizer responses
1:09 – four longer vocal phrased lines
Vocal Chorus
1:24 – "Tension in my body" refrain (A)
1:32 – "Ease the tension" refrain (B)

1:41 – "The Tension keep rising …" (C)
1:50 – repeat "Ease the tension" refrain (B)
band chorus
1:58 – Shadow ad-libs over introductory guitar/synthesizer riff and second synthesizer figure
2:06 – full synthesizer on descending line
2:15 – synthesized horn figure based on vocal verse
2:25 – vocal verse 2
2:57 – vocal chorus
3:31 – band chorus
3:56 – vocal verse 3
4:30 – vocal chorus
Tag
5:04 – Shadow ad-libs over repeated "higher, higher, higher" and "ease the tension" vocal refrains and synthesizer figures

"Tension" basic chord progression (key of E)

E-A / E-A / repeat throughout
// //   // //

Listening Highlights

- Building of groove beginning with guitar riff and adding synthesizer lines (0:09)
- Pentatonic, jagged Mirage synthesizer lines rather than live horns (0:25 and 0:42)
- Sectional vocal verses with short vocal phrased lines/synthesizer response (0:50) in contrast to longer vocal phrased lines (1:09)
- Sectional ABCB vocal chorus.

14) "Music Turns Me On" by Shadow (Straker's Records 1989)

https://www.youtube.com/watch?v=PTVklOCVjvA

Introduction
0:05 – descending synthesizer figure in C♯minor tonal setting—repeated twice

0:13 – beat established under Shadow moans; harmony stays minor
0:30 – horns enter on major harmony voicing (tonic key of Emajor), synthesizer response
0:47 – sharp horn/synthesizer line in unison, taken from "Music Turns me on" vocal chorus
0:55 – vocal verse 1
1:38 – vocal chorus
Band Chorus
2:11 – solo synthesizer line from vocal chorus
2:20 – sharp horn lines with synthesizer response
2:38 – vocal verse 2
3:18 – vocal chorus
Band Chorus/chaotic jam
3:52 – solo synthesizer line from vocal chorus
4:03 – descending synthesizer/horn lines
4:10 – texture thickens with new synthesizer sounds as harmony shifts from major to C♯minor tonal setting
4:22 – agitated, dissonant synthesizer lines dominate over swirling, minor chords
4:51 – harmony turns returns to tonic, Emajor voicing as dissonant synthesizer disappears
5:07 – vocal verse 3
5:50 – vocal chorus
Band Chorus/Tag
6:24 – solo synthesizer line from vocal chorus
6:32 – sharp horn lines with synthesizer response
6:42 – new sharp, staccato horn lines
6:57 – Shadow returns with "I don't want to wine at the party / I don't want to grind at the party / I'm feeling the rhythm inside me / I can't control the energy" refrain to fade

"Music Turns Me On" basic chord progressions (key of E):

Introduction:

```
C♯m  /  C♯m  /  repeat
////        ////
```

```
E   /  B-A  /  E   /  B-A  /  repeat
////   // //   ////   // //
```

Vocal Verse:

```
E    /  B-A  /  E    /  B-A  /  repeat
////    // //   ////    // //
```

Vocal Chorus:

```
E    /  B-A  /  E    /  B-A  /  repeat
////    // //   ////    // //
```

Listening Highlights

- Heavy decay on introductory synthesizer path creates ominous mood
- Segue from minor (C♯m) to major (E) tonality provides jarring contrast during the Introduction (0:30)
- Dissonant jam (4:10–4:51) by three clashing keyboard parts over extended C♯ bass pedal (see narrative description in chapter 6)

15) "Two to Go" by Lord Kitchener (Charlie's Records, 1988)

https://www.youtube.com/watch?v=woz22mwiUVw

Introduction
0:08 – electric piano and clavinet, bass, and drum machine establish groove (eight bars)
Introductory Band Chorus
0:24 – short, bright horn riffs enter
0:32 – lyrical low reed line eventually joined by brass for full horn crescendo on turnaround
0:37 – turnaround transition with synthesizer, bass, and reeds in unison followed by a rising line with the high brass joining in
Vocal Verse 1
0:43 – lilting voice over a I-IIm7-V-I (D-Em7-A7-D) repeated chord sequence
0:59 – voice over descending and accelerating chord sequence
Vocal Chorus
1:14 – female refrain
1:22 – Kitchener returns over second descending and accelerating chord sequence

1:30 – female chorus returns
1:38 – Kitchener returns, completes phrase with scat mimic of bass pans (at 1:44)

Band Chorus 2

1:46 – short, bright horn riffs enter
1:54 – pan figure, eventually joined by brass for full crescendo
1:59 – bridge with pan/synthesizer/bass in unison joined by horns for last measure leading into next vocal verse
2:05 – vocal verse 3
2:36 – vocal chorus

Band Chorus 3

3:08 – pan solo over funky synthesizer
3:23 – pan out and horn riffs in
3:39 – more horn riffs and synthesizer response
3:47 – synthesizer interlude
3:52 – bridge with pan/synthesizer/bass in unison joined by horns for last measure leading into next vocal verse
3:58 – vocal verse 4
4:30 – vocal chorus

Tag

5:01 – extended pan solo (four verse/chorus sections, fade on fifth chorus)

"Two Days to Go" basic chord progressions (key of D)

Band Chorus:

```
D    /  A7   /  A7   /  D    /  repeat
////    ////    ////    ////

D    /  Am-D7-G    /  D-Daug-Em-A7    /  D   /
////    / / //        / /  / /           ////

D-A7  /  D-A7  /
// //    // //
```

Vocal Verse:

```
D    /  Em7  /  A7   /  D    /  repeat
////    ////    ////    ////

Bm  /  Bm  /  A   /  A   /  G-F#7  /  F#7-Bm  /  G-D  /  A7-D /
////   ////   ////   ////   // //     // //      // //    // //
```

Vocal Chorus:

```
D    /  A7   /  A7   /  D    /  repeat
////    ////    ////    ////

D    /  C#7  /  C#7  /  F#m-Fdim-Em-A7  /  D    /  A7   /  A7  /  D   /
////    ////    ////     /    /   /   /    ////    ////    ///    ////

D    /  Am-D-G   /  D-Daug-Em-A7  /  D    /
////     /  / //      /   /   /   /    ////
```

Listening Highlights

- Chord progressions making generous use of minor sevenths, augmented, and diminished chords for coloring and jazzy big band flavor reminiscent of older calypsos
- Turnaround transition from band instrumental introduction to vocal verse 1 (0:37–0:42)
- Unusual move from I (D) to VII7 (C#7) chord on vocal chorus (1:24)

16) "Don't Back Back" by Sparrow (B's Records, 1984)

https://www.youtube.com/watch?v=R7QJbb1pVk4

Band Chorus Introduction
0:02 – bright, full horn line
0:09 – synthesizer response
0:16 – second horn line
0:22 – synthesizer bridge
0:24 – vocal verse 1
Vocal Chorus
0:38 – "Don't do that" vocal riff/synthesizer response (A)
0:45 – "Don't back back on me" vocal riff doubled with bass (B)
0:52 – "Dancing with you, man you only, jamming down the bam-bam??" Sparrow vocal doubled on the bass (C)
0:58 – "Don't do that" vocal riff/synthesizer response (A)
1:06 – "Don't back back on me" vocal riff doubled with bass (B)
1:13 – Sparrow sings ascending line over ascending chord sequences (D)
1:24 – band chorus
1:47 – vocal verse 2

2:01 – vocal chorus (A-B-C-A-B-D)
2:47 – synthesizer break
3:17 – band chorus
3:40 – vocal verse 3
3:54 – vocal chorus (A-B-C-A-B-D)
4:40 – extended synthesizer break over "Don't do that" vocal riff to fade

"Don't Back Back" basic chord progressions (key of G)

Band Chorus:

G / D7 / D7 / G / repeat
////   ////   ////   ////

Vocal Verse:

C-D / G / C-D / G /
// //   ////   // //   ////

B   / Em / C-D / G /
////   ////   // //   //

Vocal Chorus:

D7 / G / D7 / G / (A)
////   ////   ////   //

G / D7   repeat (B)
////   ////

G / C-D7 / D7-G / (C)
////   // //   // //

G / Am / Bm-C / D-E♭dim / C-D / G (D)
////   ////   // //   // //   // //   ////

Listening Highlights

- ABCABD sectional vocal chorus, ending with ascending chord progression (1:13)
- Extended synthesizer break during tag (4:40)

APPENDIX 3

JAZZING UP CALYPSO

1) "Blue Bossa" by Kenny Dorham

Boogsie Sharpe Ensemble (July 1993)

https://www.youtube.com/watch?v=eobac6qRaJE

0:00 – introductory riff
0:80 – main melody/head on steel pan, saxophone, piano
0:46 – saxophone solo
2:16 – steel pan solo (doubled by voice)
4:40 – piano solo
5:38 – bass solo
7:02 – drum solo
8:34 – repeat main interlocutory riff and melody/head
9:23 – unaccompanied improvised steel pan coda
10:04 – whole ensemble holds final chord

Basic chord progressions (key of C):

Cm7-Cm7   /   Fm7-B♭7   /
//   //   //   //

Dm7(♭5)-G7)   /   Cm7-Cm7   /
//   //   //   //

E♭m7-A♭7   /   D♭maj7-D♭maj7   /
//   //   //   //

```
Dm7(b5)-G7   /   Cm7-Dm7(b5)-G7
//      //      //    /      /
```

Listening highlights

- Generous use of minor seventh and substitute chords for jazz flavor
- Straight-ahead, 4/4 jazz tempo
- Pan solo doubled by voice for jazz vocalize effect at 2:16
- Unaccompanied, improvised pan coda at 9:23

2) "St. Thomas" by Sonny Rollings

Boogsie Sharpe Ensemble (July 1993)

https://www.youtube.com/watch?v=QXqFLBWPV2o

0:00 – main melody/head on steel pan, saxophone, piano
0:31 – steel pan solo
1:48 – saxophone solo
3:19 – piano solo
4:20 – repeat main melody/head

Basic chord progressions (key of C)

```
C6-Em7-A7   /   Dm7-G7-C6-G7   /
//    /   /       /   /   /   /

C6-Em7-A7   /   Dm7-G7-C6-G7   /
//    /   /       /   /   /   /

C6-Bb7-A7   /   rest   /   Dm7-Ab7(#5)-G7   /   rest   /
//    /   /    ///        //        /      /   ///

C6-C7(+9)   /   F6-F#dim7   /   C-G7-C   /
//    //       //   //        //   /   /
```

Listening Highlights

- Generous use of minor seventh and substitute chords for jazz flavor

- Lilting beat and syncopated head melody create an overall calypso feel
- Steel pan solo at 0:31
- Frankie's piano solo at 3:19 with tresillo/habanera rhythmic underpinnings

3) "I Love Pan" by David "Happy" Williams

Ping Pong Obsession, ROTS Records CD (2000)

https://www.youtube.com/watch?v=-R7urUJ9A-Y

0:00 – iron-driven percussion introduction
Introduction/Band Chorus
0:09 – synthesized pan theme (from vocal verse B)
0:13 – horn riffs (from vocal verse C)
0:21 – vocal verse 1(A)
0:30 – vocal verse 1 (B)
0:34 – vocal verse 1 (C)
0:38 – vocal verse 2 (ABC)
0:55 – vocal verse 3 (ABC)
1:12 – vocal chorus ("Because Carnival time is for fun /Carnival time is to jam")
1:29 – band chorus with steel pan (D, from vocal chorus)
1:45 – vocal verse 4 (ABC)
2:02 – vocal verse 5 (ABC)
2:18 – vocal verse 6 (ABC)
2:35 – vocal chorus
2:52 – band chorus with steel pan (D)
3:08 – vocal verse 7 (ABC)
3:25 – vocal verse 8 (ABC)
3:41 – vocal verse 9 (ABC)
3:59 – vocal chorus
4:15 – band chorus with steel pan (D)
4:32 – vocal verse 10 (ABC)
4:48 – vocal verse 11 (ABC)
5:05 – vocal verse 12 (ABC)
5:22 – vocal chorus (repeat and fade)

"I Love Pan" basic chord progressions (key of D)

Instrumental Intro:

```
D-F#7   /  G7-C7+9+13  /
// //      // //

D-D   /  D-A  /  repeat
// //    // //
```

Vocal Verse:

```
D-Bm  /  G-A7  /  D   /  repeat (labeled A)
// //    / /      //

D-D  /  F#7  /  G7  /  C7+9+13  /  (labeled B)
// //    //     //       /

D-D  /  D-A  /  (labeled C)
// //    // //
```

Vocal Chorus:

```
D-G  /  D-G  /  D   /  A7  /  repeat
// //   // //   ////   ////
```

Instrumental band chorus with steel pan:

```
D-G  /  D-G  /  D   /  A7  /  repeat
// //   // //   ////   ////
```

Listening Highlights

- Iron-driven percussion introduction sets Carnival/calypso tone
- Ascending I-III-IV-VII chord progression with lush major7+9+13 chords in introduction and second section of vocal verse (B) provide harmonic color and a jazzy feel
- Sectionalized verses (labeled A/B/C) add variety to overall form

4) That's the Culture" by Raf Robertson, performed by David "Happy" Williams

Ping Pong Obsession, ROTS Records CD (2000)

https://youtu.be/bNsxHrBJu_E

Introductory Band Chorus
0:00 – initial horn riffs (A)
0:08 – steel pan/synth figure (B)
0:12 – horns and steel pan synth join for final line (C)
0:17 – vocal verse 1
0:33 – vocal chorus
1:06 – band chorus
1:23 – vocal verse 2
1:40 – vocal chorus
2:13 – band chorus
2:28 – modulate up from original key of B♭ to new key of B
2:30 – vocal verse 3 (now in new key of B)
2:46 – vocal chorus
3:20 – repeat vocal chorus
Tag
3:36 – vocal ad-lib over horns and vocal chorus
3:45 – new horn lines
3:49 – "That's the spirit" vocal refrain
3:57 – vocal ad-lib over "Jump and play your mas" vocal chorus

"That's the Culture" basic chord progressions (key of B♭)

Instrumental Intro:

```
Cm7-F7   /   Dm7-G7   /   repeat (labeled A)
//   //      //   //
```

```
E♭-D7   /   Gm-C7   /   (under steel pan patch at 0:08, labeled B)
//  //      //  //
```

```
E♭-B♭   /   D♭dim-Cm-F7   /
//  //       //    /   /   (under horns and synthesizer on final line at
00:12, labelled C)
```

Vocal Verse (0:17):

```
B♭-A   /  Dm7-G7  /  Cm-A7  /  Dm-G7-Cm-F7
// //     //   //     //  //     /  /  /  /
```

Vocal Chorus (0:33):

Same as Instrumental Introduction

Listening Highlights

- Three-section instrumental introduction and vocal chorus with rapidly changing chord progressions add variety and harmonic richness
- Jazzy turnaround Cm-A7/Dm-G7-Cm-F7 cycle of fourths progression in the middle of vocal verse (0:21, at "No Panorama") add more harmonic richness
- Modulate up from original key of B♭ to new key of B at (2:28) for the rest of the song for added energy and brightness

5) "Ping Pong Obsession" by David "Happy" Williams

Ping Pong Obsession, ROTS Records CD (2000)

https://www.youtube.com/watch?v=o1BgdonG-C8&list=PLcldY-KYUdTwM_4E-rEroIUnjWi1vaMYG&index=7

0:00 – iron-driven percussion introduction
0:08 – synthesized pan theme
0:24 – vocal verse 1 (minor)
0:57 – vocal chorus (modulate to major)
1:13 – "Ah-ya-ya-ya-ya" chorus (minor)
1:29 – band chorus with flute and saxophone
1:45 – vocal verse 2 (minor)
2:18 – vocal chorus (major)
2:34 – "Ah-ya-ya-ya-ya" chorus (minor)
2:50 – band chorus with flute and saxophone
3:06 – vocal verse 3 (minor)
3:39 – vocal chorus (major)

3:55 – "Ah-ya-ya-ya-ya" chorus (minor)
4:11 – band chorus with flute
4:28 – vocal ad-lib over "Ah-ya-ya-ya-ya" chorus and flute

"Ping Pong Obsession" basic chord progressions (keys of Dm/F):

Instrumental Introduction:

Dm-A7 / A7-Dm / Dm-A7 / A7-Dm / repeat (in key of Dm)
// //   // //   // //   // //

Vocal Verse:

Dm / A7 / A7 / Dm / Dm / A7 / A7 / Dm / repeat (in key of Dm)
//// //// //// //// //// //// //// ////

Vocal Chorus:

C7 / F / D7 / Gm / B♭ / F / Gm-C7 / F-A7 / (in key of F)
//// //// //// //// //// //// // //   // //

Listening Highlights

- Instrumental introduction with strong habanera beat and tonic Dminor chord evokes an older lavway, folk-calypso style
- Modulation from minor to major key at 0:57 creates contrast and more modern feel
- Harmonic turnaround (Gminor-C7/Fmajor-A7 at 1:09) to return to the original key of D minor

6) "Pan Romance" by Garvin Blake, performed by Garvin Blake and Frankie McIntosh with David Rudder on Vocals

Belle Eau Road Blues, Basement Recordings CD (2000)

https://www.youtube.com/watch?v=Pcrx9PzOQso

0:00 – introduction on pan and bass
0:15 – vocal verse 1
0:42 – vocal chorus

1:04 – instrumental interlude on pan and bass
1:13 – vocal chorus
1:35 – vocal verse 2
2:02 – vocal chorus
2:24 – pan solo
2:55 – vocal ad-lib/percussive chanting over percussion and bass
3:30 – pan and bass return and repeat introduction theme over percussion
3:44 – vocal verse 3
4:11 – vocal chorus
4:32 – instrumental interlude on pan and bass
4:42 – vocal chorus
5:04 – vocal ad-lib over pan improv

"Pan Romance" basic chord progressions (key of C):

Instrumental Intro:

```
Dm7-G7  /  Em7-Am  /
 //  //     //  //

Dm7-G7  /  E7-A7  /
 //  //    //  //

Dm7-G7  /  A♭Maj7  /  (resolves to tonic C)
 //  //    //// (hold)
```

Vocal Verse (0:15):

```
C  /  C-Em-E♭m  /  Dm-G7  /  C  /  E7  /  Am  /  D7  /  G7  /
////   //  /  /    //  //   ////  ////  ////   ////  ////
```

Vocal Chorus (0:42):

```
G7 /  C  / G7 /  C  /
////  ////  ////  ////

F-F6  /  C  /  F-F6  /  C  /  F-F6  /  C-A7  /
// //    ////   // //    ////   // //    // //

Dm-G7  /  Em-A7  /  Dm7-G7  /  C  /
 //  //     //  //     //  //    ////
```

Listening Highlights

- Generous use of major and minor seventh chords and sixth chords for harmonic sweetening
- Ending the II-V-III-VI-II-V progression on the A♭maj7 chord at 0:12 before modulating descending down to the tonic C at 0:15 creates and resolves tension
- David Rudder's silky vocals float over airy, harmonically rich accompaniment
- Vocal ad-lib and chanting over percussion create brief ritual-like feel at 2:55

7) "Pan in A Minor" by Lord Kitchener, performed by Garvin Blake and Frankie McIntosh

Belle Eau Road Blues, Basement Recordings CD (2000)

https://www.youtube.com/watch?v=O6xYMrqMIFI&t=24s
(Kitchener original arranged by Leston Paul at: https://www.youtube.com/watch?v=DGPwBXUKK7I)

0:04 – free-meter vamp on steel pan and piano on Amin9 chord
0:24 – modal introductory riff played in unison on pan, piano, and bass
0:33 – verse melody on steel pan
1:11 – "beat pan" stop-time chorus on steel pan
1:49 – steel pan improvised solo over calypso/Latin beat
3:04 – steel pan improvised solo over straight-ahead 4/4 jazz meter
4:19 – verse melody returns on steel pan
4:56 – "beat pan" stop-time chorus returns on steel pan
5:25 – percussion/bass tag
6:02 – final unison riff on pan, bass, and piano

"Pan in A Minor" basic chord progressions (key of Am):

Instrumental Intro:

Am9 / Am (free meter)

Verse:

Am / F-E7 / E7 / Am / repeat
////   // //   ////   ////

Dm / Am / E7 / Am / Dm / Am / Adim / E7 /
////   ////   ////   /////   ////   ////   ////   ////

Chorus:

E7 / Am / E7 / Am /
//   //   //   //

E7 / E7 / Am / Am / Dm7 / G / C / E7 /
////   ////   ////   ////   ////   ////   ////   ////

E7 / Am / E7 / Am
//   //   //   //

Listening Highlights

- Generous use of minor chords and occasional diminished harmonies throughout creates tense mood
- Switch from calypso/Latin beat to straight-ahead jazz meter at 3:04 during steel pan solo
- Percussion/bass tag at 5:25

8) "Jane" by Sparrow, performed by Garvin Blake and Frankie McIntosh

Belle Eau Road Blues, Basement Recordings CD (2000)

https://www.youtube.com/watch?v=zlNWUDEEhLg
Sparrow original at: https://www.youtube.com/watch?v=sv-Yi7_lNdY

0:00 – free-meter steel pan improvisation over atmospheric piano chords
1:20 – steel pan plays embellished melody as piano chords establish 4/4 meter
1:50 – steel pan improvises more freely
3:15 – piano solo over jazzy substitute chords

4:05 – steel pan returns, improvising over piano chords in 4/4 meter
4:35 – free meter returns with steel pan improvisation over atmospheric piano chords
5:47 – steel pan melody over slow, steady piano chords
6:18 – final free-meter steel pan improvisation

"Jane" basic chord progressions (key of G)

Verse:

G-E7 / Am-D7 / Am-D7 / G /
// //   // //   // //   ////

B7 / C / G-D7 / G /
////   ////   // //   ////

Chorus (at 1:20):

Am7 / D7 / F#7 / G (b bass) / repeat
////   ////   ////   ////

A (with c# bass) / D7 (with c bass) / Gmajor (with b bass)-B♭dim / Am7-D7 / G /
////   ////   //   // //   ////

G-E7 / Am-D7 / Am-D7 / G /
// //   // //   // //   ////

B7 / Em / G-D7 / G /
////   ////   // //   ////

Listening Highlights

- Introductory, free-meter pan improvisation
- Move from free meter to steady 4/4 meter at 1:20
- Piano solo over substitute, jazzy chords at 3:15
- Return to free meter at 4:35

9) "One for Boogsie" by Frankie McIntosh, performed by Garvin Blake and Frankie McIntosh

Parallel Overtones, Khalabashmusic Music CD (2015)

https://www.youtube.com/watch?v=CtLMYsoicTk

0:00 – percussion/bass introduction sets calypso beat and evokes pan yard vibe
0:09 – jazzy piano chords enter II-V-I progression in key of Cm
0:17 – pan enters, playing jagged unison line with piano
0:32 – head—pan takes melody over piano and rhythm section in key of E♭
1:00 – stop-time bridge with piano (D7add13/D♭7add13)
1:07 – improvised piano solo (back in Cm)
1:57 – improvised pan solo
2:49 – drum solo over piano chords
3:10 – bass solo over piano chords
3:41 – pan returns, playing jagged unison line with piano in key of Cm
3:58 – repeat head—pan takes melody over piano and rhythm section in key of E♭
4:24 – stop-time bridge with piano to end

"One for Boogsie" basic chord progressions (key of Cm, modulate to E♭)

Piano Introduction (0:09):

   Ddim7-G7 / Cm-Adim / repeat
   //   //   //   //

Head (in E♭ at 0:32):

   Fm7-B♭7 / E♭-Gm-G♭m / Fm7-B♭7 / E♭-Cm-Bm /
   // //   // / /   // //   // / /

   B♭m-E♭7 / A♭-Dm-G7 / Cm-D7 / G-G♭aug-Fm7+6- E♭+9 /
   // //   // / /   // //   / / /   /

   Ddim-G7 / Cm-Bdim / B♭m-E♭7 / A♭-B-E-E♭ /
   // //   // //   //   //   / / / /

   Ddim-G7 / E-A7 /
   //   //   // //

–Descending stop time bridge (1:00) leading into piano solo (1:07):

D7+13 / rest / Db7+13 / rest /
////   ////   ////   ////

Listening Highlights

- Generous use of minor7, diminished, and augmented chords for coloring throughout
- Key switch from Cm, to Eb at 0:32, creates unexpected harmonic twist and tonal variation
- Stop-time bridge with chromatic descending extended 13th chords at 1:00
- Lyrical piano solo with light syncopation beginning at 1:07

10) "Pan in Harmony" by Lord Kitchener, performed by Garvin Blake and Frankie McIntosh

Parallel Overtones, Khalabashmusic Music CD (2015)

https://www.youtube.com/watch?v=NbO1Vguq-ro
(Kitchener original at: https://www.youtube.com/watch?v=2THO01HjUUk)

0:05 – piano introduction over bass and percussion (key of A)
0:15 – steady 6/8 rhythms established as pan plays verse melody over piano runs and rhythm section (key of C)
0:24 – melody continues on pan over modulation (key of C to key of Eb)
0:31 – repeat verse melody (modulating from key of C to key of Eb)
0:49 – pan plays chorus melody (A) (key of C)
1:04 – pan and piano play chorus melody (B)
1:19 – piano bridge/introduction (key of A)
1:28 – pan improvised solo (key of C)
2:42 – piano improvised solo
3:40 – piano bridge
3:49 – return to verse melody on pan over piano runs and rhythm section
4:05 – repeat verse melody on pan
4:22 – pan plays chorus melody (A)
4:38 – pan and piano play chorus melody (B)

5:10 – coda with pan and piano on drawn out D♭major7 and Cmajor7 chords

"Pan in Harmony" basic chord progressions
(key of A with modulations to C and E♭; 6/8 meter)

–Instrumental Introduction (in key of A at 0:05):

A / Em / A / Em / A+c♯bass / C7 / F / F / B♭7 / D♭7 /
/// /// /// ///   ///   /// /// /// /// ///

–Verse: (key of C at 0:15/key of E♭ at 0:24):

C / Am / Dm / G7 / Em / Am / Gm / C7 /
/// /// /// /// /// /// /// ///

Fm / B♭ / E♭ / D7 / Dm / G7 / Fm / B♭7 /
/// /// /// /// /// /// /// ///

C / Am / Dm / G7 / Em / Am / Gm / C7 /
/// /// /// /// /// /// /// ///

Fm / B♭ / E♭ / D7 / Dm / G7 / Fm / B♭ /
/// /// /// /// /// /// /// ///

–Chorus: (key of C at 0:49):

C / B♭maj7 / C / B♭maj7 / Aminor7 / E♭dim / Dm / G7 /
//// ///   /// ///   ///   ///   /// ///

Dm7 / G7 / Dm7 / G7 / F♯m7-B7 / Em7-Am7 / Gm7 / C7 /
/// /// /// ///   // /   // /   /// ///

G / C7 / F / Adim / Gm7 / C7 / F / F /
/// /// /// ///   ///   /// /// ///

Dm7 / G7 / Em7 / Am7 / Dm7 / G7 /   (back to introduction)
/// /// ///   ///   ///   ///

Listening Highlights

- 6/8 waltz time meter throughout creates a "jazz waltz"

- Introduction in key of A modulates to key of C at 0:15 and to key of E♭ at 0:24 for verse and finally back to key of C for chorus (labeled A at 0:49 and B at 1:04)
- Lyrical improvised piano solo with occasional melodic runs between 2:58 and 3:02 and two-over-three rhythmic figures at 2:54 and 3:12

11) "No Money, No Love" by Sparrow, performed by Garvin Blake and Frankie McIntosh

Parallel Overtones, Khalabashmusic Music CD (2015)

https://www.youtube.com/watch?v=vFZoJnsLt2Q
(Sparrow original at: https://www.youtube.com/watch?v=KMFkAuP73QQ)

0:04 – piano chords over bass and light percussion
0:14 – pan enters with melody
0:24 – straight-ahead 4/4 beat established by drums and walking bass under pan melody
0:31 – stop-time figure on pan, bass, drums, and piano with John Coltrane quotation serving as bridge
0:38 – back to straight-ahead rhythm under pan melody
0:54 – interlude as ensemble stalls and builds on extended chord with G pedal
1:02 – pan improvised solo over straight-ahead rhythm
1:40 – interlude as ensemble stalls and builds on extended chord with G pedal
1:49 – piano improvised solo over straight-ahead rhythm
2:24 – interlude as ensemble stalls and builds on extended chord with G pedal
2:33 – pan returns with main melody over straight-ahead rhythm
2:49 – stop-time figure on pan, bass, drums, and piano
2:55 – pan returns with main melody over straight-ahead rhythm
3:10 – interlude as ensemble stalls and builds on extended chord with G pedal
3:18 – rhythm changes to lilting calypso beat under pan improvisation (becomes extended tag)

"No Money No Love" basic chord progressions (key of F)

First Section: movement among temporary tonal centers F to D to G♭ to E♭ to C and finally back to F (0:14–1:01)

Tag (3:18):

C-Am/ Dm-G /
// //   // //

Listening Highlights

- Opening section movement between temporary tonal centers (0:14–1:01)
- Rhythmic quotation from John Coltrane head on "Giant Steps" between 0:31–0:37
- Rhythm change from straight-ahead 4/4 jazz meter to calypso beat at 3:18

NOTES

Introduction

1. Ray Allen and Leslie Slater, "Steel Pan Grows in Brooklyn: Trinidadian Music and Cultural Identity," in Ray Allen and Lois Wilcken, editors, *Island Sounds in the Global City: Caribbean Popular Music and Identity in New York* (University of Illinois Press, 1998), 114–37.

2. For the history of calypso as a vocal tradition see Gordon Rohlehr, *A Scuffling of Islands: Essays on Calypso* (Lexicon Trinidad Ltd., 2004); Rohlehr, *Calypso and Society in Pre-Independence Trinidad* (Port of Spain, Trinidad: published by the author, 1990); Donald Hill, *Calypso Calaloo* (University Press of Florida, 1993); and Keith Warner, *The Trinidad Calypso* (Heinmann Educational Books, 1982).

3. Jocelyne Guilbault and Roy Cape, *Roy Cape: A life on the Calypso and Soca Bandstand* (Duke University Press, 2014).

4. Jocelyne Guilbault, *Governing Sound: The Cultural Politics of Trinidad's Carnival Musics* (University of Chicago Press, 2007), 139–54; Ray Allen, *Jump Up! Caribbean Carnival Music in New York City* (Oxford University, 2019), 149–79.

5. Guilbault and Cape, *Roy Cape*; Kyle DeCoste and Stooges Brass Band, *Can't Be Faded: Twenty Years in the New Orleans Brass Band Game.* (University Press of Mississippi, 2020); Stan BH Tan-Tangbau and Quyen Van Minh, *Playing Jazz in Socialist Vietnam* (University Press of Mississippi, 2021). We follow Guilbault's lead in attempting to maintain a critical tone to avoid slipping into what could simply become a love fest for Frankie and his music. That is, while together we chronicle and laud Frankie's many accomplishments, Ray is constantly asking how and why he did what he did, and in retrospect what did and did not work for him musically. For a discussion of critical versus admirational writing in music biography, see Guilbault and Cape, *Roy Cape*, 230.

6. Dialogic or collaborative editing has become a useful approach for researchers seeking to balance their voices with those of the people with whom they partner to learn from and with (not simply to learn about). The importance of dialogic editing in writing music biography is discussed by Guilbault in *Roy Cape*, 10–11.

For another perspective on rethinking the scholar/subject relationship, see Kyle DeCoste's frank assessment of his experiences as a white researcher and trumpeter working with the Stooges, an African American brass band from New Orleans, in DeCoste and the Stooges Brass Band, *Can't Be Faded*, xii–xv. DeCoste observes that his position in the white researcher/Black subjects binary "is a problematic colonial norm, but it's a reality that is hopefully pushed back against by this collaboration" (232). Like DeCoste, our collaborative voices aim to challenge that essentialist racial binary and encourage more egalitarian partnerships in researching and writing about music cultures.

7. The Youtube channel "Art of the Soca Arranger" is found at: https://www.youtube.com/@BrooklynSoca/playlists.

Chapter 1: Making Music in Saint Vincent and Antigua

1. For historical background on Saint Vincent and the Grenadines, see Virginia Heyer Young, *Becoming West Indian: Culture, Self, and Nation in Saint Vincent* (Smithsonian Press, 1993); Gordon Lewis, *The Growth of the Modern West Indies* (Monthly Review Press, 1968), 144–66, 330–42; and B. W. Higman, *A Concise History of the Caribbean* (Cambridge University Press, 2011), 266–326. According to Young, in 1980 Saint Vincent was approximately 96 percent African and racially mixed, 1.6 percent East Indian, with the remaining population divided between Portuguese and other white Europeans (9). Saint Vincent's East Indian population was significantly smaller than some other West Indian nations such as Trinidad and Guyana.

2. For a full account of the 1935 labor riots and their aftermath, see Adrian Fraser, *The 1935 Riots in St. Vincent: From Riots to Adult Suffrage* (University of the West Indies Press, 2016).

3. For more on secondary education in Saint Vincent and the Boys Grammar School, see Philip Nanton, *Riff: The Shake Keane Story* (Papillote Press, 2021), 13–14.

4. A photograph dated 1893 pictures twenty-four formally dressed Black and mixed-race musicians with the title "Georgetown Orchestral Society." They are holding trumpets, baritone horns, clarinets, string bass, a bass drum, a snare drum, violins, and violas. For more on this group and the later Saint Vincent Philharmonic Orchestra, see Nanton, *Riff: The Shake Keane Story*, 15. By the time Frankie and his father occasionally played with the Philharmonic Orchestra in the 1950s, they were primarily a marching ensemble of brass, reeds, and percussion instruments. Frankie surmises this was because wind and brass instruction were available through the police bands, while there was a shortage of string instructors (and hence players) on the island at the time.

5. "Music icon Patrick Prescod, to be buried Thursday, July 18." *Searchlight* (16 July 2013): http://testwp05.tecnavia.com/searchlight/news/news/2013/07/16/music-icon-patrick-prescod-to-be-buried-thursday-july-18/.

6. These Saint Vincent groups were typical of vernacular dance ensembles throughout the Caribbean and in Caribbean immigrant communities. See Lara Putman, *Radical Moves: Caribbean Migrants and the Politics in the Jazz Age* (University of North Carolina Press, 2013), 153–95. For a broader discussion of these dance bands and their global impact between the World Wars, see Michael Denning, *Noise Uprising: The Audiopolitics of a World Music Revolution* (Verso Press, 2015), 171–215.

7. Roger Abrahams, "Christmas and Carnival on St. Vincent," *Western Folklore* (vol. 31, no. 4, October 1972).

8. For background on Carnival masquerading and music, see Errol Hill, *The Trinidad Carnival* (University of Texas Press, 1972). A more recent account of Trinidad's Carnival music is found in Ray Allen, *Jump Up! Caribbean Carnival Music in New York City* (Oxford University Press, 2019), 14–31.

9. Adrian Fraser, "Calypso and Politics in St Vincent and the Grenadines," 2. Paper presented to at the "Seminar on the Calypso," 10 January 1986, University of the West Indies, St. Augustine, Trinidad.

10. These early calypso contests are described by Olsen "Caribbean Pete" Peters in "Singing for the Pole," *The News*, September 14, 1993.

11. Anthony Williams, *The Vincentian* (26 October 1990). Quoted in Young, *Becoming West Indian*, 175. Williams's account was partially confirmed by Frankie's Uncle Harold McIntosh.

The elder McIntosh told him that Raphael "Raffaye" Davis, a onetime drummer for the Melotones orchestra, brought news to Saint Vincent of a new Trinidad percussion instrument called a "ping pong" that could produce multiple pitches.

12. Background on Saint Vincent's early calypso contests is drawn from Cauldric Forbes's unpublished manuscript, *Calypso Stories for SVG*, courtesy of author. In addition to Victoria Park, Forbes reports that Kingstown's calypso contests were occasionally held in the downtown Russell Cinema and Lyric Cinema.

Young reports that the 1962 steelband contest was won by the local Police Steel Orchestra, in *Becoming West Indian*, 175. The 1962 police orchestra victory is collaborated by the *When Steel Talks* website. See "The Story of Steelbands and the Steelband Art Form in St. Vincent," When Steel Talks, https://www.panonthenet.com/history/st-vincent/the-story-of-pan-in-st-vincent.htm. This may have been the year that Frankie competed with the Tuborg Steel band, as described later in this chapter.

13. For more on post-1960 Saint Vincent calypso, see Forbes, *Calypso Stories for SVG*. See also Olson "Caribbean Pete" Peters, "The Calypso Monarchy," *The Vincentian News*, 16 July 1993. Information on Cauldirc Forbes's calypso career and on the Melotones and Latinaires calypso orchestras is found in Olsen "Caribbean Pete" Peters, "Musical Exploits of Recording Artist, Cauldric Forbes," *The Vincentian News*, clipping ca. April 1999. Additional information on Saint Vincent Carnival in the 1960s comes from the author's interview with Cauldric Forbes, 1 April 2021.

14. Fraser, "Calypso and Politics in St Vincent and the Grenadines," 5.

15. An account of Shake Keane's migration to Great Britain is found in Nanton, *Riff: The Shake Keane Story*.

16. For background on post-1965 West Indian migration to New York, see Philip Kasinitz, *Caribbean New York: Black Immigrants and the Politics of Race* (Cornell University Press, 1992). The establishment of steelband and soca music in Brooklyn during this period is discussed in Allen, *Jump Up!*, 112–88.

17. A summary of Antigua's turn to tourism including its implications for Carnival is found in Frank E. Manning, "Carnival in Antigua (Caribbean Sea): An Indigenous Festival in a Tourist Economy," *Anthropos* 73 (1978): 191–204. Manning points out that while tourism brings economic gain, it also "erodes the sense of autonomy by tending to relegate the native population to the role of servitude and paternalism" (198).

18. Leroy "Jughead" Gordon, "The Story of Pan in Antigua." When Steel Talks: https://www.panonthenet.com/history/antigua/the-story-of-pan-in-antigua.htm.

The LPs *Steel Band Clash* (Cook 1040, 1955) and *Brute Force Steelbands from Antigua* (Cook 1042, 1955) feature the early recordings by Brute Force, Hells Gate, and the Big Shells Steelbands. The two Ps are available digitally at folkways.si.edu.

19. Llewellyn Joseph, "History of Calypso Singing in Antigua," *Antigua Calypso Review 1974* (1974), 3.

20. "Antigua and Barbuda Calypso Results," geographia.com, http://www.geographia.com/antigua-barbuda/calypsoresults.htm.

Chapter Two: Brooklyn is Meh Home

1. "The Revolution and CUNY: Remembering the 1969 Fight for Open Admissions," *The Advocate* (3 May 2021).

2. Philip Kasinitz, *Caribbean New York: Black Immigrants and the Politics of Race* (Cornell University Press, 1992), 54.

3. Nancy Foner, "Introduction," in Nancy Foner, editor, *Islands in the City: West Indian Migration to New York* (University of California Press, 2001), 4.

4. According to the 1980 census, 1,340 Vincentians (including Frankie) arrived legally in New York between 1965 and 1974. A total of 156,920 Caribbean migrants arrived from the English-speaking islands and Haiti during that period. Kasintz, 54.

5. While the notion of a West Indian entrepreneurial ethos may have been exaggerated, there is data suggesting that average income of West Indian New Yorkers in the 1980s was higher than that of their African Americans counterparts. See Philip Kasintz, "Invisible No More? West Indian Americans in the Social Scientific Imagination," in Foner, *Islands in the City*, 260–61. There is clear evidence that West Indians were more apt to own their own homes than were their African American neighbors. See Eleanor Marie Lawrence Brown, "Why Black Homeowners Are More Likely to Be Caribbean American than African American in New York: A Theory of How Early West Indian Migrants Broke Racial Cartels in Housing, George Washington Law / Scholarly Commons, 2016. https://scholarship.law.gwu.edu/cgi/viewcontent.cgi?article=2465&context=faculty_publications.

6. For a discussion of the relationship between Black Caribbean immigrants and native-born Black Americans and the intersection of multiple cultural identities for immigrants, see Philip Kasintz, "Invisible No More?" 257–75.

7. See Kasinitz, *Caribbean New York*, 133–59, for background on the establishment of Brooklyn Carnival.

8. See Allen, *Jump Up*, for the history of Brooklyn's Carnival music and calypso/soca recording industries.

9. Robin Kelley, "Brooklyn's Jazz Renaissance," *ISAM Newsletter* Vol. XXXIII, no. 2 (Spring 2004). See also Jeffrey Taylor, "Across the East River: Searching for Brooklyn's Jazz History," *American Music Review* Vol. XXXVIII, no. 2 (Spring 2009); and Jeffrey Taylor, "'Live From the East: Pharoah Sanders in Brooklyn," *American Music Review* Vol. XLII, no. 2 (Spring 2013).

10. Walter Laning Barr, "NAJE Directory to Jazz Studies in Higher Education," *Jazz Educator's Journal* (February–March 1983): 14–16; (April–May 1983): 68–71.

11. For a discussion of the status of jazz in American colleges and universities, see Charles Beale, "Jazz Education," in *The Oxford Compendium to Jazz*, edited by Bill Kirchner (Oxford University Press, 2000), 756–65.

12. The first Brooklyn College jazz ensemble, established sometime in 1973, was run by the jazz bassist and founder of the National Jazz Ensemble, Charles Israels. See John S. Wilson, "The Great Jazz Dream—Can It Come True?" *New York Times*, 18 November 1973. https://www.nytimes.com/1973/11/18/archives/the-great-jazz-dreamcan-it-come-true-will-new-yorkers-support-jazz.html. The Conservatory continued to run jazz ensembles under the direction of Stafford Horne and Paul Sheldon in the 1980s and 1990s and Salim Washington in the 2000s. A Global jazz MM program was established in 2016. Email communication with Professor Bruce McIntyre, 30 June 2021.

Chapter Three: The Saint Vincent Connection

1. The transition from calypso to soca in the 1970s and early 1980s is recounted in Jocelyne Guilbault, *Governing Sound: The Cultural Politics of Trinidad's Carnival Musics* (University of Chicago Press, 2007), 169–201; Gordon Rohlehr, *A Scuffling of Islands: Essays on Calypso* (Lexicon Trinidad Ltd, 2004), 1–21; Shannon Dudley, *Carnival Music in Trinidad: Experiencing Music, Expressing Culture* (Oxford University Press, 2004), 87–92; and Ray Allen, *Jump Up! Caribbean Carnival Music in New York City* (Oxford University Press, 2019), 143–88.

2. The stylistic characteristics differentiating soca from calypso are discussed by Shannon Dudley in "Judging 'By the Beat': Calypso versus Soca," *Ethnomusicology* 40 (1996: 2): 269–98.

3. Background on influential calypso arrangers Frankie Francis and Art De Coteau is found in Guilbault, *Governing Sound*, 138–54. Background on soca arrangers Ed Watson, Leston Paul, Pelham Goddard, Clive Bradley, and Errol Ince is found in Allen, *Jump Up!*, 160–79.

4. For background on Brooklyn record producers Granville Straker, Rawlston Charles, and Michael Gould, as well as the borough's emergence as a center of soca music in the 1970s and 1980s, see Allen, *Jump Up!*, 143–88.

Chapter Four: The Art of the Soca Arranger

1. For an overview of jazz arranging, see Gunther Schuller, "Arranging," in *The New Grove Dictionary of Jazz*, 2nd ed., Vol. 1, edited by Barry Kernfeld (Macmillan Press, 2003), 75–81. Jazz arranging in the prewar years is surveyed in John Wriggles, *Blue Rhythm Fantasy: Big Band Jazz Arranging in the Swing Era* (University of Illinois Press, 2016). For jazz arranging in the postwar period, see Doug Ramsey, "Big Bands and Jazz Composing and Arranging After World War II" in *The Oxford Companion to Jazz*, edited by Bill Kirchner (Oxford University Press, 2000), 403–17. See also the following biographies: David Hajdu, *Lush Life: A Biography of Billy Strayhorn* (North Point Press, 1997); Larry Hicock, *Castles Made Of Sound: The Story Of Gil Evans* (Da Capo Press, 2002); and Mark Tucker, *Ellington: The Early Years* (University of Illinois Press, 1995). For an accounting of the role of arrangers in postwar American popular music, see Richard Niles, *The Invisible Artist: American Arrangers in Popular Music (1950–2000)* (Niles Smiles Music, 2014).

2. Wriggles, *Blue Rhythm Fantasy*, 1.

3. Wriggles, *Blue Rhythm Fantasy*, 197.

4. Schuller, "Arranging," 75.

5. See Niles, *The Invisible Artist*, 1–10. See also his discussion of collective arranging with Atlantic Record producer Jerry Wexler, 89–101.

6. Jocelyne Guilbault, *Governing Sound: The Cultural Politics of Trinidad's Carnival Music* (University of California Press, 2007), 138.

7. Three Calypsonians who did often work with their own bands were Sparrow (with the Troubadours), David Rudder (with Charlie's Roots), and Black Stalin (with the Roy Cape Allstars). These three were the exceptions for the 1970s and 1980s. See Guilbault, *Governing Sound*, 137.

Chapter Five: Arranging with the Small Island Calypsonians

1. See for example, Gordon Rohlehr, *Calypso and Society in Pre-Independence Trinidad* (Port of Spain, Trinidad: published by the author, 1990); Donald Hill, *Calypso Calaloo* (University Press of Florida, 1993); and Keith Warner, *The Trinidad Calypso* (Heinmann Educational Books, 1982).

2. A useful overview of the mixing of various African, European, and Indigenous folk styles across the Caribbean Islands to create new syncretic musics (including calypso) is found in Peter Manuel, *Caribbean Currents: Caribbean Music form Rumba to Reggae* (Temple University Press, 1995), 1–16.

3. Dorbrene O'Marde, *Short Shirt, Nobody Go Run Me: The Life and Times of Sir Maclean Emanuel* (Hansib Publications, 2014), 22.

4. We recognize the category "small island" carries a negative connotation for some residents of East Caribbean Islands other than Trinidad and Jamaica. For them, "small island" is often read as a derogatory term, while they regard the concept of "big island" as an oxymoron. In this work we use the term purely as a categorical distinction of geographic locations in the Eastern Caribbean other than Trinidad. These so called "small islands" have yielded a number of big-time calypsonians.

5. Background on Alston Becket Cyrus is drawn from Dawad Philip, "Beckett: A Major Calypso Talent Climbing High," *Amsterdam News*, 24 September 1977; Nelson King, "Lord Nelson, Becket to receive UWI honorary Doctor of Letters," *Caribbean Life* (8 September 2022): https://www.caribbeanlife.com/lord-nelson-becket-to-receive-uwi-honorary-doctor-of-letters/; and personal interview with Ray Allen, 19 August 2013.

6. Winston Soso's biography is drawn from Nelson King, "Leading Artists Pay Tribute to 'The Rolls Royce of Calypso,' Winston Soso," *Caribbean Life*, 20 July 2012: https://www.caribbeanlifenews.com/leading-artistes-pay-tribute-to-the-rolls-royce-of-calypso-winston-soso/; Nelson King, "Clymax Band Leader Pays Tribute to Winston Soso," *Caribbean Life*, 3 August, 2021: https://www.caribbeanlifenews.com/clymax-band-leader-pays-tribute-to-the-rolls-royce-of-calypso/; and interview with Bonnie Brown by Ray Allen, 5 August 2021.

7. Scorcher's biography is drawn from Nelson King, "Cyril 'Scorcher' Thomas," *Caribbean Life*, 8 November 2017: https://www.caribbeanlifenews.com/cyril-scorcher-thomas/; and interviews with Ray Allen, 19 and 20 August 2021, Brooklyn, NY.

8. Gordon Rohlehr, *A Scuffling of Islands: Essays on Calypso* (Lexicon Trinidad Ltd., 2004), 66–67. Rohlehr notes that prominent calypsonians Sparrow, Kitchener, Duke, and Melody publicly opposed the ban.

9. Short Shirt's biography is drawn from O'Marde, *King Short Shirt, Nobody Go Run Me*.

10. "Sir Rupert Philo—The Mighty Swallow," madeingrenada, 12 September, 2020: https://madeingrenadawordpresscom.wordpress.com/2020/09/12/sir-rupert-philo-the-mighty-swallow/.

11. Swallow's biography is drawn from interview with Ray Allen, Brooklyn, 4 September 2015. See also "Antigua/Barbuda Mourns For King Swallow," *The Vincentian*, 18 September 2020: https://thevincentian.com/antiguabarbuda-mourns-for-king-swallow-p20336-116.htm; and Hollis Liverpool, "Hail King Swallow," *Trinidad Daily Express*, 14 September 2020: https://trinidadexpress.com/opinion/columnists/hail-king-swallow/article_1751f892-f6ec-11ea-932c-672ab906abb2.html.

12. Obsinate's biography is drawn from "Conversations with King Obstinate" (2021): https://www.youtube.com/watch?v=pMe4jix7keo; "ABS Archives, Focus" (c1985): https://www.youtube.com/watch?v=UKc1j9nhNtA&t=115s; O'Marde, *King Short Shirt, Nobody Go Run Me*, 147–48; and interview with Ray Allen, 2 November 2021.

Chapter Six: Arranging with the Trinidad Stars

1. Hollis Liverpool's biography is drawn from Hollis Liverpool, *Thoughts Along the Kaiso Road* (Juba Publications, 2017), 363–66; and interview with Ray Allen, 5 October 2014, Brooklyn.

2. Linda "Calypso Rose" McArthur Sandy Lewis's biography is drawn from interview with Ray Allen, 23 July 2014, Queens, NY; Hope Munro, *What She Go Do: Women in Afro-Trinidadian Music* (University Press of Mississippi, 2016), 97–106; and Jocelyne Guilbault, *Governing Sound: The Cultural Politics of Trinidad's Carnival Music* (University of Chicago Press, 2007), 102–11.

3. Kelvin "Mighty Duke" Pope's biography is drawn from "Chalkdust's Eulogy for the Mighty Duke," TriniSoca.com, 25 January 2009: http://www.trinisoca.com/duke/220109b.html; "Kelvin 'Mighty Duke' Passes Away," Trinidad and Tobago News, 14 January 2009: https://www.trinidadandtobagonews.com/blog/?p=848; Keith Smith, "A Pope, a King and a Duke: Remembering the Mighty Duke," *Caribbean Beat* (May/June, 2009): https://www.caribbean-beat.com/issue-97/pope-king-and-duke#axzz7EelLJeuK; and Dave Thompson, "Mighty Duke," in *Reggae and Caribbean Music* (Backbeat Books, 2002), 183–84.

4. Winston "Explainer" Henry's biography is drawn from Anupal Sraban Neog, "Who was Explainer? Tributes pour in as Calypsonian legend dies aged 74," SKPop, 8 October 2022: https://www.sportskeeda.com/pop-culture/news-who-explainer-tributes-pour-calypsonian-legend-dies-aged-74; and interview with Ray Allen, 25 February 2015, Port of Spain.

5. Winston "Shadow" Bailey's biography is drawn from Peter Mason, "Mighty Shadow Obituary," *Trinidad Guardian*, 30 October 2018: https://www.theguardian.com/music/2018/oct/30/mighty-shadow-obituary; Patricia Meschino, "Calypso Legend Winston 'Shadow' Bailey Dies at 77," *Billboard*, 10 October 2018; and Guilbault, *Governing Sound*, 158–62.

6. Aldwyn "Lord Kitchener" Roberts's biography is drawn from Gordon Rohlehr, *Calypso and Society in Pre-Independence Trinidad* (Tunapuna, Trinidad: self-published, 1990), 457–65; Guilbault, *Governing Sound*, 174; Thompson, *Reggae and Caribbean Music*, 149–54; Jon Pareles, "Lord Kitchener, 77, Calypso Songwriter Who Mixed Party Tunes with Deeper Messages," *New York Times*, 14 February 2000.

7. Slinger "Might Sparrow" Francisco's biography is drawn from Gordon Rohlehr, *My Whole Life Is Calypso: Essays on Sparrow* (Tunapuna, Trinidad: self-published by, 2015), 3–40; Guilbault, *Governing Sound*, 2007, 154–58; and phone interview with Ray Allen, 26 March 2018.

Chapter Seven: Jazzing Up Calypso in the New Millennium

1. The April 2016 Brooklyn College panel discussion on calypso jazz and improvisation can be found at: https://www.youtube.com/watch?v=TrjHdCDUrwM.

2. Frankie's arrangement of Raf Robertson's "That's the Culture," performed by the Brooklyn Big Band, can be heard at: https://www.youtube.com/watch?v=Iag4-B1vI80.

3. "One for Boogsie" and "Rose," performed by the Frankie McIntosh/Garvin Black Ensemble with Etienne Charles at Brooklyn College can be heard at: https://www.youtube.com/watch?v=Xe4KXioO4pw.

4. According to music historian Nigel Campbell, the term "calypso jazz" surfaced in the early 1960s from the Queens Royal College Jazz Club, a Trinidad organization founded by educator Scofield Pilgrim. The term loosely referred to the mixing of indigenous Caribbean music, grounded in calypso rhythms, with elements of American jazz. The steel pan emerged as the lead instrument in the related subgenre "pan jazz." Nigel Campbell, "Jazz in Trinidad and Tobago: An Improvised Existence in the Islands," paper presented at the 40th Annual Conference of the Caribbean Studies Association in New Orleans, May 2015.

Musicologist Warren Pinkney Jr. employed the broader term "Caribbean jazz" in reference to "an improvisory musical idiom based on the use of various native and folkloric traditions found on islands throughout the [Caribbean] region." Warren Pinckney Jr., "Jazz in Barbados," *American Music* (Spring 1994): 69.

Record producer Emory Cook used the term "*patois* jazz" in reference to the music of Trinidad drummer Rupert Celmendore, pianist Bertram Inniss, and band leader John "Buddy" Williams that he recorded in the early 1960s. Cook described their distinctive style as "jazz improvisation with a Trinidadian touch." Liner notes to *Le Jazz Primatif from Trinidad*, Cook Records, COK01082, 1961.

While the terms calypso, Caribbean, and patois jazz came into common currency in the early 1960s, clearly the symbiotic relationship between Caribbean calypso and American jazz goes back much further to the early decades of the twentieth century. Trinidad expatriate bandleader Gerald Clark drew on the syncopated rhythms and bluesy improvisations of early New Orleans jazz, as revealed in his early 1930s recordings made in New York. Trinidad-based bands the Harmony Kings and Codallo's Top Hatters Orchestra employed the call-and-response brass/reed voicings of American swing bands of the 1930s. See Ray Allen, *Jump Up! Caribbean Carnival Music in New York* (Oxford University Press, 2019), 35–37. As discussed throughout this book, bands of the late 1950s led by Frankie Francis, Bertram Inniss, and John "Buddy" Williams brought big band brass voicings and occasional jazz solos into their calypso arrangements. For the contributions of Francis see Jocelyne Guilbault, *Governing Sound: The Cultural Politics of Trinidad's Carnival Musics* (University of Chicago Press, 2008), 139–44.

The brass band orchestra tradition has been continued into the twenty-first century by the Roy Cape All Stars, a Trinidad-based band whose calypso arrangements and instrumental solos borrow from American jazz. See Jocelyne Guilbault and Roy Cape, *Roy Cape: A Life on the Calypso and Soca Bandstand* (Duke University Press, 2014).

5. At the time of the 2016 Calypso Jazz concert, the Brooklyn College Conservatory supported two jazz ensembles while offering classes in jazz history, jazz arranging, and world music. In the fall of 2016, the Conservatory announced an MA in Global Jazz, a program initiated by Ray Allen and jazz historian Jeffrey Taylor, and directed by jazz pianist and band leader Arturo O'Farrill. Despite these inroads, funding difficulties have left the jazz program in limbo. In 2017 O'Farrill departed from Brooklyn College and the administration refused to replace his position in the Conservatory, citing an ongoing CUNY austerity mandate. The MA Global Jazz program was eventually placed into hiatus, where it stands at the time of this writing. The divide between those faculty who favor Western art music and those advocating for more jazz and world music continues to hamper a robust jazz presence in the Conservatory.

6. Garvin Blake response quoted from email from Blake to Ray Allen, 2 February 2022. Internal quote from liner notes to the CD *Garvin Blake: Parallel Overtones* (Khalabashmusic, 2015).

Epilogue

1. Pelham Goddard, interview with Ray Allen, 4 September 2021, Brooklyn.
2. Leston Paul, phone interview with Ray Allen, 19 June 2021.
3. Dawad Philip, "Becket: A Major Calypso Talent 'Climbing High,'" *Amsterdam News* (24 September 1977).
4. Leslie Slater, "Frankie McIntosh, Master Musician," *Class Magazine* (July/August 1991).
5. *Trinidad and Tobago Guardian* (October 1, 2015). Quoted from Nelson King, "Frankie 'The Maestro' McIntosh to be Honored," *The Vincentian*, 28 September 2018. The *Guardian*'s claim of 2,500 song arrangements is a rough estimate and difficult to verify.
6. Herman Hall, interview with Ray Allen, 27 August 2022, Brooklyn.
7. "Sir Frankie," *The Punch* magazine, 18 September 1988. Frankie was regularly referred to as "The Maestro" in the credits on Straker Record releases.
8. Quotes from Calypso Rose, phone interview with Ray Allen, 27 July 2022; Errol Ince, zoom interview with Ray Allen, September 13, 2022; MacLean "Short Shirt" Emanuel, phone interview with Ray Allen, 4 September 2022; Alston "Becket" Cyrus, phone interview with Ray Allen, 24 July 2021; Cyril "Scorcher" Thomas, interview with Ray Allen, 19 August 2021, Brooklyn; Winston "Explainer" Henry, interview with Ray Allen, 25 February 2015, Port of Spain, Trinidad.

9. Quotes from Hollis "Chalkdust" Liverpool, interview with Ray Allen, 5 October 2014, Brooklyn; Rawlston Charles, interview with Ray Allen, 26 August 2022, Brooklyn; and interview with Hall, 27 August 2022, Brooklyn.

10. Phone interview with Becket, 24 July 2021.

11. Christopher Washburne offers a provocative discussion of the problems of musical genre labeling, focusing on the so-called "Latin jazz" style. He cautions that the "institutional game of naming" too often ignores the complex process of cross-cultural exchange that lies at the heart of so much music, especially that of the multicultural Caribbean. This inevitably leads to a discrepancy "between actual lived experience and its idolized projection." Like Frankie and Garvin, Washburne argues for syncretic process over stylistic categories, concluding that what we call jazz "resounds in a new creolized space, marked by a fusion of cultural elements drawn from Caribbean, American, African, and European cultures." See Washburne, *Latin Jazz: The Other Jazz* (Oxford University Press, 2020), 25–26, 176.

12. Chalkdust makes this point in his 1988 song "Two Chords and Leston Paul," which Frankie arranged. See Frankie's comments in chapter 6. See also Jocelyne Guilbault's discussion of the song in *Governing Sound: The Cultural Politics of Trinidad's Carnival Musics* (University of Chicago Press, 2007), 137–38.

INTERVIEWS

This book is based on approximately one hundred hours of taped conversations (in person and via Zoom) between the authors that took place from August 2020 through October 2022.

The following interviews, conducted by Ray Allen unless otherwise noted, provided additional information:

1) Blake, Garvin, and David "Happy" Williams. 18 March 2021 (zoom).
2) Brown, Bonnie. 5 August 2021 (phone).
3) Charles, Rawlston. 26 August 2022, Brooklyn.
4) Cyrus, Alston Becket. 19 August 2013, Brooklyn (with Ray Allen and Ray Funk).
5) Emanuel, Maclean "Short Shirt." 4 September 2022 (phone).
6) Forbes, Cauldric. 1 April 2021 (phone).
7) Francisco, Slinger "Sparrow." 26 March 2018 (phone).
8) Hall, Herman. 27 August 2022, Brooklyn.
9) Henry, Winston "Explainer." 25 February 2015, Port of Spain.
10) Ince Errol. 13 September 2022 (phone).
11) Lewis, Linda McArthur Sandy "Calypso Rose." 27 July 2022 (phone).
12) Lewis, Linda McArthur Sandy "Calypso Rose." 23 July 2014, Queens.
13) Liverpool, Hollis "Chalkdust." 5 October 2014, Brooklyn.
14) McIntosh, Frankie. 23 July 2013, Brooklyn.
15) McIntosh, Frankie. 24 October 2014, Brooklyn.
16) Philip, Dawad. 16 June 2022. Brooklyn.
17) Straker, Granville. 18 July 2013, Brooklyn.
18) Richards, Paul "King Obstinate." 2 November 2021 (phone).
19) Thomas, Cyril "Scorcher." 19 August 2021 and 20 August 2021, Brooklyn.

REFERENCES

Books and Articles

Abrahams, Roger. 1972. "Christmas and Carnival on Saint Vincent." *Western Folklore*. 31 October.
Allen, Ray. 2019. *Jump Up! Caribbean Carnival Music in New York City*. Oxford University Press.
Allen, Ray. 2014. "The Brooklyn Connection: Frankie McIntosh and Straker Records." *American Music Review* 44 (Fall): 9–14.
Allen, Ray, and Les Slater. 1998. "Steel Band Grows in Brooklyn: Trinidadian Music and Cultural Identity." In *Island Sounds in the Global City: Caribbean Music in New York*, edited by Ray Allen and Lois Wilcken, 114–37. University of Illinois Press.
Barr, Walter Laning. February–March 1983; April–May 1983. "NAJE Directory to Jazz Studies in Higher Education." *Jazz Educator's Journal*, 14–16; 68–71.
Beale, Charles. 2000. "Jazz Education." In *The Oxford Compendium to Jazz*, edited by Bill Kirchner. Oxford University Press, 756–65.
Campbell, Nigel. May 2015. "Jazz in Trinidad and Tobago: An Improvised Existence in the Islands." Paper presented to the 40th Annual Conference of the Caribbean Studies Association, New Orleans. Retrieved December 1, 2022. https://www.academia.edu/12835158/Jazz_in_Trinidad_and_Tobago_An_Improvised_existence_in_the_Islands.
DeCoste, Kyle, and Stooges Brass Band. 2020. *Can't Be Faded: Twenty Years in the New Orleans Brass Band Game*. University Press of Mississippi.
Denning, Michael. 2015. *Noise Uprising: The Audiopolitics of a World Musical Revolution*. Verso Press.
Dudley, Shannon. 2004. *Carnival Music in Trinidad: Experiencing Music, Expressing Culture*. Oxford University Press.
Dudley, Shannon. 1996. "Judging 'By the Beat': Calypso versus Soca." *Ethnomusicology* 40 (2): 269–98.
Foner, Nancy. 2001. "Introduction: West Indian Migration to New York." In *Islands in the City: West Indian Migration to New York*, edited by Nancy Foner, 1–22. University of California Press.
Fraser, Adrian. 2016. *The 1935 Riots in St Vincent: From Riots to Adult Suffrage*. University of the West Indies Press.
Guilbault, Jocelyne. 2007. *Governing Sound: The Cultural Politics of Trinidad's Carnival Musics*. University of Chicago Press.

Guilbault, Jocelyne, and Roy Cape. 2014. *Roy Cape: A Life on the Calypso and Soca Bandstand*. Duke University Press.

Hajdu, David. 1997. *Lush Life: A Biography of Billy Strayhorn*. North Point Press.

Hicock, Larry. 2002. *Castles Made Of Sound: The Story of Gil Evans*. De Capo Press.

Higman, B. W. 2011. *A Concise History of the Caribbean*. Cambridge University Press.

Hill, Donald. 1998. "I am Happy in This Sweet Land of Liberty: The New York Calypso Craze of the 1930s and 1940s." In *Island Sounds in the Global City: Caribbean Popular Music in New York*, edited by Ray Allen and Lois Wilcken, 74–92. University of Illinois Press.

Hill, Donald. 1993. *Calypso Calaloo*. University Press of Florida.

Hill, Errol. 1972. *The Trinidad Carnival*. Austin: University of Texas Press, 2nd edition, 1997. London: New Beacon Books.

Kasintz, Philip. 1992. *Caribbean New York: Black Immigrants and the Politics of Race*. Cornell University Press.

Kasinitz, Philip, 2001. "Invisible No More? West Indian Americans in the Social Scientific Imagination." In *Islands in the City: West Indian Migration to New York*, edited by Nancy Foner, 257–75. University of California Press. Kelley, Robin. 2004. "Brooklyn's Jazz Renaissance." *ISAM Newsletter* Vol. XXXIII, no. 2 (Spring).

Kelley, Robin. 2004. "Brooklyn's Jazz Renaissance." *ISAM Newsletter* Vol. XXXIII, no. 2 (Spring).

Lewis, Gordon. 1968. *The Growth of the Modern West Indies*. Monthly Review Press.

Liverpool, Hollis. 2017. *Thoughts Along the Kaiso Road*. Juba Publications.

Manning, Frank E. 1978. "Carnival in Antigua (Caribbean Sea): An Indigenous Festival in a Tourist Economy." *Anthropos* 73, 191–204.

Munro, Hope. 2016. *What She Go Do: Women in Afro-Trinidadian Music*. University Press of Mississippi.

Nanton, Philip. 2021. *Riff: The Shake Keane Story*. Papillote Press.

Niles, Richard. 2014. The *Invisible Artist: American Arrangers in Popular Music (1950–2000)*. Niles Smiles Music.

O'Marde, Dorbrene. 2014. *Short Shirt, Nobody Go Run Me: The Life and Times of Sir Maclean Emanuel*. Hansib Publications.

Pinckney Jr., Warren. Summer 1994. "Jazz in Barbados." *American Music*, 58–87.

Putman, Lara. 2013. *Radical Moves: Caribbean Migrants and the Politics of Race in the Jazz Age*. University of North Carolina Press.

Ramsey, Doug. 2000. "Big Bands and Jazz Composing and Arranging After World War II." In *The Oxford Companion to Jazz*, edited by Bill Kirchner. Oxford University Press, 403–17.

Rohlehr, Gordon. 2015. *My Whole Life Is Calypso: Essays on Sparrow*. Tunapuna, Trinidad: published by the author.

Rohlehr, Gordon. 2004. *A Scuffling of Islands: Essays on Calypso*. Lexicon Trinidad Ltd.

Rohlehr, Gordon. 1990. *Calypso and Society in Pre-Independence Trinidad*. Port of Spain, Trinidad: published by the author.

Schuller, Gunther. 2003. "Arranging." In *The New Grove Dictionary of Jazz*, 2nd ed., Volume 1, edited by Barry Kernfeld. Macmillan Press, 75–81.

Sutton, Constance. 1997. "The Caribbeanization of New York City and the Emergence of a Transnational Socio-Cultural System." In *Caribbean Life in New York City: Sociocultural Dimensions*, edited by Constance Sutton and Elsa Chaney, 15–30. New York: Center for Migration Studies.

Tan-Tangbau, Stan BH, and Quyen Van Minh. 2021. *Playing Jazz in Socialist Vietnam*. University Press of Mississippi.

Taylor, Jeffrey. 2013. "Live From the East: Pharoah Sanders in Brooklyn." *American Music Review* Vol. XLII, no. 2 (Spring).
Taylor, Jeffrey. 2009. "Across the East River: Searching for Brooklyn's Jazz History." *American Music Review* Vol. XXXVIII, no. 2 (Spring).
Thompson, Dave. 2002. *Reggae and Caribbean Music*. Backbeat Books.
Tucker, Mark. 1995. *Ellington: The Early Years*. University of Illinois Press.
Warner, Keith. 1982. *The Trinidad Calypso*. Heinmann Educational Books.
Washburne, Christopher. 2020. *Latin Jazz: The Other Jazz*. Oxford University Press.
Wriggles, John. 2016. *Blue Rhythm Fantasy: Big Band Jazz Arranging in the Swing Era*. University of Illinois Press.
Young, Virginia Heyer. 1993. *Becoming West Indian: Culture, Self, and Nation in St. Vincent*. Smithsonian Press.

Websites, Magazines, Newspapers, and Liner Notes

Allen, Ray. Fall 2021. "Winston Soso, Clymax, and Small Island Calypso in Brooklyn." *Everybody's Caribbean Magazine*, 21–22.
"Antigua/Barbuda Mourns for King Swallow." September 18, 2020. *The Vincentian*. Retrieved November 29, 2022.https://thevincentian.com/antiguabarbuda-mourns-for-king-swallow-p20336-116.htm
Blake, Garvin. February 22, 2022. "What Is Calypso Jazz?" Unpublished document sent to authors via email.
Blake, Garvin. 2015. Liner notes to *Parallel Overtones*. Khalabashmusic Music CD.
Brown, Eleanor Marie Lawrence. 2016. "Why Black Homeowners Are More Likely to Be Caribbean American than African American in New York: A Theory of How Early West Indian Migrants Broke Racial Cartels in Housing." George Washington Law / Scholarly Commons. Retrieved November 29, 2022. https://scholarship.law.gwu.edu/cgi/viewcontent.cgi?article=2465&context=faculty_publi cations
Cook, Emory. 1961. Liner notes to *Le Jazz Primatif from Trinidad*. Cook Records COK01082.
"Conversations with King Obstinate." 2021. Retrieved November 29, 2022. https://www.youtube.com/watch?v=pMe4jix7keo
King, Nelson. September 8, 2022. "Lord Nelson, Becket to receive UWI honorary Doctor of Letters." *Caribbean Life*. Retrieved November 29, 2022. https://www.caribbeanlife.com/lord-nelson-becket-to-receive-uwi-honorary-doctor-of-letters/
King, Nelson. June 23, 2022. "Franklyn 'Frankie' McIntosh, Pre-eminent Musical Arranger." *Caribbean Life*. Retrieved November 29, 2022. https://www.caribbeanlife.com/franklyn-frankie-mcintosh-pre-eminent-caribbean-musical-arranger/
King, Nelson. January 28, 2022. "McIntosh Marks 25th Anniversary of Commemorative Stamp." *The Vincentian*. Retrieved November 29, 2022. https://thevincentian.com/mcintosh-marks-th-anniversary-of-commemorative-stamp-p23509-133.htm
King, Nelson. August 3, 2021. "Clymax Band Leader Pays Tribute to Winston Soso." *Caribbean Life*. Retrieved November 29, 2022. https://www.caribbeanlifenews.com/clymax-band-leader-pays-tribute-to-the-rolls-royce- of-calypso/
King, Nelson. September 28, 2018. "Frankie 'The Maestro' McIntosh to be Honored." *Vincentian*. Retrieved November 29, 2022. https://thevincentian.com/frankie-the-maestro-mcintosh-to-be-honoured-p15899-133.htm

King, Nelson. November 8, 2017. "Cyril 'Scorcher' Thomas." *Caribbean Life*. Retrieved November 29, 2022. https://www.caribbeanlifenews.com/cyril-scorcher-thomas/

King, Nelson. July 20, 2012. "Leading Artists Pay Tribute to 'The Rolls Royce of Calypso,' Winston Soso." *Caribbean Life*. Retrieved November 29, 2022. https://www.caribbeanlifenews.com/leading-artistes-pay-tribute- to-the-rolls-royce-of-calypso-winston-soso/

Forbes, Cauldric. *Calypso Stories for SVG*. Unpublished manuscript, courtesy of author.

"Frankie in the Spotlight." October 5, 2019. *The Vincentian*. Retrieved November 29, 2022. https://thevincentian.com/frankie-in-the-spotlight-p15943-133.htm

Funk, Ray, and Ray Allen. October 1, 2015. "Soca Legend McIntosh Gets Sunshine Award." *Trinidad Guardian*. Retrieved November 29, 2022. https://www.guardian.co.tt/article-6.2.369942.e41e397ea6

Joseph, Llewellyn. 1974. "History of Calypso Singing in Antigua." *Antigua Calypso Review 1974*, 3.

Liverpool, Hollis. September 14, 2020. "Hail King Swallow." *Trinidad Daily Express*. Retrieved November 29, 2022. https://trinidadexpress.com/opinion/columnists/hail-king-swallow/article_1751f892-f6ec- 11ea-932c-672ab906abb2.html

Liverpool, Hollis. January 25, 2009. "Chalkdust's Eulogy for the Mighty Duke." TriniSoca.com. http://www.trinisoca.com/duke/220109b.html

Mason, Peter. October 30, 2018. "Mighty Shadow Obituary." *Trinidad Guardian*. Retrieved November 29, 2022. https://www.theguardian.com/music/2018/oct/30/mighty-shadow-obituary

McIntosh, Frankie, with Ray Allen, Garvin Blake, Etienne Charles, and David "Happy" Williams discuss the state of Calypso Jazz at Brooklyn College, April 21, 2016. Youtube.com. Retrieved December 1, 2022. https://www.youtube.com/watch?v=TrjHdCDUrwM

Meshchino, Patricia. October 10, 2018. "Calypso Legend Winston 'Shadow' Bailey Dies at 77." *Billboard*. Retrieved November 29, 2022. https://www.billboard.com/music/music-news/calypso-legend-winston- shadow-bailey-dead-8481783/

Neog, Anupal Sraban. October 8, 2022. "Who was Explainer? Tributes pour in as Calypsonian legend dies aged 74." *SK Pop*. Retrieved November 29, 2022. https://www.sportskeeda.com/pop-culture/news-who-explainer-tributes-pour-calypsonian-legend-dies-aged-74

Pareles, Jon. February 14, 2000. "Lord Kitchener, 77, Calypso Songwriter Who Mixed Party Tunes with Deeper Messages." *New York Times*. Retrieved November 29, 2022. https://www.nytimes.com/2000/02/14/arts/lord-kitchener-77-calypso-songwriter-who-mixed-party-tunes-with-deeper-messages.html

Persad, Seeta. July 18, 2008. "Frankie McIntosh and Friends Take Spotlight in San Fernando." *Trinidad and Tobago's Newsday*.

Peters, Olsen "Caribbean Pete." Ca. April 1999. "Musical Exploits of Recording Artist, Cauldric Forbes." *The Vincentian*, clipping.

Peters, Olsen "Caribbean Pete." July 16, 1993. "The Calypso Monarchy." *The Vincentian*, clipping.

Peters, Olsen "Caribbean Pete." September 14, 1993. "Singing for the Pole." *The Vincentian*, clipping.

Philip, Dawad. September 24, 1977. "Beckett: A Major Calypso Talent 'Climbing High.'" *New York Amsterdam News*.

Scaramuzzo, Gene, and Bill Nowlin. 1996. Liner notes to *Best of Straker's: Ah Feel to Party*. Rounder CD5066167.

"Sir Frankie." September 18, 1988. *Punch Magazine*.

"Sir Rupert Philo—The Mighty Swallow." September 12, 2020. Madeingrenada. Retrieved November 29, 2022. https://madeingrenadawordpresscom.wordpress.com/2020/09/12/sir-rupert-philo-the- mighty-swallow/

Slater, Les. 2015. "'Parallel Overtones': An Infectious Garvin Blake CD." *When Steel Talks*. Retrieved November 29, 2022. https://www.panonthenet.com/news/2015/mar/parellel-overtones-slater-3-8-2015.htm

Slater, Les. July/August 1991. "Frankie McIntosh—Master Musicians." *Class Magazine*, 16, 20.

Smith, Keith. May/June 2009. "A Pope, a King and a Duke: Remembering the Mighty Duke." *Caribbean Beat*. https://www.caribbean-beat.com/issue-97/pope-king-and-duke#axzz7EelLJeuK

Wilson, John S. 18 November 1973. "The Great Jazz Dream—Can It Come True?" *New York Times*. Retrieved November 29, 2022. https://www.nytimes.com/1973/11/18/archives/the-great-jazz-dreamcan-it-come- true-will-new-yorkers-support-jazz.html

Wong, Melissa. November 20, 2020. "Honorary UWI doctorate for Vincentian Musical Legend Frankie McIntosh." *Loop News*. Retrieved November 29, 2022. https://caribbean.loopnews.com/content/honorary-uwi- doctorate-Vincentian-musical-legend-Frankie-McIntosh

INDEX

Antigua: calypso music, 39, 135; history, 36–37; steelbands, 39–41
arrangers (music): in American R&B and pop, 91; in calypso and soca, 91–93, 97–113; in jazz, 90–91
arranging versus composing, 90–91, 112–13, 245
Ayoung, Edwin "Crazy," 78–79

Bailey, Winston. *See* Shadow (Winston Bailey)
band chorus, 100–101
bass lines (in soca), 104–5
Becket (Alston Cyrus): career, 115–16; "Coming High," 76, 116–19, 253–55; *Coming Higher* LP, 77–78; *Disco Calypso* LP, 75–76; on Frankie as arranger, 244; Frankie on Becket, 74–78; meeting Frankie, 74–75; "Tony," 121–22, 257–58; "Wine Down Kingstown," 119–21, 244, 255–57
Birdsong Academy (Trinidad), 213–14
Blake, Garvin: *Bella Eau Road Blues* CD, 224; "Jane," 227–28, 308–9; meeting Frankie, 224; "No Money No Love," 231–32; "One for Boogsie," 229, 310–11; "Pan in A Minor," 226, 307–8; "Pan in Harmony," 230–31, 311–13; "Pan Romance," 225, 305–7; *Parallel Overtones* CD, 229; on relationship of calypso, steel pan, and jazz, 233
Boras, Tom, 61, 94–95
Bradley, Clive, 224, 227, 240
B's Records, 81, 87. *See also* Gould, Michael
Brooklyn: as calypso and soca production/distribution hub, 79, 240; Caribbean neighborhoods, 44–45, 48–51

Brooklyn Carnival: calypso tents, 3–4, 67; Eastern Parkway parade, 3, 45–46, 66
Brooklyn College: Conservatory of Music, 5, 47, 94, 207, 208, 318n12, 322n5 (chap. 7); jazz programs and performances, 59–60, 207–9, 322n5 (chap. 7); open admissions, 56, 57; piano instruction, 57–58

calypso jazz (Caribbean jazz): Brooklyn College concert, 207–9; on defining the term, 233–34, 245, 321–22n4
calypso music: in Antigua, 36–37; characteristics of, 73–74; in Saint Vincent, 15–16, 317n2; "small island" calypso, 114–15, 320n4; in Trinidad, 114
Calypso Rose (Linda McArthur Sandy Lewis): "Back to Africa,"169–70, 282–84; career, 164–66; on Frankie as arranger, 242; Frankie on Calypso Rose, 166; "No Mister, No," 167–68, 279–80; "Side Man Sweet," 168–69, 280–82; "Tempo," 73
calypso tents: in Brooklyn, 3, 4, 67; in Saint Vincent, 15, 33, 37
Cape, Roy, 6, 248
Caribbean Pete (Peter Olson), 15
Carnival: in Antigua, 36, 39; in Brooklyn, 3–4, 45–46, 66; in Saint Vincent, 33–36
Chalkdust (Hollis Liverpool): "Ash Wednesday Jail," 161–62, 276–77; "Black Inventions," 160–62, 275–76; career, 156–57; on Frankie as arranger, 157–58; Frankie on Chalkdust, 157–63; *Origins* LP, 158–60; "Two Chords and Leston Paul," 162–63, 278–79
Charles, Etienne, 234–36

Charles, Rawlston "Charlie:" career, 80–81; working with Frankie, 86–87, 142, 179–80
Charlie's Records, 80–81
City College, CUNY (jazz program), 46–47, 60
Clymax (Saint Vincent band), 83, 123–24
Collins, Victor, 79, 118
Crazy (Edwin Ayoung), 78–79
Crown Heights Brooklyn, 9, 43, 44, 51, 200
Cyrus, Alston. *See* Becket (Alston Cyrus)

decolonizing knowledge, 10, 315n6
De Coteau, Art, 74, 134, 186, 200, 242, 278
De Vlugt, Ottmar, 96–97
dialogic editing, 11, 315n6
"Don't Stop the Party" (Swallow), 141, 247
Dougherty, Charles, 204–5, 208, 237–38
drum machines, 89, 102, 105–6, 169, 210
Duke (Kelvin "Mighty Duke" Pope): career, 171–72; Frankie on Duke, 173–74; "How Many More Must Die," 174–75, 284–85; "Is Thunder," 175–76, 285–86; "Total Disorder," 176–77, 287–88
Dutchy Brothers Orchestra, 56, 96–97, 230

Eastern Parkway Carnival Parade (Brooklyn), 3, 45–46, 66
Emanuel, MacLean Leroy. *See* Short Shirt (MacLean Leroy Emanuel)
Equitables (studio band), 8, 80, 81–82, 181
Explainer (Winston Henry): career, 178–79; "Celebration," 183–84, 291–92; Frankie on Explainer, 180; "Heroes," 182–83, 289–91; "Lorraine," 180–82, 288–89; *Man from the Ghetto* LP, 179

Fishbein, Zenon, 57–58
Forbes, Cauldric, 15, 25–26, 317n12
Frankie McIntosh Orchestra, 30–32, 35
Francis, Frankie, 7, 65, 91, 97, 148, 230, 322n4 (chap. 7)
Francisco, Slinger. *See* Sparrow (Slinger "Mighty Sparrow" Francisco)
Furnace, Sam, 77, 79, 112, 122

Ghana tour with Sparrow, 204–6
Grant, Eddy, 177–78
Goddard, Pelham, 73, 74, 80, 91, 165, 200, 240
Gould, Michael, 81, 87, 240

Gouveia, Max, 9, 237–38, 239, 248, 251
Griffith, Beverly, 96, 247
Guilbault, Jocelyne, 6, 10, 91, 315nn5–6

habanera rhythm, 105
Hall, Herman, 241–42, 243
Henry, Winston. *See* Explainer (Winston Henry)
Horne, Eunice, 14, 20, 23, 24

Ice Records, 177–78
Ince, Errol, 4, 67, 96, 110, 147, 200, 204, 235, 240, 242
Innis, Bertram, 91, 96, 107, 139

J&W Records, 87
Jefferson, Jean, 84, 112, 158, 168, 175, 212
John, Trevor, 224

Keane, Shake, 14, 16, 18, 25, 84, 316n4
Kimbro, Howard, 63, 68, 78, 212
Kingstown, Saint Vincent, 13–15, 16, 18, 19, 20, 23, 24, 25, 27, 29, 35, 50, 66, 119

Laviscount Brass, 37, 38–39, 40, 41, 135, 142
Lio Smith Orchestra, 62–63, 64, 77, 78, 79, 112, 208, 210, 212; "Rasta Man," 64
Liverpool, Hollis. *See* Chalkdust (Hollis Liverpool)
Lord Kitchener (Aldwyn Roberts): career, 193–95; Frankie on Kitchener, 195–96; *The Master and the Grandmaster* LP, 193, 194; "Sugar Bum Bum," 73, 194; "Two to Go," 196–98, 295–97
Lorrainey, Mikey, 62, 69, 70–71

Maldonado, Ray, 119–20
McIntosh family: Arlene (sister), 22; Belle Cordice (mother), 21–22; Clarence Arthur (father), 17, 20, 21; Cheryl (sister), 22; Ethel Warren (grandmother), 17–18; George Agustus (grandfather), 18, 19–20; Harold (uncle), 14, 25, 26, 48, 49; Jim (uncle), 25, 27–28; Patsy Olivacce (wife), 49, 52, 53, 54, 239; Syl (cousin), 14, 25, 81–82, 247; Tony (brother), 14, 22, 24, 52, 53, 77, 121
McNeely, Jim, 61, 94–95
Melotones Orchestra, 26, 27, 28

New York University (jazz program), 45, 47, 60–62, 94–95
Niles, Anthony "Buggs," 66, 105, 106, 204

Obstinate (Paul "King Obstinate" Richards): "Antiguan Independence," 151–52, 273–74; career, 147–48; Frankie on Obstinate, 135, 149–51; "Shiny Eyes," 151–53, 272–73
Olson, Peter "Caribbean Pete," 15

pan jazz, 208, 215, 224
Paul, Leston, 72, 80, 81, 91, 107, 141, 142, 162–63, 194, 198, 240, 241, 249
Payne, Eddie, 22, 158–59
Philip, Dawad, 3, 241
Philo, Rupert. *See* Swallow (Rupert Philo)
Pope, Kelvin. *See* Duke (Kelvin "Mighty Duke" Pope)
Prescod, Pat, 14

Quarless, Eddy, 212–13

reggae music, 45, 46, 96, 102, 170
Richards, Paul. *See* Obstinate (Paul "King Obstinate" Richards)
Roberts, Aldwyn. *See* Lord Kitchener (Aldwyn Roberts)
Robertson, Raff, 35, 208, 212–13, 220, 222, 224, 228; "That's the Culture," 222, 303–4
Rohlehr, Gordon, 134
Rollins, Sonny, 217–18
Rudder, David, 67, 225, 226

Saint Vincent: calypso music, 15–16, 317n12; Carnival, 15; history, 13–14
Saint Vincent Boy's Grammar School, 14, 29
Sanders, "Montego Joe," 92
Scorcher (Cyril Thomas): career, 127–28; "East 95th Street," 129–30, 261–62; Frankie on Scorcher, 128–29; *The Hoper* LP, 128; "I'm a Hoper," 131–32, 263–64; "Party Fever," 130–31, 262–63
Shadow (Winston Bailey): "Bass Man," 185–86; career, 185–86; Frankie on Shadow, 186–87, 192; "Music Turns Me On," 190–92, 293–95; "Tempo," 189; "Tension," 187–89, 292–93

Sharpe, Len "Boogsie," 208; Frankie on Boogsie, 215–16; "Blue Bossa," 216–17, 299–300; "St Thomas," 217–19, 300–301
Short Shirt (MacLean Leroy Emanuel): career, 133–34; "The Champion," 137–38, 266–67; Frankie on Short Shirt, 134–36; meeting Frankie in Antigua, 40–41; "Push," 136–37, 264–66; Short Shirt on Frankie as an arranger, 242; "Tourist Leggo," 134; 2023 studio work with Short Shirt, 238, 251; "World in Distress," 138–40, 267–69
Slater, Leslie, 4, 241
soca arranging: form, 99–102; harmony, 107–11; history, 91–92; orchestration, 102–7
soca music: in Brooklyn, 79–81; characteristics of, 73–74; transmission from calypso to soca, 73–74
Soso, Winston: career, 123–24; Frankie on Soso, 124; "I Don't Mind," 109, 125–26, 259–61; "Soca Diane," 83–84, 123; "Too Much Corruption," 124–25, 258–59; *Too Much Corruption* LP, 124
Sparrow (Slinger "Mighty Sparrow" Francisco): African tour with Frankie, 204–6; career, 199–201; "Don't Back Back," 202–4, 297–98; Frankie on Sparrow, 201–2; "Mas in Brooklyn," 45, 200; *25th Anniversary* LP, 73, 200
steelbands: in Antigua, 39, 40; in Saint Vincent, 15, 34–35, 317n11
Straker, Granville: career, 80; working with Frankie, 81–85
Straker's Records, 80
studio sessions: mixing, 85, 86–87, 250–51; recording, 84–85, 87, 88, 201–2
Swallow (Rupert Philo): career, 140–41; "Find the Spot," 143–44, 269–70; "Fire in the Backseat," 144–47, 271–72; Frankie on Swallow, 142
"Sweet Music" (Lord Shorty), 73
Syd Joe Orchestra, 64–65, 210–11
synthesizers, 102–3

tag section of a calypso, 100, 101–2
Taylor, Ron, 130
Thomas, Cyril. *See* Scorcher (Cyril Thomas)
Tyler, Jimmy, 71–72

Watson, Ed, 73, 91, 194, 240
Williams, David "Happy:" Frankie on Happy, 219–20; "I Love Pan," 221–22, 301–2; "Ping Pong Obsession," 222–23, 304–5; *Ping Pong Obsession* CD, 221; "That's the Culture," 222, 303–4
Williams, John "Buddy," 219, 223, 322n4 (chap. 7)
Weeks, Daphne, 46, 214
Wilson, Teddy, 41
Wonderful World of Charlie Brown and Yvonne, The, 53, 70–71

ABOUT THE AUTHORS

Frankie McIntosh is recognized internationally as one of the architects of the popular West Indian soca style that emerged in the late 1970s. A pianist and music arranger, he served as music director for Brooklyn-based Straker's Records for three decades. During that time, he composed musical arrangements and oversaw the recordings of close to one thousand calypso/soca albums for Straker and other Brooklyn-based calypso labels. He recently was awarded an honorary doctorate from the University of the West Indies and became a grandfather for the ninth time with the arrival of Kymani.

Ray Allen is professor of music and American studies emeritus at Brooklyn College, CUNY, and worked as a senior research associate at the Hitchcock Institute for the Study of American Music. His books include *Singing in the Spirit: African-American Sacred Quartets in New York City*; *Gone to the Country: The New Lost City Ramblers and the Urban Folk Music Revival*; *Island Sounds in the Global City: Caribbean Popular Music and Identity in New York*, coedited with Lois Wilcken; and *Jump Up! Caribbean Carnival Music in New York City*. He recently became a grandfather for the first time with the arrival of Cooper.

www.ingramcontent.com/pod-product-compliance
Lightning Source LLC
Chambersburg PA
CBHW021913180426
43198CB00035B/454